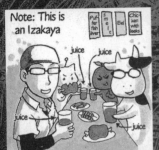

Note: This is
an Izakaya

Puf fer fish liver · smelt · Eel · Chicken with leeks

juice · juice · juice · juice

When my comic artist friends and I gather at an Izakaya (restaurant/bar), we always have lively conversations about manga. Sometimes we talk so much that we miss the last train—some people might think, "What are a bunch of grown-ups doing wasting time like that?" But when I hear my friends saying things like, "This is the kind of manga that I want to do!!" I really feel reenergized. This time Mr. Moritaishi, who is a passionate and talented fellow of the best sort, was kind enough to do the bonus comic for this volume. Yaaay!! (Bliss)

—Hiromu Arakawa, 2004

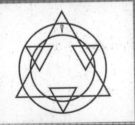

Born in Hokkaido (northern Japan), Hiromu Arakawa first attracted national attention in 1999 with her award-winning manga *Stray Dog*. Her series *Fullmetal Alchemist* debuted in 2001 in Square Enix's monthly manga anthology *Shonen Gangan*.

FULLMETAL ALCHEMIST
VOL. 9

Story and Art by Hiromu Arakawa

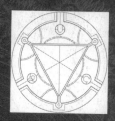

Translation/Akira Watanabe
English Adaptation/Jake Forbes
Touch-up Art & Lettering/Wayne Truman
Design/Amy Martin
Editor/Urian Brown

Editor in Chief, Books/Alvin Lu
Editor in Chief, Magazines/Marc Weidenbaum
VP, Publishing Licensing/Rika Inouye
VP, Sales & Product Marketing/Gonzalo Ferreyra
VP, Creative/Linda Espinosa
Publisher/Hyoe Narita

Hagane no RenkinJutsushi vol. 9 © 2004 Hiromu Arakawa/SQUARE ENIX. First published in Japan in 2004 by SQUARE ENIX CO., LTD. English translation rights arranged with SQUARE ENIX CO., LTD. and VIZ Media, LLC. The stories, characters and incidents mentioned in this publication are entirely fictional.

Printed in the U.S.A.

Published by VIZ Media, LLC
P.O. Box 77010
San Francisco, CA 94107

10 9 8 7 6 5 4 3 2
First printing, September 2006
Second printing, August 2008

www.viz.com

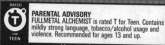

PARENTAL ADVISORY
FULLMETAL ALCHEMIST is rated T for Teen. Contains mildly strong language, tobacco/alcohol usage and violence. Recommended for ages 13 and up.
ratings.viz.com

store.viz.com

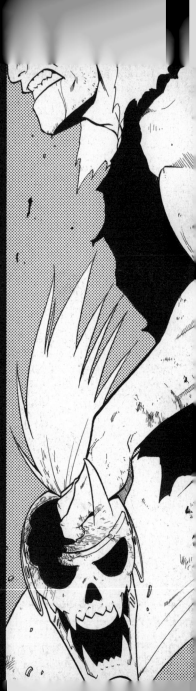

鋼の錬金術師

FULLMETAL ALCHEMIST

HIROMU ARAKAWA

荒川弘

9

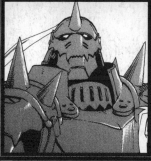

□ アルフォンス・エルリック

Alphonse Elric

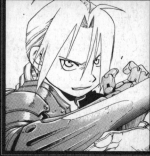

□ エドワード・エルリック

Edward Elric

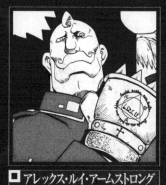

□ アレックス・ルイ・アームストロング

Alex Louis Armstrong

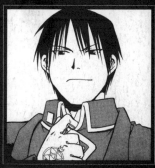

□ ロイ・マスタング

Roy Mustang

OUTLINE
FULLMETAL ALCHEMIST

Using a forbidden alchemical ritual, the Elric Brothers attempted to bring their dead mother back to life. But the ritual went wrong, consuming Edward Elric's leg and Alphonse Elric's entire body. At the cost of his arm, Edward was able to graft his brother's soul into a suit of armor. Equipped with mechanical "auto-mail" to replace his missing limbs, Edward becomes a state alchemist, serving the military on deadly missions. Now, the two brothers roam the world in search of the philosopher, the legendary substance with the power to restore what they have lost…

After a traumatic visit to Dublith and a run in with the rogue homunculus Greed, Al's memory of "the truth" is unlocked. Now, like his brother and their teacher Izumi, the younger Elric can perform alchemy without a transmutation circle. The traumatic battle left Ed's auto-mail broken, So once again they go to Winry for repairs. In Rush Valley, the Elric brothers are joined by Lin, a prince from Xing who also seeks the philosopher's stone. As they set off for central, Winry joins the boys in the hopes of visiting Lt. Colonel Hughes. Little do they know that Hughes was murdered shortly after they last saw him…

鋼の錬金術師
FULLMETAL ALCHEMIST

CHARACTERS
FULLMETAL ALCHEMIST

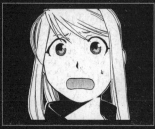

□ ウィンリィ・ロックベル

Winry Rockbell

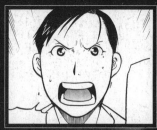

□ マリア・ロス

Maria Ross

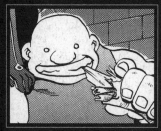

□ グラトニー

Gluttony

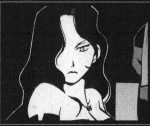

□ ラスト

Lust

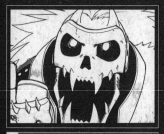

□ 66

66

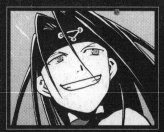

□ エンヴィー

Envy

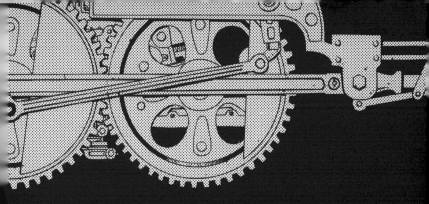

CONTENTS

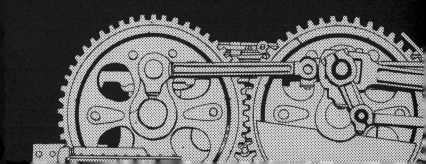

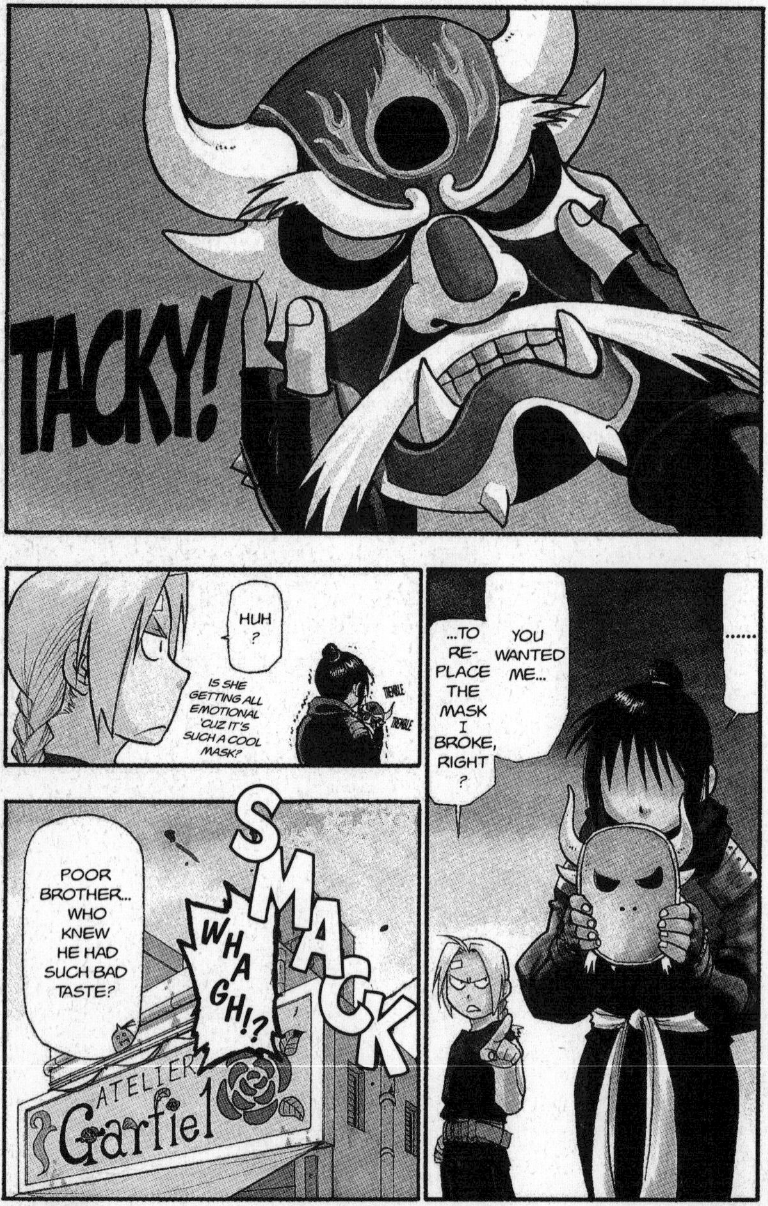
TACKY!
......
YOU WANTED ME...
...TO RE-PLACE THE MASK I BROKE, RIGHT?
HUH?
IS SHE GETTING ALL EMOTIONAL 'CUZ IT'S SUCH A COOL MASK?
TREMBLE
TREMBLE
SMACK
WHAGH!?
POOR BROTHER... WHO KNEW HE HAD SUCH BAD TASTE?
ATELIER Garfiel

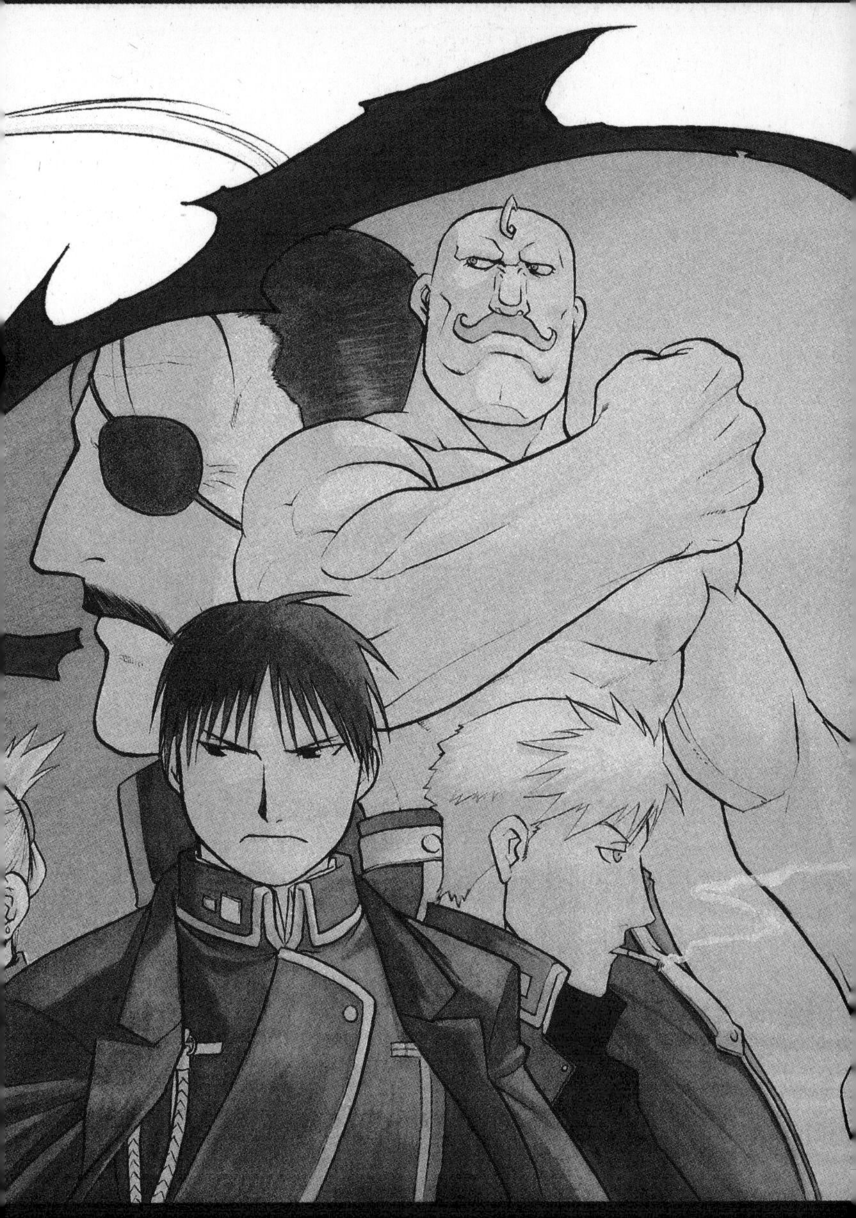

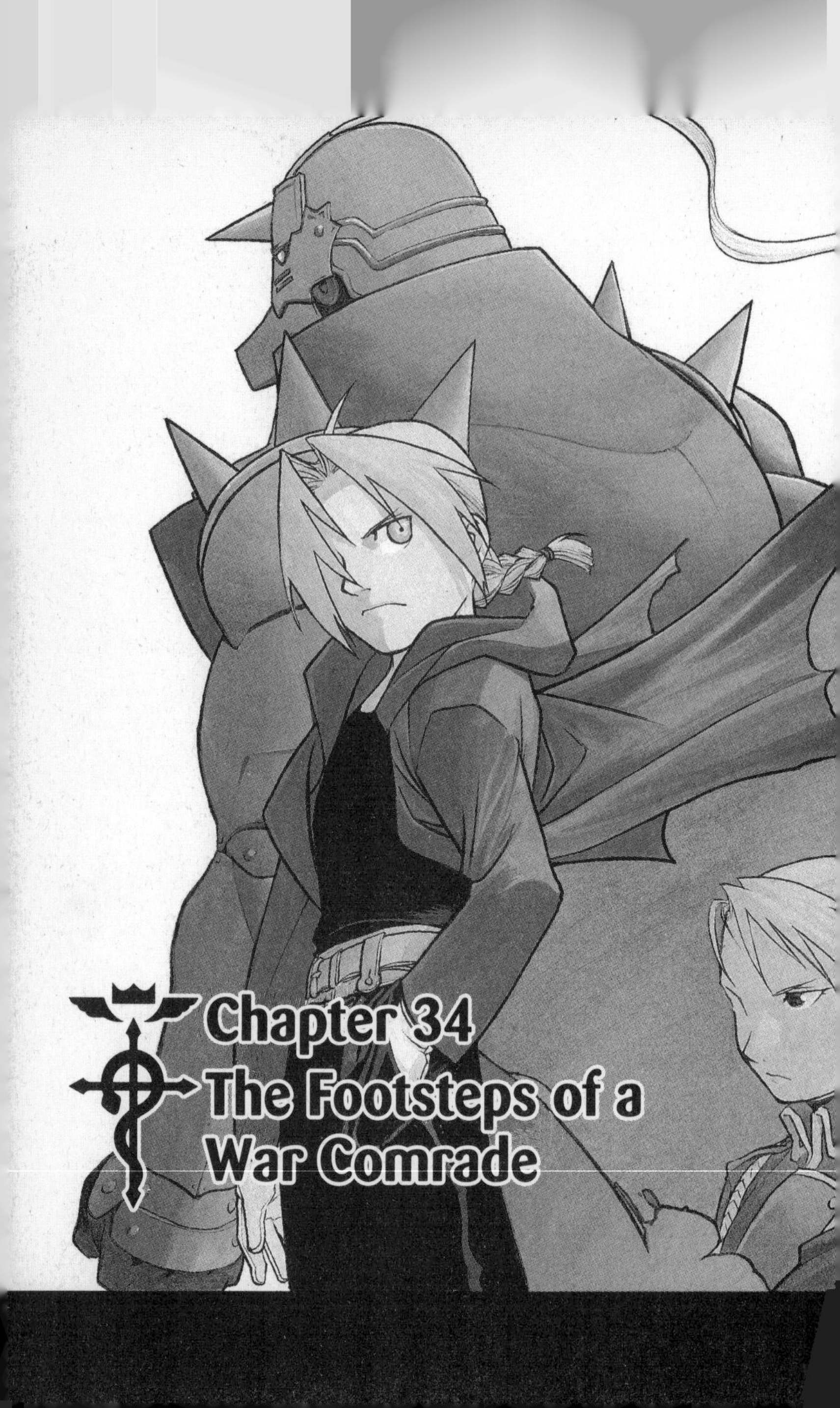
Chapter 34
The Footsteps of a
War Comrade

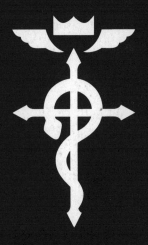

FULLMETAL
ALCHEMIST

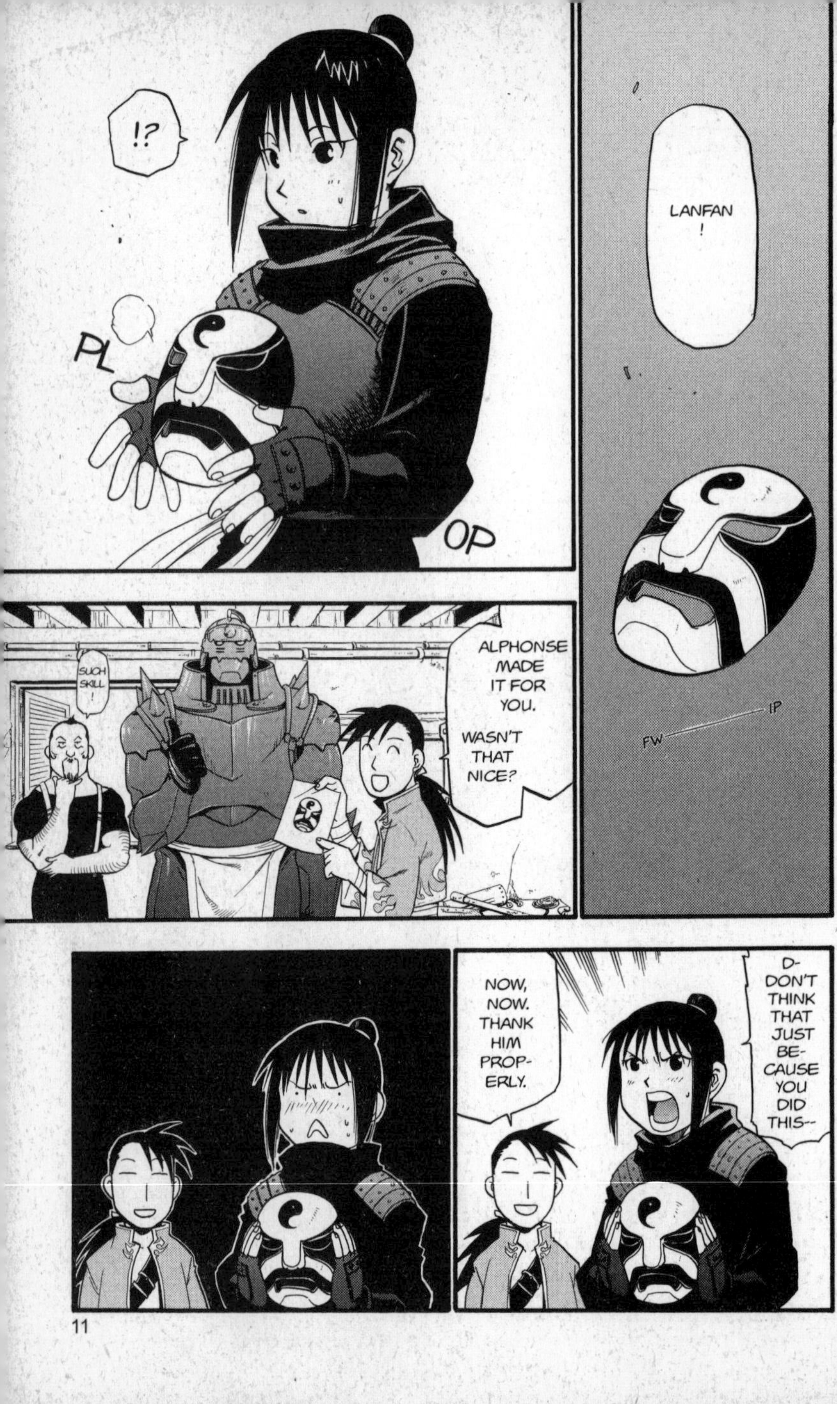
LANFAN !
FW IP
!?
PL OP
ALPHONSE MADE IT FOR YOU.
WASN'T THAT NICE?
SUCH SKILL !
D- DON'T THINK THAT JUST BE- CAUSE YOU DID THIS--
NOW, NOW. THANK HIM PROP- ERLY.

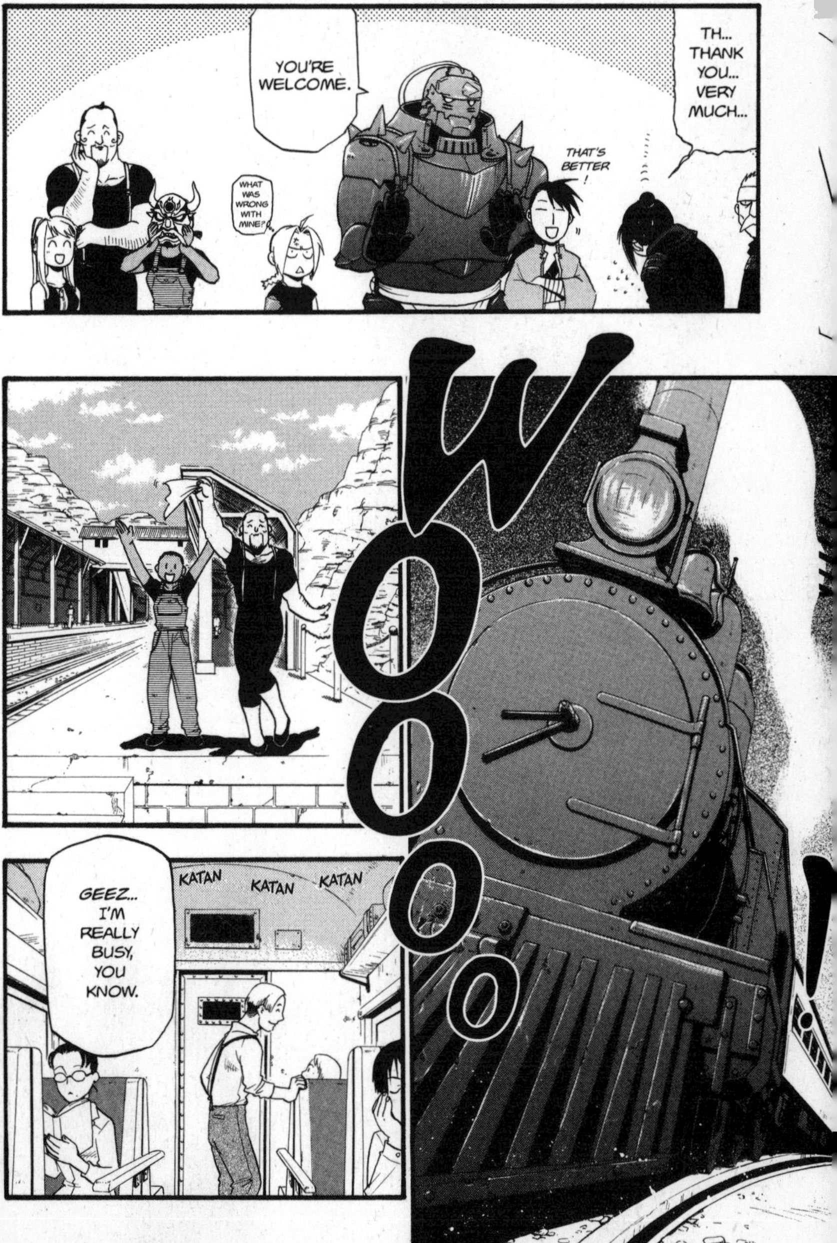
TH... THANK YOU... VERY MUCH...
THAT'S BETTER!
WHAT WAS WRONG WITH MINE?
YOU'RE WELCOME.
WOOOO!
KATAN KATAN KATAN
GEEZ... I'M REALLY BUSY, YOU KNOW.

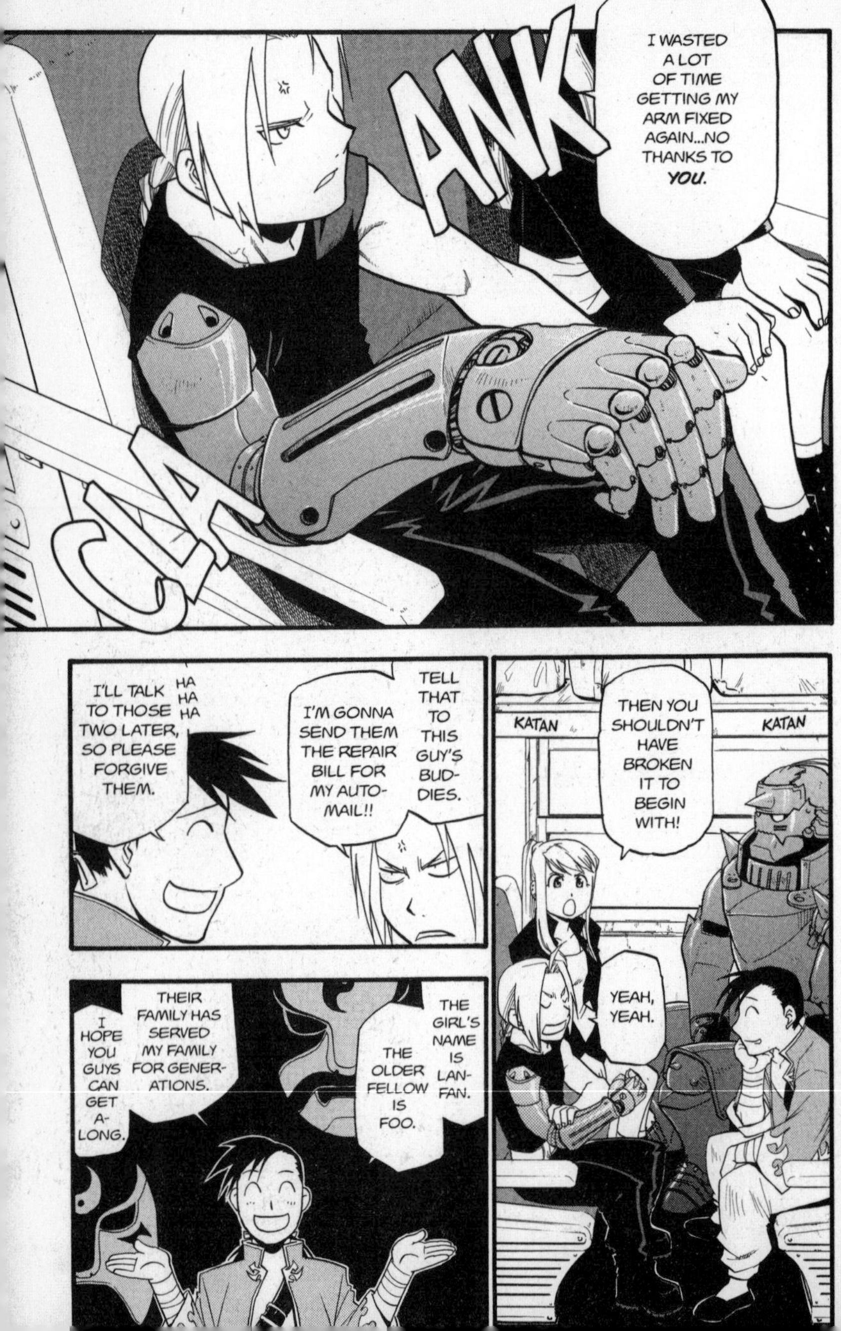
I WASTED A LOT OF TIME GETTING MY ARM FIXED AGAIN...NO THANKS TO *YOU*.
ANK
CLA
KATAN
KATAN
THEN YOU SHOULDN'T HAVE BROKEN IT TO BEGIN WITH!
YEAH, YEAH.
TELL THAT TO THIS GUY'S BUD-DIES.
I'M GONNA SEND THEM THE REPAIR BILL FOR MY AUTO-MAIL!!
HA HA HA
I'LL TALK TO THOSE TWO LATER, SO PLEASE FORGIVE THEM.
THE GIRL'S NAME IS LAN-FAN.
THE OLDER FELLOW IS FOO.
THEIR FAMILY HAS SERVED MY FAMILY FOR GENER-ATIONS.
I HOPE YOU GUYS CAN GET A-LONG.

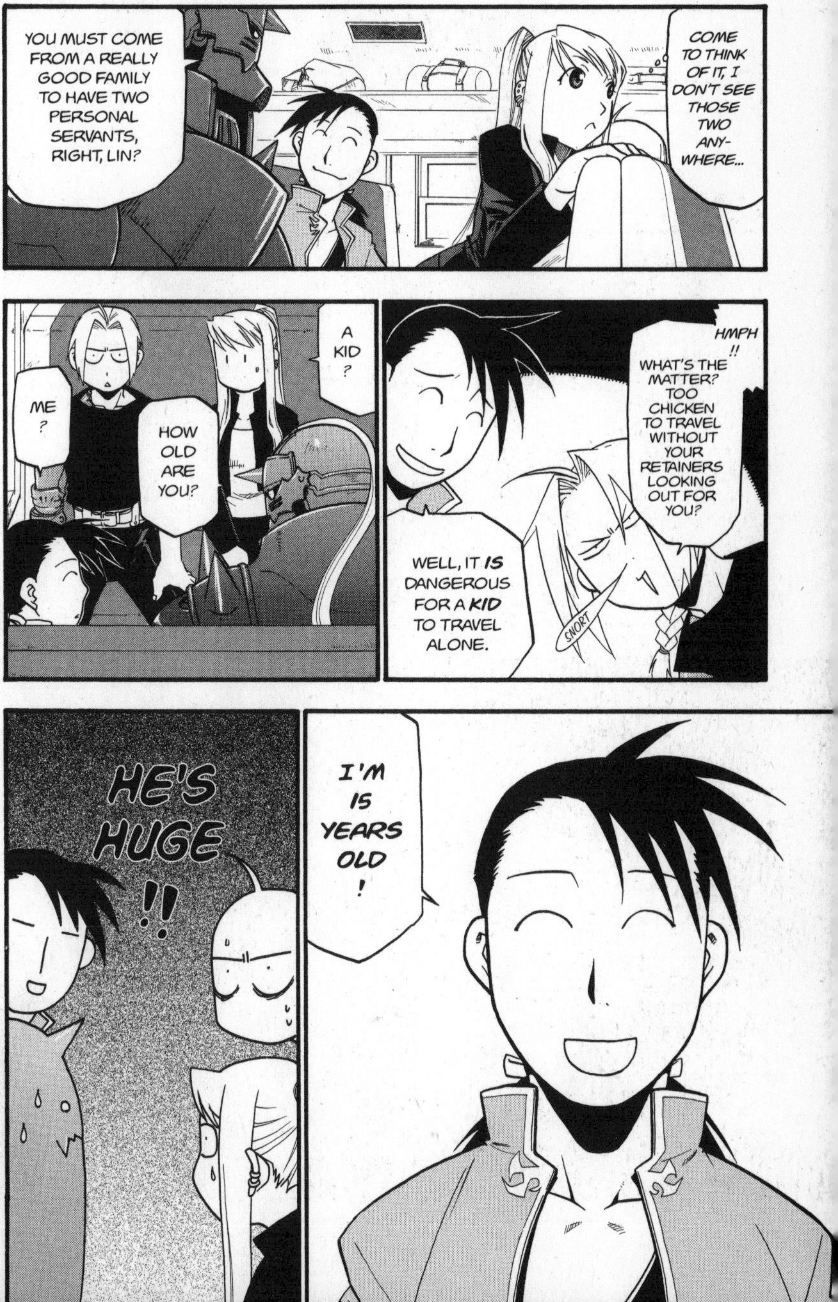
COME TO THINK OF IT, I DON'T SEE THOSE TWO ANY-WHERE...
YOU MUST COME FROM A REALLY GOOD FAMILY TO HAVE TWO PERSONAL SERVANTS, RIGHT, LIN?
HMPH!!
WHAT'S THE MATTER? TOO CHICKEN TO TRAVEL WITHOUT YOUR RETAINERS LOOKING OUT FOR YOU?
SNORT
WELL, IT IS DANGEROUS FOR A KID TO TRAVEL ALONE.
A KID?
HOW OLD ARE YOU?
ME?
I'M 15 YEARS OLD!
HE'S HUGE!!

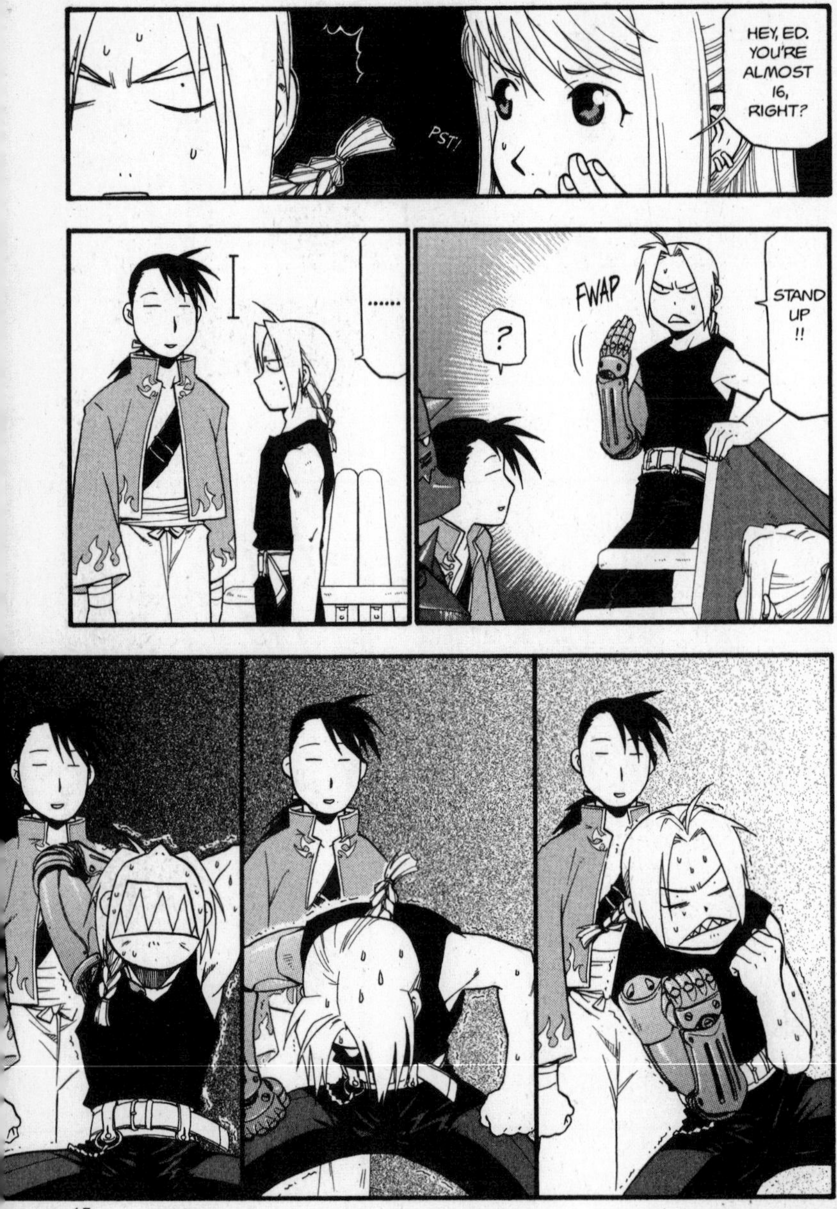
HEY, ED. YOU'RE ALMOST 16, RIGHT?
PST!
STAND UP !!
FWAP
?
......

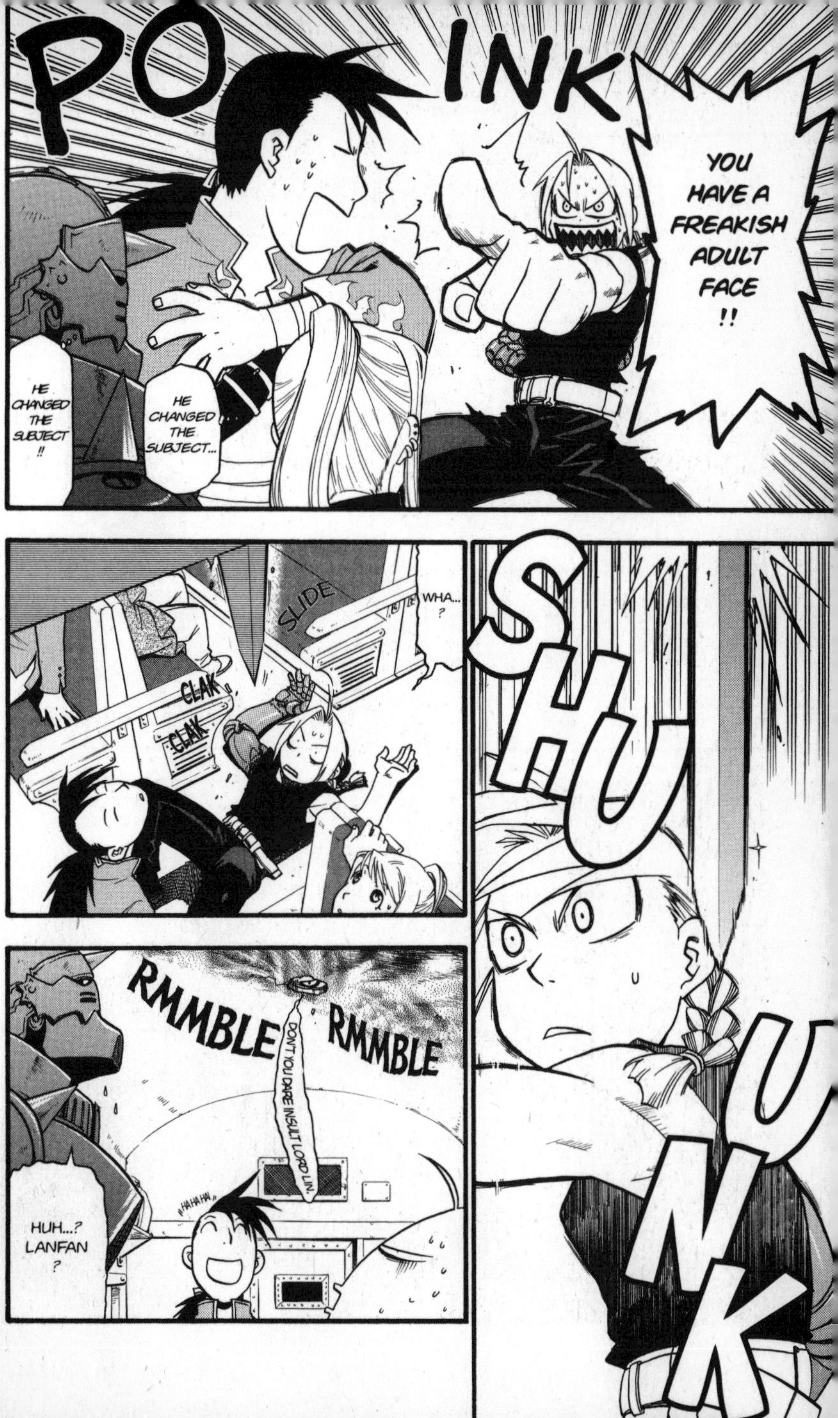
POINK
YOU HAVE A FREAKISH ADULT FACE !!
HE CHANGED THE SUBJECT...
HE CHANGED THE SUBJECT !!
SHUNK
WHA...?
SLIDE
CLAK
CLAK
RMMBLE RMMBLE
DON'T YOU DARE INSULT LORD LIN!
HA HA HA!
HUH...? LANFAN ?

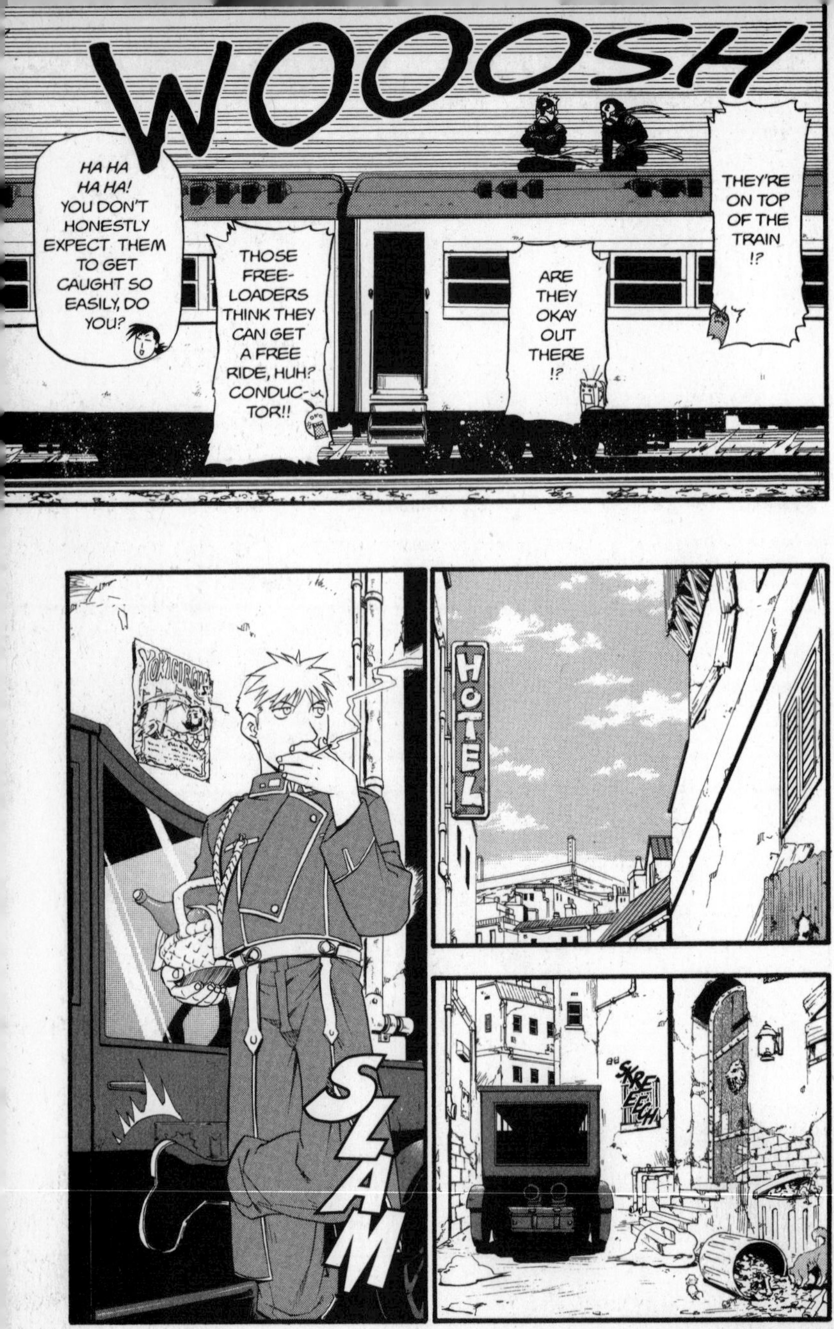
WOOOSH
THEY'RE ON TOP OF THE TRAIN !?
ARE THEY OKAY OUT THERE !?
THOSE FREE-LOADERS THINK THEY CAN GET A FREE RIDE, HUH? CONDUCTOR!!
HA HA HA HA! YOU DON'T HONESTLY EXPECT THEM TO GET CAUGHT SO EASILY, DO YOU?
HOTEL
SKREEECH
SLAM

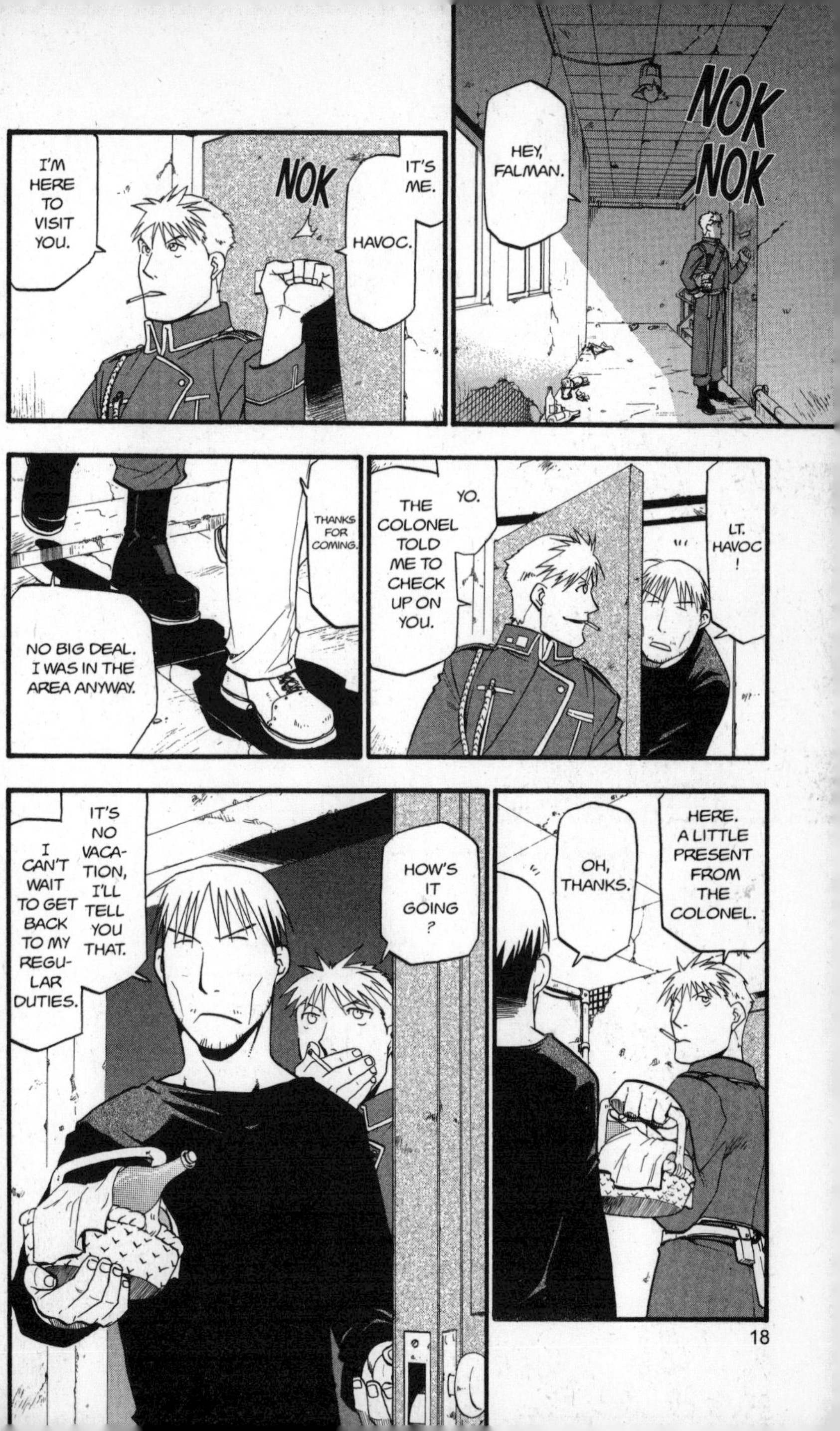
NOK NOK NOK
HEY, FALMAN.
IT'S ME.
NOK
HAVOC.
I'M HERE TO VISIT YOU.
LT. HAVOC!
YO.
THE COLONEL TOLD ME TO CHECK UP ON YOU.
THANKS FOR COMING.
NO BIG DEAL. I WAS IN THE AREA ANYWAY.
HERE. A LITTLE PRESENT FROM THE COLONEL.
OH, THANKS.
HOW'S IT GOING?
IT'S NO VACATION, I'LL TELL YOU THAT.
I CAN'T WAIT TO GET BACK TO MY REGULAR DUTIES.

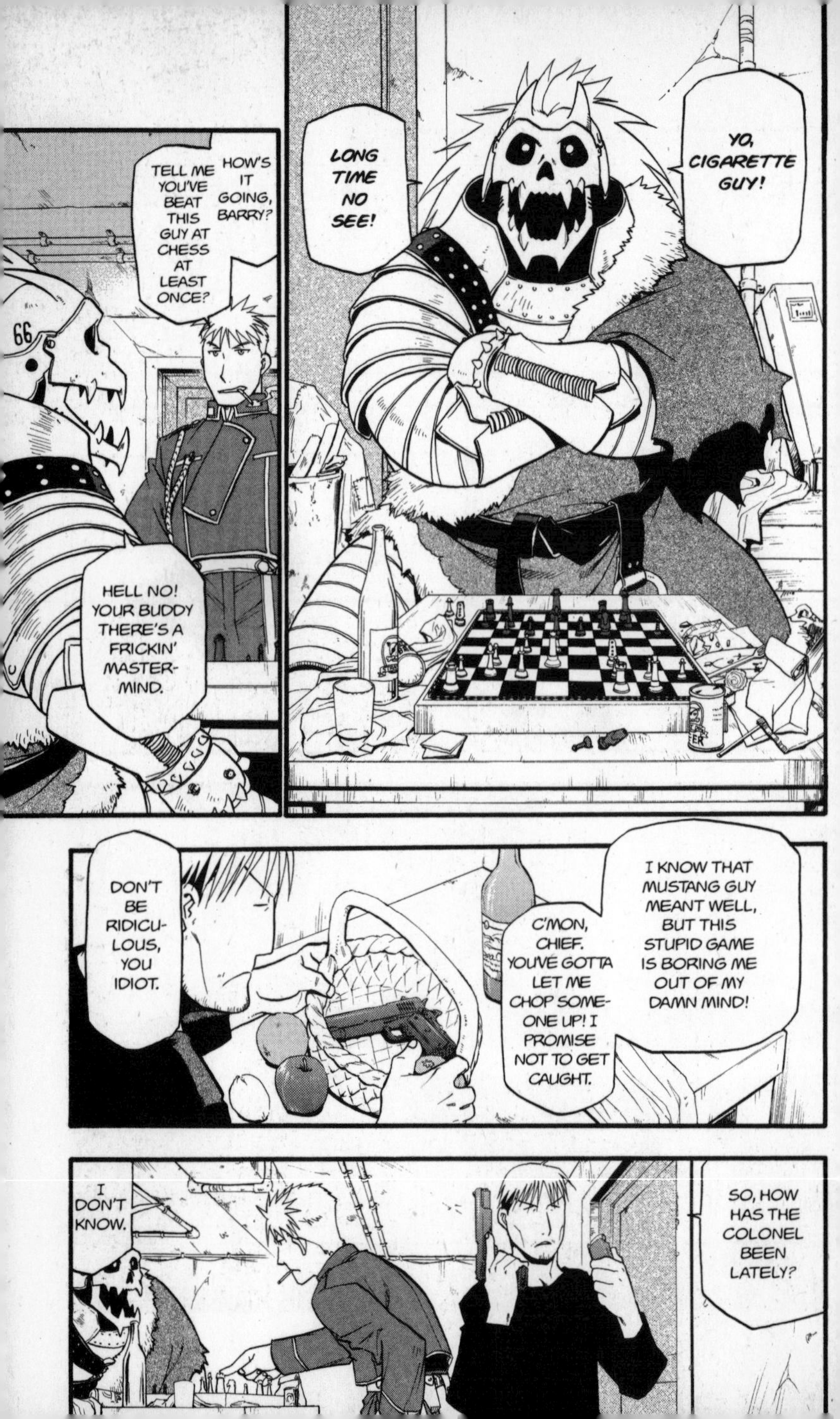
YO, CIGARETTE GUY!
LONG TIME NO SEE!
HOW'S IT GOING, BARRY?
TELL ME YOU'VE BEAT THIS GUY AT CHESS AT LEAST ONCE?
HELL NO! YOUR BUDDY THERE'S A FRICKIN' MASTER-MIND.
I KNOW THAT MUSTANG GUY MEANT WELL, BUT THIS STUPID GAME IS BORING ME OUT OF MY DAMN MIND!
C'MON, CHIEF. YOU'VE GOTTA LET ME CHOP SOME-ONE UP! I PROMISE NOT TO GET CAUGHT.
DON'T BE RIDICU-LOUS, YOU IDIOT.
SO, HOW HAS THE COLONEL BEEN LATELY?
I DON'T KNOW.

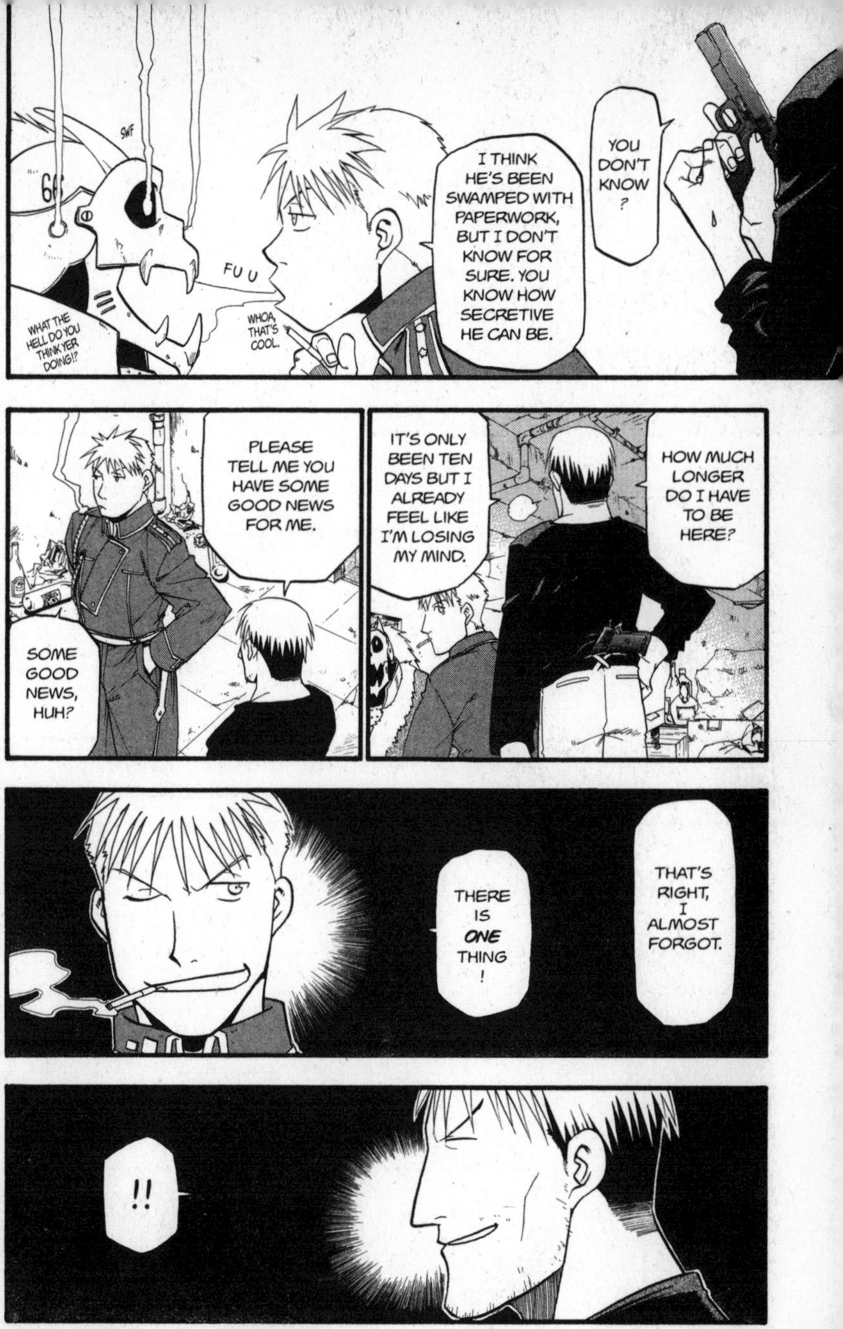
YOU DON'T KNOW?
I THINK HE'S BEEN SWAMPED WITH PAPERWORK, BUT I DON'T KNOW FOR SURE. YOU KNOW HOW SECRETIVE HE CAN BE.
SWF
FU U
WHOA, THAT'S COOL.
WHAT THE HELL DO YOU THINK YER DOING!?
HOW MUCH LONGER DO I HAVE TO BE HERE?
IT'S ONLY BEEN TEN DAYS BUT I ALREADY FEEL LIKE I'M LOSING MY MIND.
PLEASE TELL ME YOU HAVE SOME GOOD NEWS FOR ME.
SOME GOOD NEWS, HUH?
THAT'S RIGHT, I ALMOST FORGOT.
THERE IS *ONE* THING!
!!

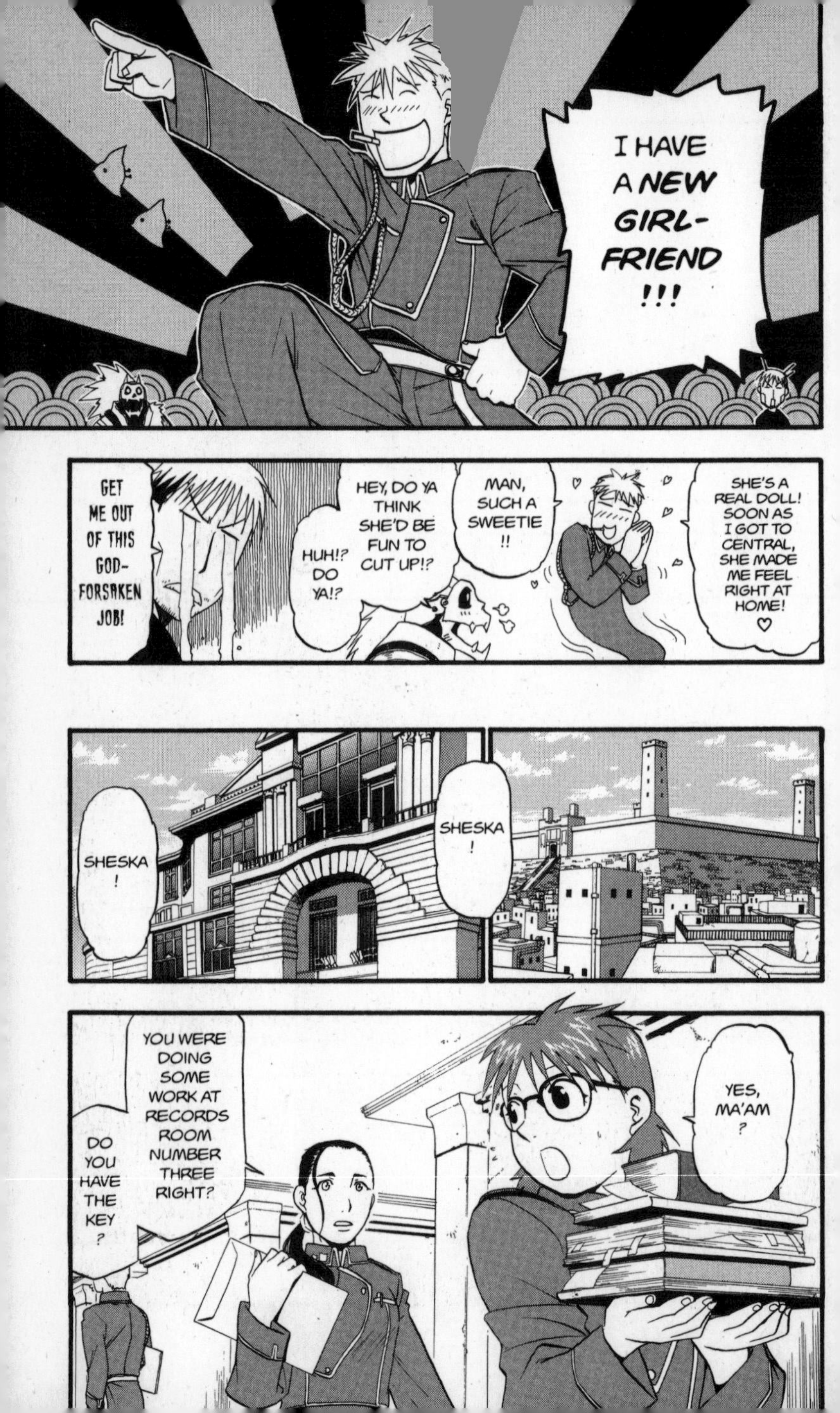
I HAVE A NEW GIRL-FRIEND !!!
SHE'S A REAL DOLL! SOON AS I GOT TO CENTRAL, SHE MADE ME FEEL RIGHT AT HOME! ♡
MAN, SUCH A SWEETIE !!
HEY, DO YA THINK SHE'D BE FUN TO CUT UP!?
HUH!? DO YA!?
GET ME OUT OF THIS GOD-FORSAKEN JOB!
SHESKA !
SHESKA !
YES, MA'AM ?
YOU WERE DOING SOME WORK AT RECORDS ROOM NUMBER THREE RIGHT?
DO YOU HAVE THE KEY ?

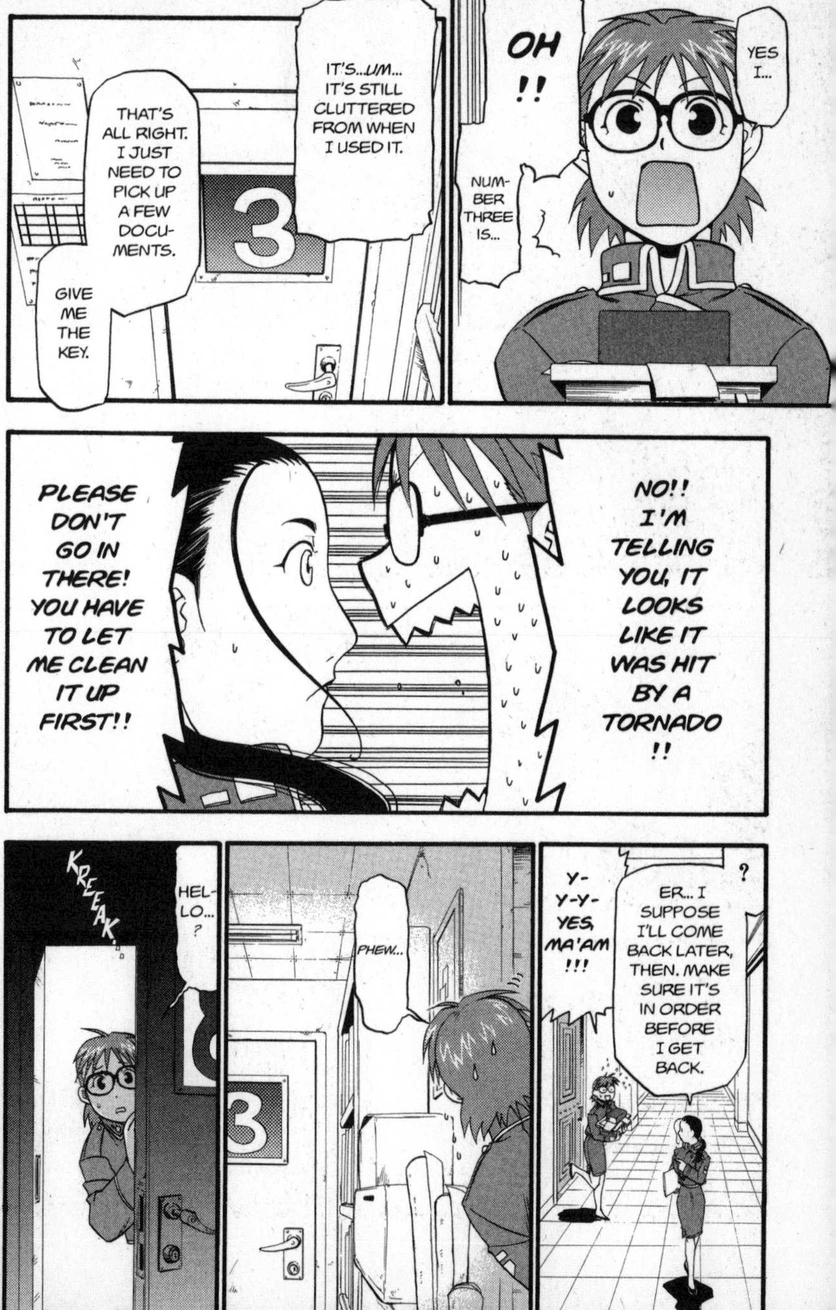
YES I...
OH !!
NUMBER THREE IS...
IT'S...UM... IT'S STILL CLUTTERED FROM WHEN I USED IT.
THAT'S ALL RIGHT. I JUST NEED TO PICK UP A FEW DOCUMENTS.
GIVE ME THE KEY.
NO!! I'M TELLING YOU, IT LOOKS LIKE IT WAS HIT BY A TORNADO !!
PLEASE DON'T GO IN THERE! YOU HAVE TO LET ME CLEAN IT UP FIRST!!
?
ER... I SUPPOSE I'LL COME BACK LATER, THEN. MAKE SURE IT'S IN ORDER BEFORE I GET BACK.
Y- Y-Y- YES, MA'AM !!!
PHEW...
HELLO... ?
KREEAK..

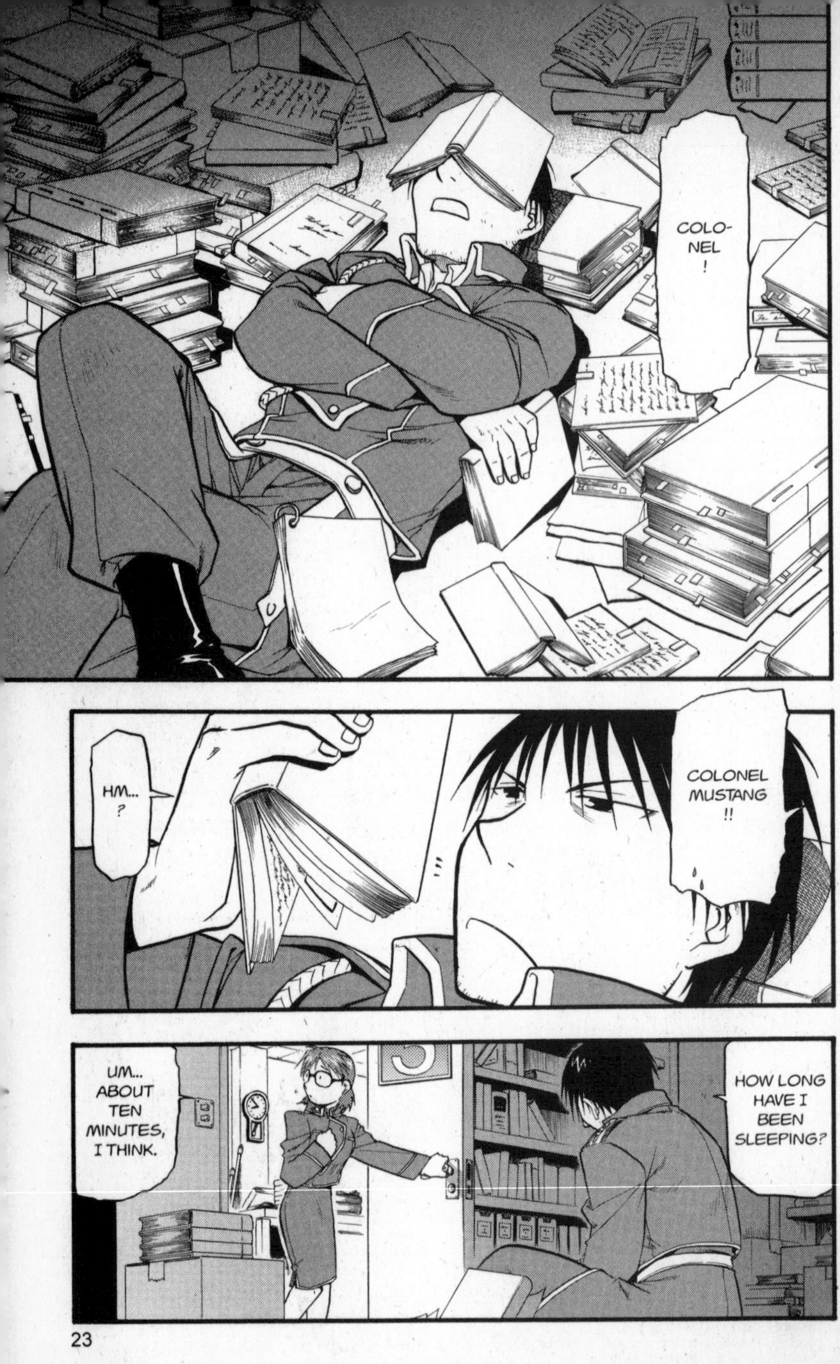
COLO-
NEL
!
COLONEL MUSTANG !!
HM... ?
HOW LONG HAVE I BEEN SLEEPING?
UM... ABOUT TEN MINUTES, I THINK.

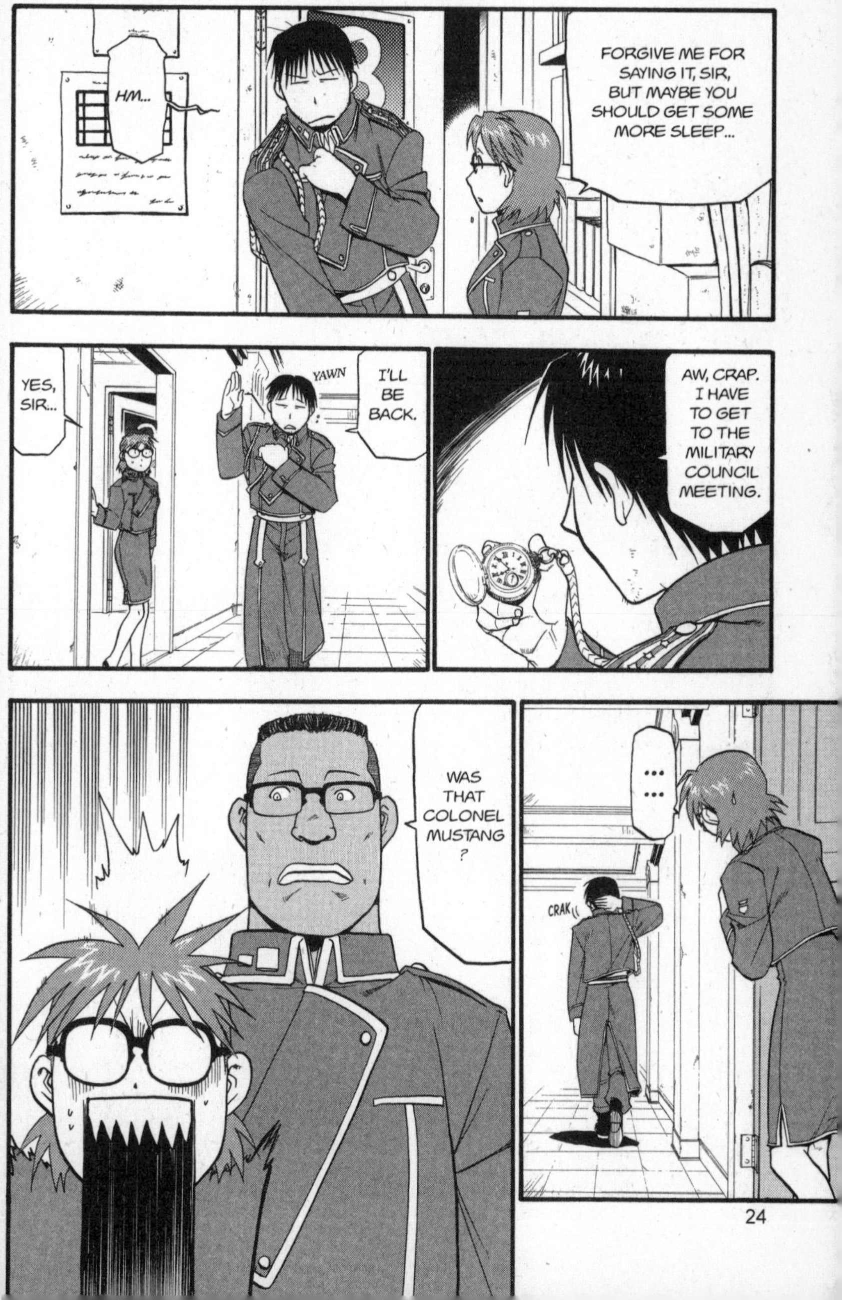
FORGIVE ME FOR SAYING IT, SIR, BUT MAYBE YOU SHOULD GET SOME MORE SLEEP...
HM...
AW, CRAP. I HAVE TO GET TO THE MILITARY COUNCIL MEETING.
I'LL BE BACK.
YAWN
YES, SIR...
...
...
CRAK
WAS THAT COLONEL MUSTANG?

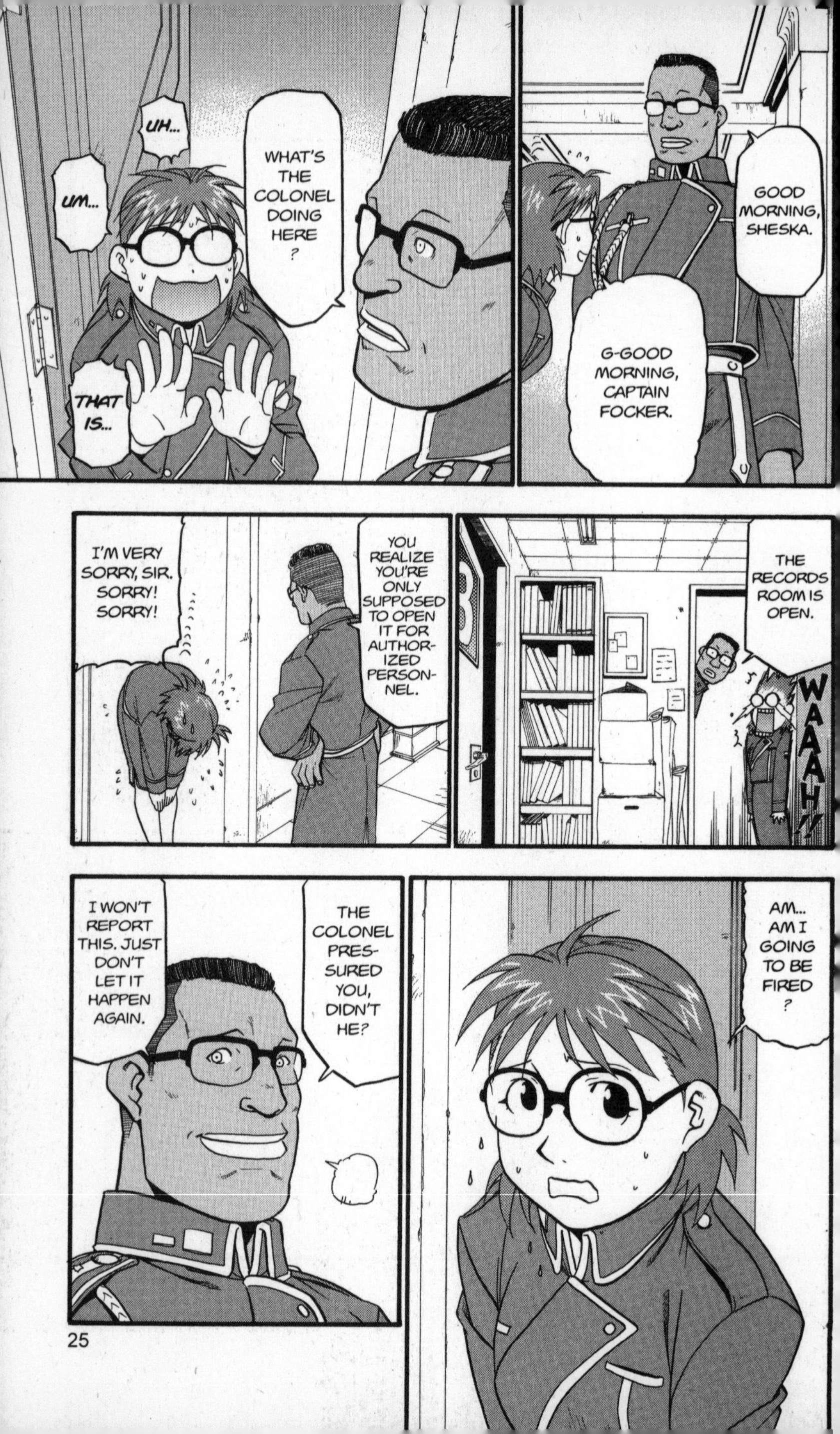
GOOD MORNING, SHESKA.
G-GOOD MORNING, CAPTAIN FOCKER.
WHAT'S THE COLONEL DOING HERE?
UH...
UM...
THAT IS...
THE RECORDS ROOM IS OPEN.
WAAAH!!
YOU REALIZE YOU'RE ONLY SUPPOSED TO OPEN IT FOR AUTHORIZED PERSONNEL.
I'M VERY SORRY, SIR. SORRY! SORRY!
AM... AM I GOING TO BE FIRED?
THE COLONEL PRESSURED YOU, DIDN'T HE?
I WON'T REPORT THIS. JUST DON'T LET IT HAPPEN AGAIN.

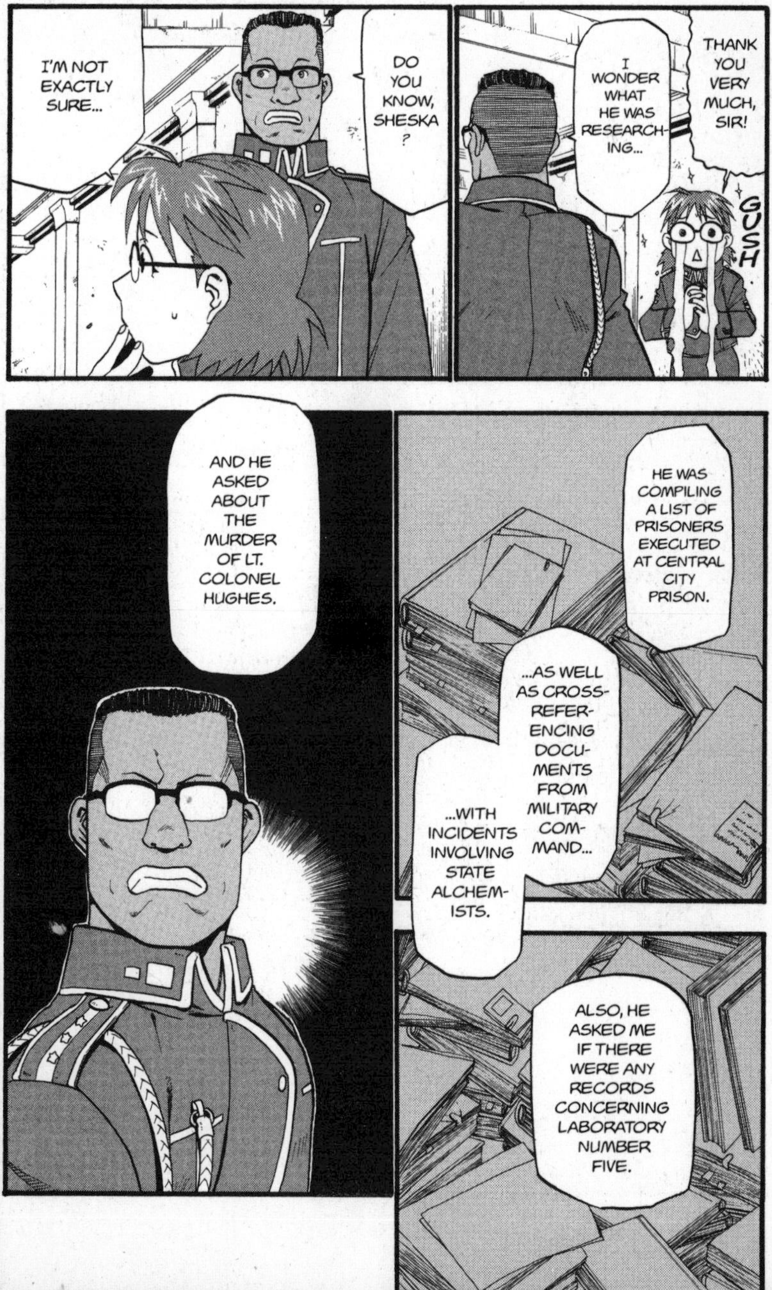
THANK YOU VERY MUCH, SIR!
I WONDER WHAT HE WAS RESEARCHING...
GUSH
DO YOU KNOW, SHESKA?
I'M NOT EXACTLY SURE...
HE WAS COMPILING A LIST OF PRISONERS EXECUTED AT CENTRAL CITY PRISON.
...AS WELL AS CROSS-REFERENCING DOCUMENTS FROM MILITARY COMMAND...
...WITH INCIDENTS INVOLVING STATE ALCHEMISTS.
ALSO, HE ASKED ME IF THERE WERE ANY RECORDS CONCERNING LABORATORY NUMBER FIVE.
AND HE ASKED ABOUT THE MURDER OF LT. COLONEL HUGHES.

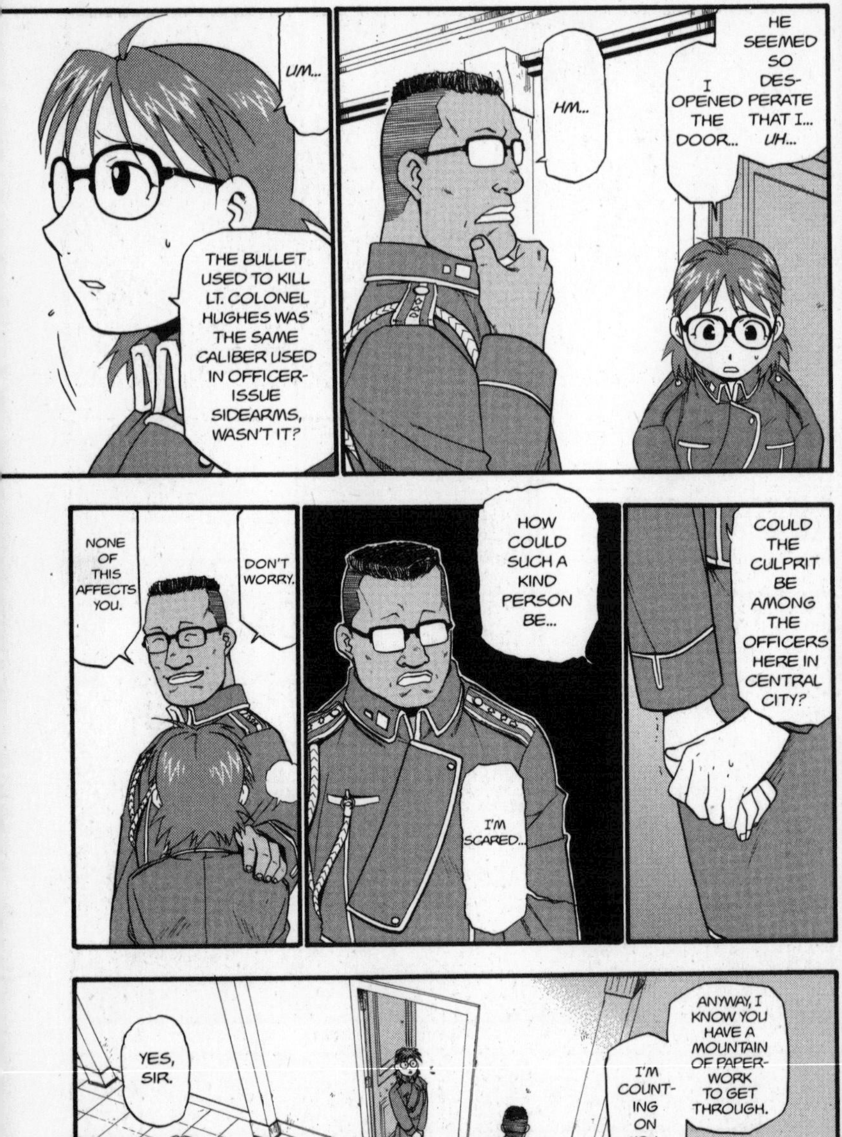
HE SEEMED SO DES-PERATE THAT I... UH...
I OPENED THE DOOR...
HM...
UM...
THE BULLET USED TO KILL LT. COLONEL HUGHES WAS THE SAME CALIBER USED IN OFFICER-ISSUE SIDEARMS, WASN'T IT?
COULD THE CULPRIT BE AMONG THE OFFICERS HERE IN CENTRAL CITY?
HOW COULD SUCH A KIND PERSON BE...
I'M SCARED...
DON'T WORRY.
NONE OF THIS AFFECTS YOU.
ANYWAY, I KNOW YOU HAVE A MOUNTAIN OF PAPER-WORK TO GET THROUGH.
I'M COUNT-ING ON YOU.
YES, SIR.

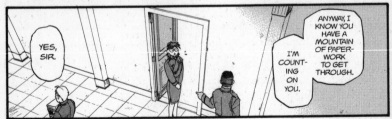

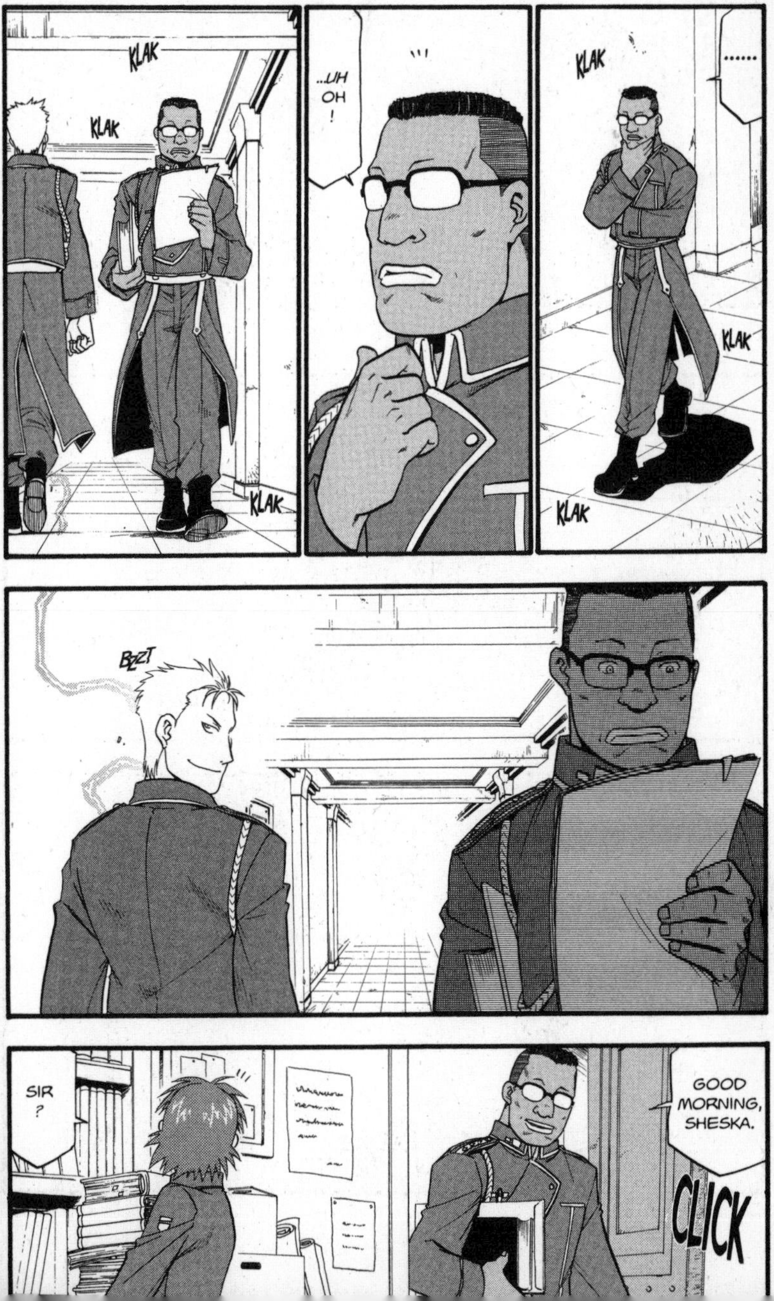
KLAK
......
KLAK
KLAK
..UH OH !
KLAK
KLAK
KLAK
BZZT
GOOD MORNING, SHESKA.
CLICK
SIR ?

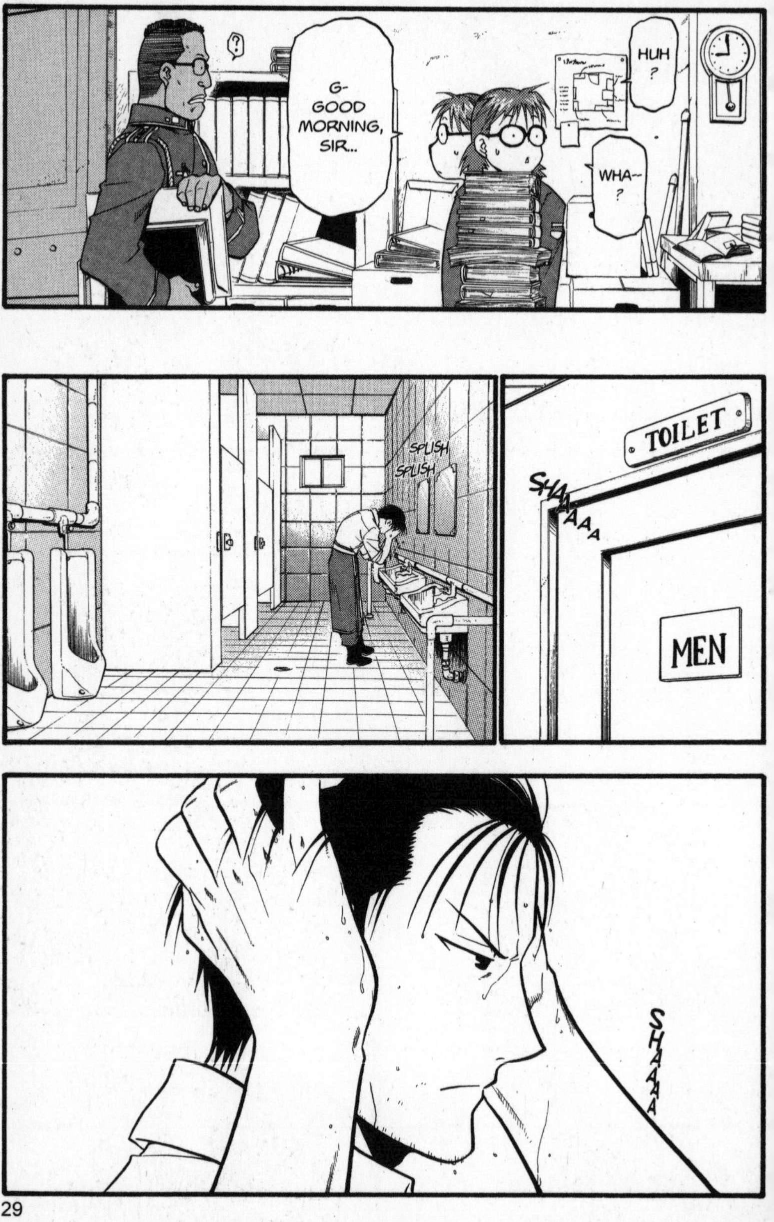
HUH ?
WHA-- ?
G- GOOD MORNING, SIR...
?
TOILET
SHAAAAA
MEN
SPLISH
SPLISH
SHAAAA

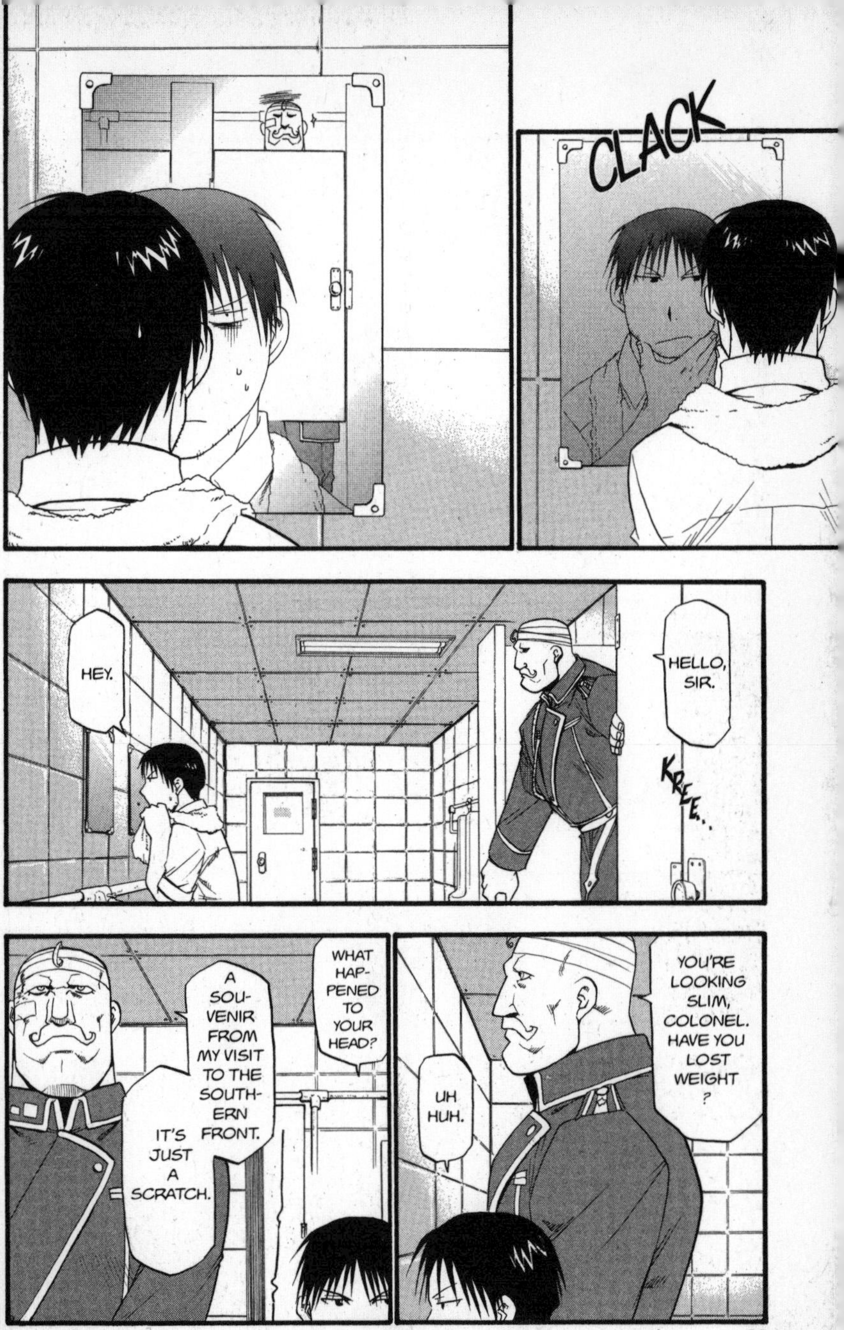
CLACK
HELLO, SIR.
KREEE...
HEY.
YOU'RE LOOKING SLIM, COLONEL. HAVE YOU LOST WEIGHT?
UH HUH.
WHAT HAPPENED TO YOUR HEAD?
A SOUVENIR FROM MY VISIT TO THE SOUTHERN FRONT.
IT'S JUST A SCRATCH.

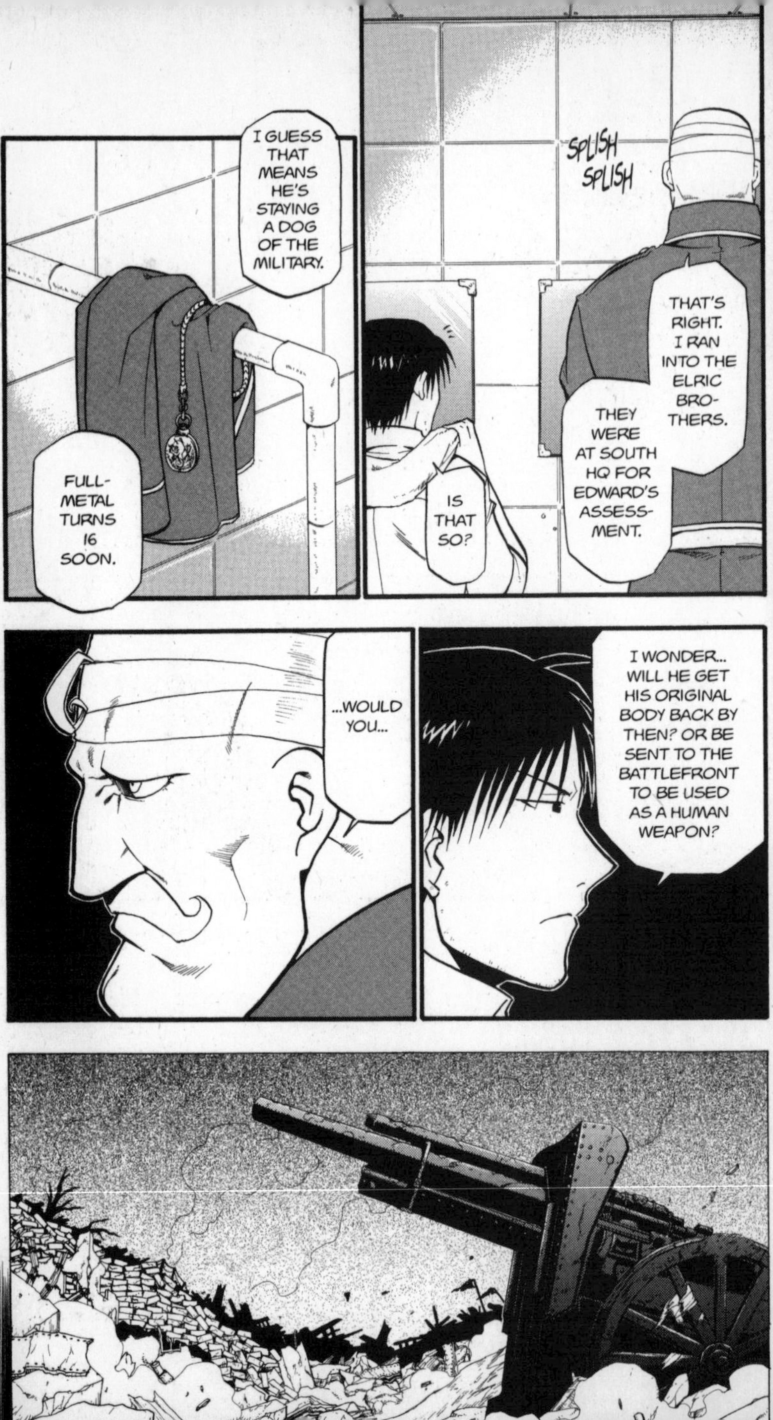
SPLISH SPLISH
THAT'S RIGHT. I RAN INTO THE ELRIC BROTHERS.
THEY WERE AT SOUTH HQ FOR EDWARD'S ASSESSMENT.
IS THAT SO?
I GUESS THAT MEANS HE'S STAYING A DOG OF THE MILITARY.
FULL-METAL TURNS 16 SOON.
I WONDER... WILL HE GET HIS ORIGINAL BODY BACK BY THEN? OR BE SENT TO THE BATTLEFRONT TO BE USED AS A HUMAN WEAPON?
...WOULD YOU...

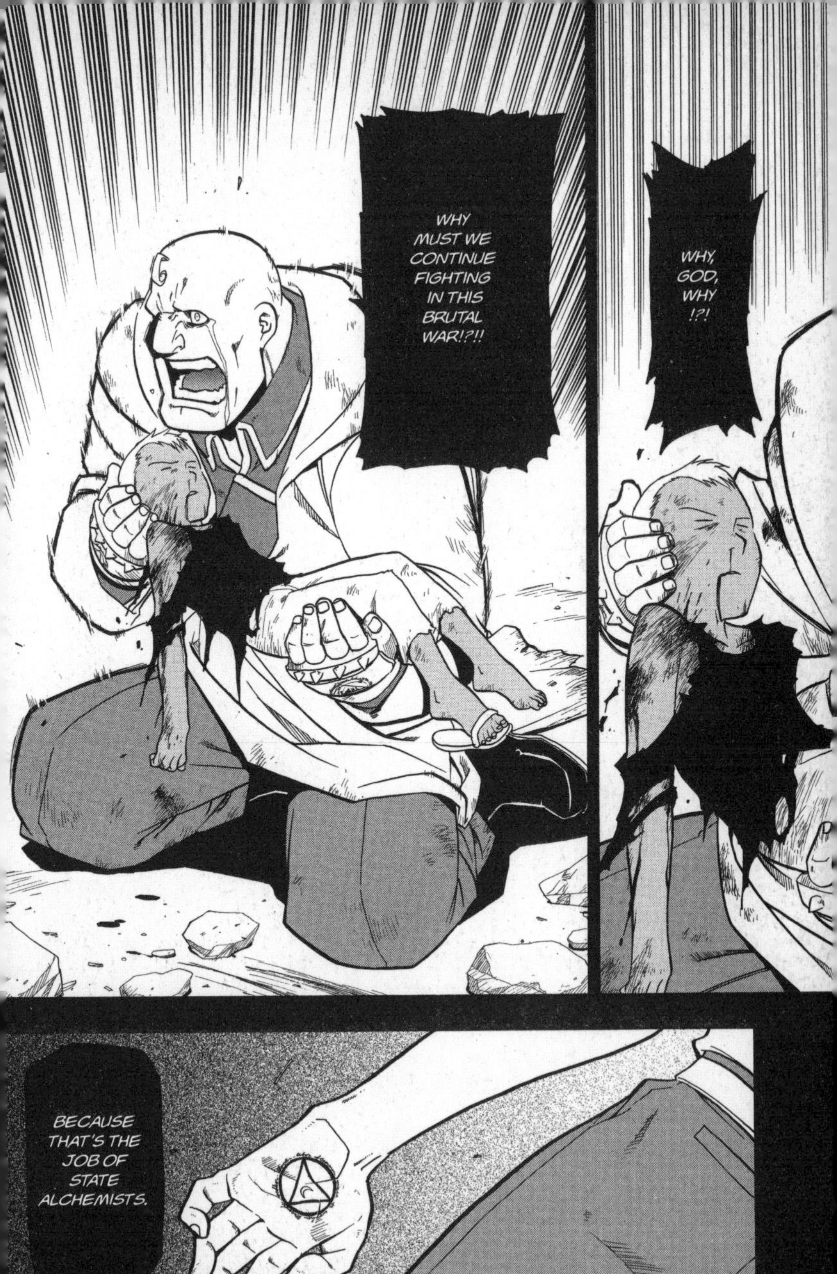
WHY, GOD, WHY !?!
WHY MUST WE CONTINUE FIGHTING IN THIS BRUTAL WAR!?!!
BECAUSE THAT'S THE JOB OF STATE ALCHEMISTS.

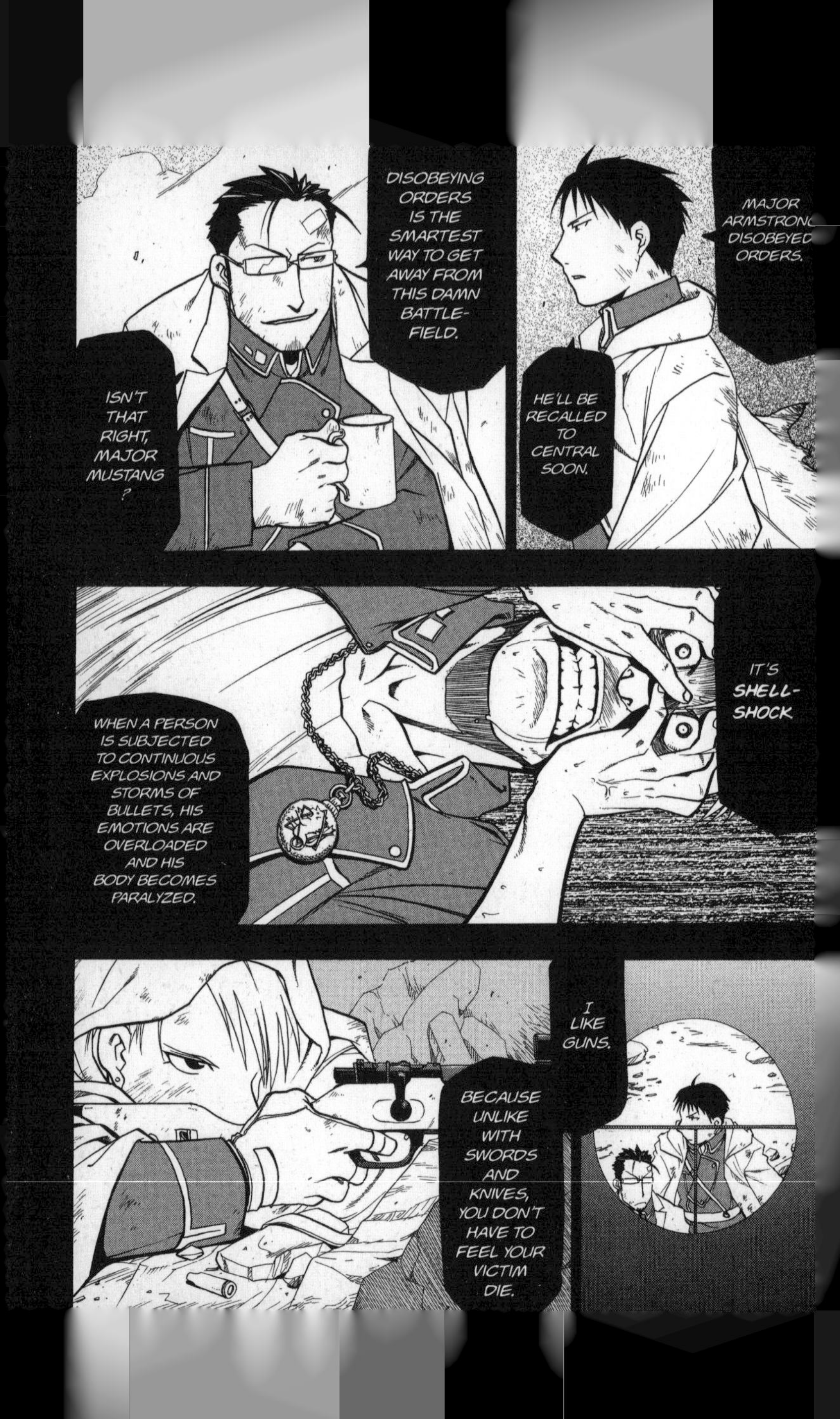
MAJOR ARMSTRONG DISOBEYED ORDERS.
HE'LL BE RECALLED TO CENTRAL SOON.
DISOBEYING ORDERS IS THE SMARTEST WAY TO GET AWAY FROM THIS DAMN BATTLE-FIELD.
ISN'T THAT RIGHT, MAJOR MUSTANG?
IT'S **SHELL-SHOCK**
WHEN A PERSON IS SUBJECTED TO CONTINUOUS EXPLOSIONS AND STORMS OF BULLETS, HIS EMOTIONS ARE OVERLOADED AND HIS BODY BECOMES PARALYZED.
I LIKE GUNS.
BECAUSE UNLIKE WITH SWORDS AND KNIVES, YOU DON'T HAVE TO FEEL YOUR VICTIM DIE.

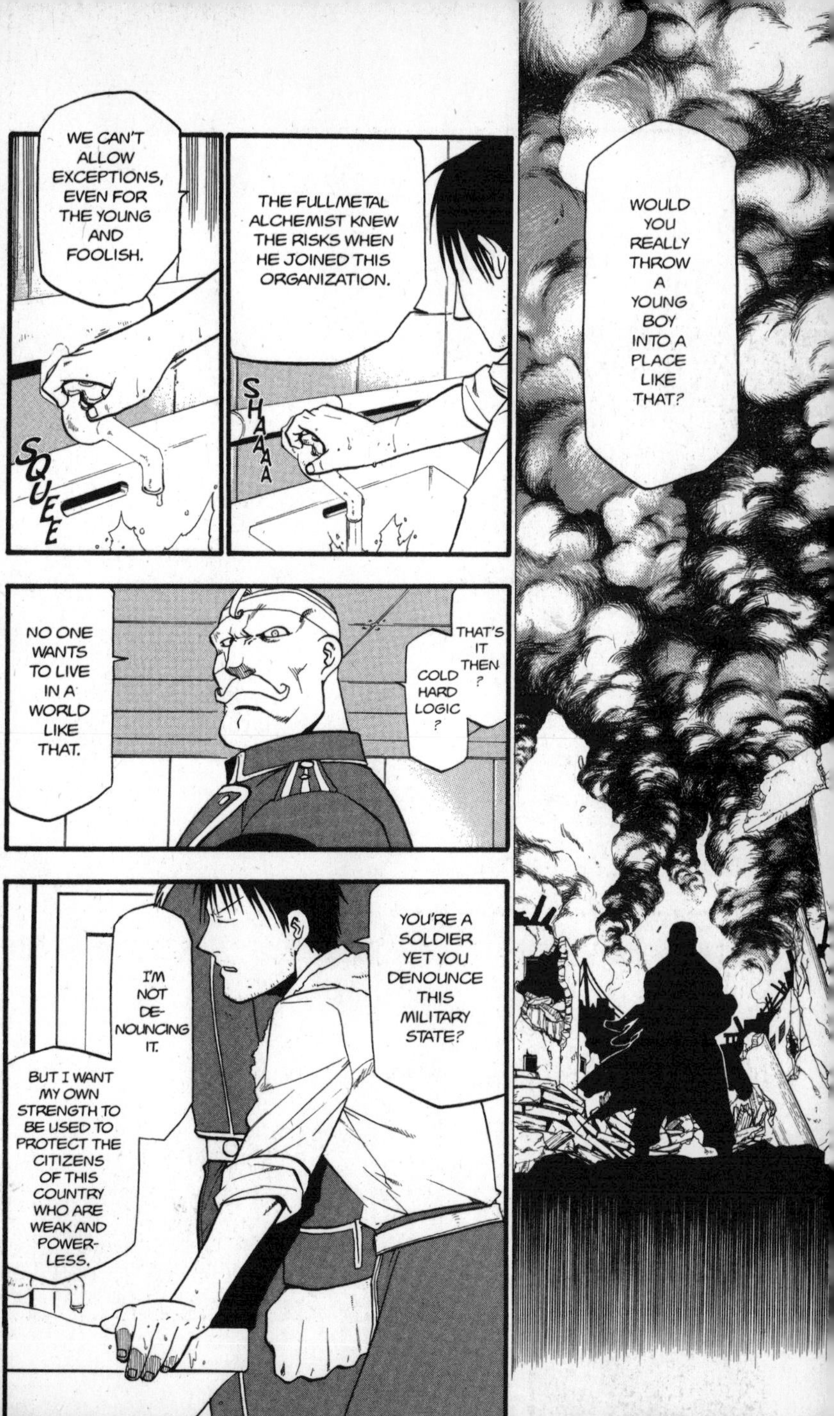
WOULD YOU REALLY THROW A YOUNG BOY INTO A PLACE LIKE THAT?
THE FULLMETAL ALCHEMIST KNEW THE RISKS WHEN HE JOINED THIS ORGANIZATION.
SHAAAA
WE CAN'T ALLOW EXCEPTIONS, EVEN FOR THE YOUNG AND FOOLISH.
SQUEE
THAT'S IT THEN?
COLD HARD LOGIC?
NO ONE WANTS TO LIVE IN A WORLD LIKE THAT.
YOU'RE A SOLDIER YET YOU DENOUNCE THIS MILITARY STATE?
I'M NOT DE-NOUNCING IT.
BUT I WANT MY OWN STRENGTH TO BE USED TO PROTECT THE CITIZENS OF THIS COUNTRY WHO ARE WEAK AND POWER-LESS.

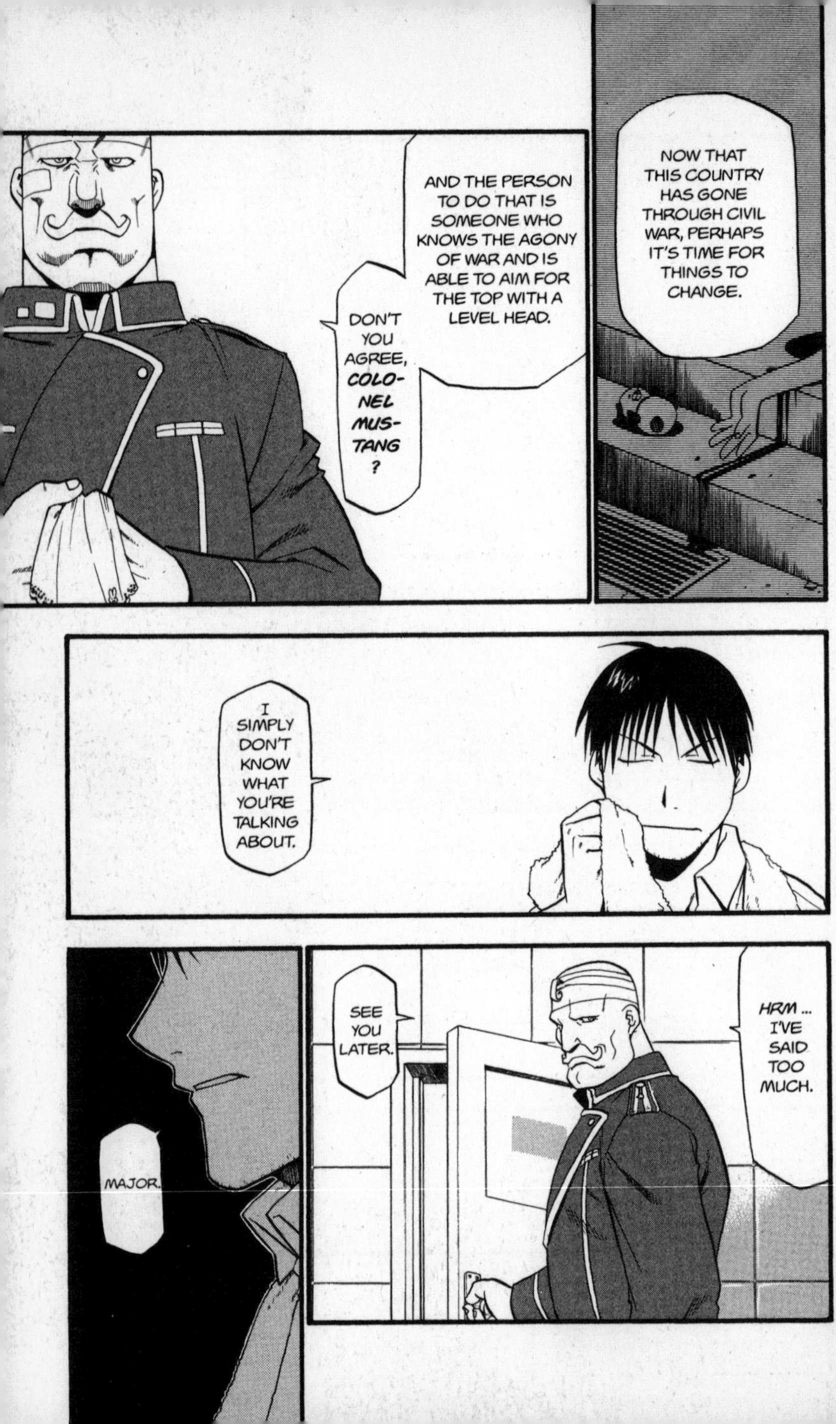
NOW THAT THIS COUNTRY HAS GONE THROUGH CIVIL WAR, PERHAPS IT'S TIME FOR THINGS TO CHANGE.
AND THE PERSON TO DO THAT IS SOMEONE WHO KNOWS THE AGONY OF WAR AND IS ABLE TO AIM FOR THE TOP WITH A LEVEL HEAD.
DON'T YOU AGREE, ***COLONEL MUSTANG***?
I SIMPLY DON'T KNOW WHAT YOU'RE TALKING ABOUT.
HRM ... I'VE SAID TOO MUCH.
SEE YOU LATER.
MAJOR.

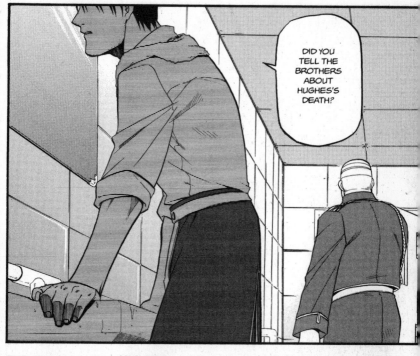

DID YOU TELL THE BROTHERS ABOUT HUGHES'S DEATH?

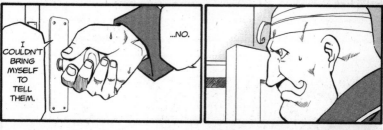

I COULDN'T BRING MYSELF TO TELL THEM.

...NO.

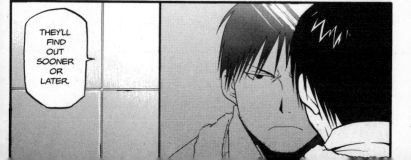

THEY'LL FIND OUT SOONER OR LATER.

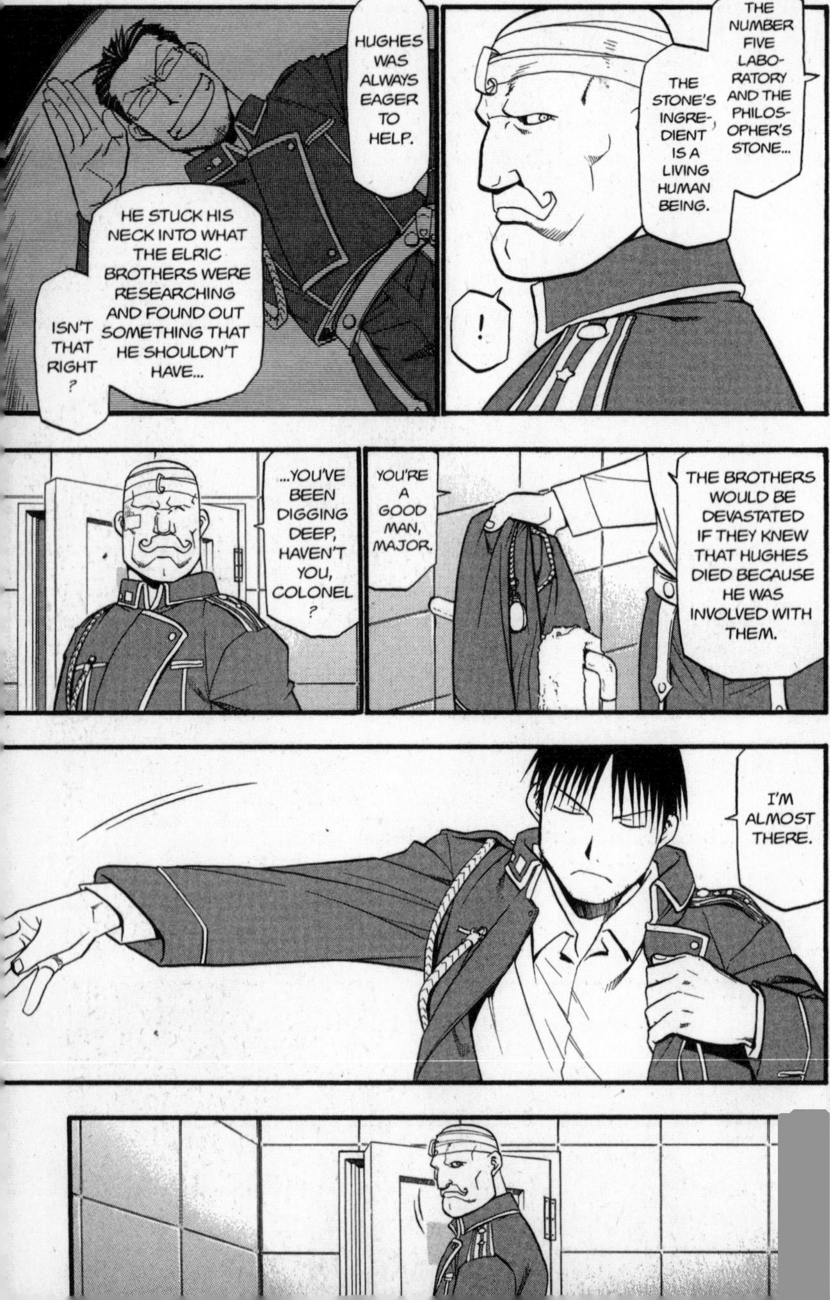
THE NUMBER FIVE LABORATORY AND THE PHILOSOPHER'S STONE...
THE STONE'S INGREDIENT IS A LIVING HUMAN BEING.
!
HUGHES WAS ALWAYS EAGER TO HELP.
HE STUCK HIS NECK INTO WHAT THE ELRIC BROTHERS WERE RESEARCHING AND FOUND OUT SOMETHING THAT HE SHOULDN'T HAVE...
ISN'T THAT RIGHT?
THE BROTHERS WOULD BE DEVASTATED IF THEY KNEW THAT HUGHES DIED BECAUSE HE WAS INVOLVED WITH THEM.
YOU'RE A GOOD MAN, MAJOR.
...YOU'VE BEEN DIGGING DEEP, HAVEN'T YOU, COLONEL?
I'M ALMOST THERE.

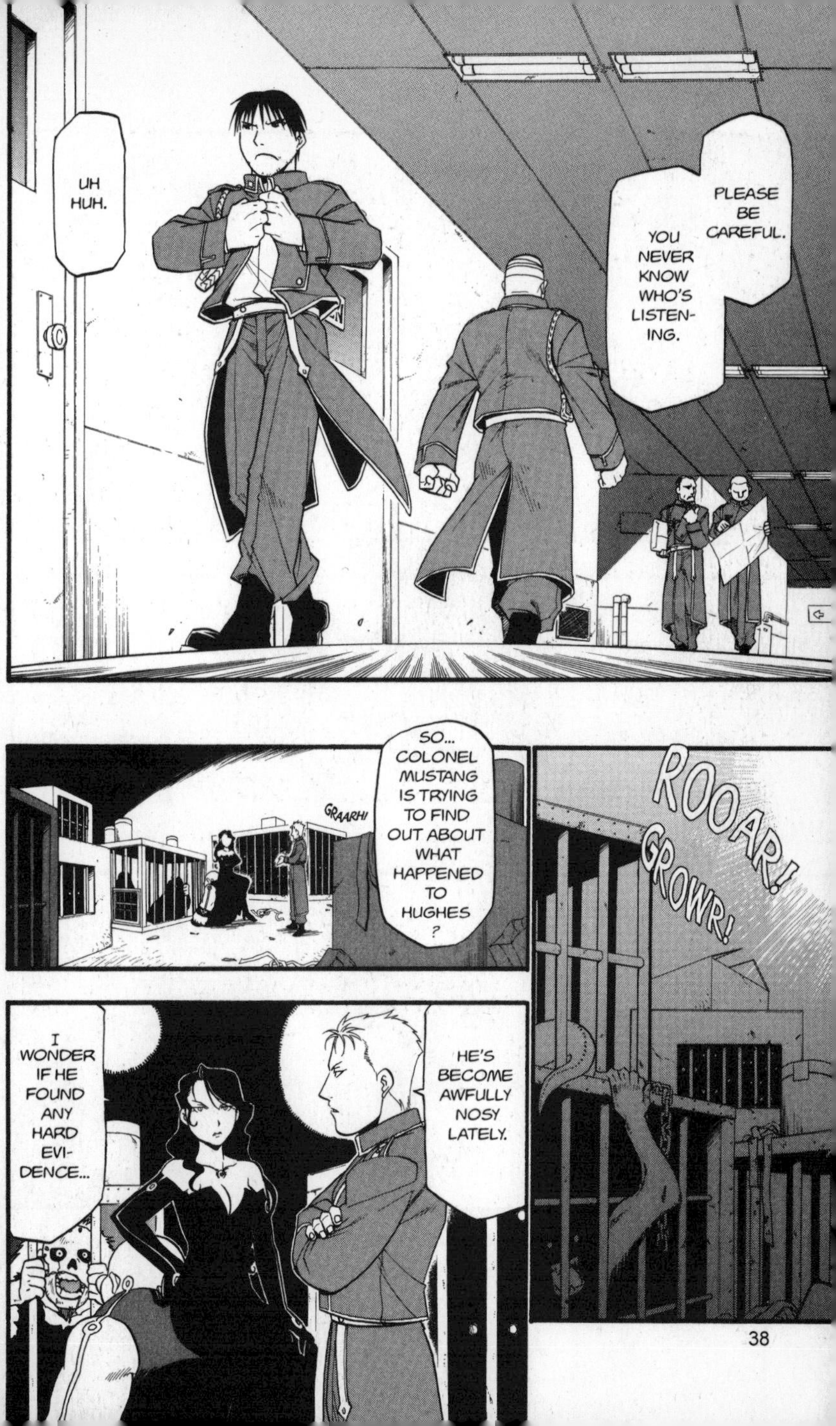
PLEASE BE CAREFUL.
YOU NEVER KNOW WHO'S LISTEN-ING.
UH HUH.
ROOAR!
GROWR!
GRAARH!
SO... COLONEL MUSTANG IS TRYING TO FIND OUT ABOUT WHAT HAPPENED TO HUGHES?
HE'S BECOME AWFULLY NOSY LATELY.
I WONDER IF HE FOUND ANY HARD EVI-DENCE...

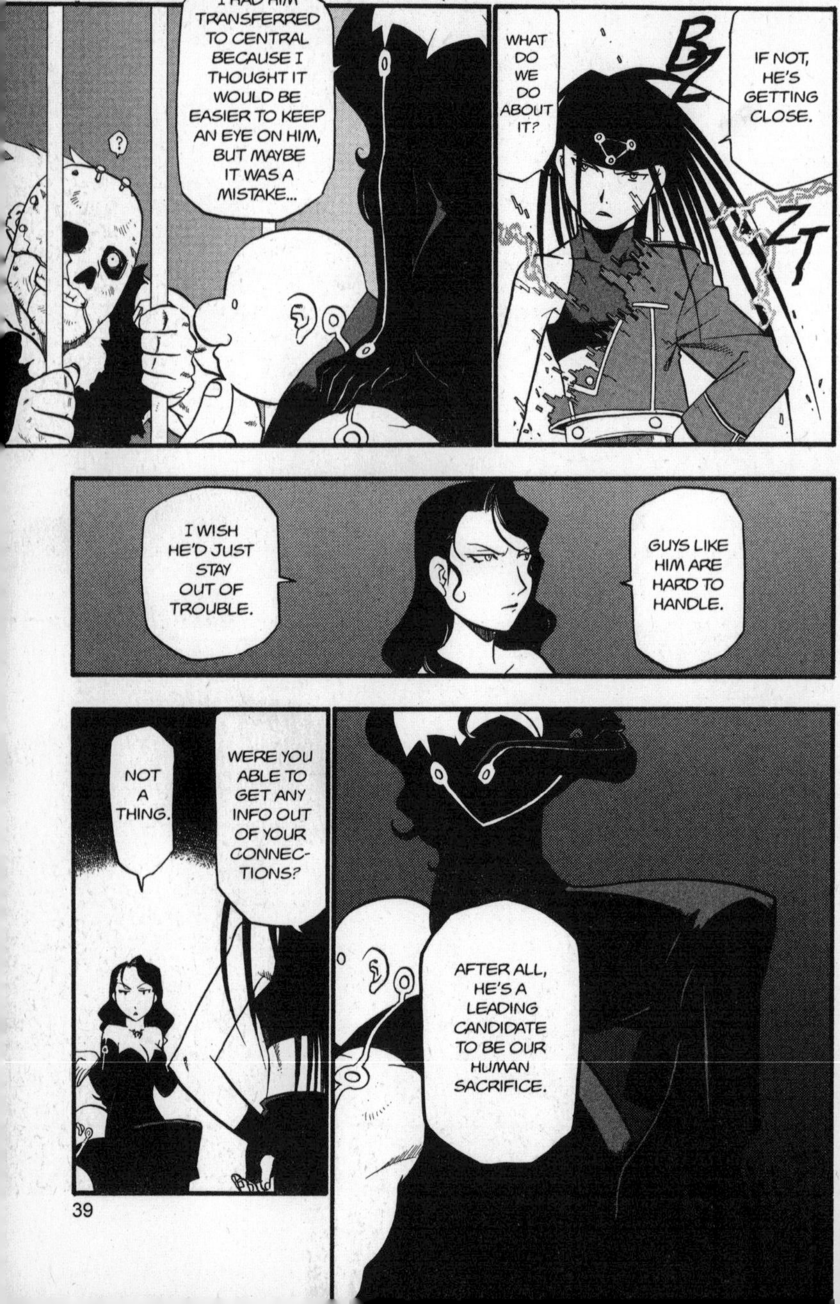

IF NOT, HE'S GETTING CLOSE.
BZZT
WHAT DO WE DO ABOUT IT?
I HAD HIM TRANSFERRED TO CENTRAL BECAUSE I THOUGHT IT WOULD BE EASIER TO KEEP AN EYE ON HIM, BUT MAYBE IT WAS A MISTAKE...
?
GUYS LIKE HIM ARE HARD TO HANDLE.
I WISH HE'D JUST STAY OUT OF TROUBLE.
AFTER ALL, HE'S A LEADING CANDIDATE TO BE OUR HUMAN SACRIFICE.
WERE YOU ABLE TO GET ANY INFO OUT OF YOUR CONNECTIONS?
NOT A THING.

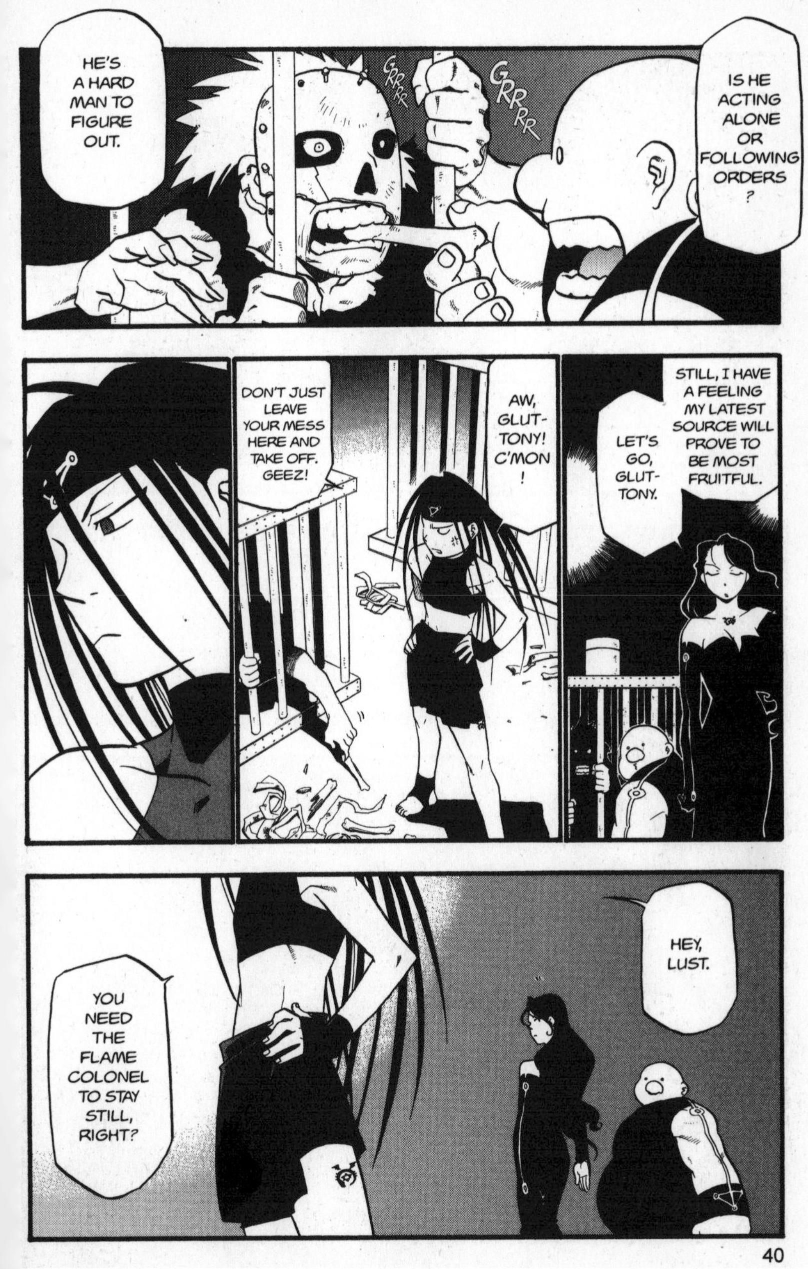
IS HE ACTING ALONE OR FOLLOWING ORDERS?
GRRRR
GRRR
HE'S A HARD MAN TO FIGURE OUT.
STILL, I HAVE A FEELING MY LATEST SOURCE WILL PROVE TO BE MOST FRUITFUL.
LET'S GO, GLUTTONY.
AW, GLUTTONY! C'MON!
DON'T JUST LEAVE YOUR MESS HERE AND TAKE OFF. GEEZ!
HEY, LUST.
YOU NEED THE FLAME COLONEL TO STAY STILL, RIGHT?

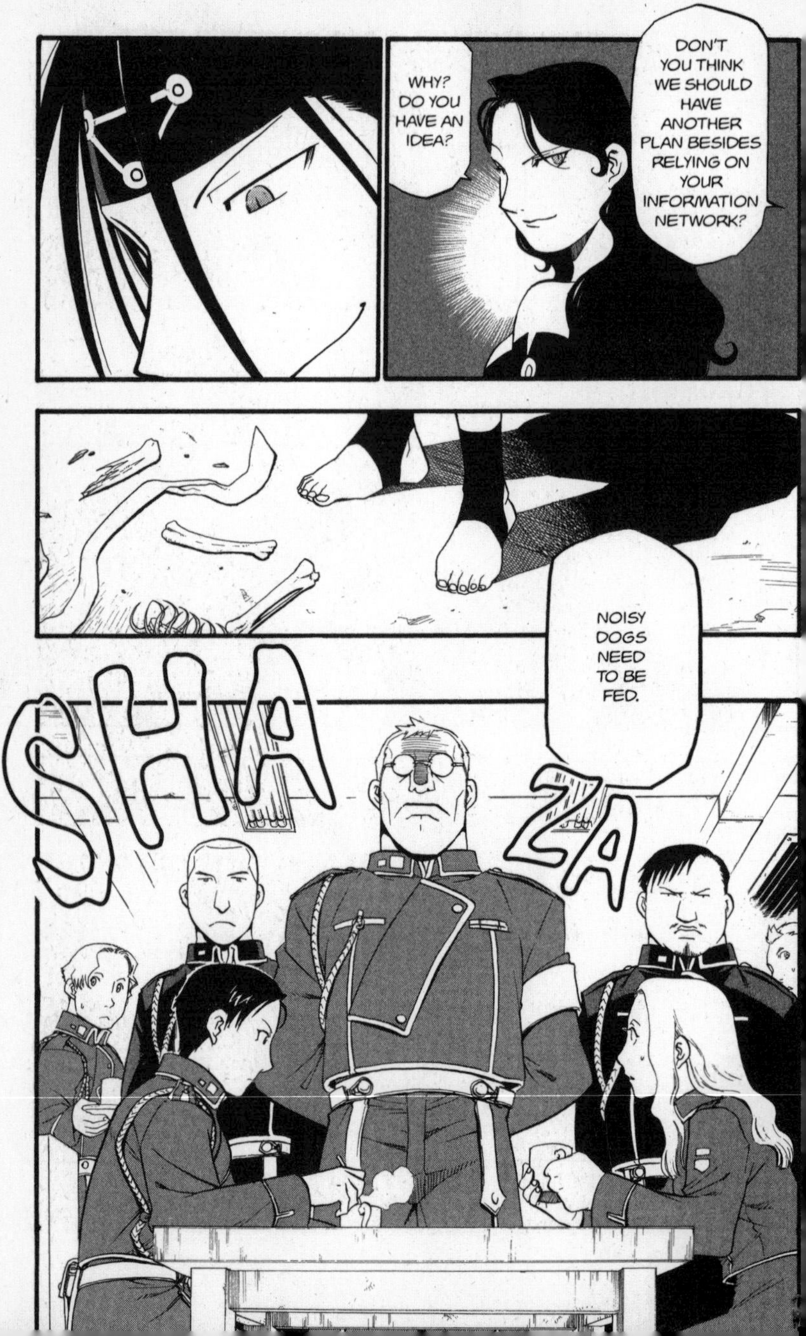
DON'T YOU THINK WE SHOULD HAVE ANOTHER PLAN BESIDES RELYING ON YOUR INFORMATION NETWORK?
WHY? DO YOU HAVE AN IDEA?
NOISY DOGS NEED TO BE FED.
SHA
ZA

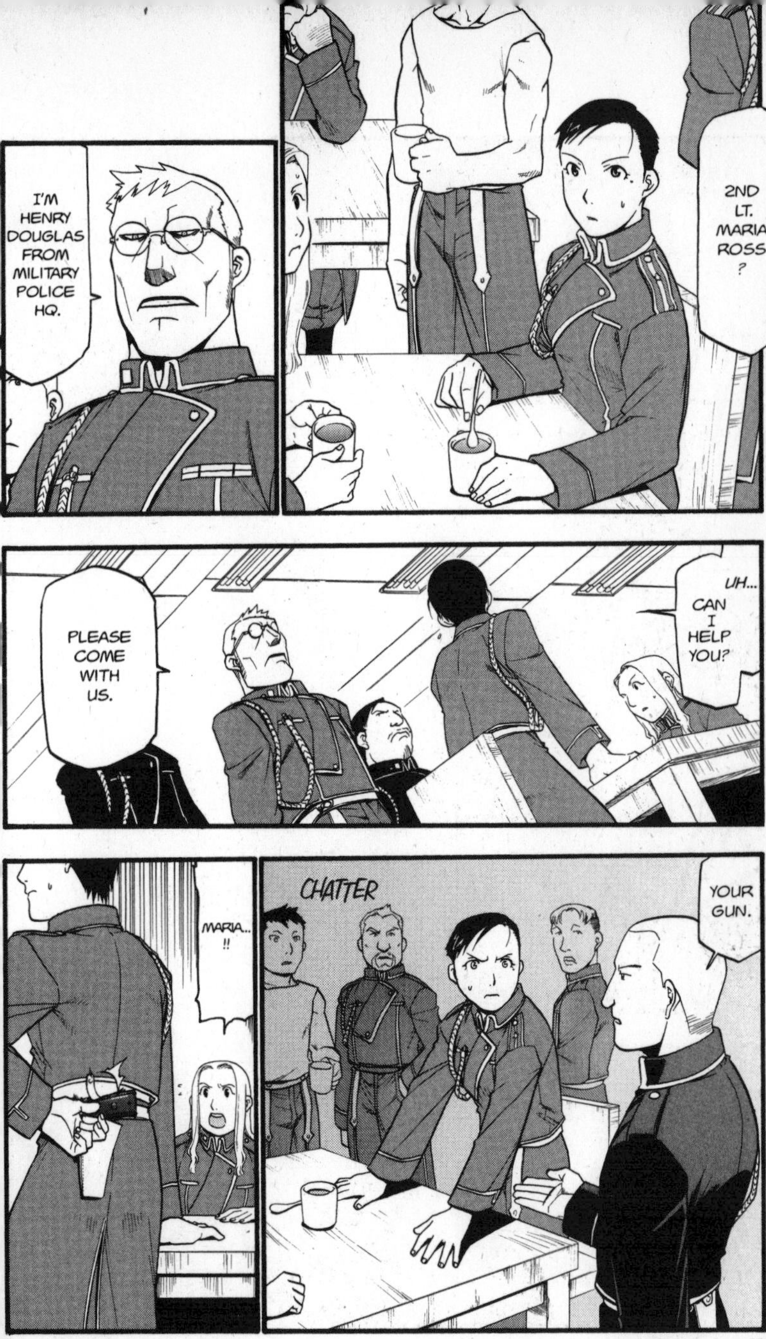
2ND LT. MARIA ROSS ?
I'M HENRY DOUGLAS FROM MILITARY POLICE HQ.
UH... CAN I HELP YOU?
PLEASE COME WITH US.
YOUR GUN.
CHATTER
MARIA... !!

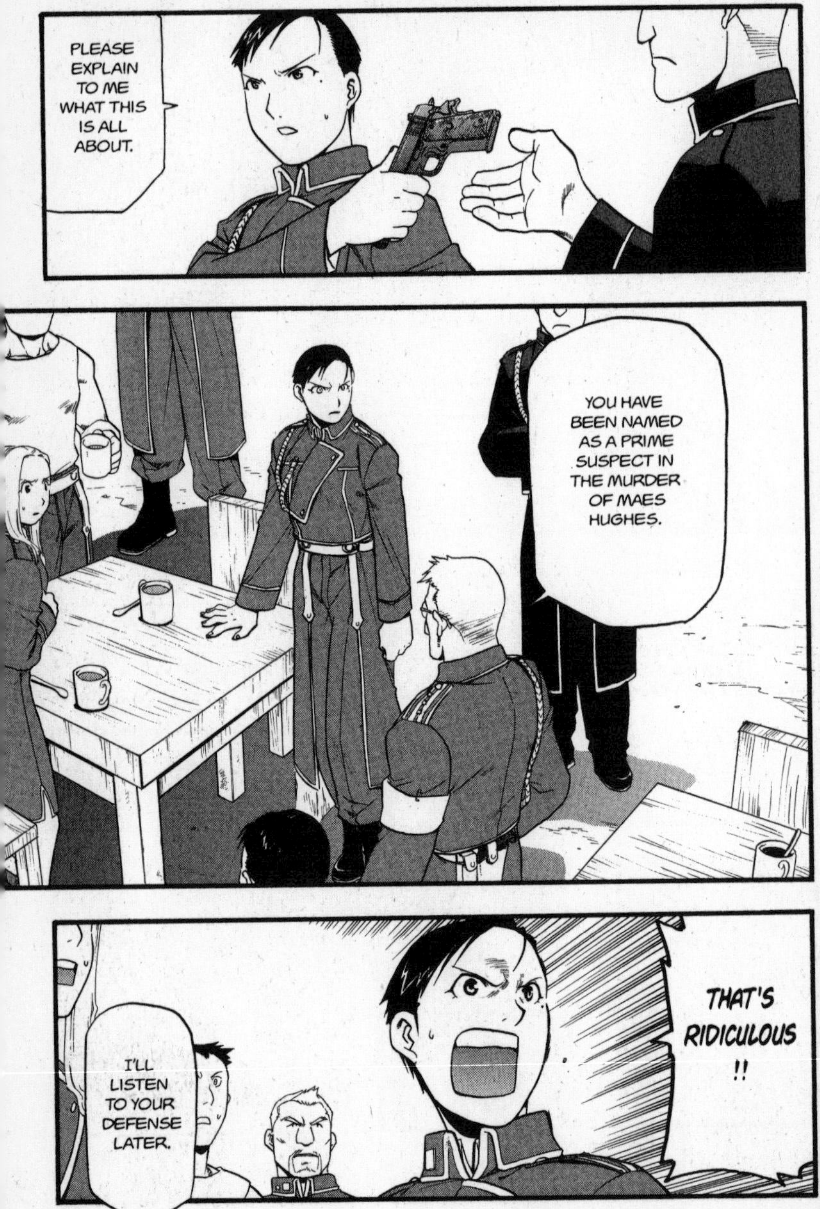
PLEASE EXPLAIN TO ME WHAT THIS IS ALL ABOUT.
YOU HAVE BEEN NAMED AS A PRIME SUSPECT IN THE MURDER OF MAES HUGHES.
THAT'S RIDICULOUS !!
I'LL LISTEN TO YOUR DEFENSE LATER.

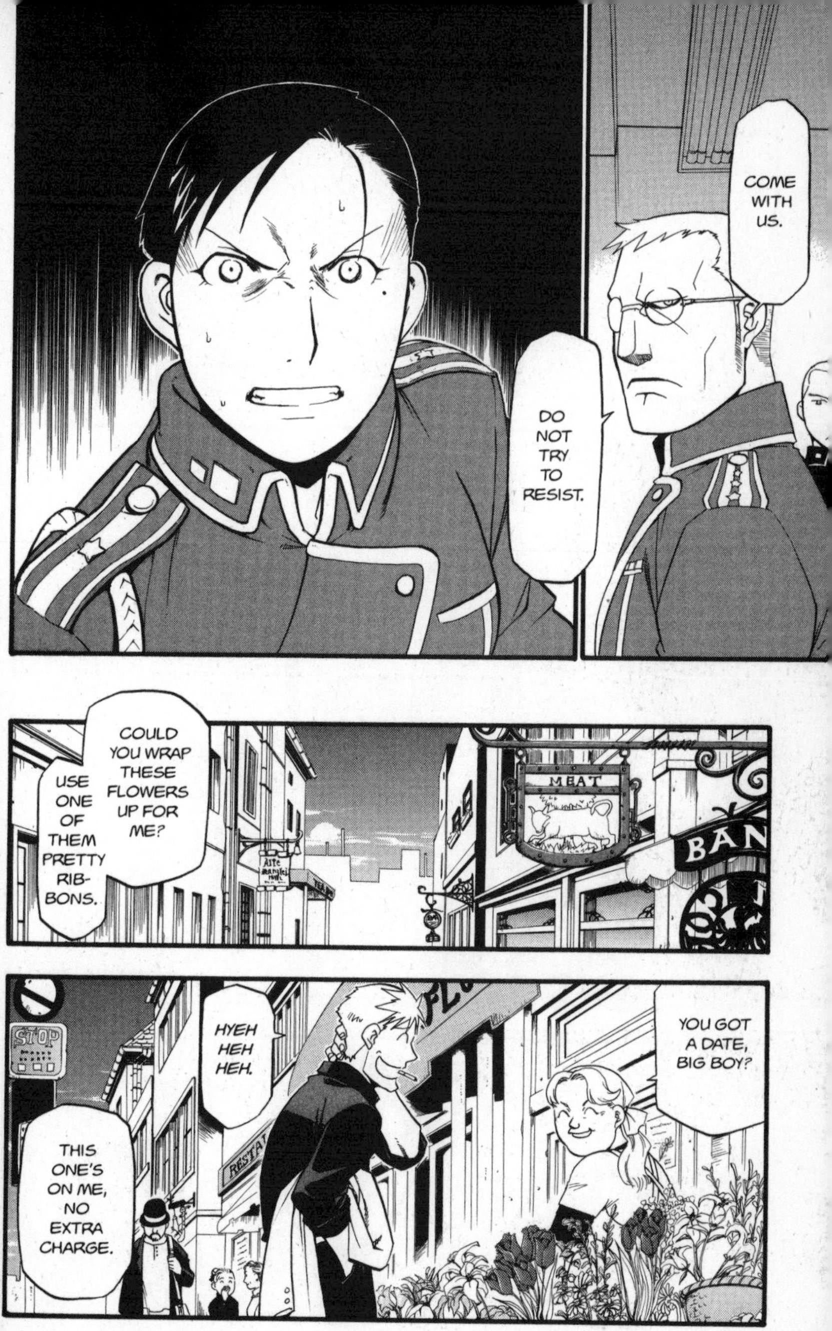
COME WITH US.
DO NOT TRY TO RESIST.
COULD YOU WRAP THESE FLOWERS UP FOR ME?
USE ONE OF THEM PRETTY RIB-BONS.
MEAT
YOU GOT A DATE, BIG BOY?
HYEH HEH HEH.
THIS ONE'S ON ME, NO EXTRA CHARGE.
STOP

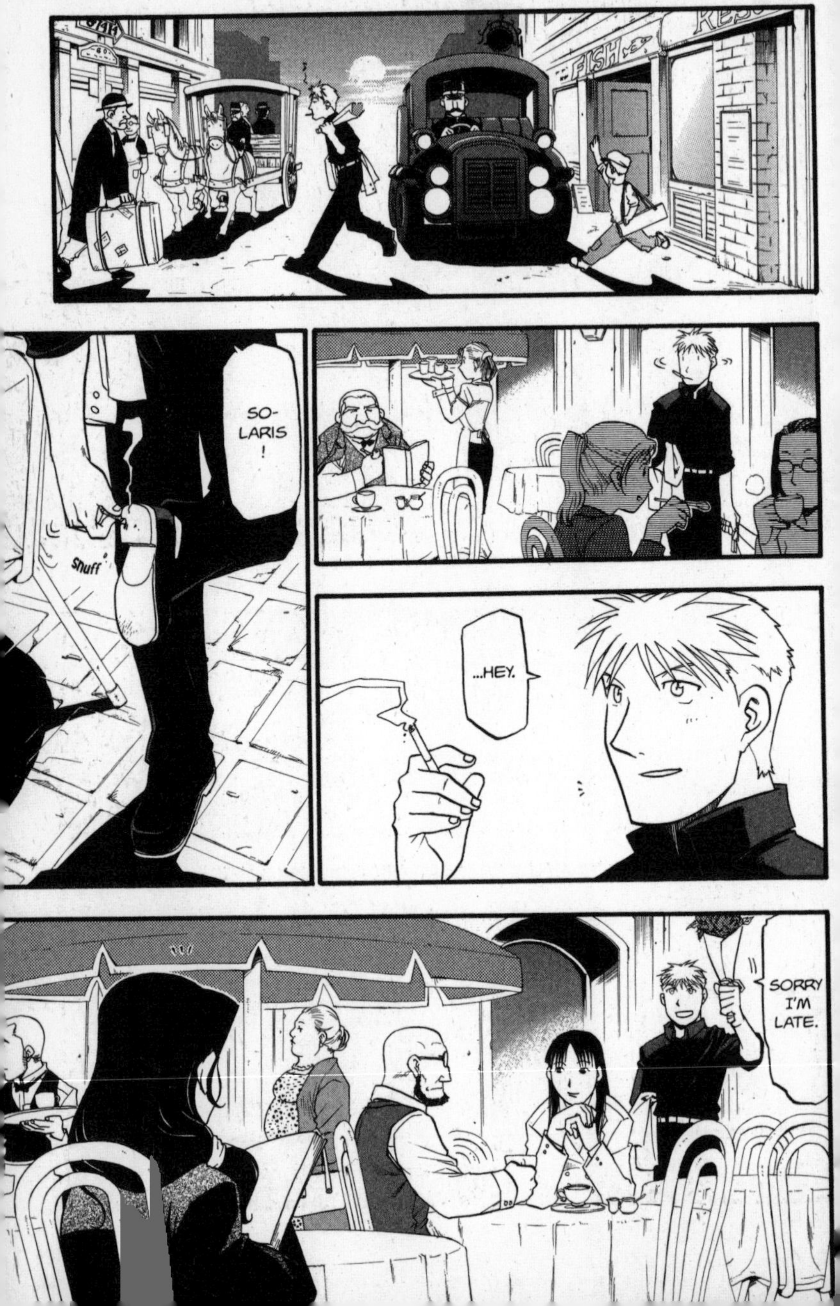
FISH
...HEY.
SO-LARIS!
snuff
SORRY I'M LATE.

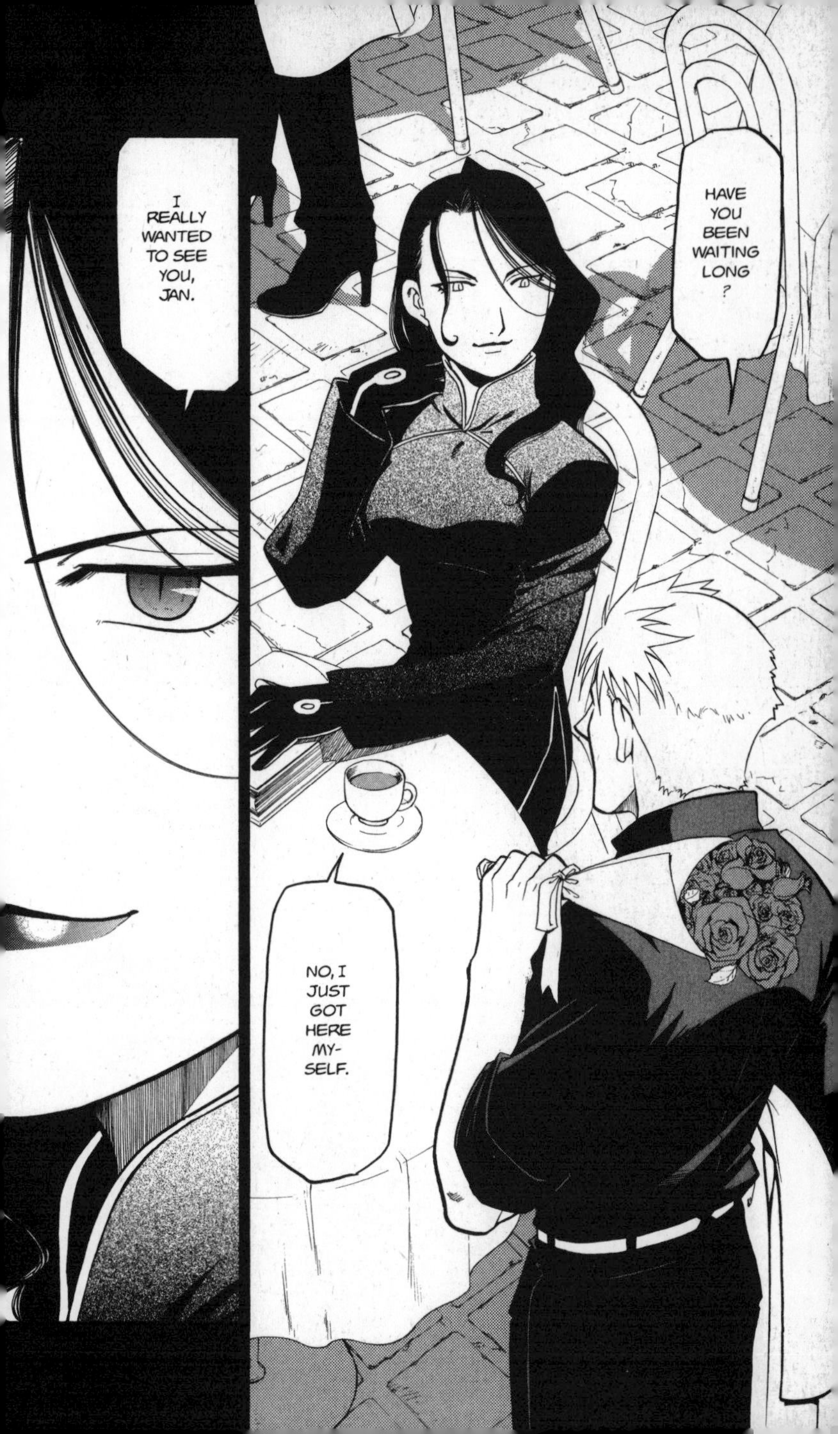
HAVE YOU BEEN WAITING LONG?
NO, I JUST GOT HERE MY-SELF.
I REALLY WANTED TO SEE YOU, JAN.

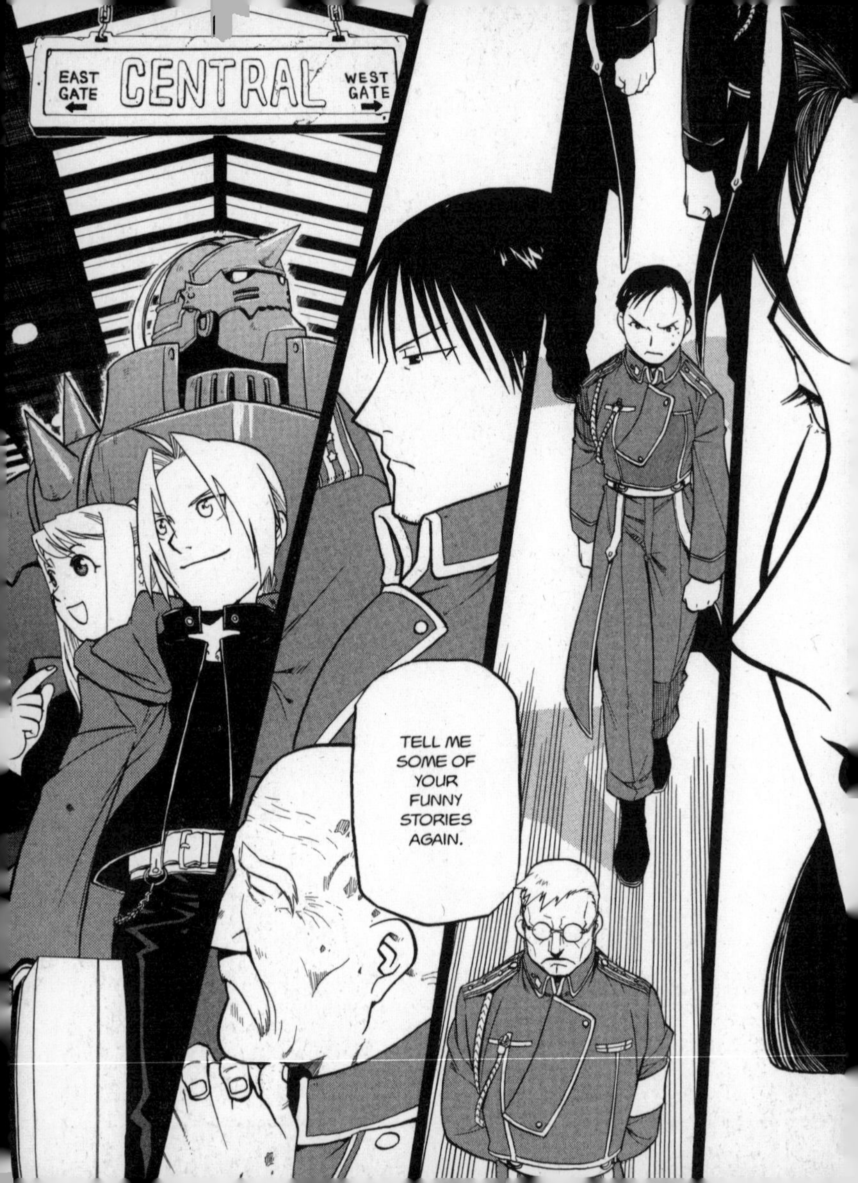
EAST GATE
CENTRAL
WEST GATE
TELL ME SOME OF YOUR FUNNY STORIES AGAIN.

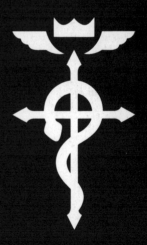

FULLMETAL
ALCHEMIST

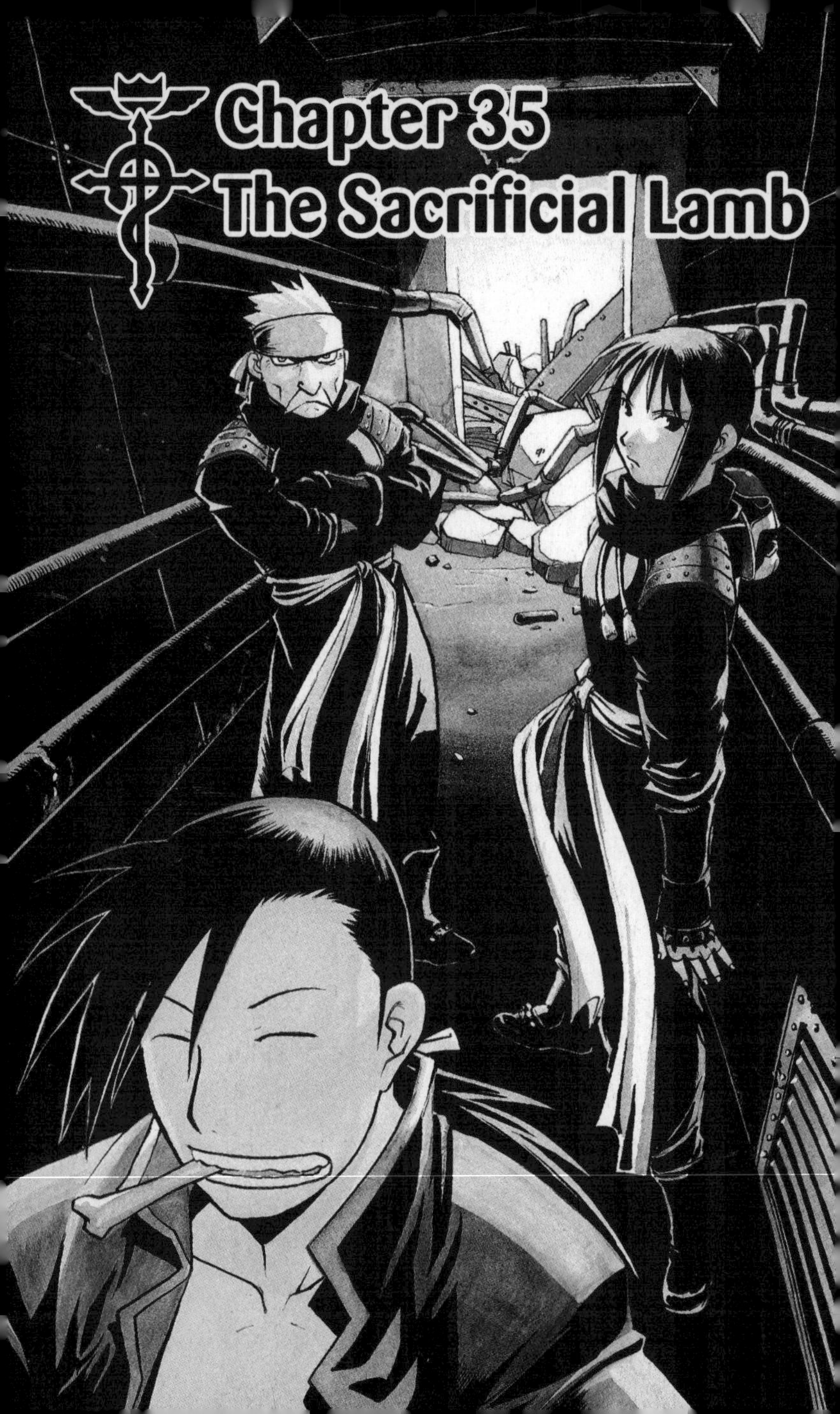
Chapter 35
The Sacrificial Lamb

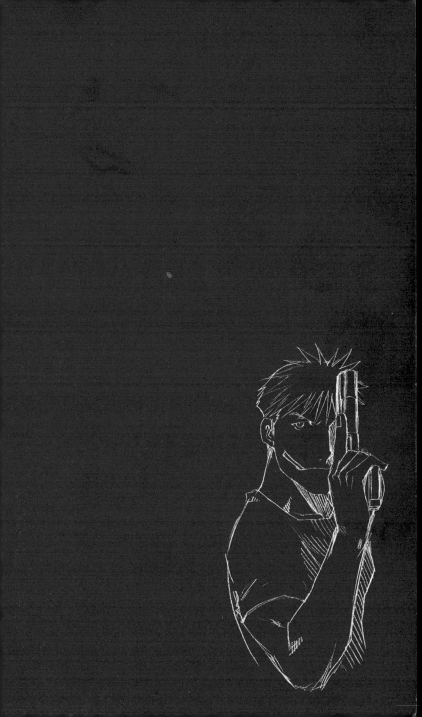

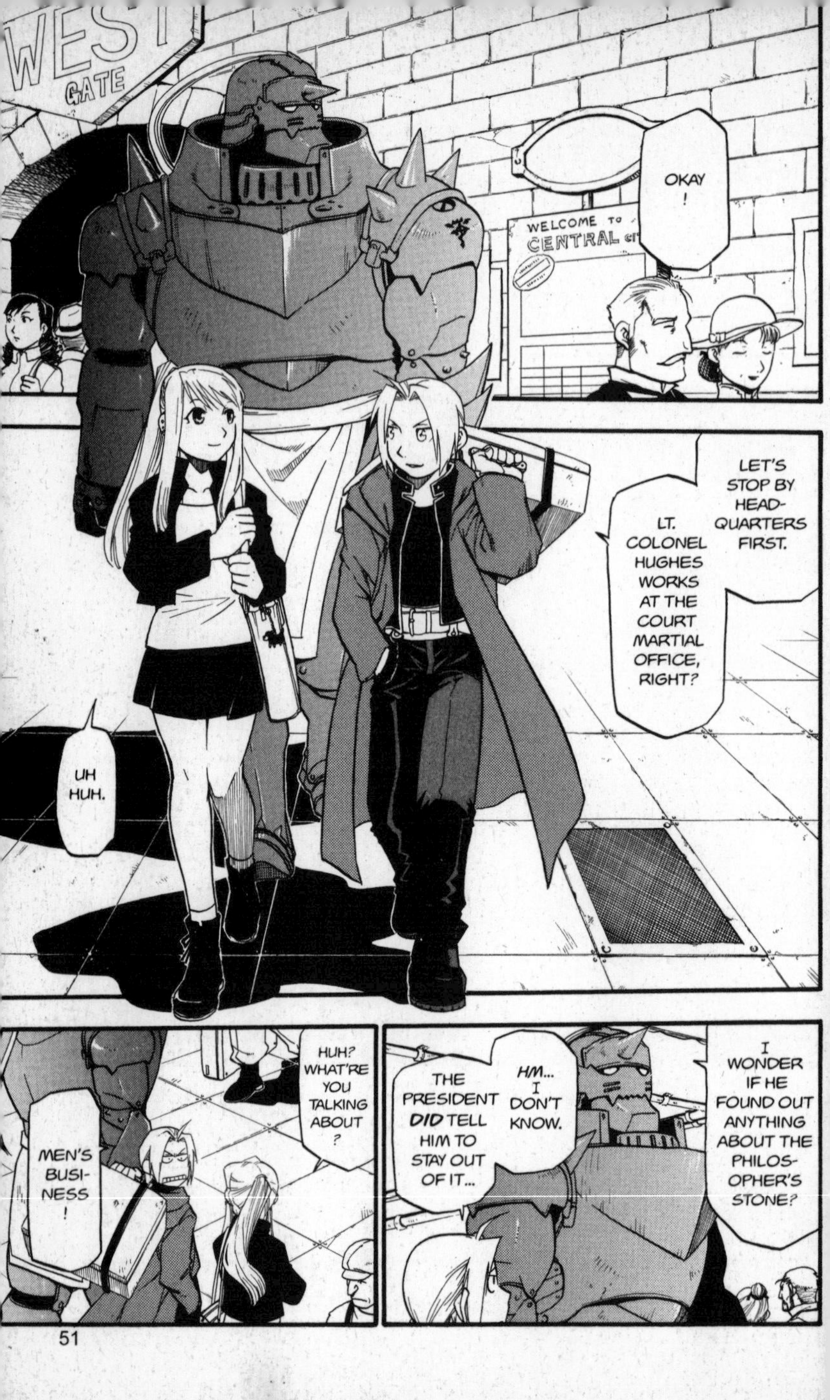
WEST
GATE
WELCOME TO
CENTRAL
OKAY!
LET'S STOP BY HEAD-QUARTERS FIRST.
LT. COLONEL HUGHES WORKS AT THE COURT MARTIAL OFFICE, RIGHT?
UH HUH.
I WONDER IF HE FOUND OUT ANYTHING ABOUT THE PHILOS-OPHER'S STONE?
HM... I DON'T KNOW.
THE PRESIDENT DID TELL HIM TO STAY OUT OF IT...
HUH? WHAT'RE YOU TALKING ABOUT?
MEN'S BUSI-NESS!

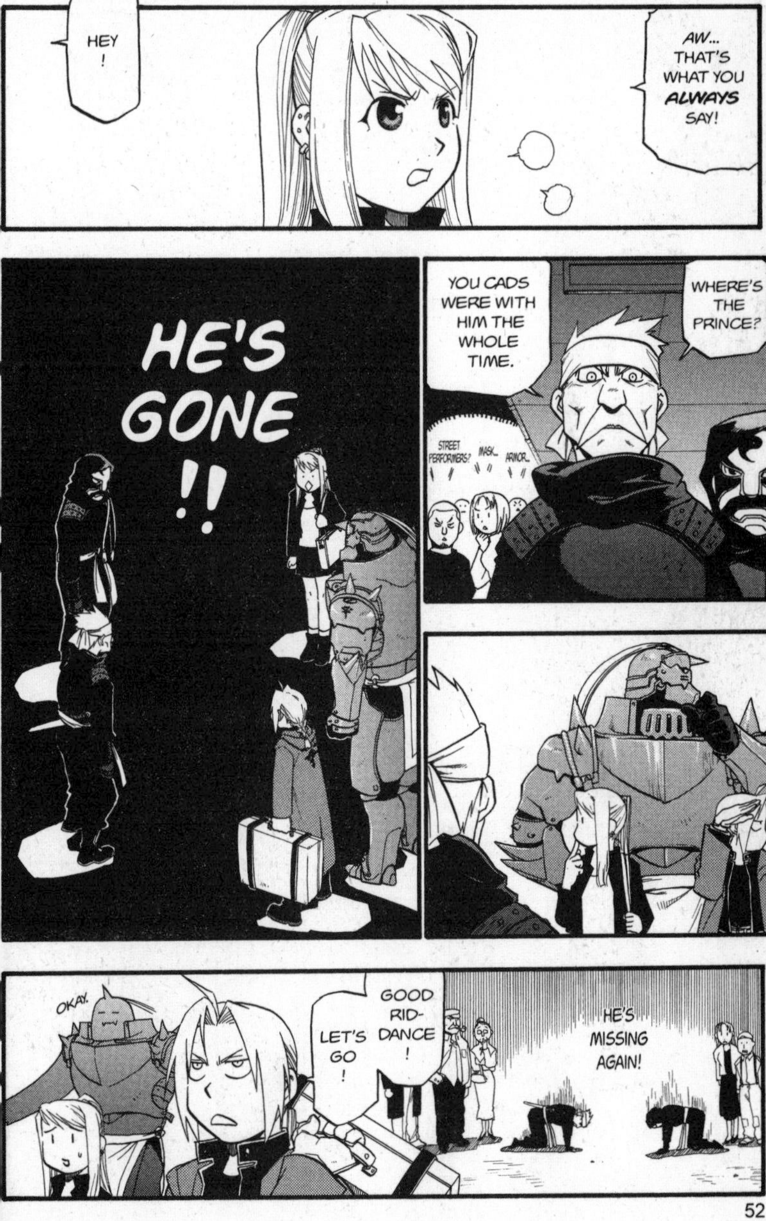
AW... THAT'S WHAT YOU ALWAYS SAY!
HEY!
WHERE'S THE PRINCE?
YOU CADS WERE WITH HIM THE WHOLE TIME.
STREET PERFORMERS?
MASK...
ARMOR...
HE'S GONE!!
HE'S MISSING AGAIN!
GOOD RID-DANCE!
LET'S GO!
OKAY.

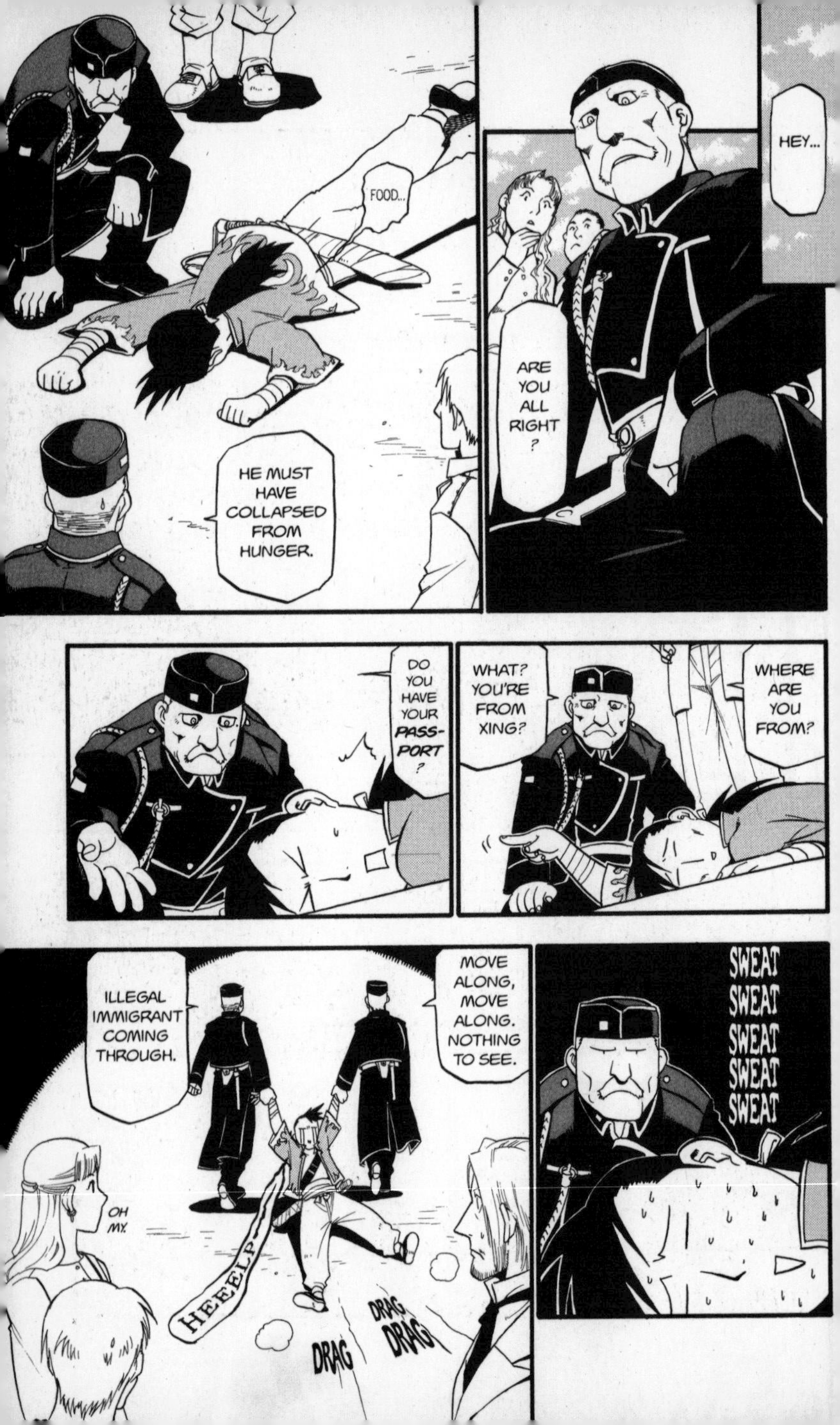
HEY...
ARE YOU ALL RIGHT?
FOOD...
HE MUST HAVE COLLAPSED FROM HUNGER.
WHERE ARE YOU FROM?
WHAT? YOU'RE FROM XING?
DO YOU HAVE YOUR PASSPORT?
SWEAT SWEAT SWEAT SWEAT SWEAT
MOVE ALONG, MOVE ALONG. NOTHING TO SEE.
ILLEGAL IMMIGRANT COMING THROUGH.
OH MY.
HEEELP
DRAG DRAG
DRAG

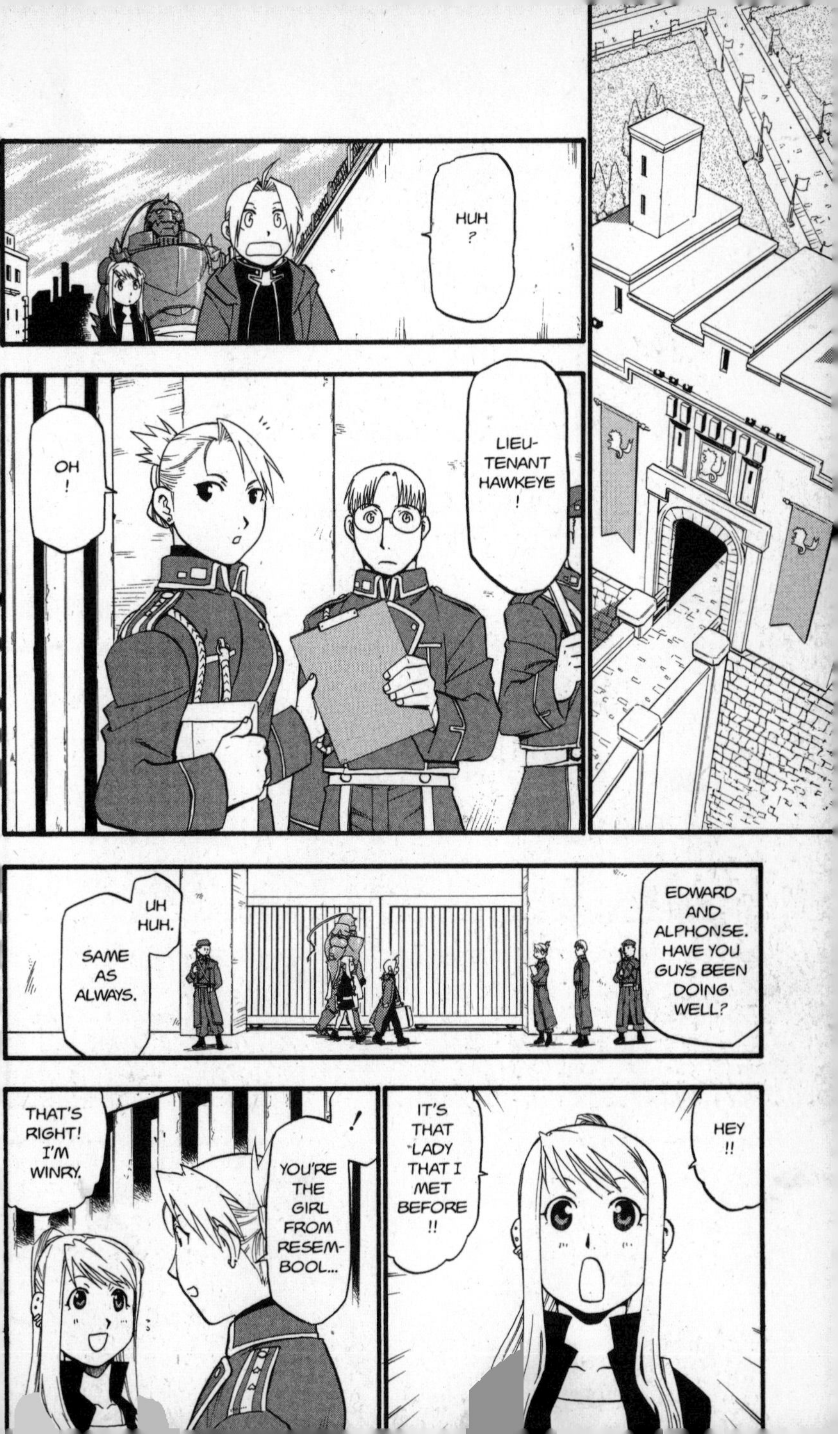
HUH?
LIEU-TENANT HAWKEYE!
OH!
EDWARD AND ALPHONSE. HAVE YOU GUYS BEEN DOING WELL?
UH HUH.
SAME AS ALWAYS.
HEY!!
IT'S THAT LADY THAT I MET BEFORE!!
!
YOU'RE THE GIRL FROM RESEM-BOOL...
THAT'S RIGHT! I'M WINRY.

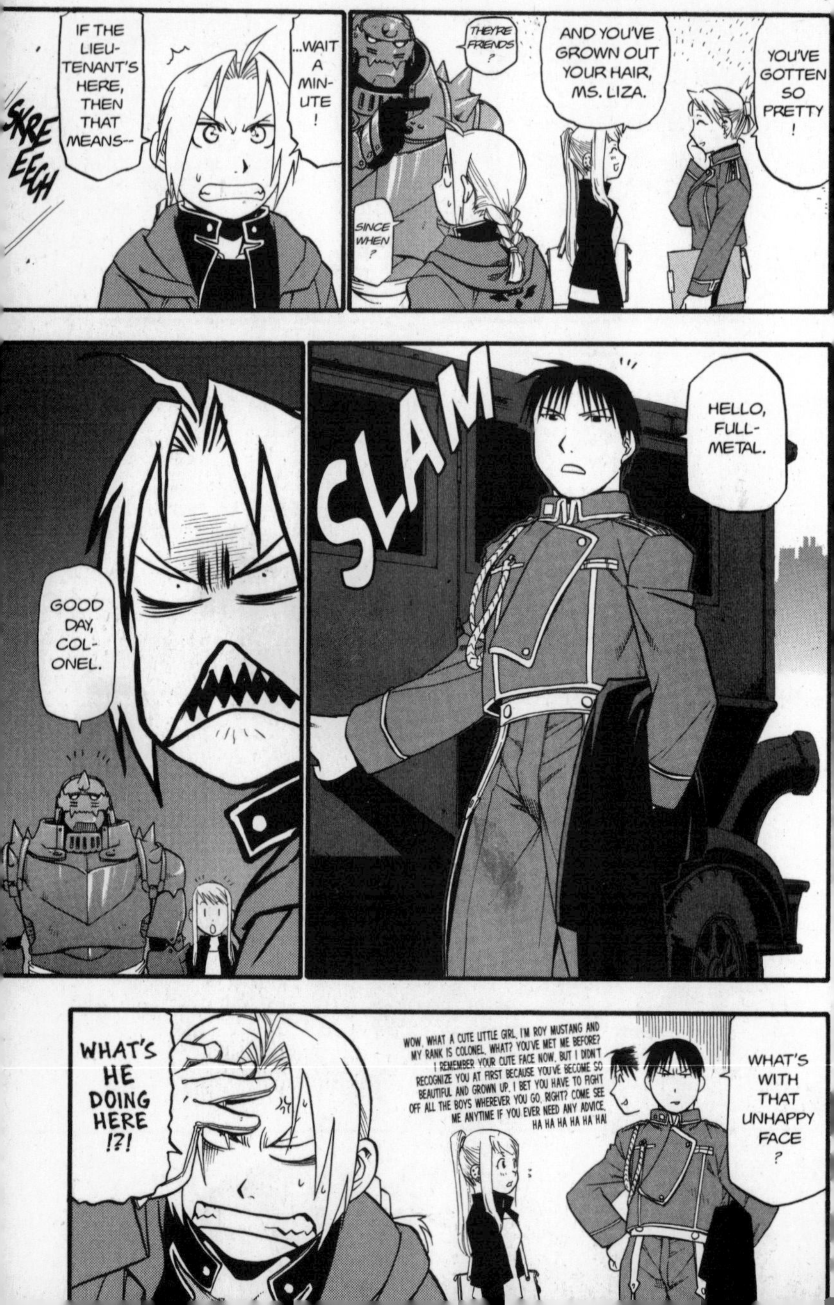
YOU'VE GOTTEN SO PRETTY!
AND YOU'VE GROWN OUT YOUR HAIR, MS. LIZA.
THEY'RE FRIENDS?
SINCE WHEN?
...WAIT A MINUTE!
IF THE LIEUTENANT'S HERE, THEN THAT MEANS--
SKREEECH
SLAM
HELLO, FULLMETAL.
GOOD DAY, COLONEL.
WHAT'S WITH THAT UNHAPPY FACE?
WOW, WHAT A CUTE LITTLE GIRL. I'M ROY MUSTANG AND MY RANK IS COLONEL. WHAT? YOU'VE MET ME BEFORE? I REMEMBER YOUR CUTE FACE NOW, BUT I DIDN'T RECOGNIZE YOU AT FIRST BECAUSE YOU'VE BECOME SO BEAUTIFUL AND GROWN UP. I BET YOU HAVE TO FIGHT OFF ALL THE BOYS WHEREVER YOU GO, RIGHT? COME SEE ME ANYTIME IF YOU EVER NEED ANY ADVICE. HA HA HA HA HA HA!
WHAT'S HE DOING HERE!?!

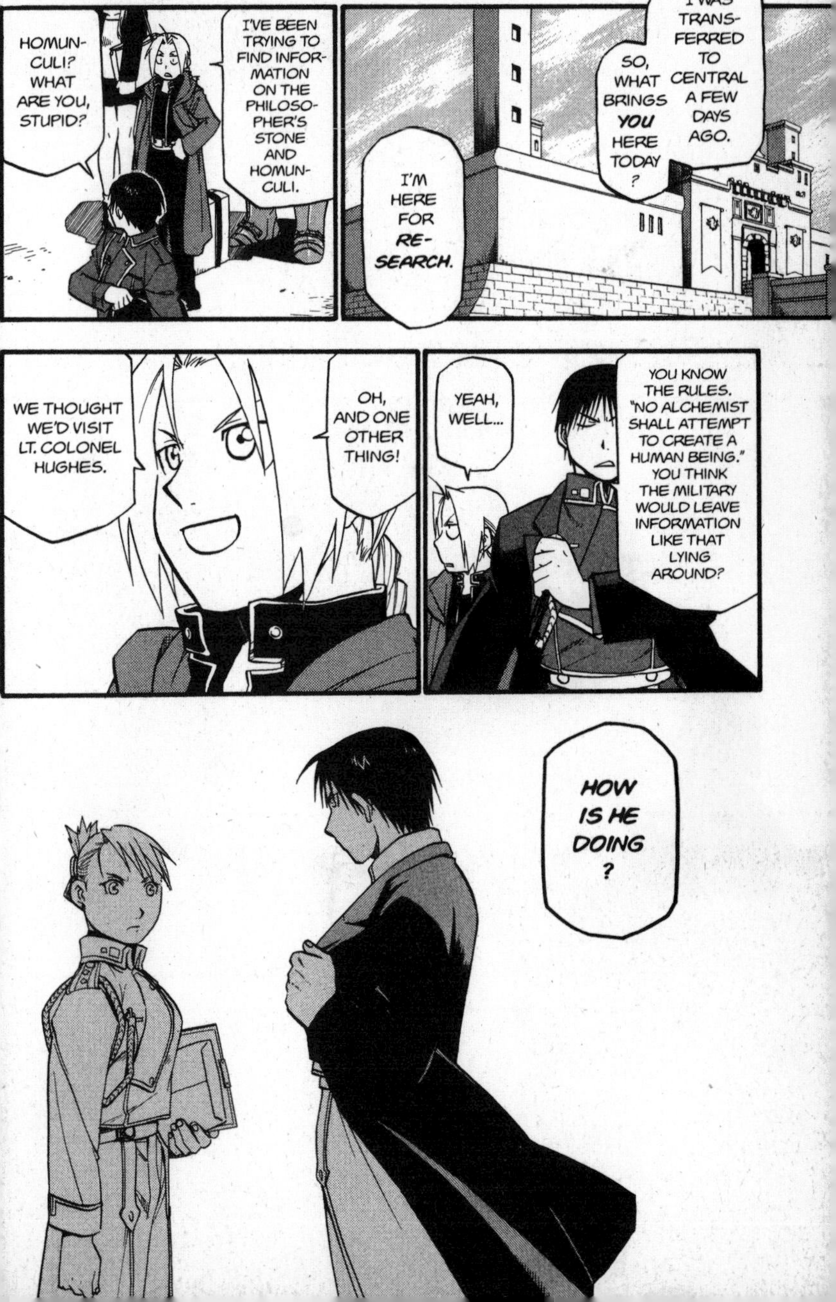
I WAS TRANSFERRED TO CENTRAL A FEW DAYS AGO.
SO, WHAT BRINGS *YOU* HERE TODAY?
I'M HERE FOR *RESEARCH.*
I'VE BEEN TRYING TO FIND INFORMATION ON THE PHILOSOPHER'S STONE AND HOMUNCULI.
HOMUNCULI? WHAT ARE YOU, STUPID?
YOU KNOW THE RULES. "NO ALCHEMIST SHALL ATTEMPT TO CREATE A HUMAN BEING." YOU THINK THE MILITARY WOULD LEAVE INFORMATION LIKE THAT LYING AROUND?
YEAH, WELL...
OH, AND ONE OTHER THING!
WE THOUGHT WE'D VISIT LT. COLONEL HUGHES.
HOW IS HE DOING?

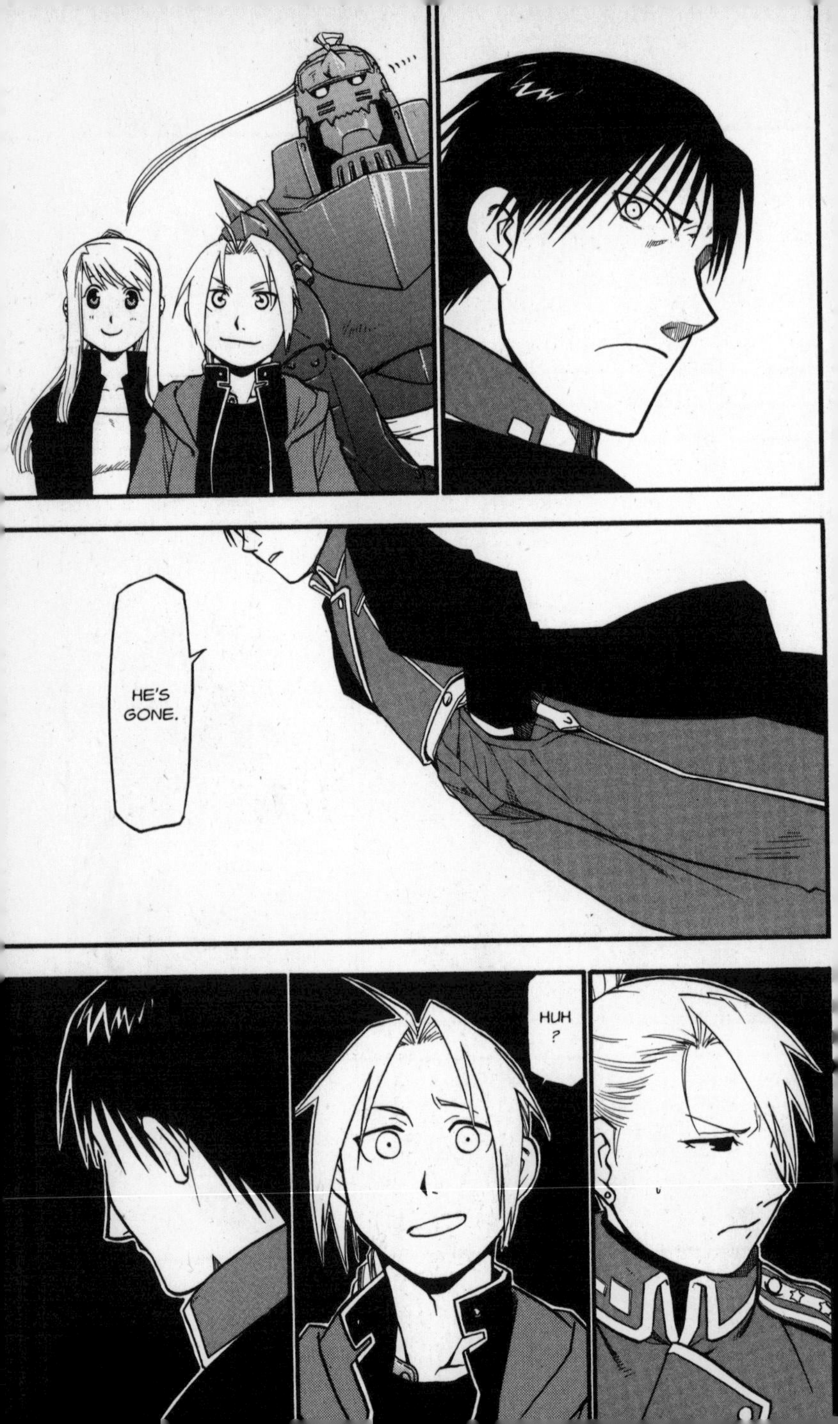
HE'S GONE.
HUH ?

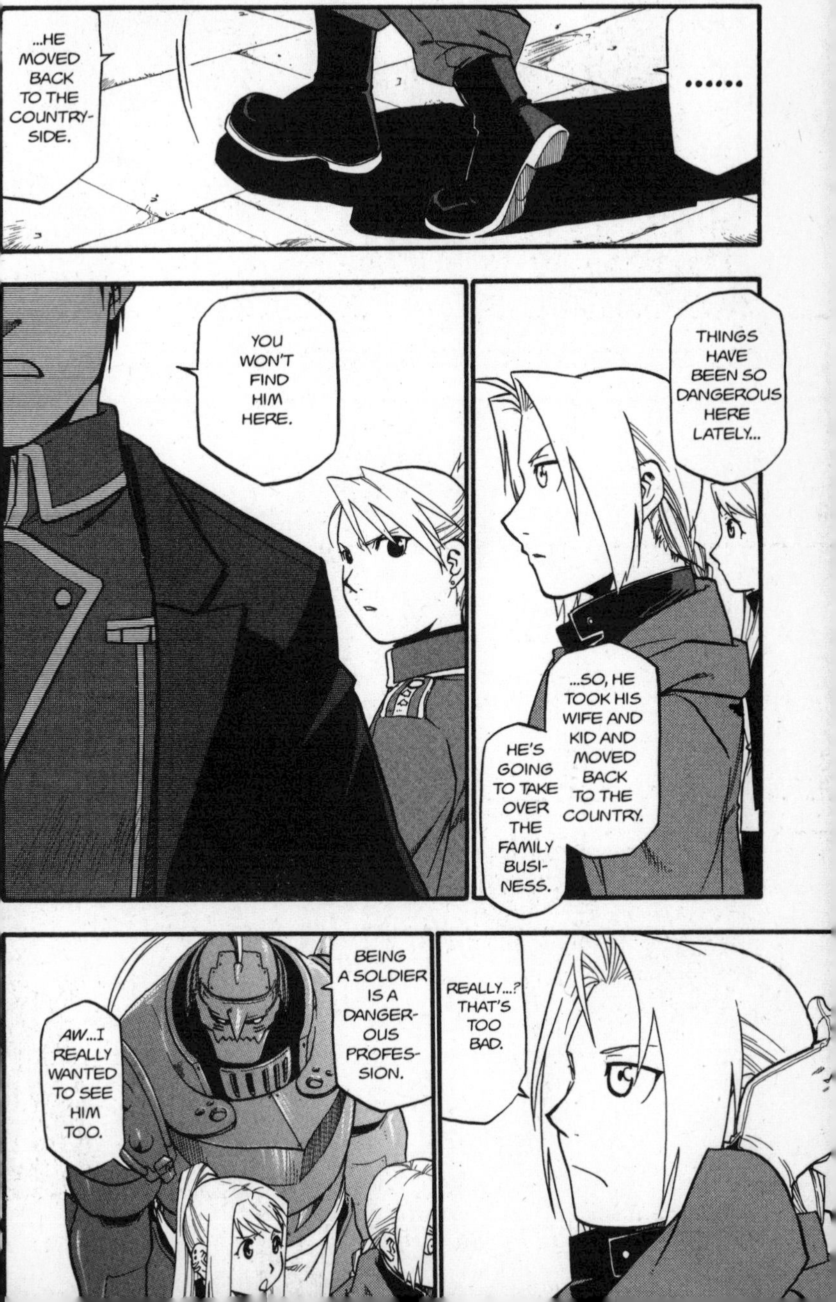

......
...HE MOVED BACK TO THE COUNTRY-SIDE.
THINGS HAVE BEEN SO DANGEROUS HERE LATELY...
...SO, HE TOOK HIS WIFE AND KID AND MOVED BACK TO THE COUNTRY.
HE'S GOING TO TAKE OVER THE FAMILY BUSI-NESS.
YOU WON'T FIND HIM HERE.
REALLY...? THAT'S TOO BAD.
BEING A SOLDIER IS A DANGER-OUS PROFES-SION.
AW...I REALLY WANTED TO SEE HIM TOO.

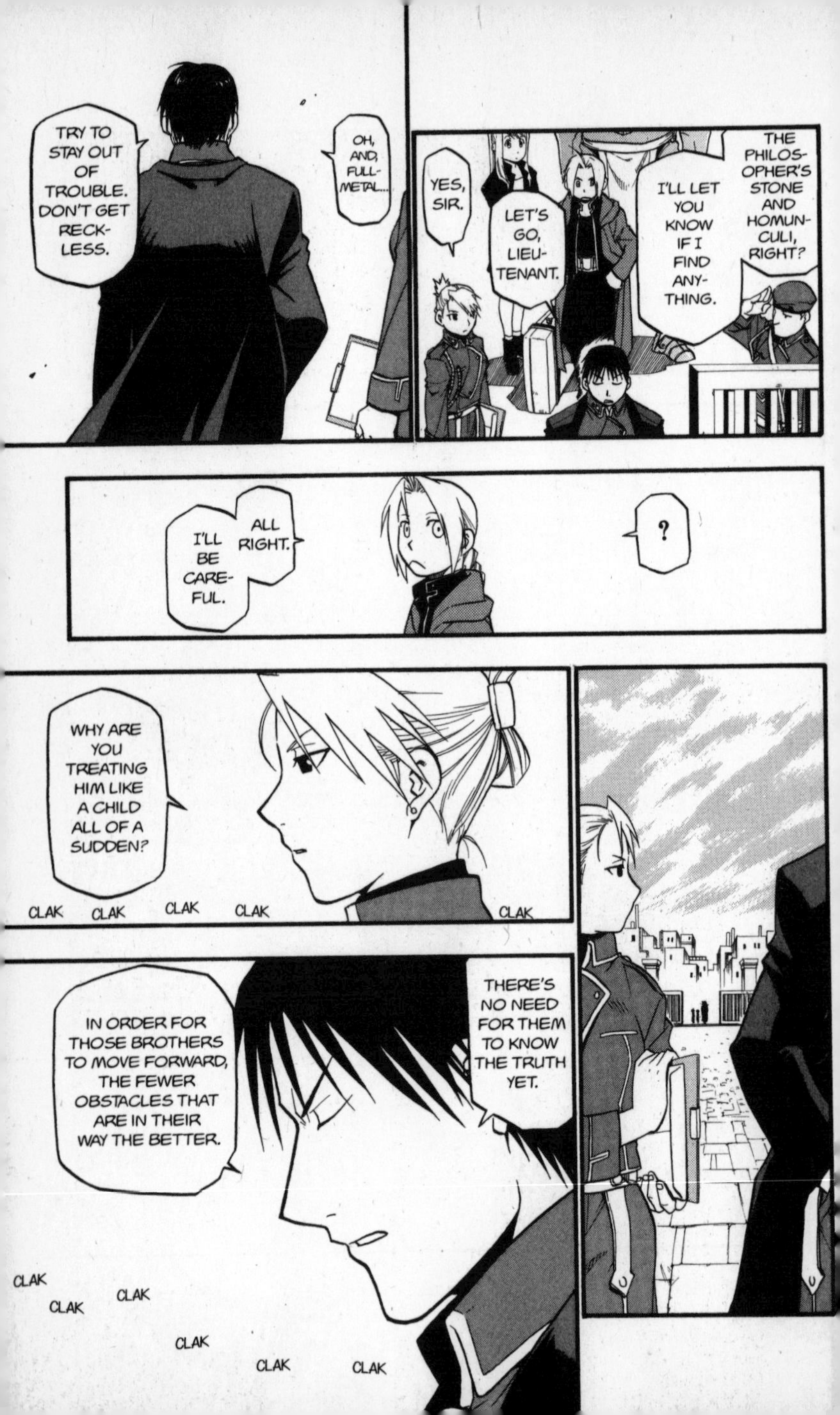
THE PHILOSOPHER'S STONE AND HOMUNCULI, RIGHT?
I'LL LET YOU KNOW IF I FIND ANYTHING.
LET'S GO, LIEUTENANT.
YES, SIR.
OH, AND, FULLMETAL...
TRY TO STAY OUT OF TROUBLE. DON'T GET RECKLESS.
?
ALL RIGHT.
I'LL BE CAREFUL.
WHY ARE YOU TREATING HIM LIKE A CHILD ALL OF A SUDDEN?
CLAK CLAK CLAK CLAK CLAK
THERE'S NO NEED FOR THEM TO KNOW THE TRUTH YET.
IN ORDER FOR THOSE BROTHERS TO MOVE FORWARD, THE FEWER OBSTACLES THAT ARE IN THEIR WAY THE BETTER.
CLAK CLAK CLAK CLAK CLAK CLAK

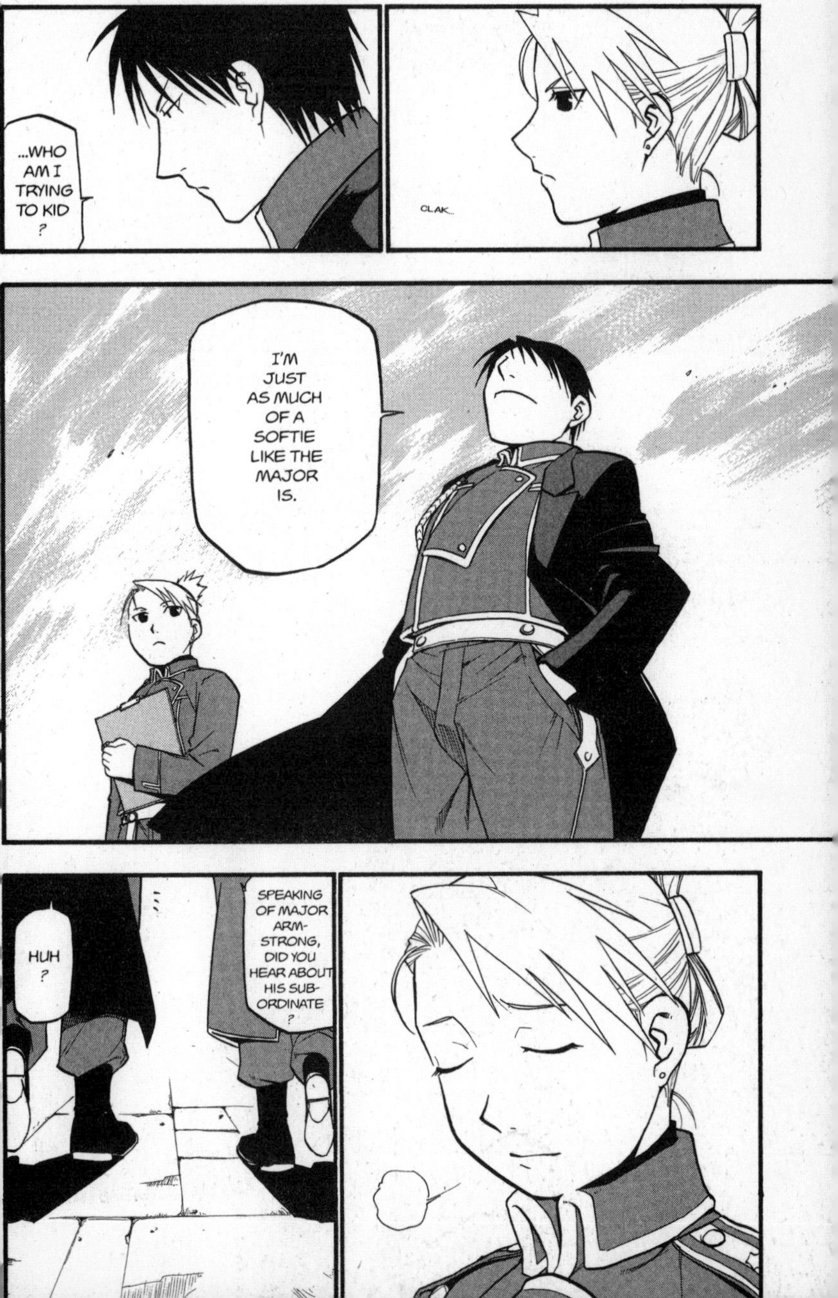
CLAK...
...WHO AM I TRYING TO KID?
I'M JUST AS MUCH OF A SOFTIE LIKE THE MAJOR IS.
SPEAKING OF MAJOR ARM-STRONG, DID YOU HEAR ABOUT HIS SUB-ORDINATE?
...
HUH?

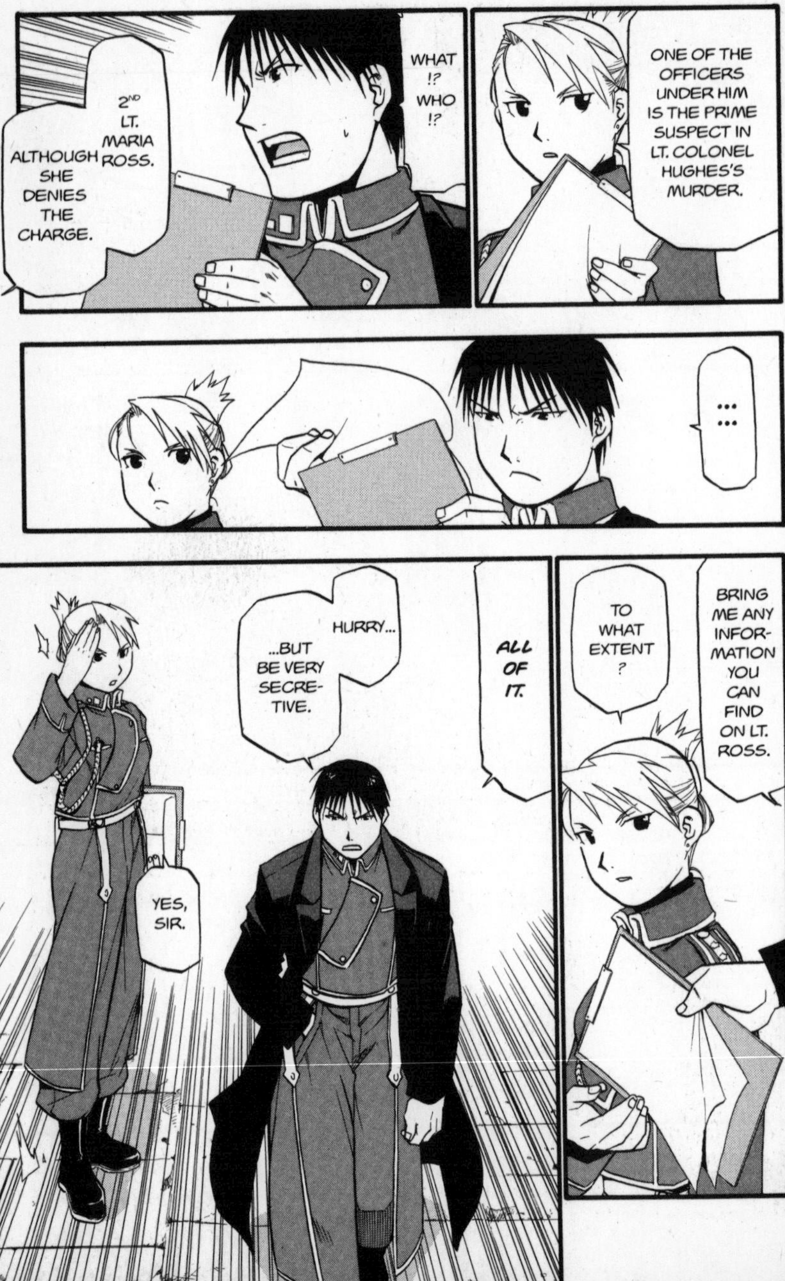
ONE OF THE OFFICERS UNDER HIM IS THE PRIME SUSPECT IN LT. COLONEL HUGHES'S MURDER.
WHAT !? WHO !?
2ND LT. MARIA ROSS.
ALTHOUGH SHE DENIES THE CHARGE.
......
BRING ME ANY INFOR-MATION YOU CAN FIND ON LT. ROSS.
TO WHAT EXTENT ?
ALL OF IT.
HURRY...
...BUT BE VERY SECRE-TIVE.
YES, SIR.

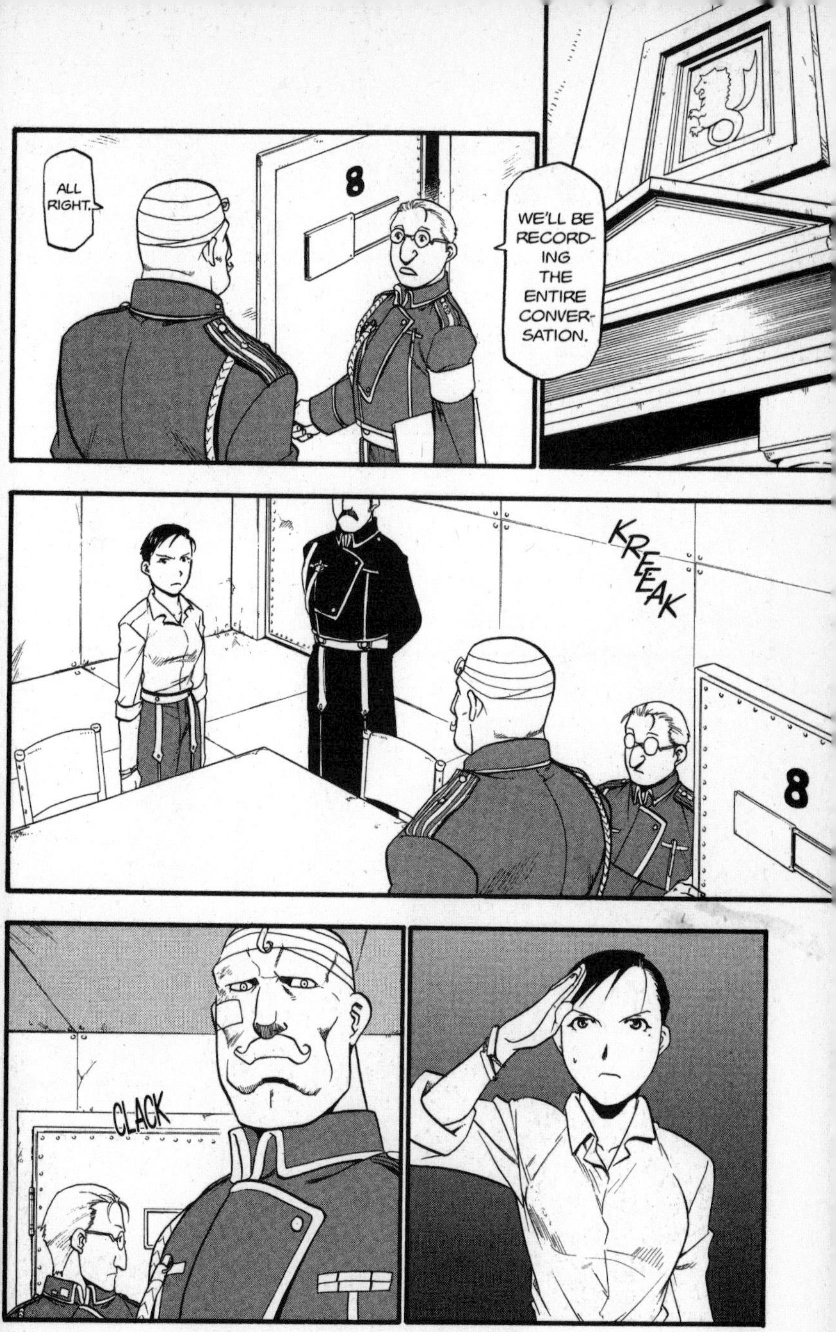
WE'LL BE RECORDING THE ENTIRE CONVERSATION.
ALL RIGHT.
KREEAK
CLACK

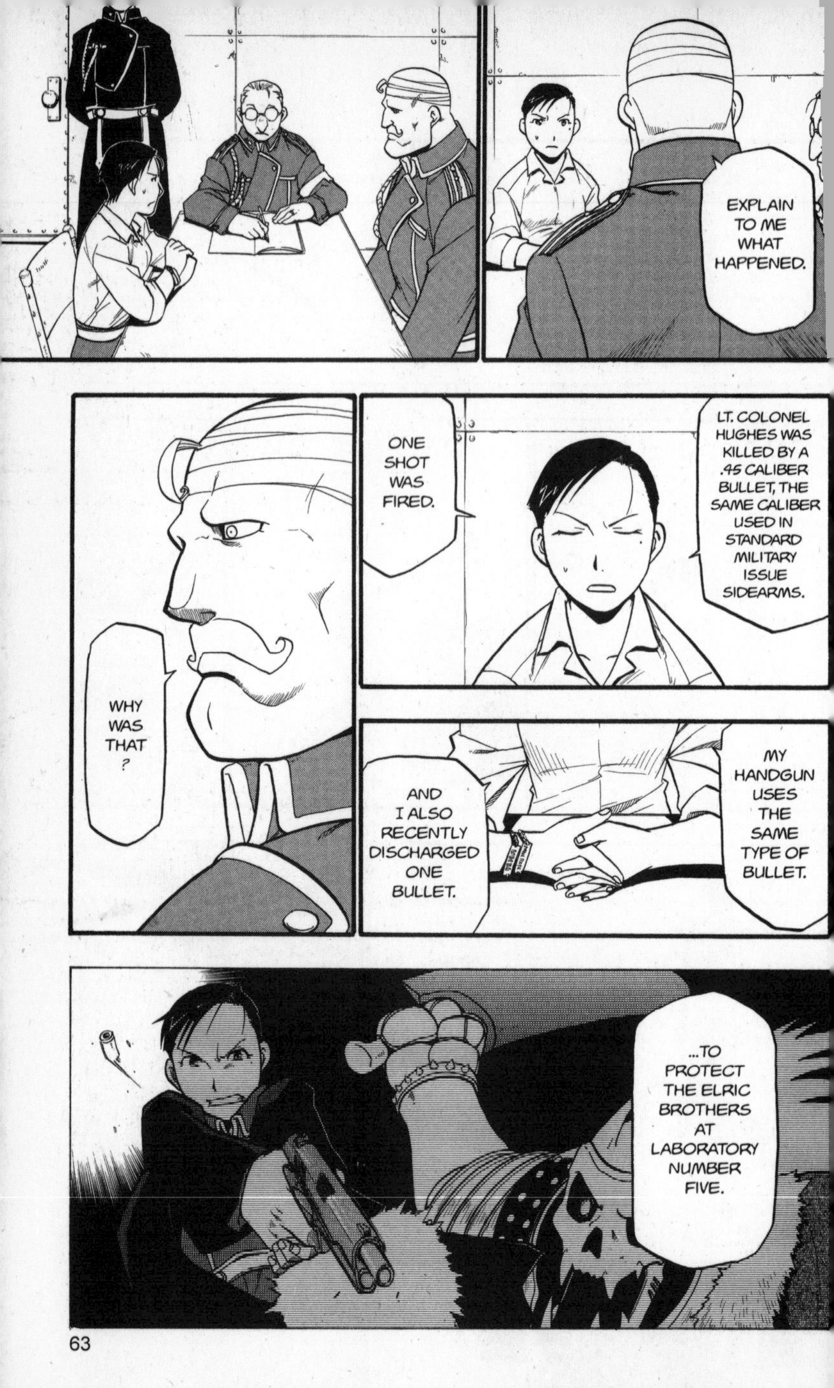
EXPLAIN TO ME WHAT HAPPENED.
LT. COLONEL HUGHES WAS KILLED BY A .45 CALIBER BULLET, THE SAME CALIBER USED IN STANDARD MILITARY ISSUE SIDEARMS.
ONE SHOT WAS FIRED.
MY HANDGUN USES THE SAME TYPE OF BULLET.
AND I ALSO RECENTLY DISCHARGED ONE BULLET.
WHY WAS THAT?
...TO PROTECT THE ELRIC BROTHERS AT LABORATORY NUMBER FIVE.

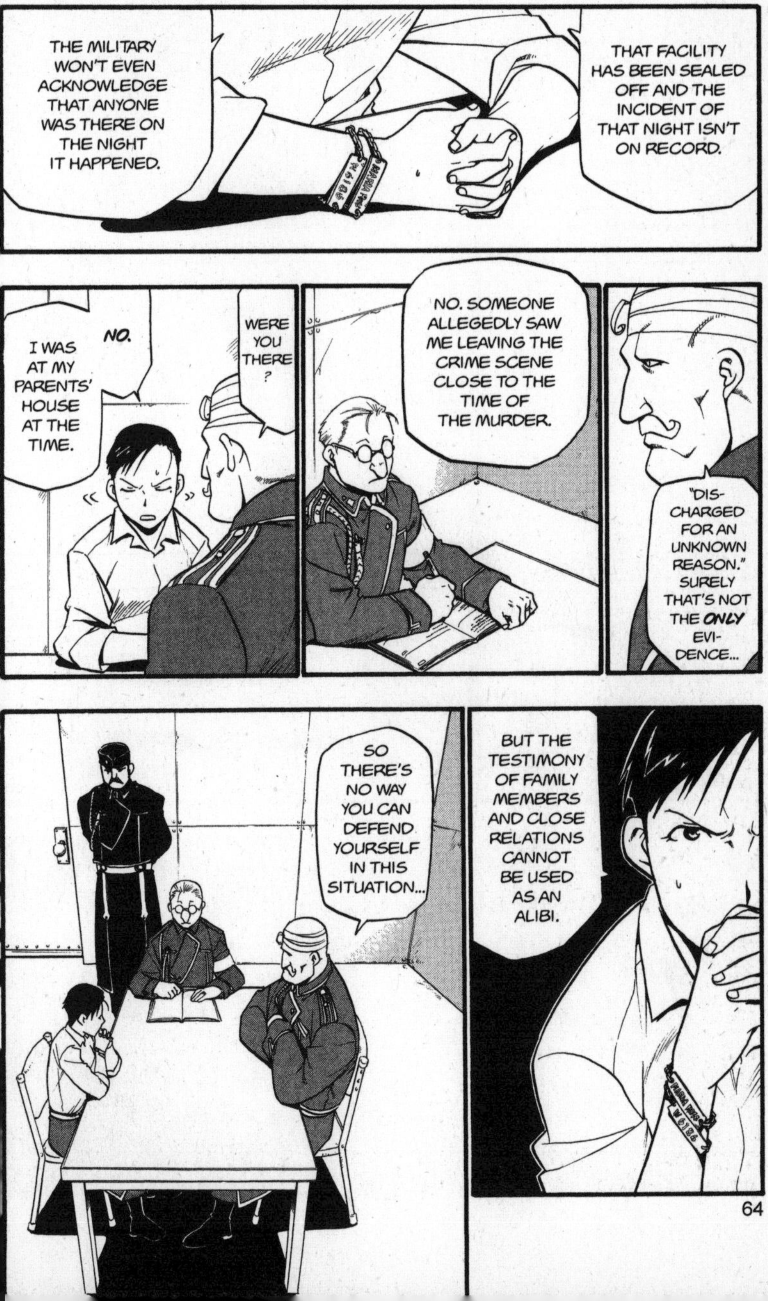
THAT FACILITY HAS BEEN SEALED OFF AND THE INCIDENT OF THAT NIGHT ISN'T ON RECORD.
THE MILITARY WON'T EVEN ACKNOWLEDGE THAT ANYONE WAS THERE ON THE NIGHT IT HAPPENED.
"DIS-CHARGED FOR AN UNKNOWN REASON." SURELY THAT'S NOT THE ***ONLY*** EVI-DENCE...
NO. SOMEONE ALLEGEDLY SAW ME LEAVING THE CRIME SCENE CLOSE TO THE TIME OF THE MURDER.
WERE YOU THERE?
NO.
I WAS AT MY PARENTS' HOUSE AT THE TIME.
BUT THE TESTIMONY OF FAMILY MEMBERS AND CLOSE RELATIONS CANNOT BE USED AS AN ALIBI.
SO THERE'S NO WAY YOU CAN DEFEND YOURSELF IN THIS SITUATION...

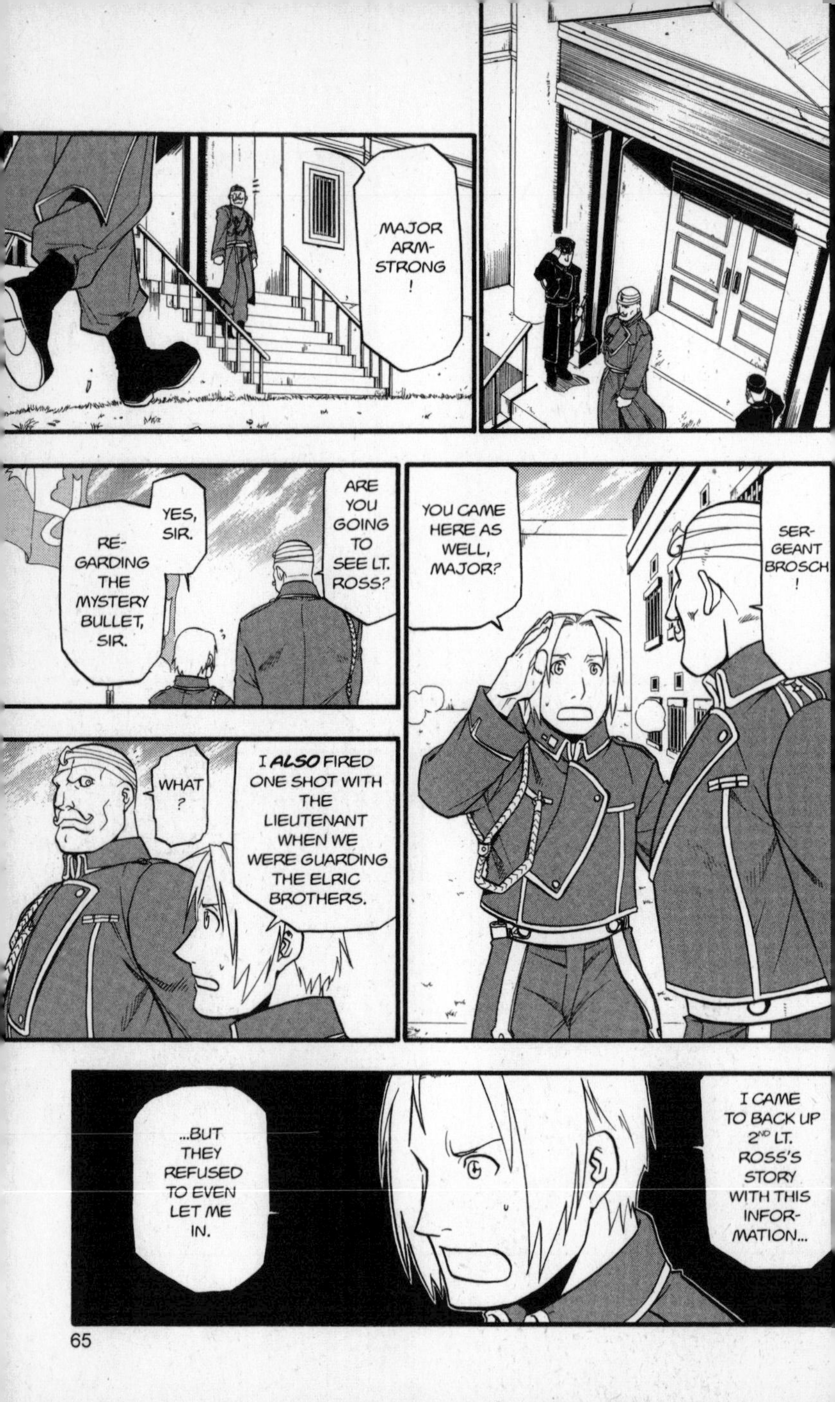
MAJOR ARM-STRONG !
SER-GEANT BROSCH !
YOU CAME HERE AS WELL, MAJOR?
ARE YOU GOING TO SEE LT. ROSS?
YES, SIR.
RE-GARDING THE MYSTERY BULLET, SIR.
I **ALSO** FIRED ONE SHOT WITH THE LIEUTENANT WHEN WE WERE GUARDING THE ELRIC BROTHERS.
WHAT ?
I CAME TO BACK UP 2ND LT. ROSS'S STORY WITH THIS INFOR-MATION...
...BUT THEY REFUSED TO EVEN LET ME IN.

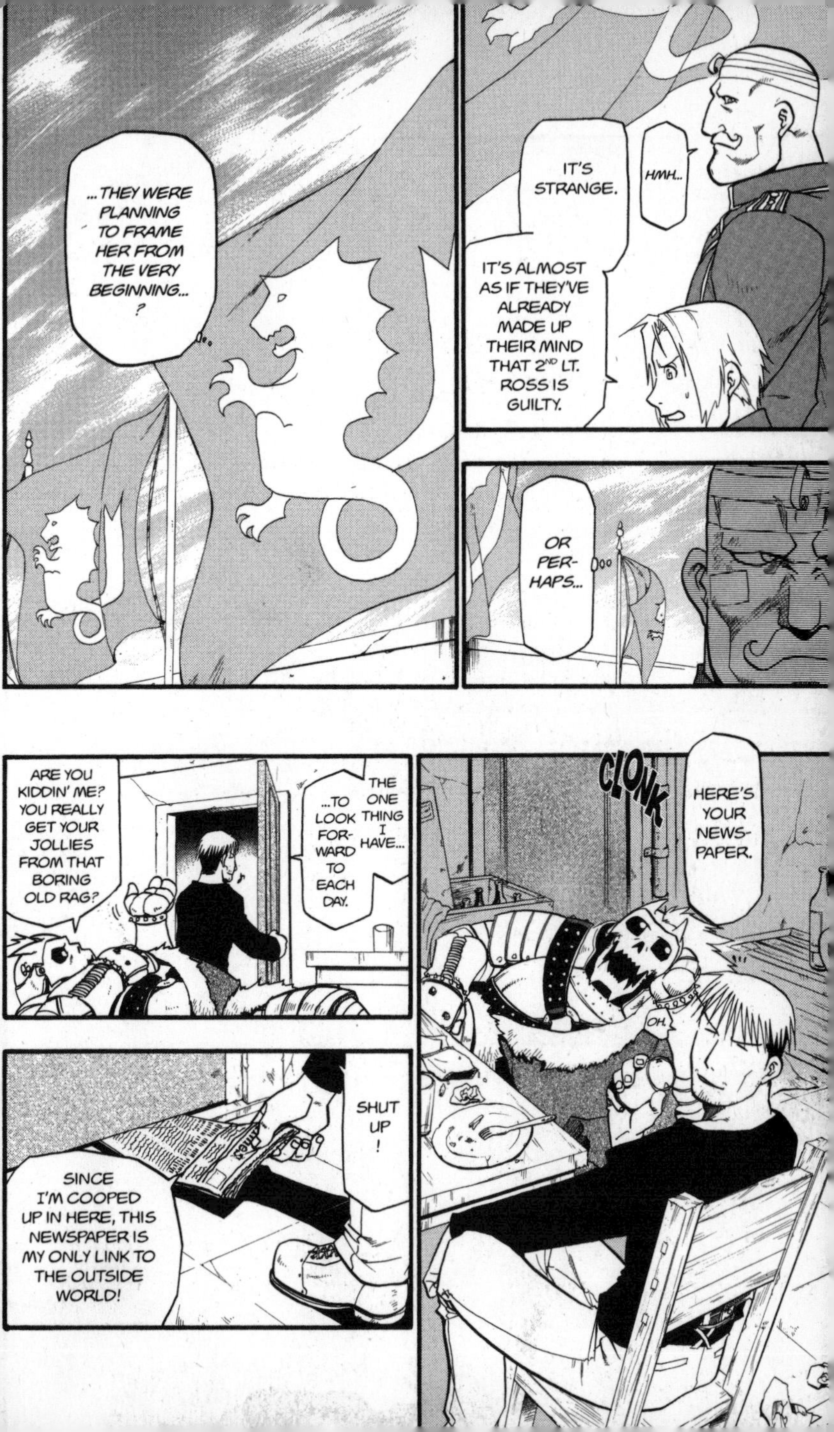
HMH..
IT'S STRANGE.
IT'S ALMOST AS IF THEY'VE ALREADY MADE UP THEIR MIND THAT 2ND LT. ROSS IS GUILTY.
OR PER-HAPS...
...THEY WERE PLANNING TO FRAME HER FROM THE VERY BEGINNING...?
CLONK
HERE'S YOUR NEWS-PAPER.
OH.
THE ONE THING I HAVE...
...TO LOOK FOR-WARD TO EACH DAY.
ARE YOU KIDDIN' ME? YOU REALLY GET YOUR JOLLIES FROM THAT BORING OLD RAG?
SHUT UP!
SINCE I'M COOPED UP IN HERE, THIS NEWSPAPER IS MY ONLY LINK TO THE OUTSIDE WORLD!

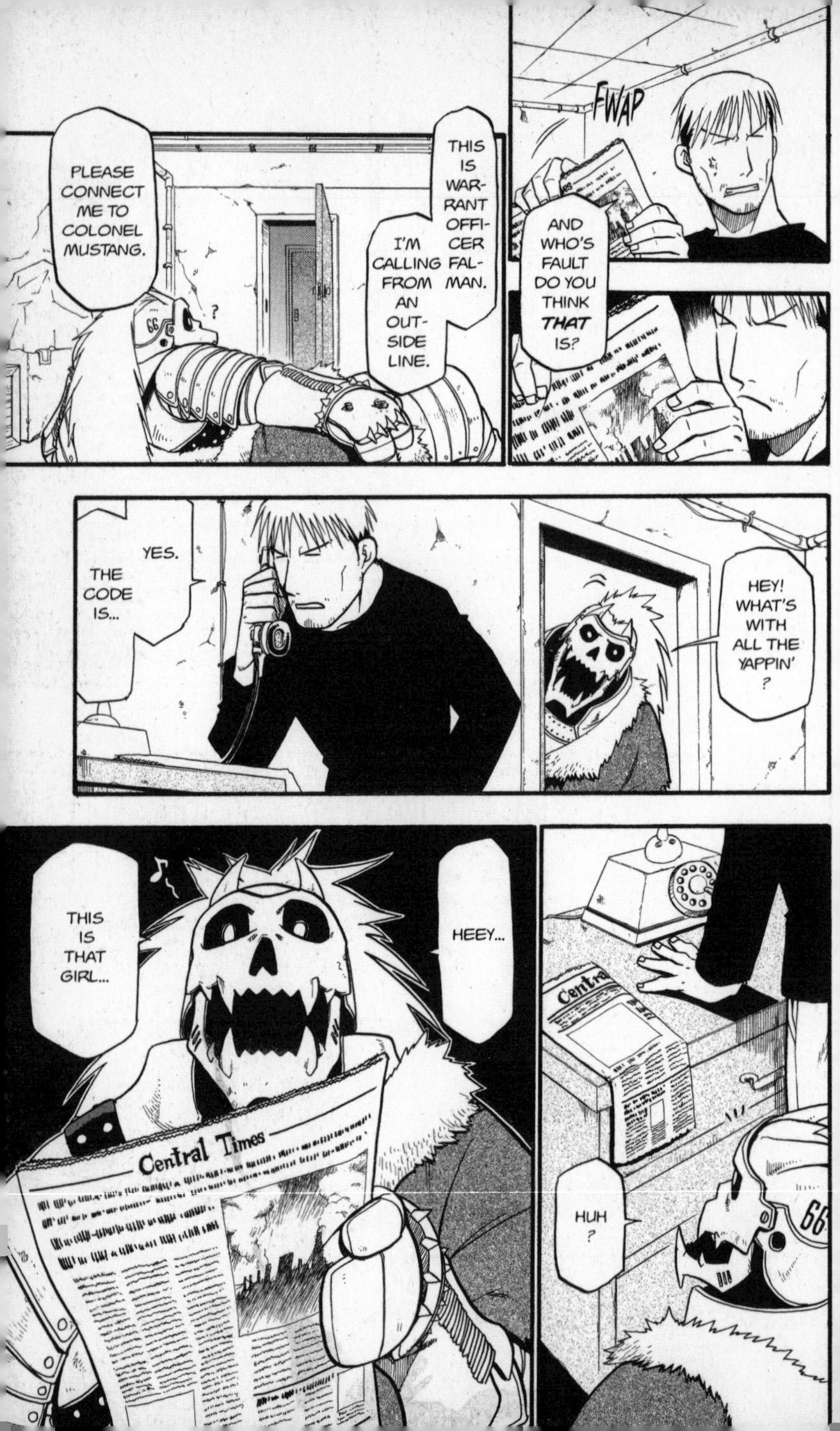
FWAP
AND WHO'S FAULT DO YOU THINK THAT IS?
THIS IS WARRANT OFFICER FALMAN.
I'M CALLING FROM AN OUTSIDE LINE.
PLEASE CONNECT ME TO COLONEL MUSTANG.
?
66
HEY! WHAT'S WITH ALL THE YAPPIN'?
YES.
THE CODE IS...
HUH?
66
HEEY...
THIS IS THAT GIRL...
Central Times

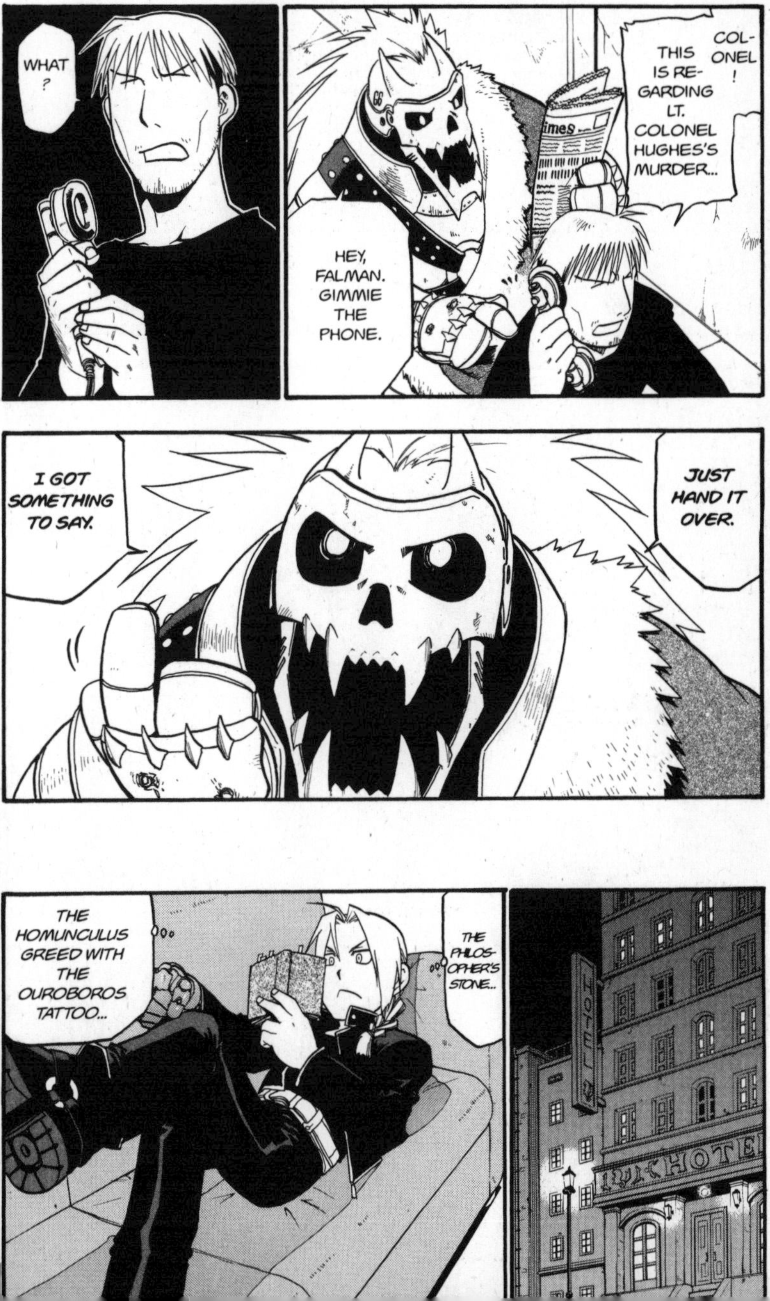
COLONEL! THIS IS REGARDING LT. COLONEL HUGHES'S MURDER...
HEY, FALMAN. GIMMIE THE PHONE.
WHAT?
JUST HAND IT OVER.
I GOT SOMETHING TO SAY.
HOTEL
THE PHILOSOPHER'S STONE...
THE HOMUNCULUS GREED WITH THE OUROBOROS TATTOO...

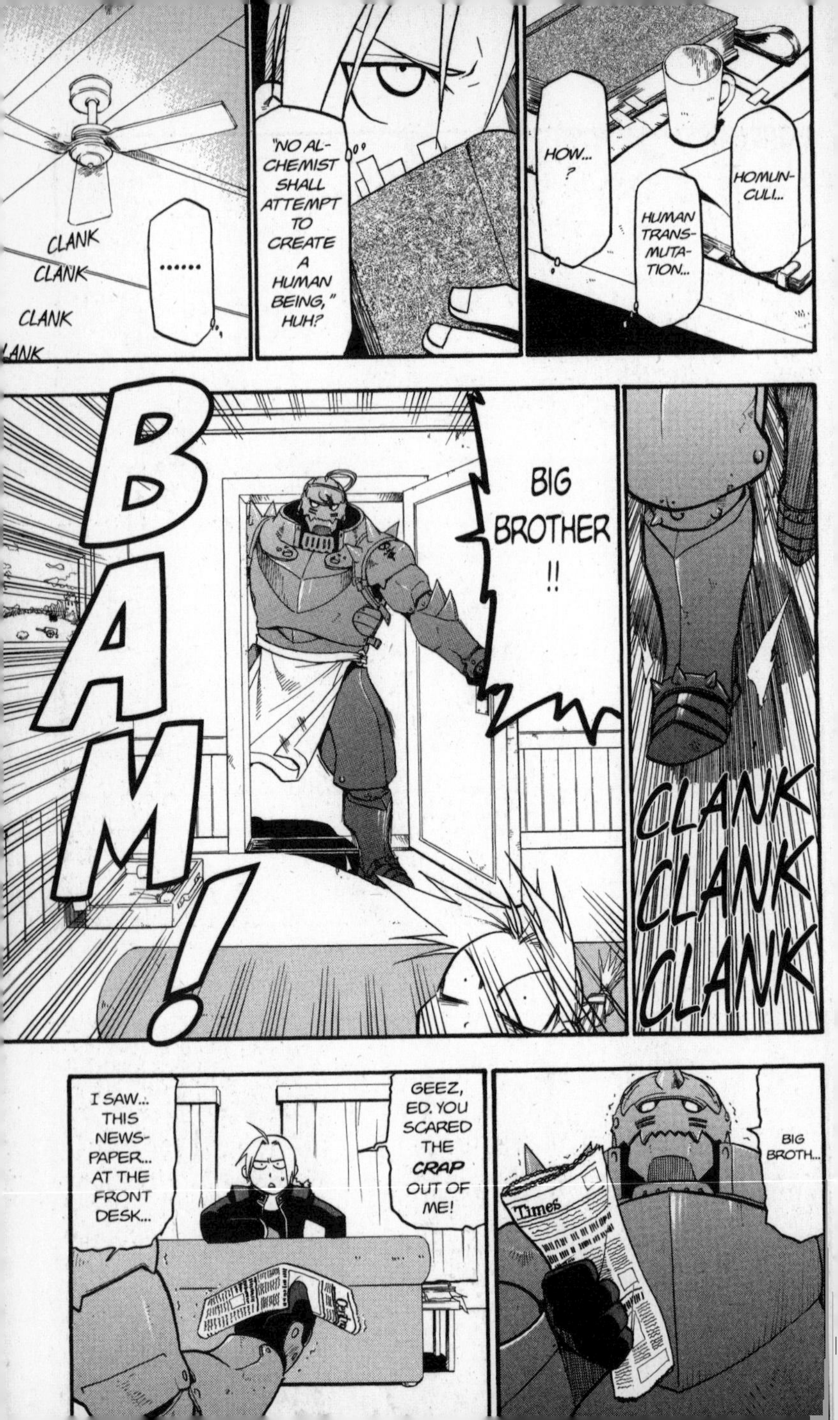
HOMUN-CULI...
HUMAN TRANS-MUTA-TION...
HOW... ?
"NO AL-CHEMIST SHALL ATTEMPT TO CREATE A HUMAN BEING," HUH?
CLANK
CLANK
CLANK
LANK
......
CLANK CLANK CLANK
BIG BROTHER !!
BAM!
BIG BROTH...
GEEZ, ED. YOU SCARED THE CRAP OUT OF ME!
I SAW... THIS NEWS-PAPER... AT THE FRONT DESK...
Times

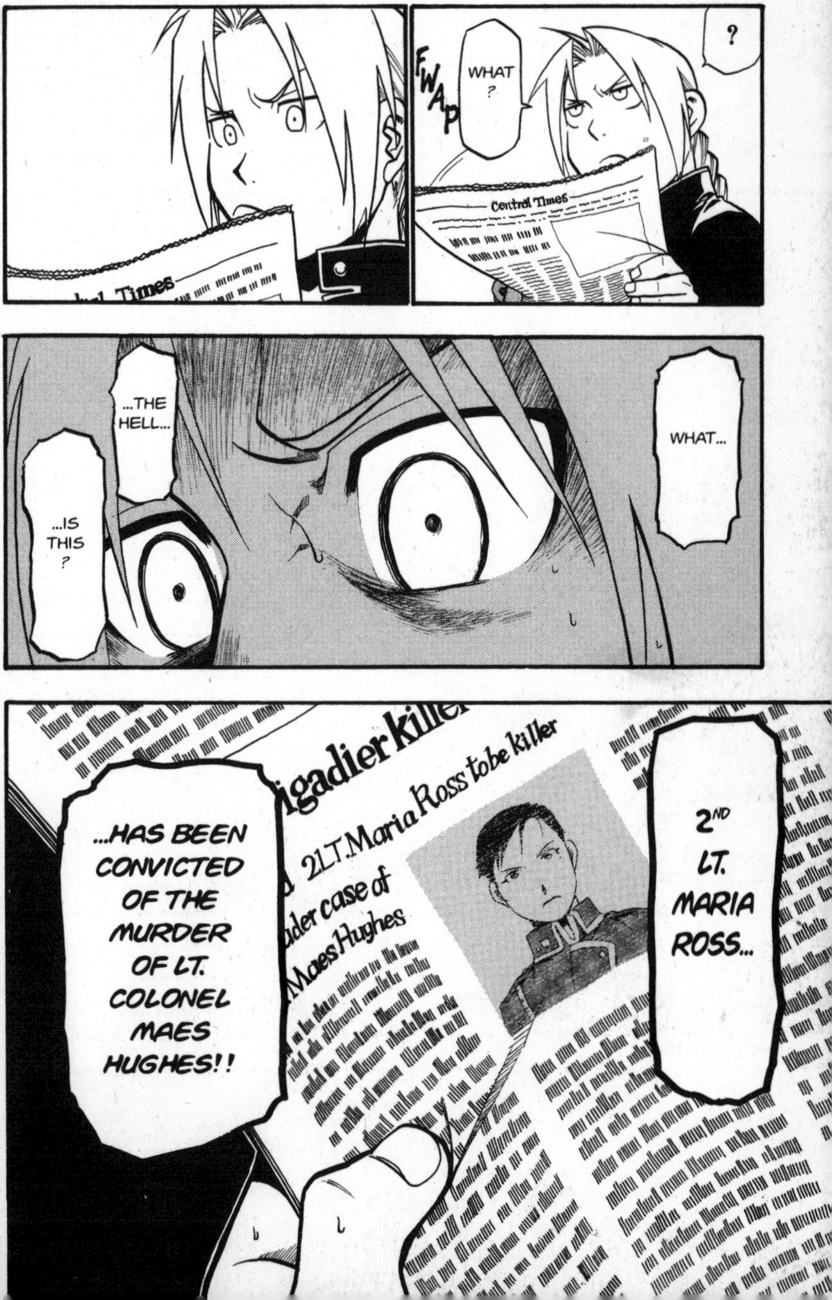
?
WHAT ?
FWAP
Central Times
WHAT...
...THE HELL...
...IS THIS ?
2ND LT. MARIA ROSS...
2LT.Maria Ross tobe killer
Maes Hughes
...HAS BEEN CONVICTED OF THE MURDER OF LT. COLONEL MAES HUGHES!!

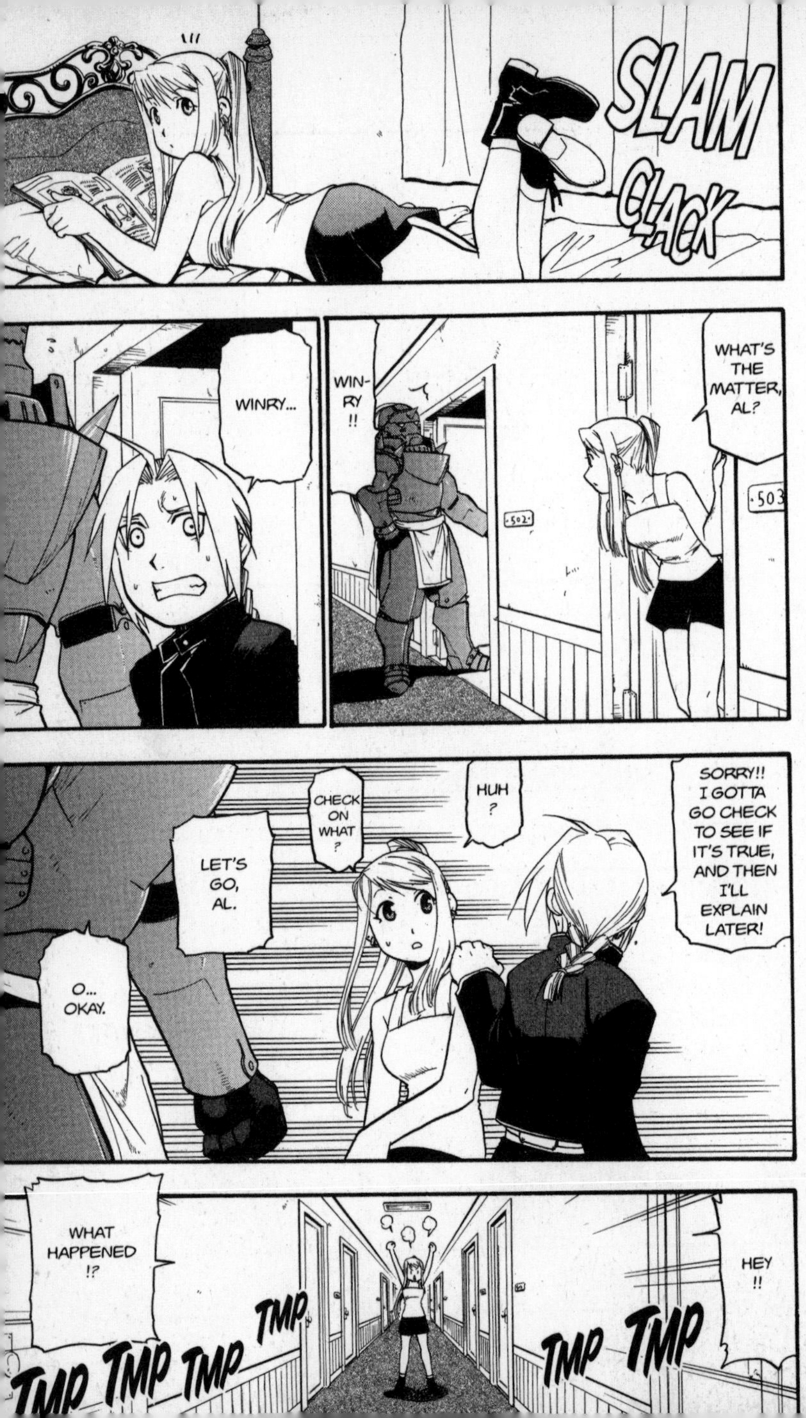
SLAM
CLACK
WHAT'S THE MATTER, AL?
WIN-RY!!
WINRY...
SORRY!! I GOTTA GO CHECK TO SEE IF IT'S TRUE, AND THEN I'LL EXPLAIN LATER!
HUH?
CHECK ON WHAT?
LET'S GO, AL.
O... OKAY.
HEY!!
TMP TMP
TMP
WHAT HAPPENED!?
TMP TMP TMP

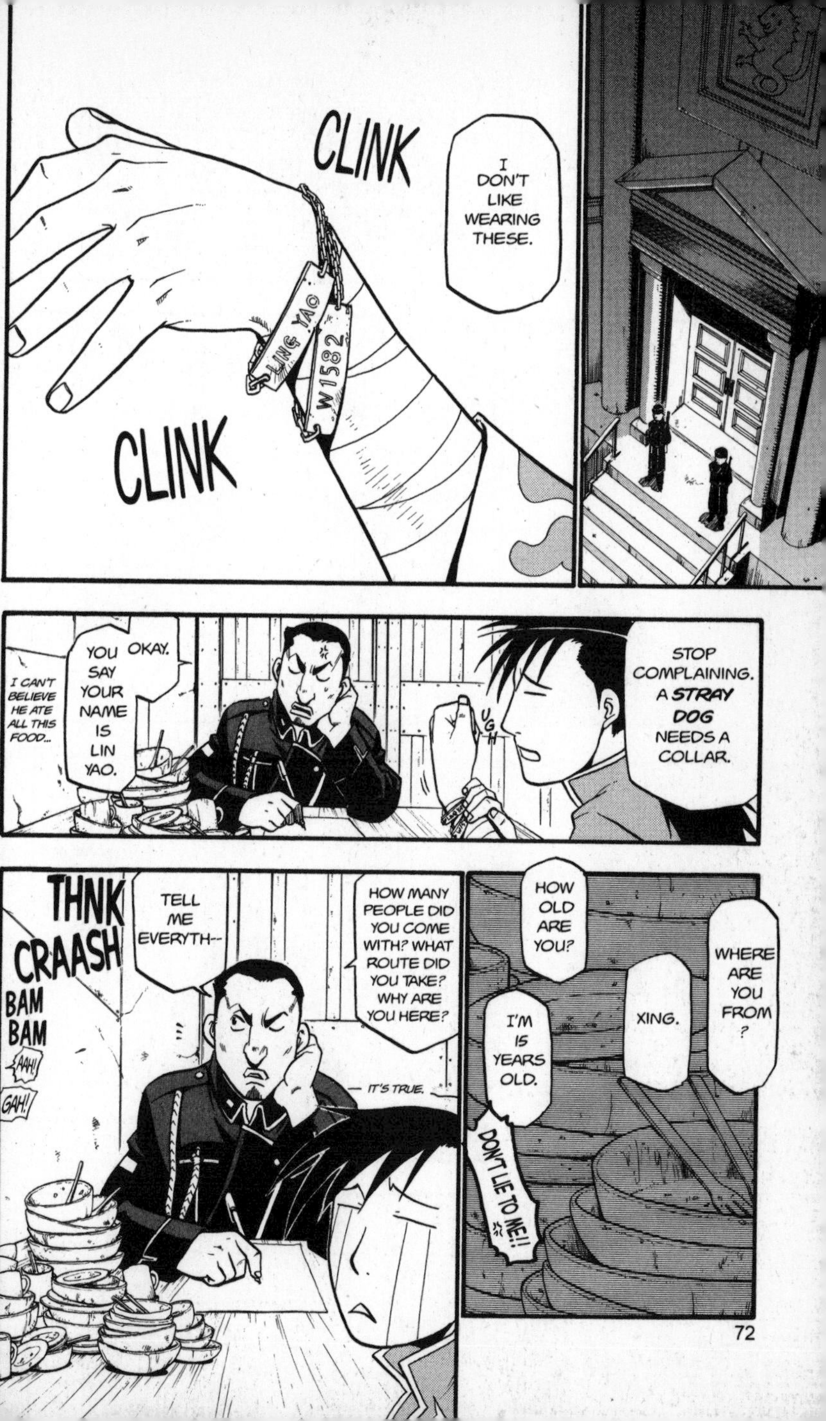
CLINK
I DON'T LIKE WEARING THESE.
LING YAO
W1582
CLINK
STOP COMPLAINING. A STRAY DOG NEEDS A COLLAR.
UGH
OKAY.
YOU SAY YOUR NAME IS LIN YAO.
I CAN'T BELIEVE HE ATE ALL THIS FOOD...
WHERE ARE YOU FROM?
XING.
HOW OLD ARE YOU?
I'M 15 YEARS OLD.
DON'T LIE TO ME!!
HOW MANY PEOPLE DID YOU COME WITH? WHAT ROUTE DID YOU TAKE? WHY ARE YOU HERE?
TELL ME EVERYTH--
IT'S TRUE.
THNK
CRAASH
BAM BAM
AAH!
GAH!

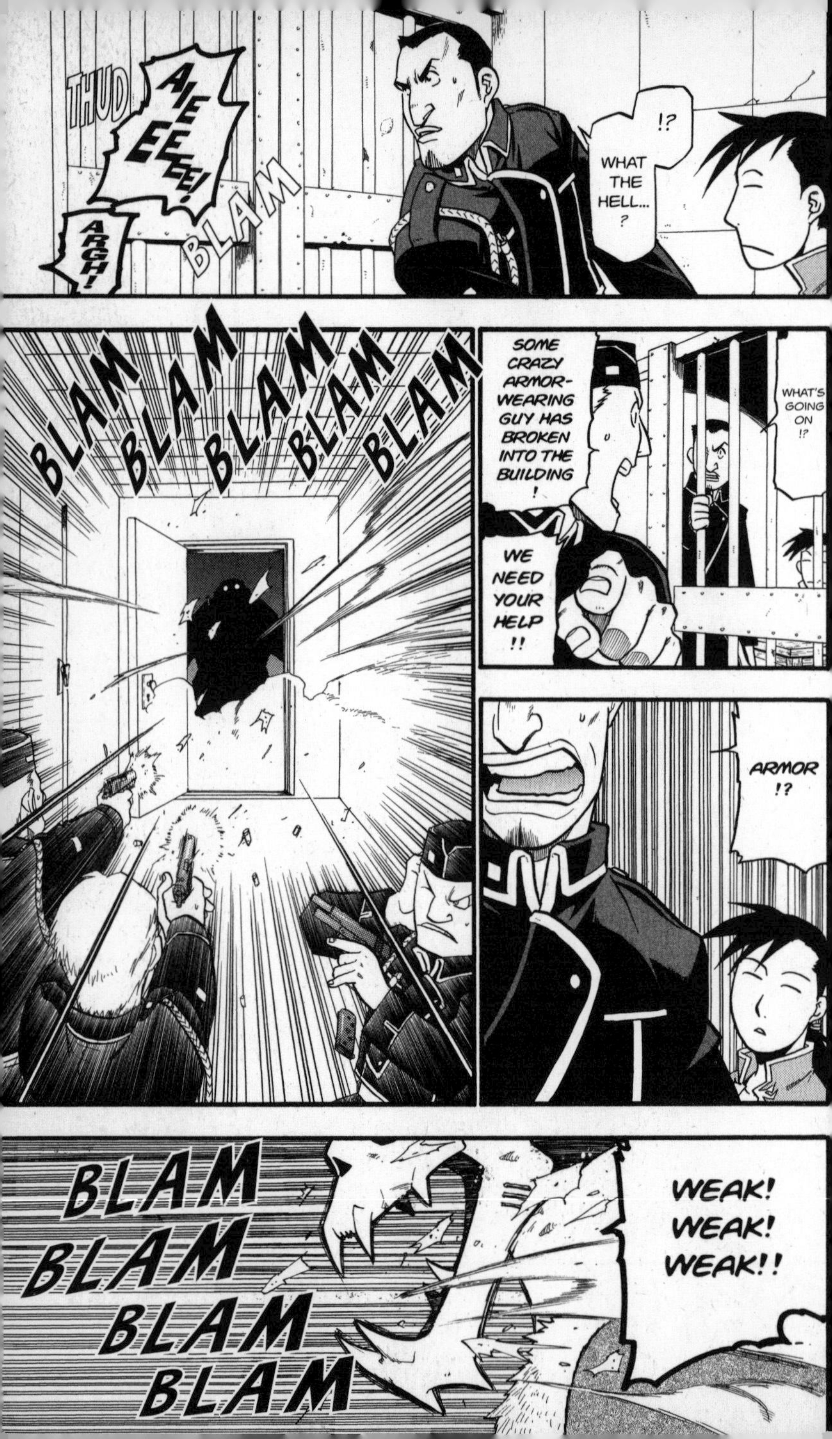
!?
WHAT THE HELL...?
THUD
AIEEEEEE!
BLAM
ARGH!
WHAT'S GOING ON!?
SOME CRAZY ARMOR-WEARING GUY HAS BROKEN INTO THE BUILDING!
WE NEED YOUR HELP!!
ARMOR!?
BLAM BLAM BLAM BLAM BLAM BLAM
WEAK! WEAK! WEAK!!
BLAM BLAM BLAM BLAM

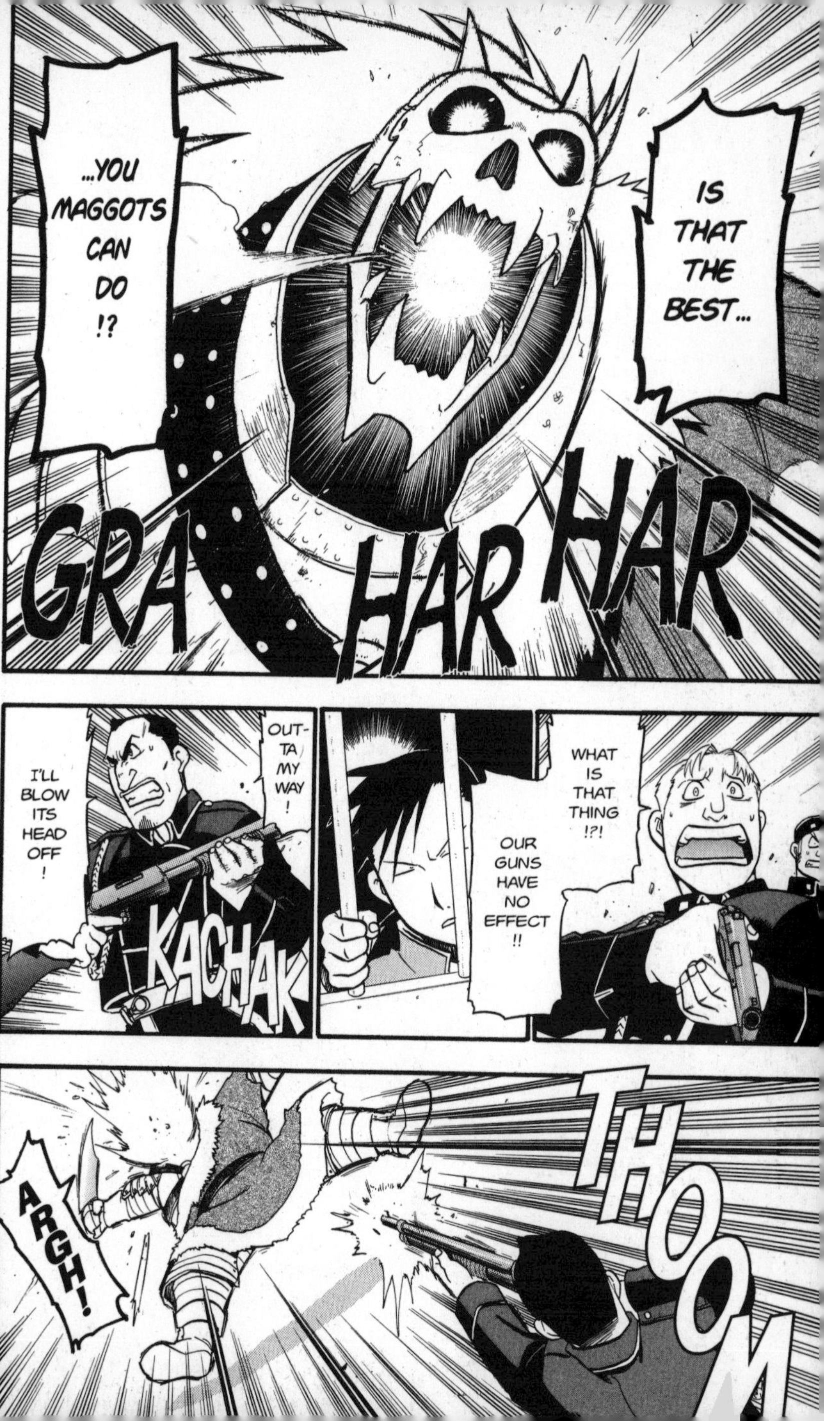
IS THAT THE BEST...
...YOU MAGGOTS CAN DO !?
GRA HAR HAR
WHAT IS THAT THING !?!
OUR GUNS HAVE NO EFFECT !!
OUTTA MY WAY !
I'LL BLOW ITS HEAD OFF !
KACHAK
THOOOM
ARGH!

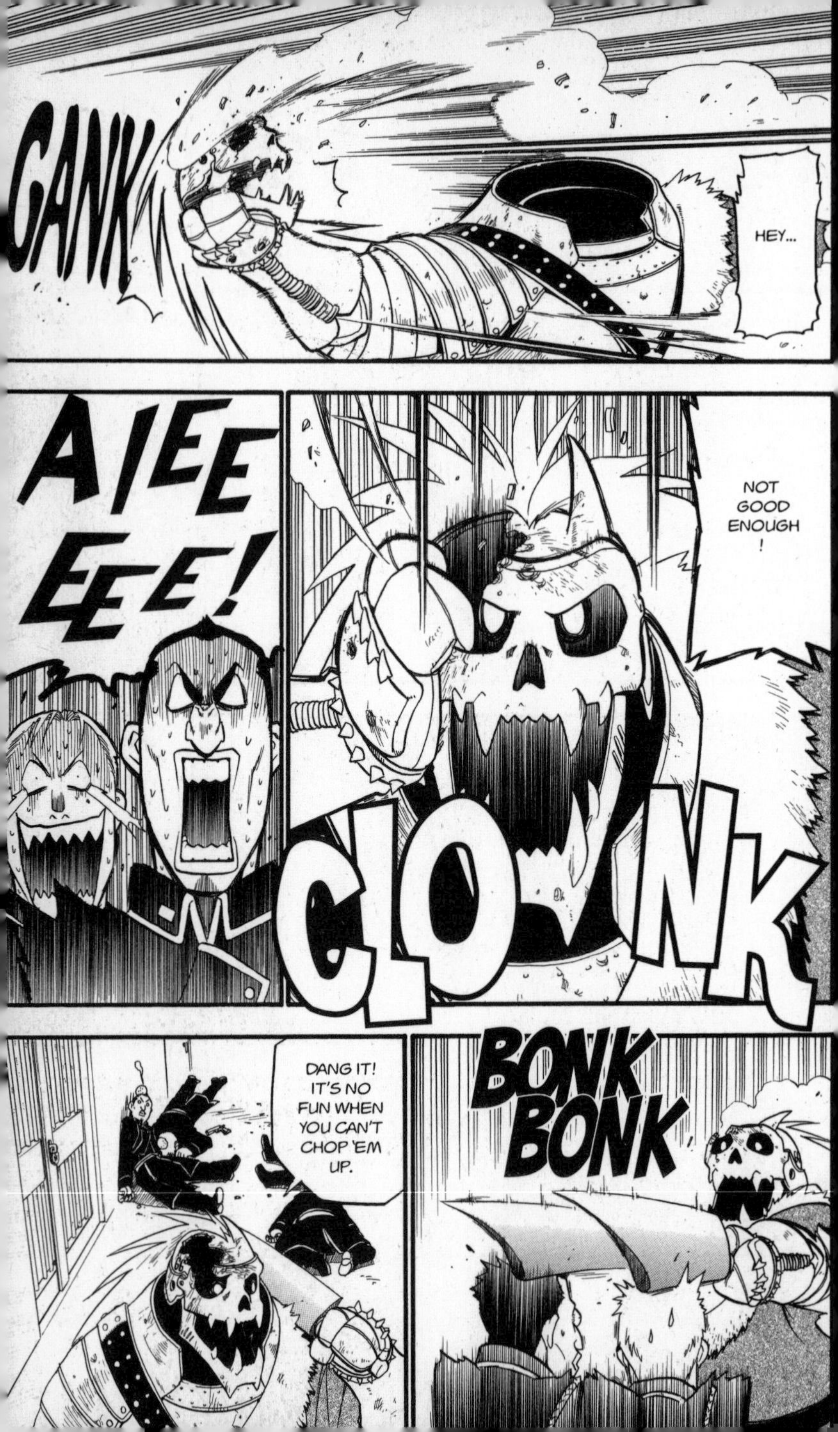
HEY...
GANK
NOT GOOD ENOUGH !
CLONK
AIEEEEE!
BONK BONK
DANG IT! IT'S NO FUN WHEN YOU CAN'T CHOP 'EM UP.

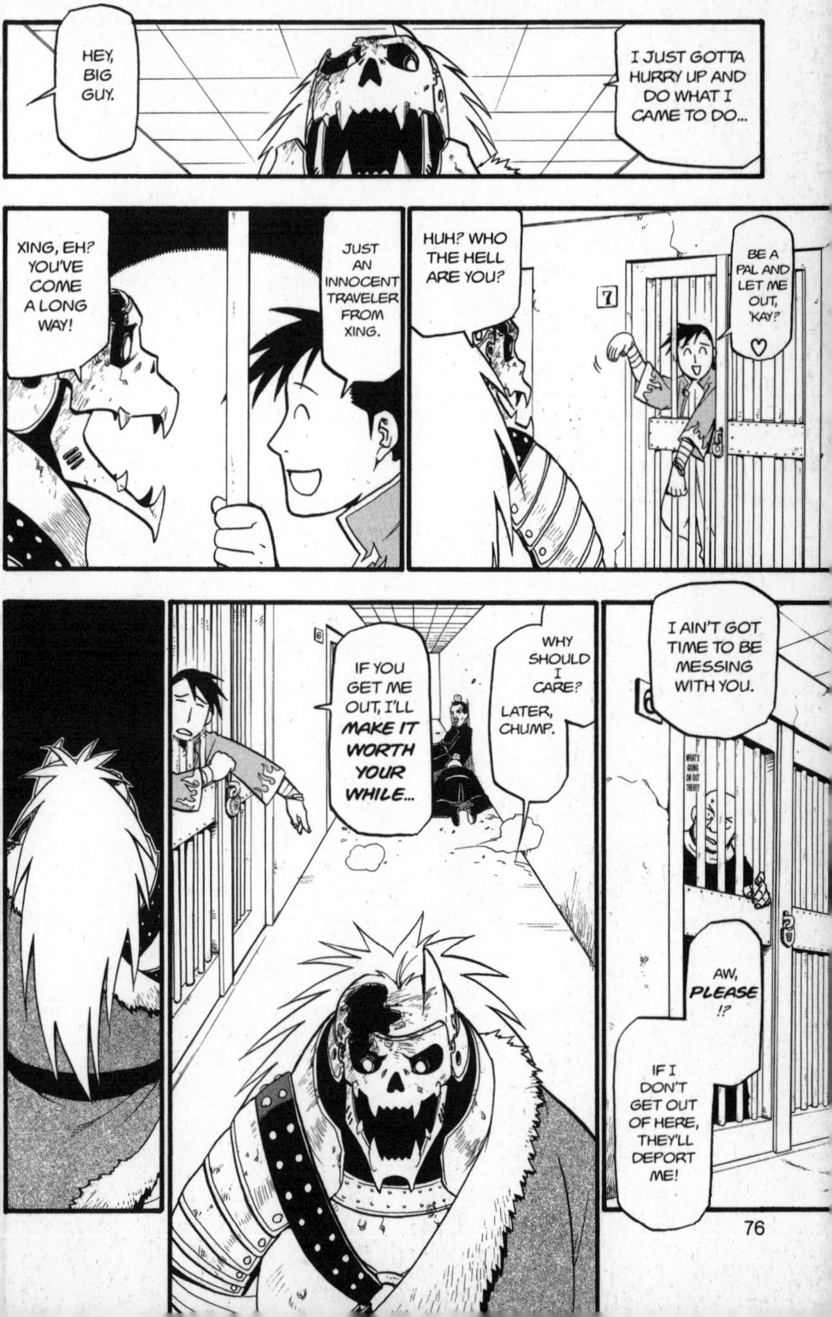
I JUST GOTTA HURRY UP AND DO WHAT I CAME TO DO...
HEY, BIG GUY.
BE A PAL AND LET ME OUT, 'KAY? ♡
HUH? WHO THE HELL ARE YOU?
JUST AN INNOCENT TRAVELER FROM XING.
XING, EH? YOU'VE COME A LONG WAY!
I AIN'T GOT TIME TO BE MESSING WITH YOU.
WHAT'S GOING ON OUT THERE?
AW, PLEASE!?
IF I DON'T GET OUT OF HERE, THEY'LL DEPORT ME!
WHY SHOULD I CARE? LATER, CHUMP.
IF YOU GET ME OUT, I'LL MAKE IT WORTH YOUR WHILE...

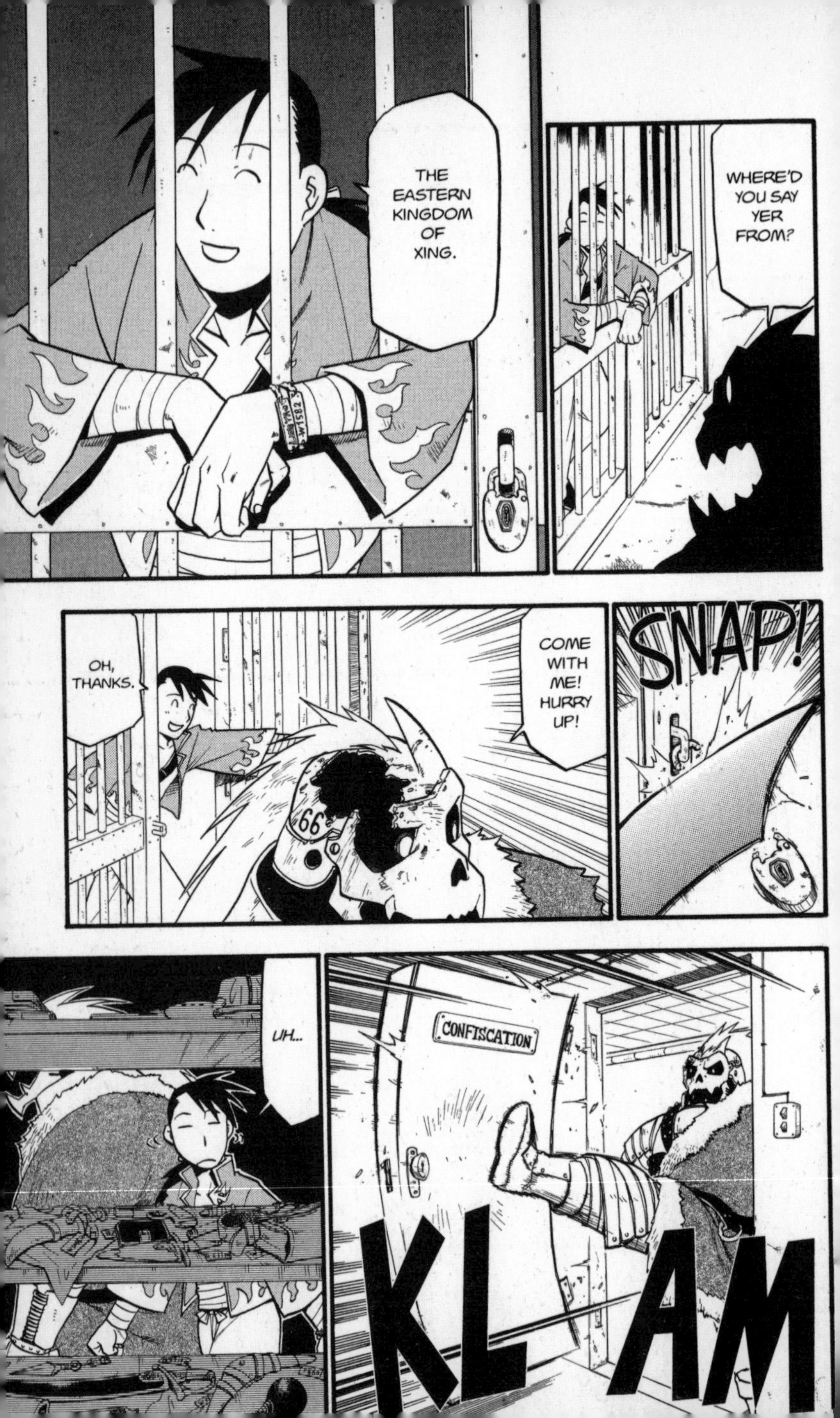
WHERE'D YOU SAY YER FROM?
THE EASTERN KINGDOM OF XING.
SNAP!
COME WITH ME! HURRY UP!
OH, THANKS.
CONFISCATION
KLAM
UH...

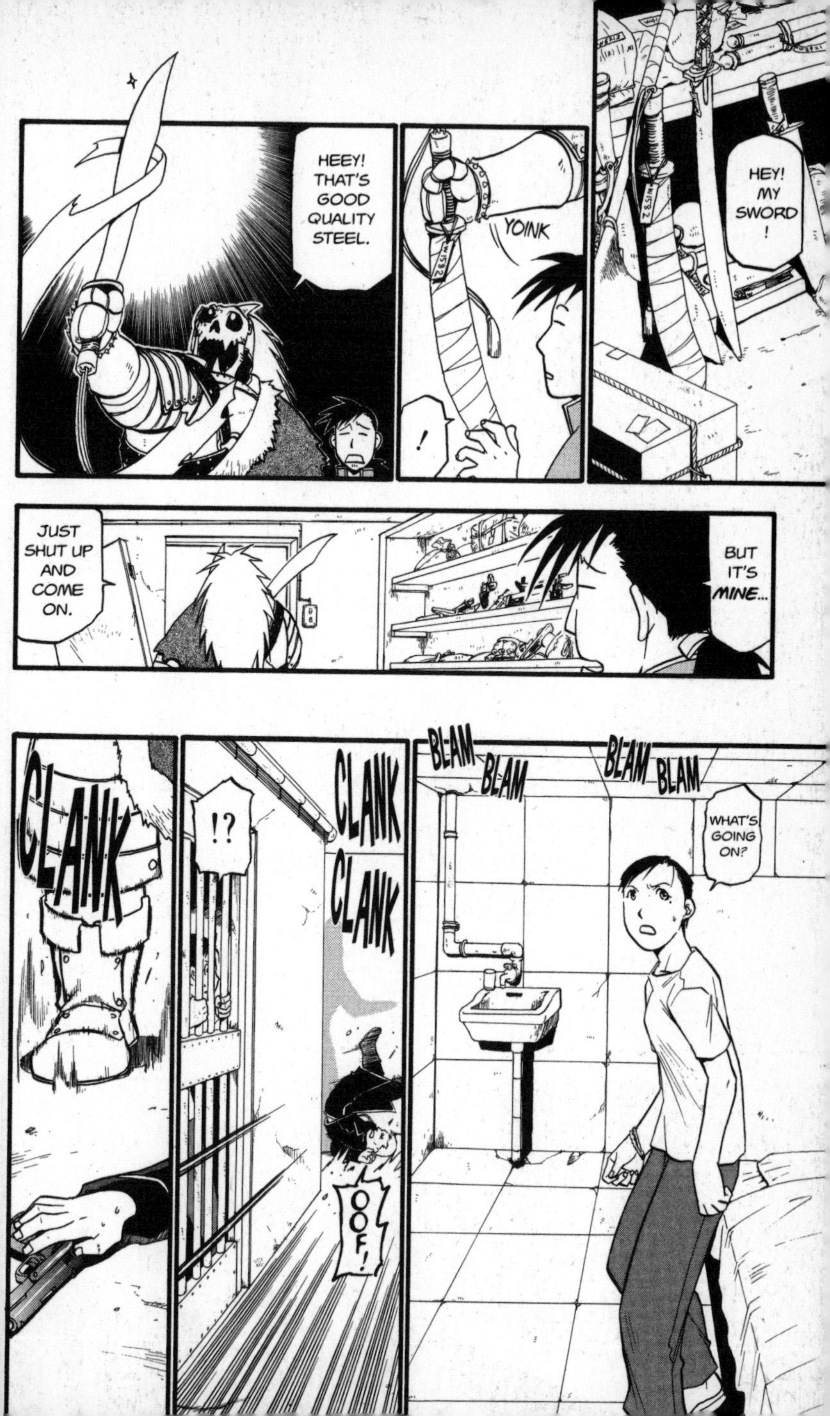
HEY! MY SWORD!
YOINK
!
HEEY! THAT'S GOOD QUALITY STEEL.
BUT IT'S *MINE*...
JUST SHUT UP AND COME ON.
BLAM BLAM
BLAM BLAM
WHAT'S GOING ON?
CLANK
CLANK
!?
OOF!
CLANK

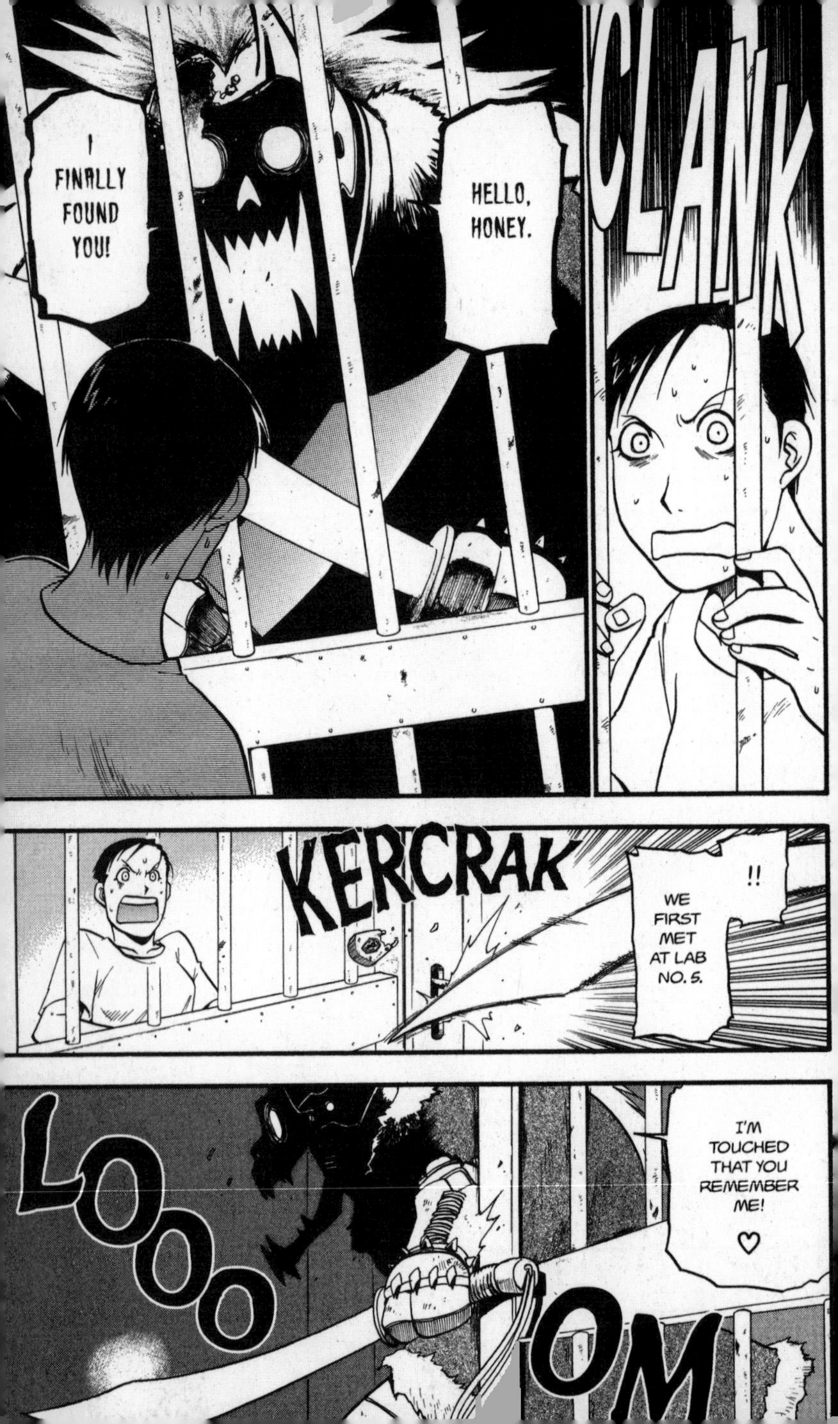
CLANK
HELLO, HONEY.
I FINALLY FOUND YOU!
!!
WE FIRST MET AT LAB NO. 5.
KERCRAK
I'M TOUCHED THAT YOU REMEMBER ME! ♡
LOOOOOM

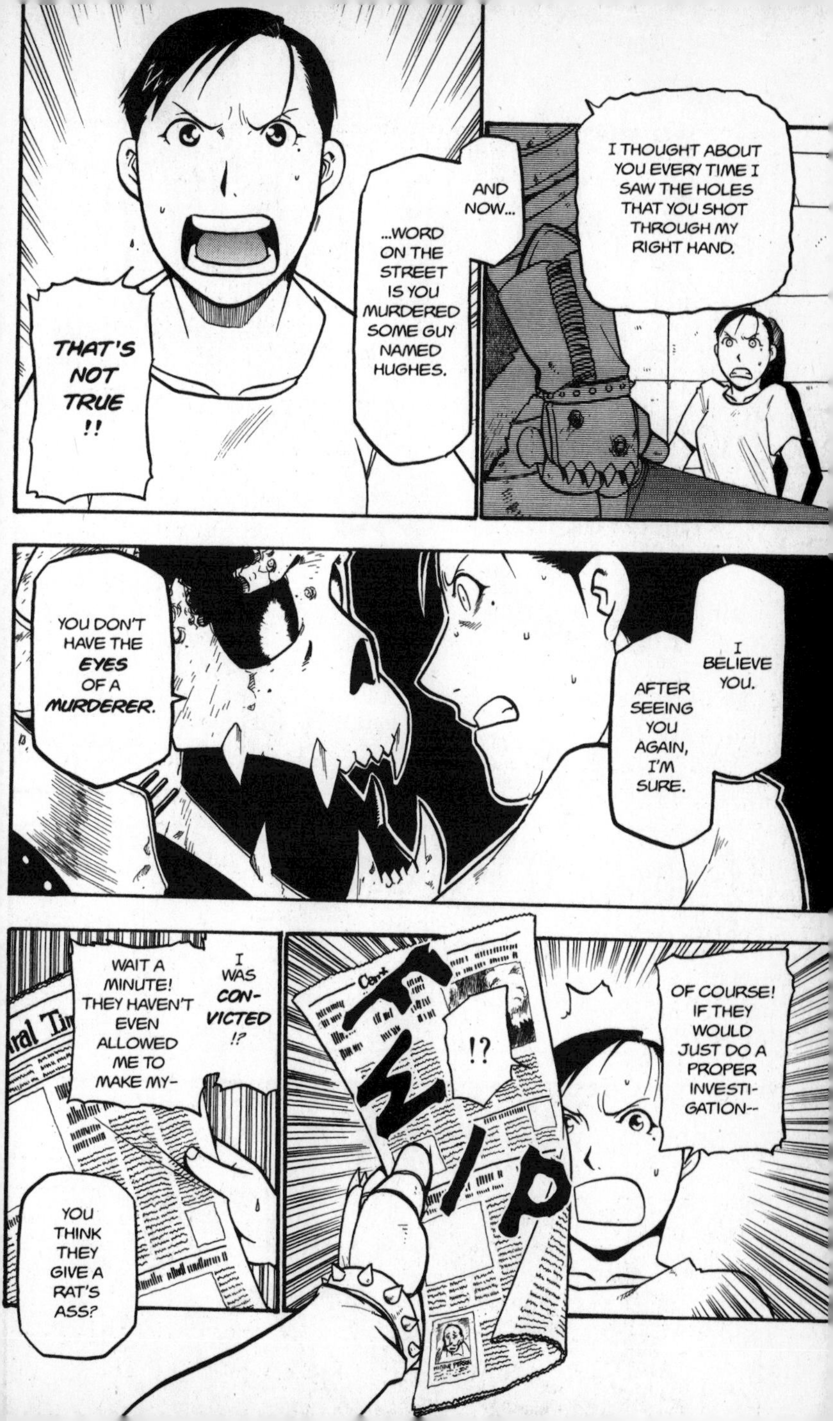
I THOUGHT ABOUT YOU EVERY TIME I SAW THE HOLES THAT YOU SHOT THROUGH MY RIGHT HAND.
AND NOW...
...WORD ON THE STREET IS YOU MURDERED SOME GUY NAMED HUGHES.
THAT'S NOT TRUE !!
I BELIEVE YOU.
AFTER SEEING YOU AGAIN, I'M SURE.
YOU DON'T HAVE THE EYES OF A MURDERER.
OF COURSE! IF THEY WOULD JUST DO A PROPER INVESTIGATION--
FWIP
!?
I WAS CONVICTED !?
WAIT A MINUTE! THEY HAVEN'T EVEN ALLOWED ME TO MAKE MY-
YOU THINK THEY GIVE A RAT'S ASS?

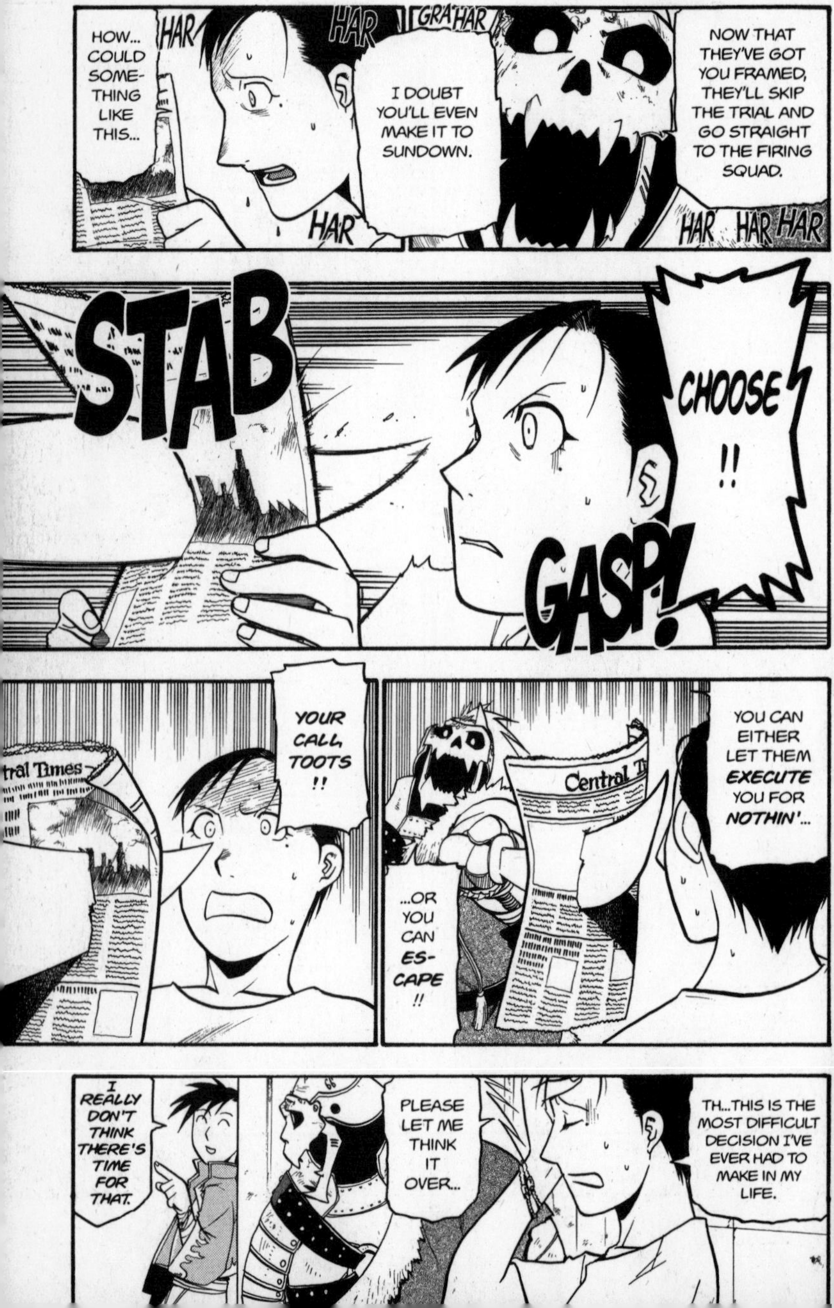
GRA HAR
HAR
NOW THAT THEY'VE GOT YOU FRAMED, THEY'LL SKIP THE TRIAL AND GO STRAIGHT TO THE FIRING SQUAD.
I DOUBT YOU'LL EVEN MAKE IT TO SUNDOWN.
HAR HAR HAR
HOW... COULD SOME-THING LIKE THIS...
HAR
HAR
CHOOSE!!
GASP!
STAB
YOU CAN EITHER LET THEM *EXECUTE* YOU FOR *NOTHIN'*...
...OR YOU CAN *ES-CAPE*!!
Central Times
YOUR CALL, TOOTS!!
TH...THIS IS THE MOST DIFFICULT DECISION I'VE EVER HAD TO MAKE IN MY LIFE.
PLEASE LET ME THINK IT OVER...
I REALLY DON'T THINK THERE'S TIME FOR THAT.

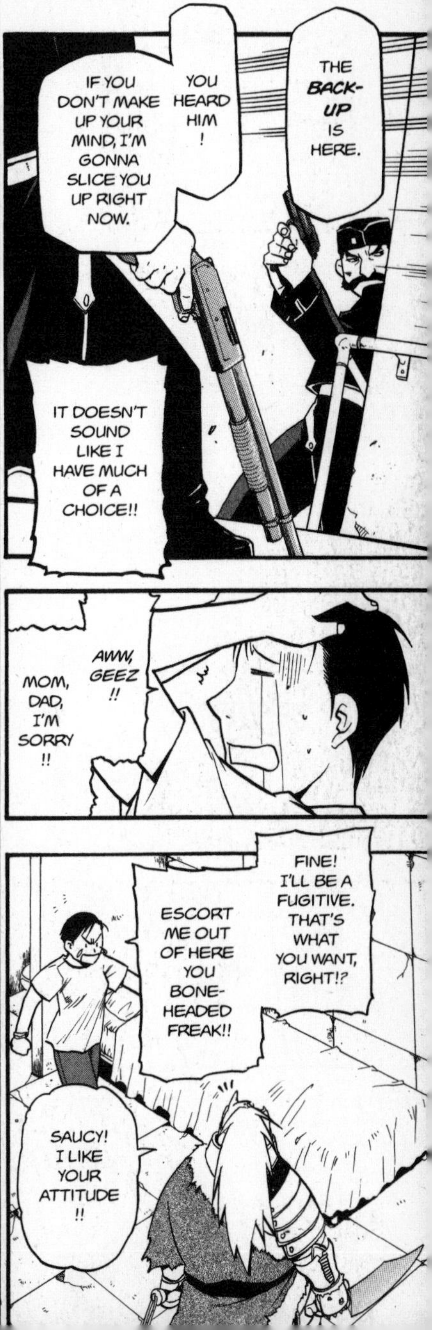
THE BACK-UP IS HERE.
YOU HEARD HIM!
IF YOU DON'T MAKE UP YOUR MIND, I'M GONNA SLICE YOU UP RIGHT NOW.
IT DOESN'T SOUND LIKE I HAVE MUCH OF A CHOICE!!
AWW, GEEZ!!
MOM, DAD, I'M SORRY!!
FINE! I'LL BE A FUGITIVE. THAT'S WHAT YOU WANT, RIGHT!?
ESCORT ME OUT OF HERE YOU BONE-HEADED FREAK!!
SAUCY! I LIKE YOUR ATTITUDE!!

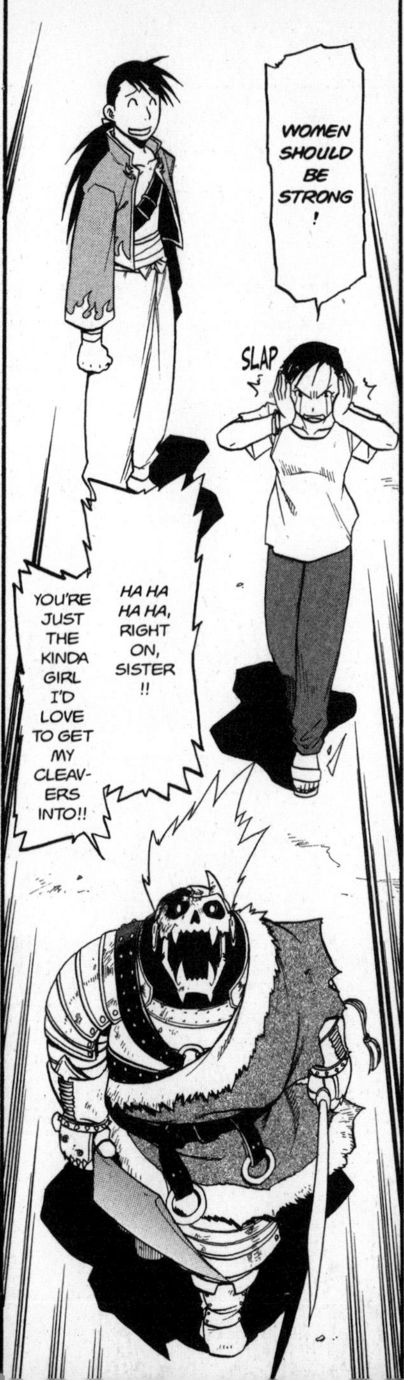
WOMEN SHOULD BE STRONG!
SLAP
HA HA HA HA, RIGHT ON, SISTER!!
YOU'RE JUST THE KINDA GIRL I'D LOVE TO GET MY CLEAVERS INTO!!

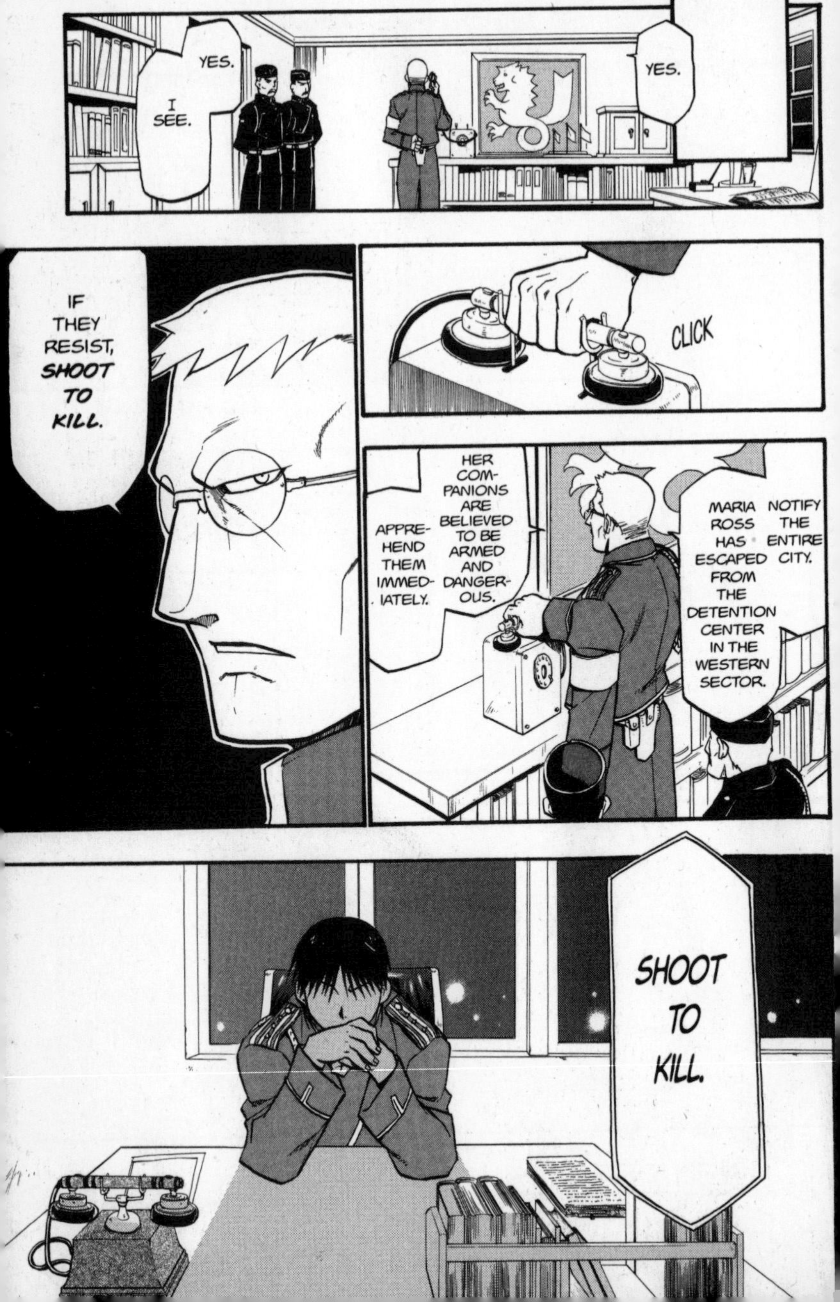
YES.
YES. I SEE.
CLICK
NOTIFY THE ENTIRE CITY.
MARIA ROSS HAS ESCAPED FROM THE DETENTION CENTER IN THE WESTERN SECTOR.
HER COMPANIONS ARE BELIEVED TO BE ARMED AND DANGEROUS.
APPREHEND THEM IMMEDIATELY.
IF THEY RESIST, **SHOOT TO KILL.**
SHOOT TO KILL.

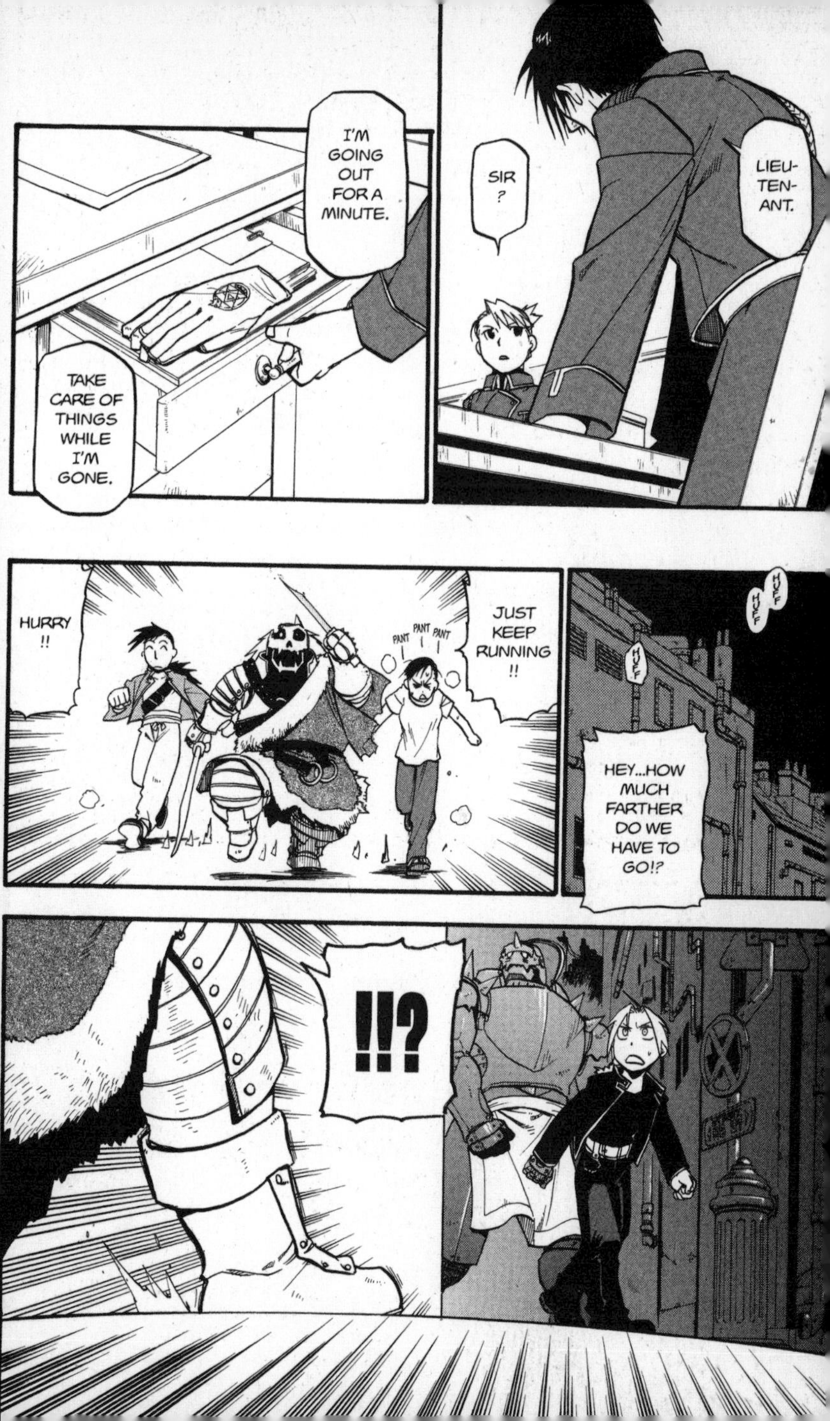
LIEU-TEN-ANT.
SIR ?
I'M GOING OUT FOR A MINUTE.
TAKE CARE OF THINGS WHILE I'M GONE.
HUFF HUFF
HUFF
HEY...HOW MUCH FARTHER DO WE HAVE TO GO!?
JUST KEEP RUNNING !!
PANT PANT PANT
HURRY !!
!!?

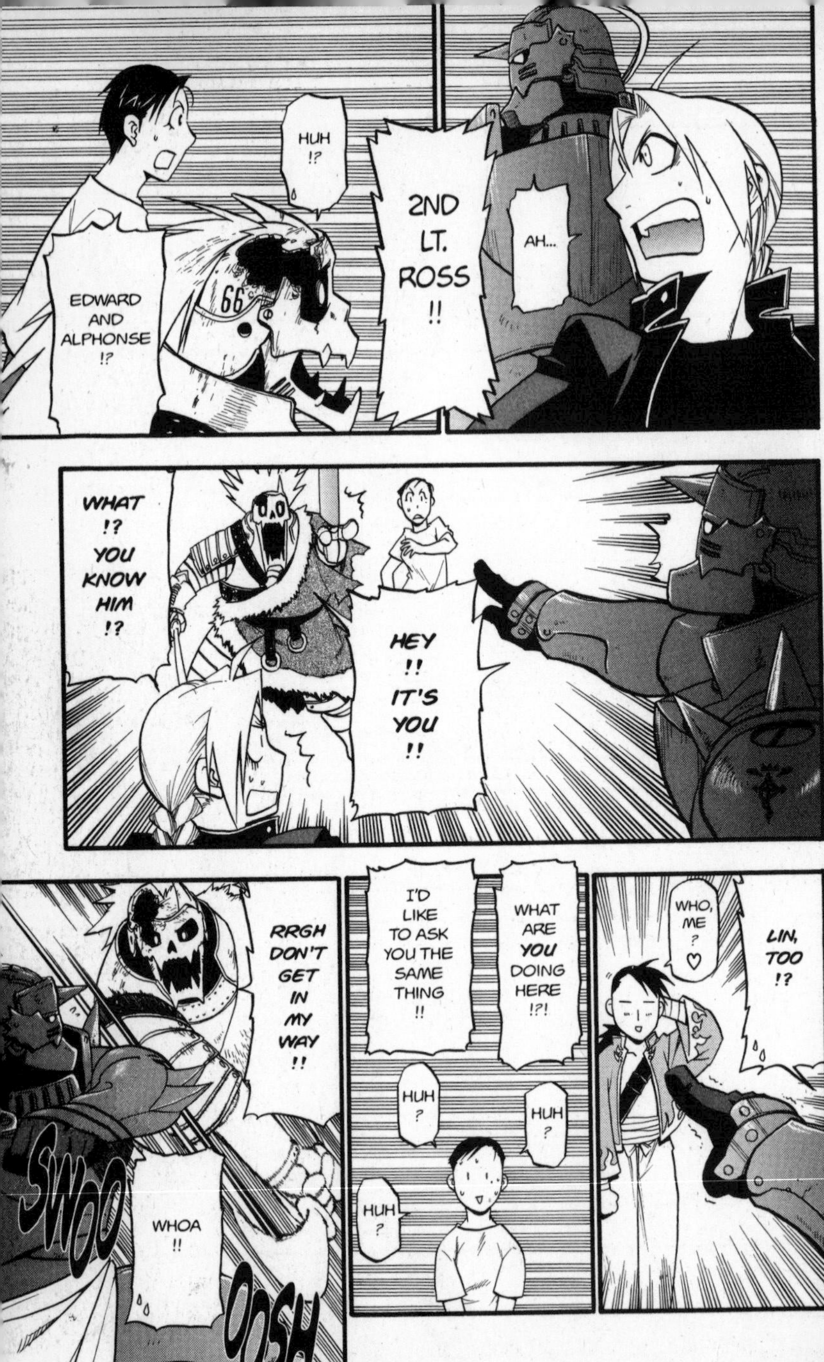
AH...
2ND LT. ROSS !!
HUH !?
EDWARD AND ALPHONSE !?
HEY !! IT'S YOU !!
WHAT !? YOU KNOW HIM !?
LIN, TOO !?
WHO, ME ? ♡
WHAT ARE YOU DOING HERE !?!
I'D LIKE TO ASK YOU THE SAME THING !!
HUH ?
HUH ?
HUH ?
RRGH DON'T GET IN MY WAY !!
WHOA !!
SWOOOOSH

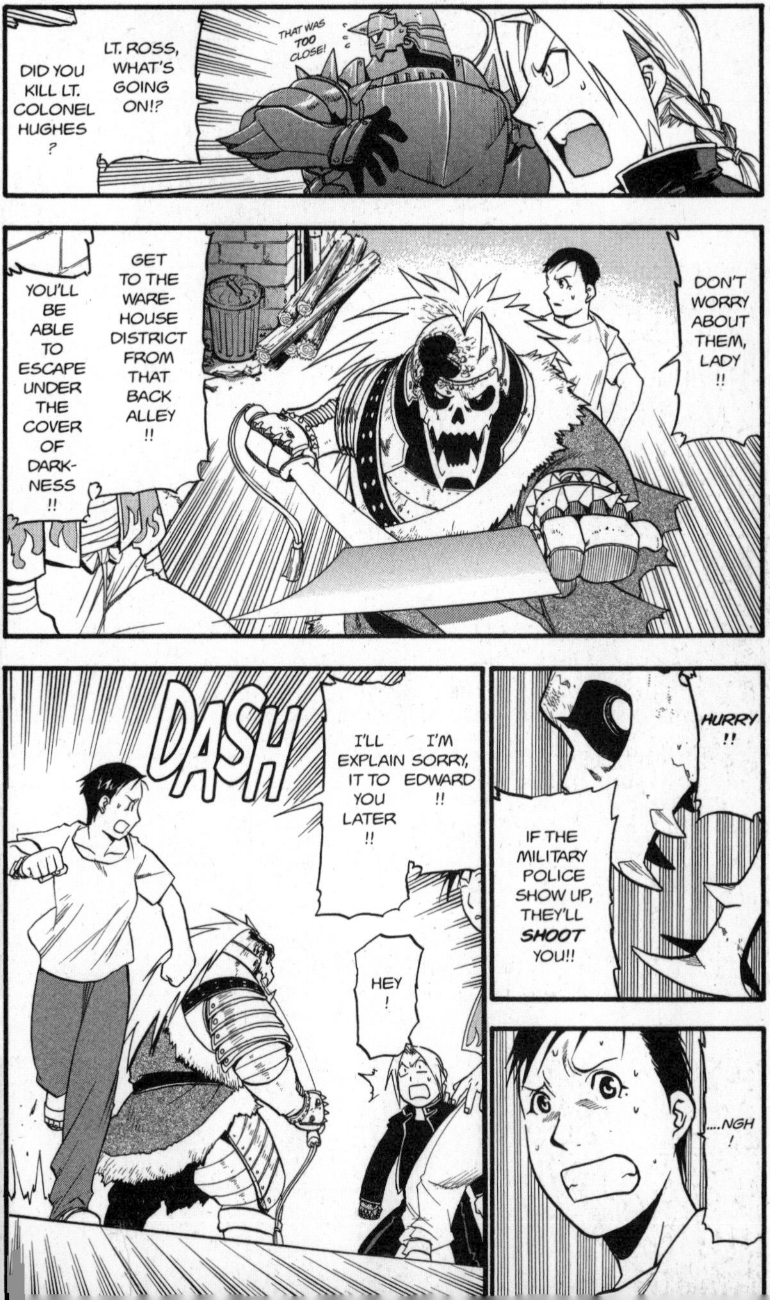
THAT WAS TOO CLOSE!
LT. ROSS, WHAT'S GOING ON!?
DID YOU KILL LT. COLONEL HUGHES?
DON'T WORRY ABOUT THEM, LADY!!
GET TO THE WAREHOUSE DISTRICT FROM THAT BACK ALLEY!!
YOU'LL BE ABLE TO ESCAPE UNDER THE COVER OF DARKNESS!!
HURRY!!
IF THE MILITARY POLICE SHOW UP, THEY'LL ***SHOOT*** YOU!!
....NGH!
I'M SORRY, EDWARD!!
I'LL EXPLAIN IT TO YOU LATER!!
DASH
HEY!

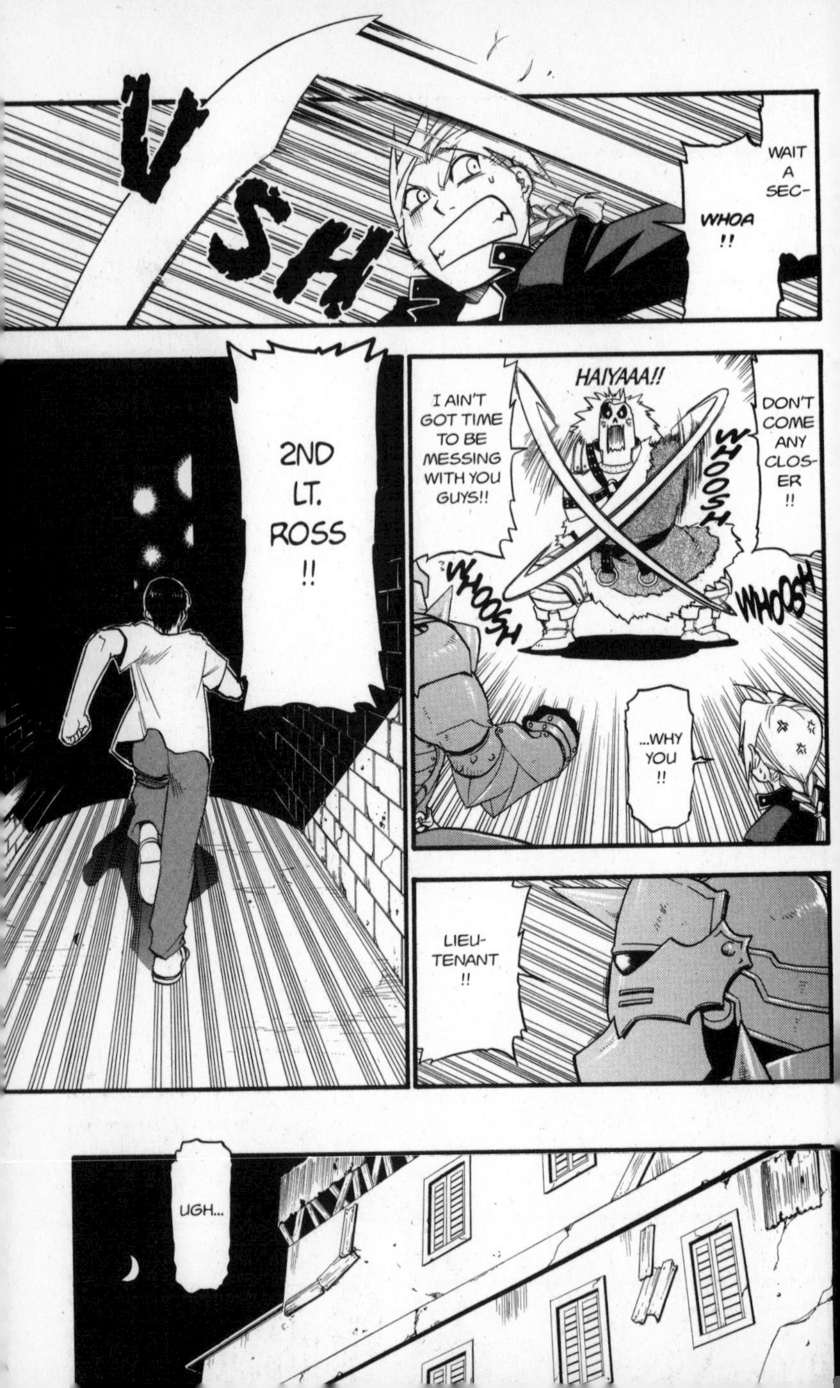
WAIT A SEC-
WHOA !!
VSH
DON'T COME ANY CLOSER !!
WHOOSH
HAIYAAA!!
I AIN'T GOT TIME TO BE MESSING WITH YOU GUYS!!
WHOOSH
WHOOSH
...WHY YOU !!
LIEUTENANT !!
2ND LT. ROSS !!
UGH...

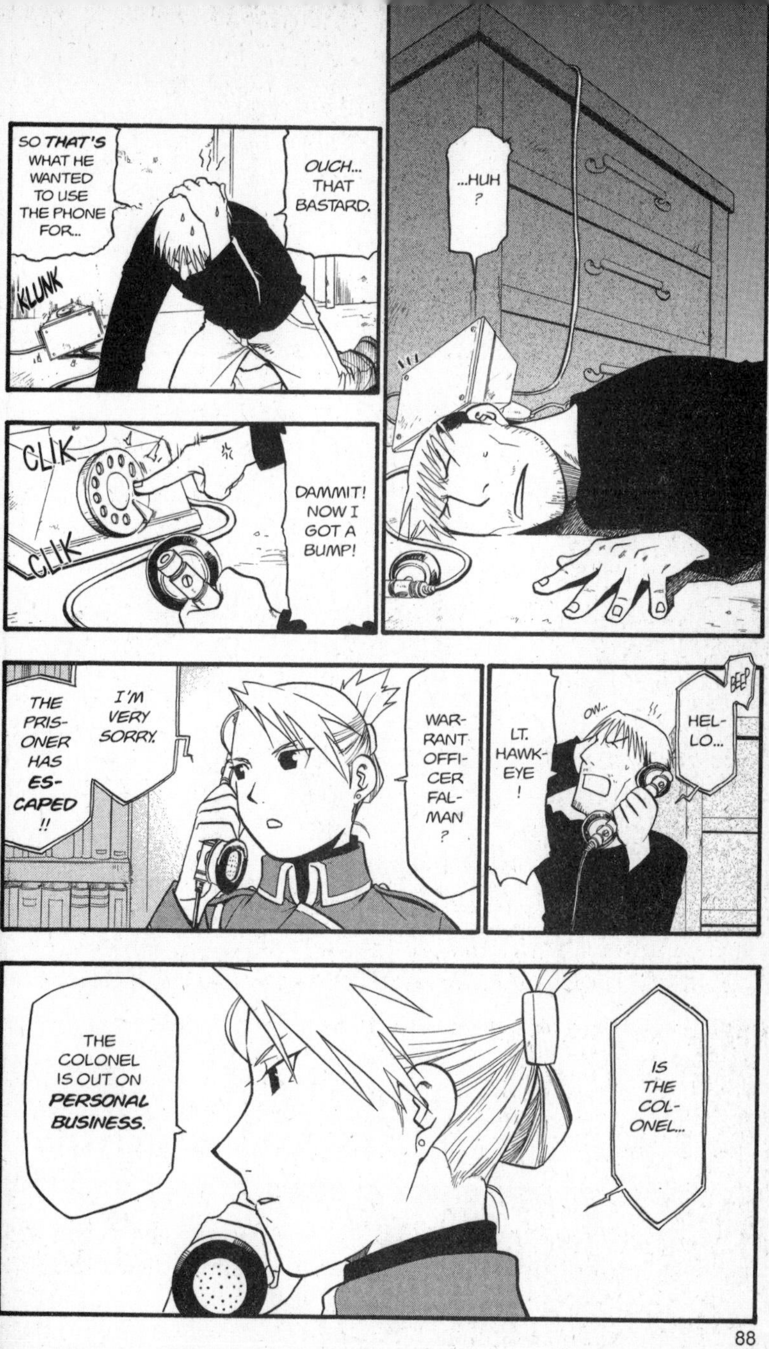
...HUH ?
OUCH... THAT BASTARD.
SO THAT'S WHAT HE WANTED TO USE THE PHONE FOR...
KLUNK
DAMMIT! NOW I GOT A BUMP!
CLIK
CLIK
BEEP
HEL-LO...
OW...
LT. HAWK-EYE!
WAR-RANT OFFI-CER FAL-MAN ?
I'M VERY SORRY.
THE PRIS-ONER HAS ES-CAPED !!
IS THE COL-ONEL...
THE COLONEL IS OUT ON PERSONAL BUSINESS.

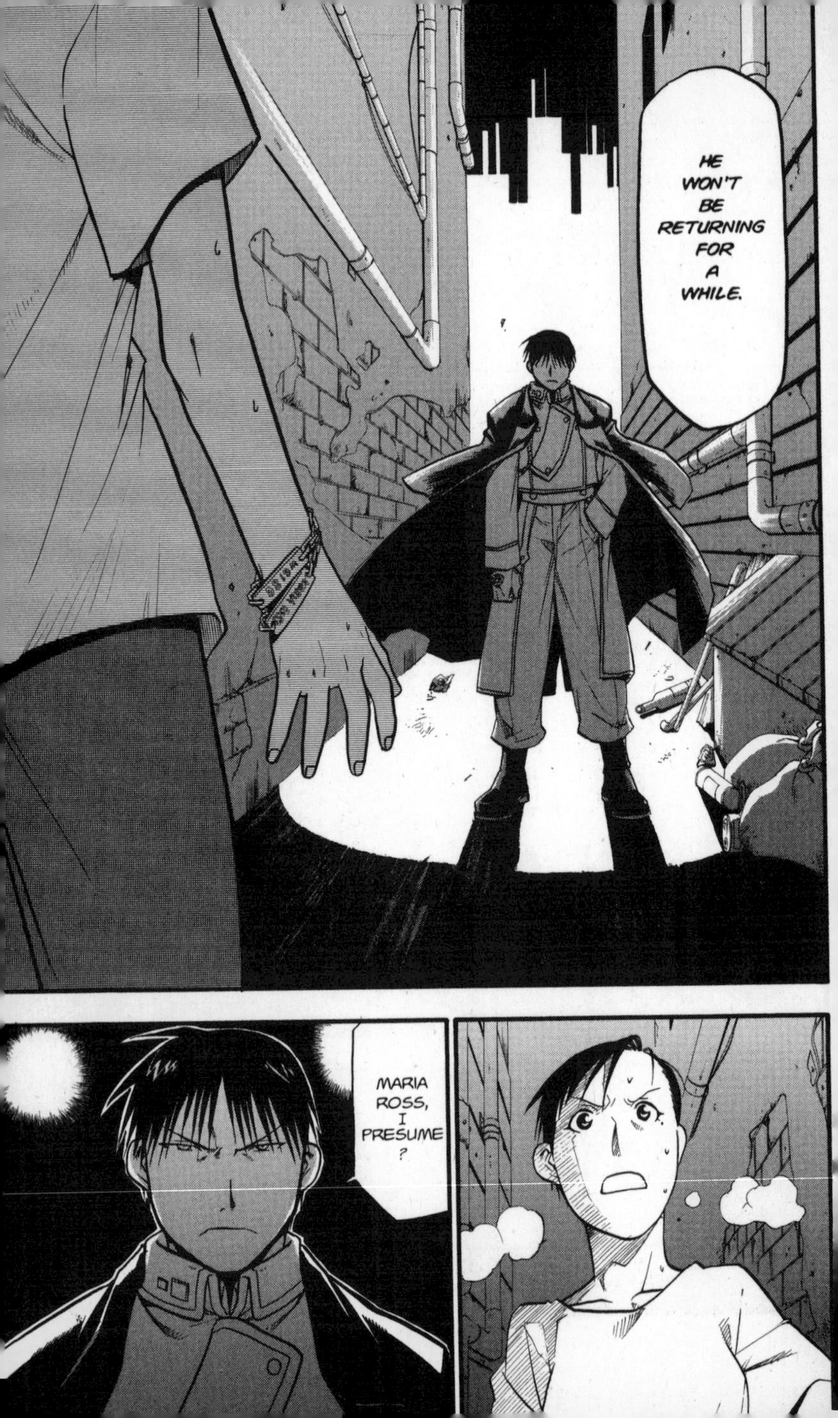
HE WON'T BE RETURNING FOR A WHILE.
MARIA ROSS, I PRESUME?

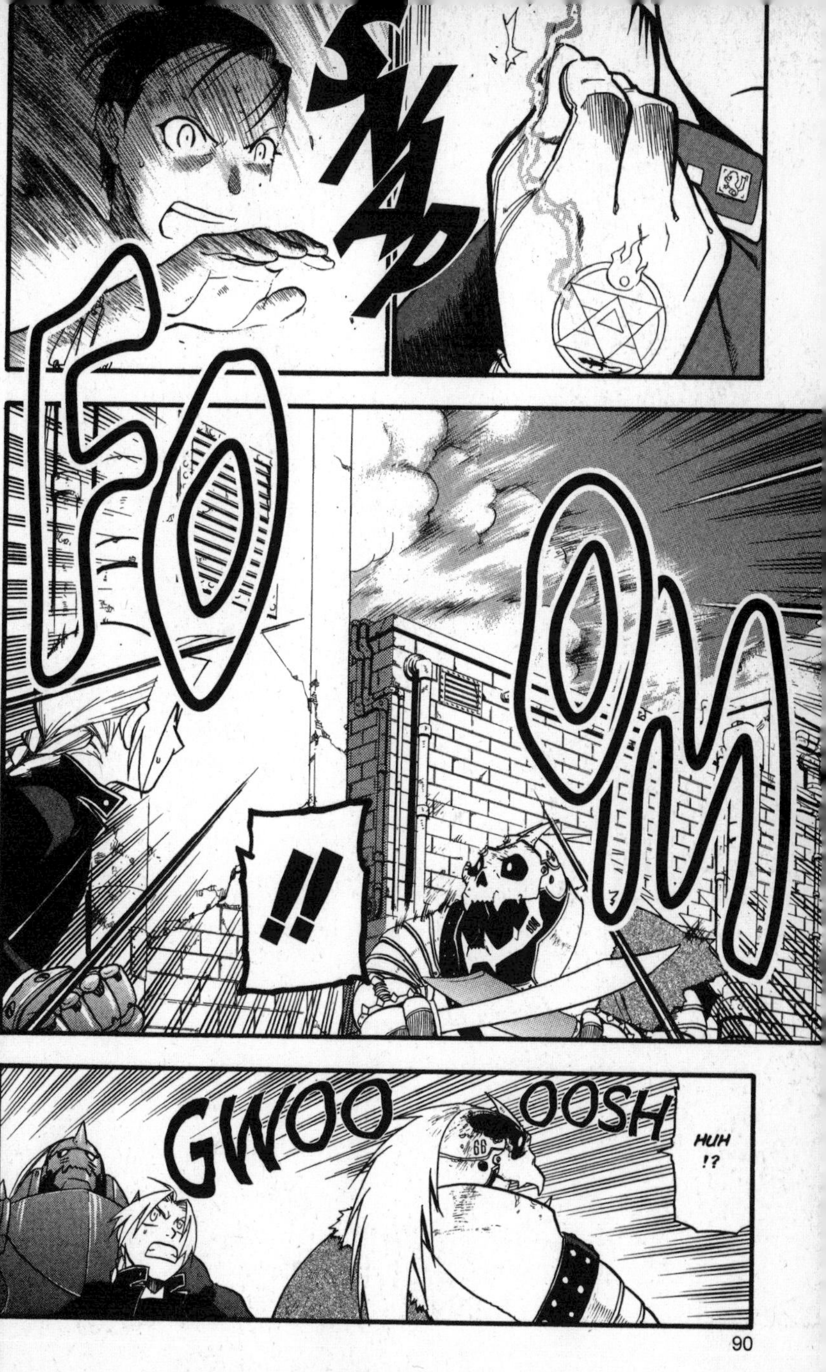
SNAP
FOOM
!!
GWOOOOSH
HUH !?

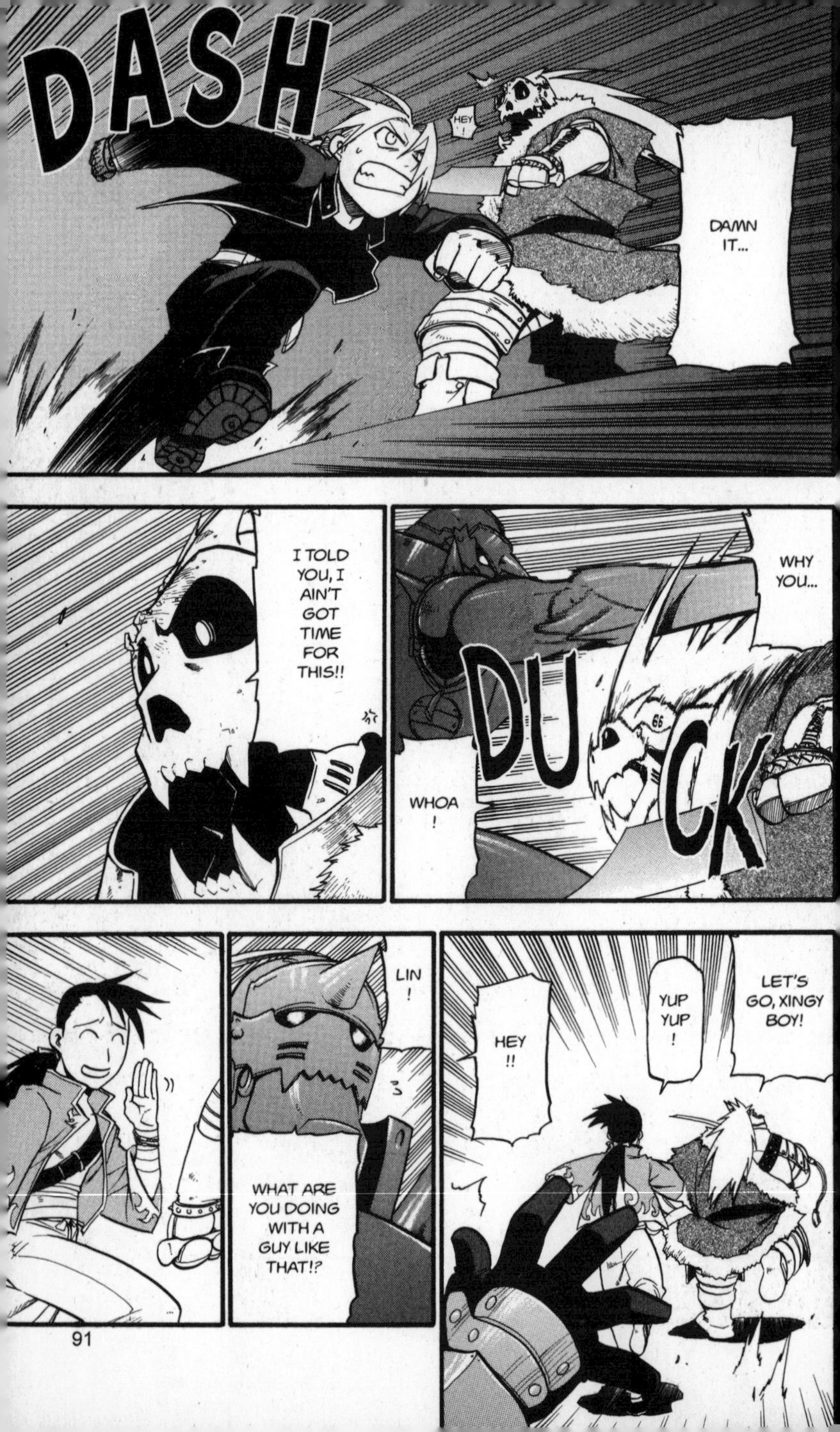
HEY!
DAMN IT...
DASH
WHY YOU...
DUCK
WHOA!
I TOLD YOU, I AIN'T GOT TIME FOR THIS!!
LET'S GO, XINGY BOY!
YUP YUP!
HEY!!
LIN!
WHAT ARE YOU DOING WITH A GUY LIKE THAT!?

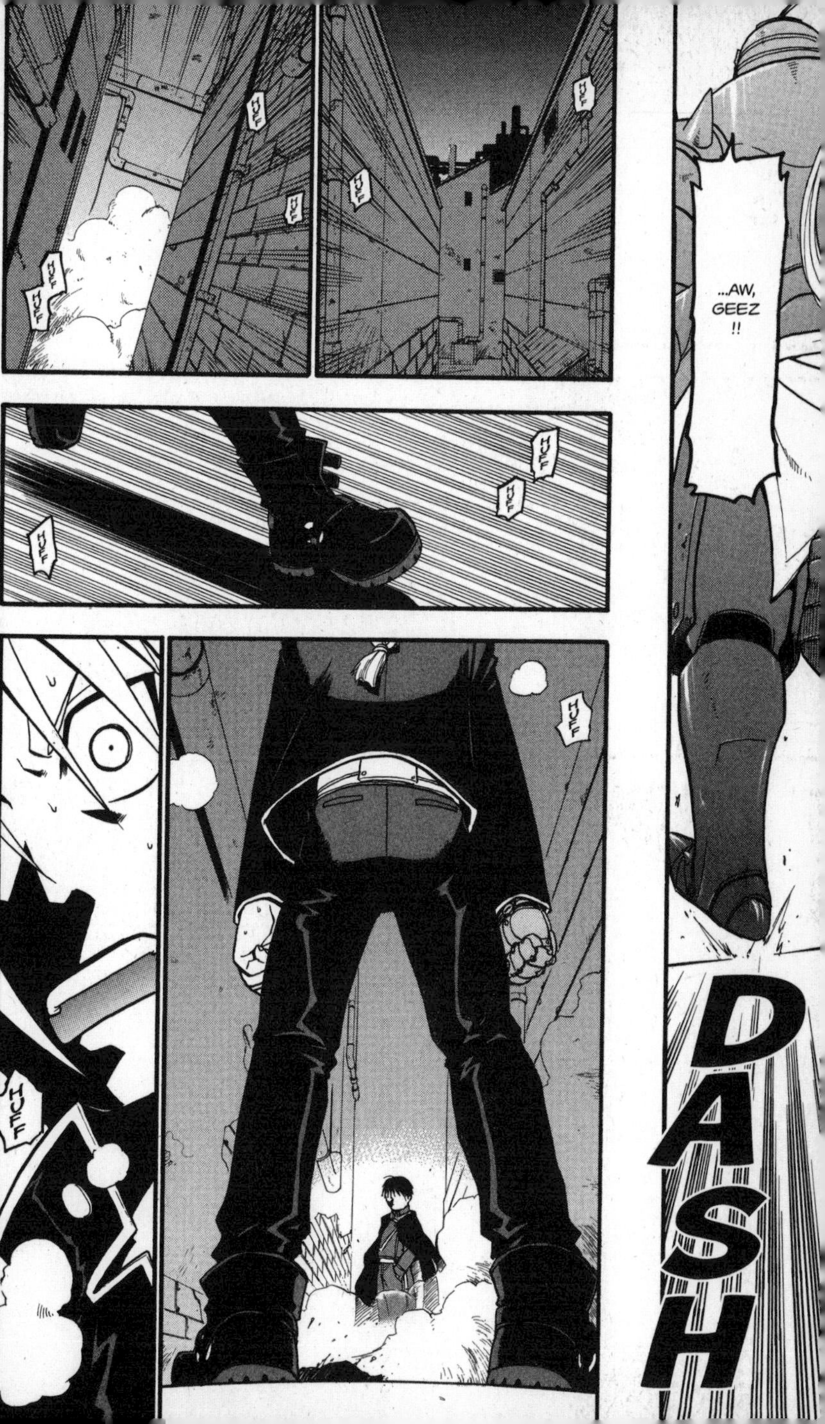
...AW, GEEZ !!
DASH
HUFF
HUFF
HUFF
HUFF
HUFF
HUFF
HUFF
HUFF
HUFF
HUFF
HUFF
HUFF

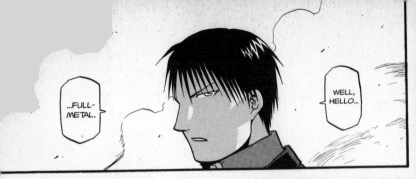

...FULL-METAL.

WELL, HELLO...

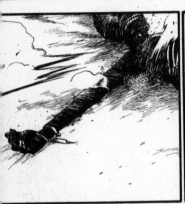

...UGH...

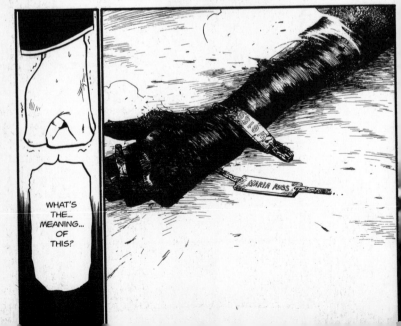

WHAT'S THE... MEANING... OF THIS?

MARIA ROSS

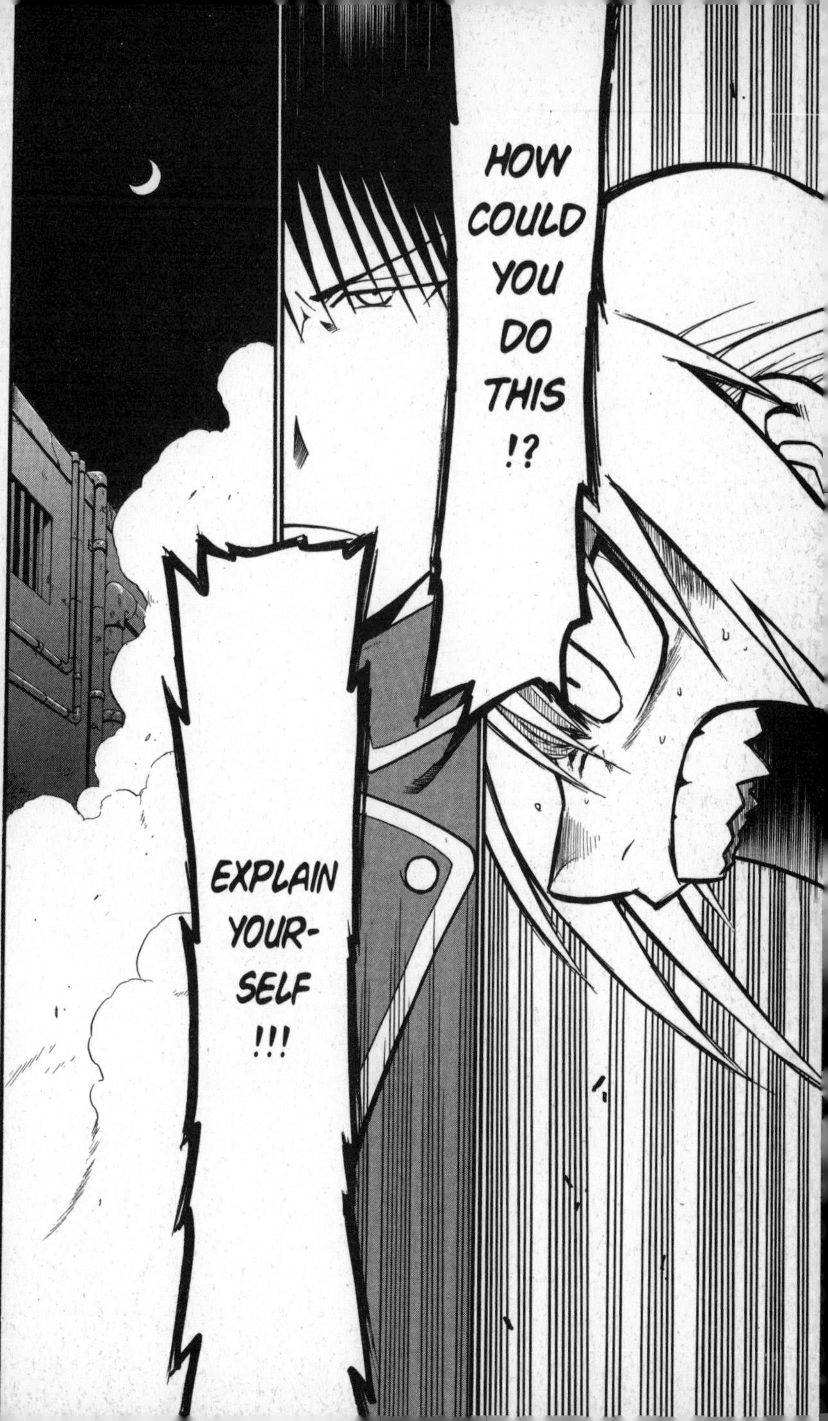
HOW COULD YOU DO THIS !?
EXPLAIN YOUR-SELF !!!

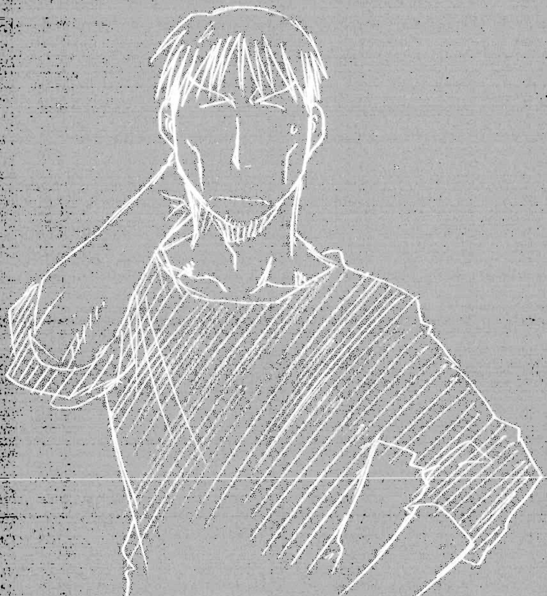

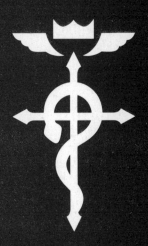

FULLMETAL
ALCHEMIST

WHEN... ?
WHY WAS LIEUTENANT COLONEL HUGHES KILLED?
WHY DID 2ND LT. ROSS HAVE TO...
WHY DIDN'T YOU TELL ME !!?

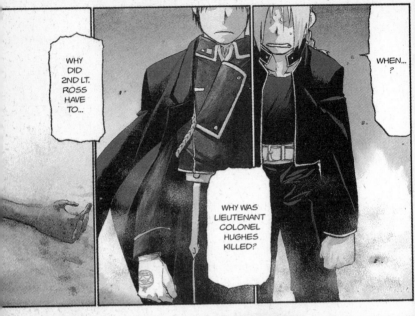

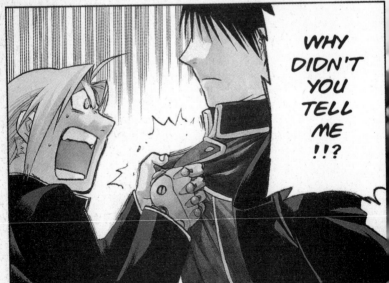

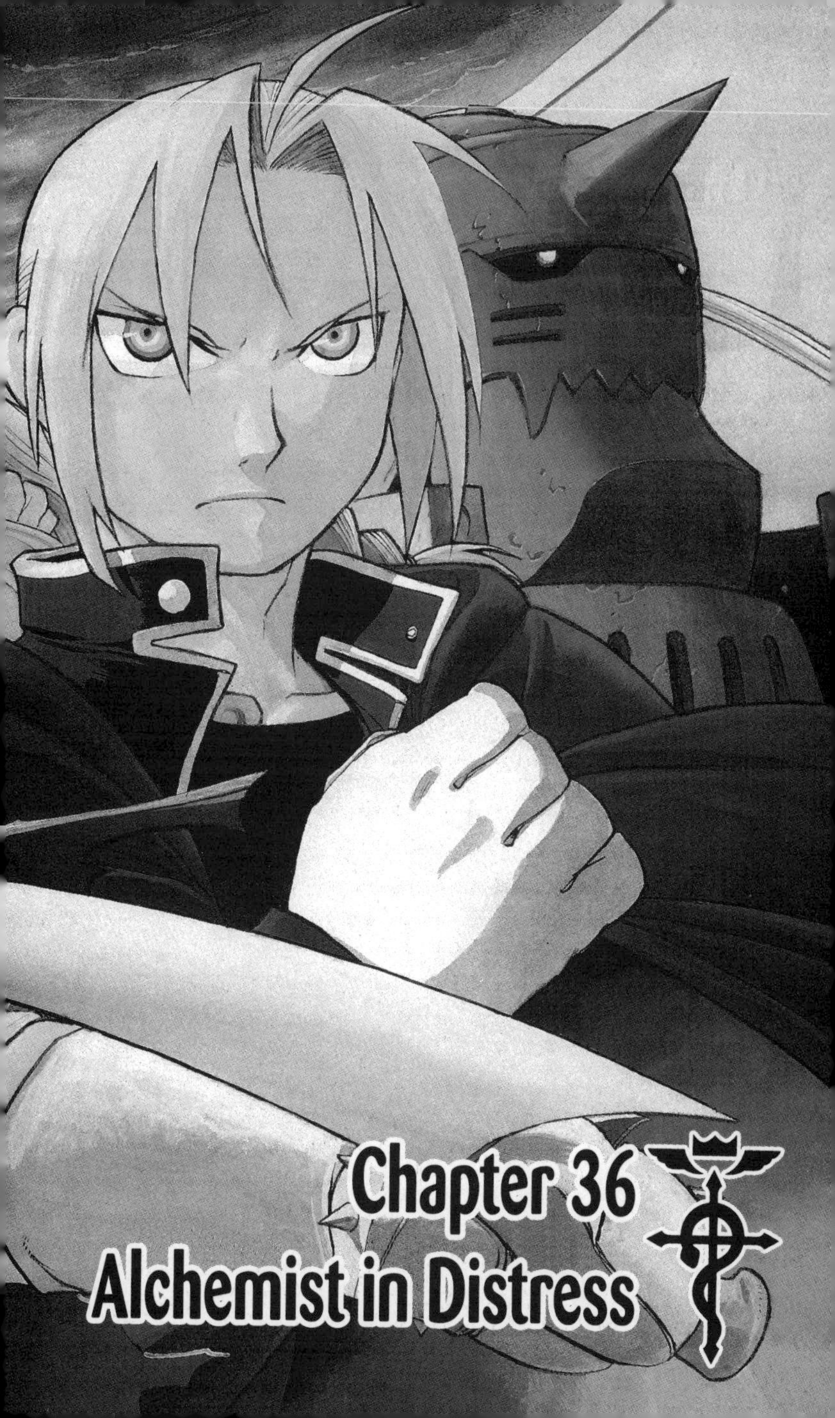
Chapter 36
Alchemist in Distress

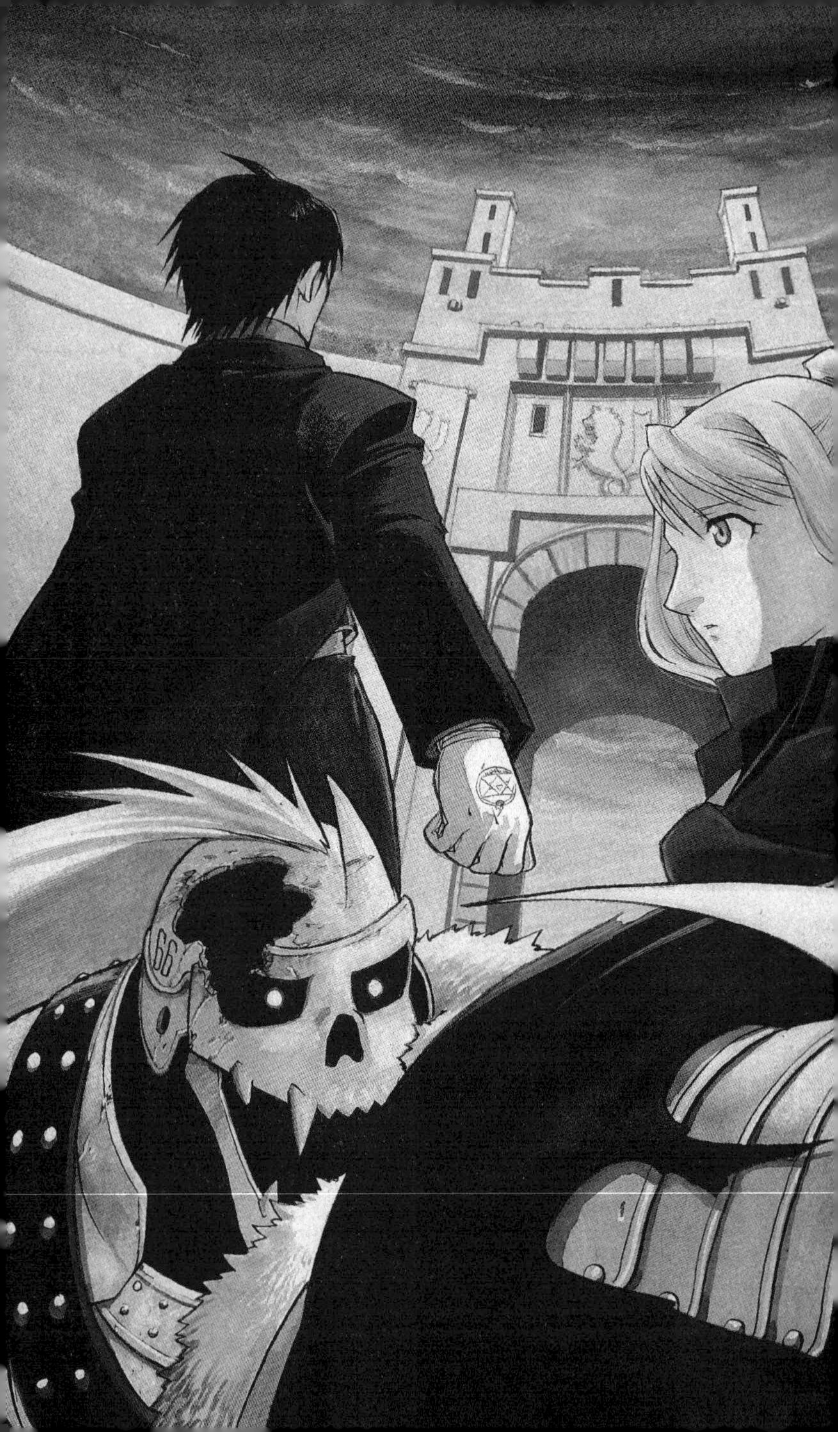

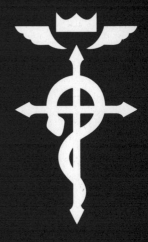

FULLMETAL
ALCHEMIST

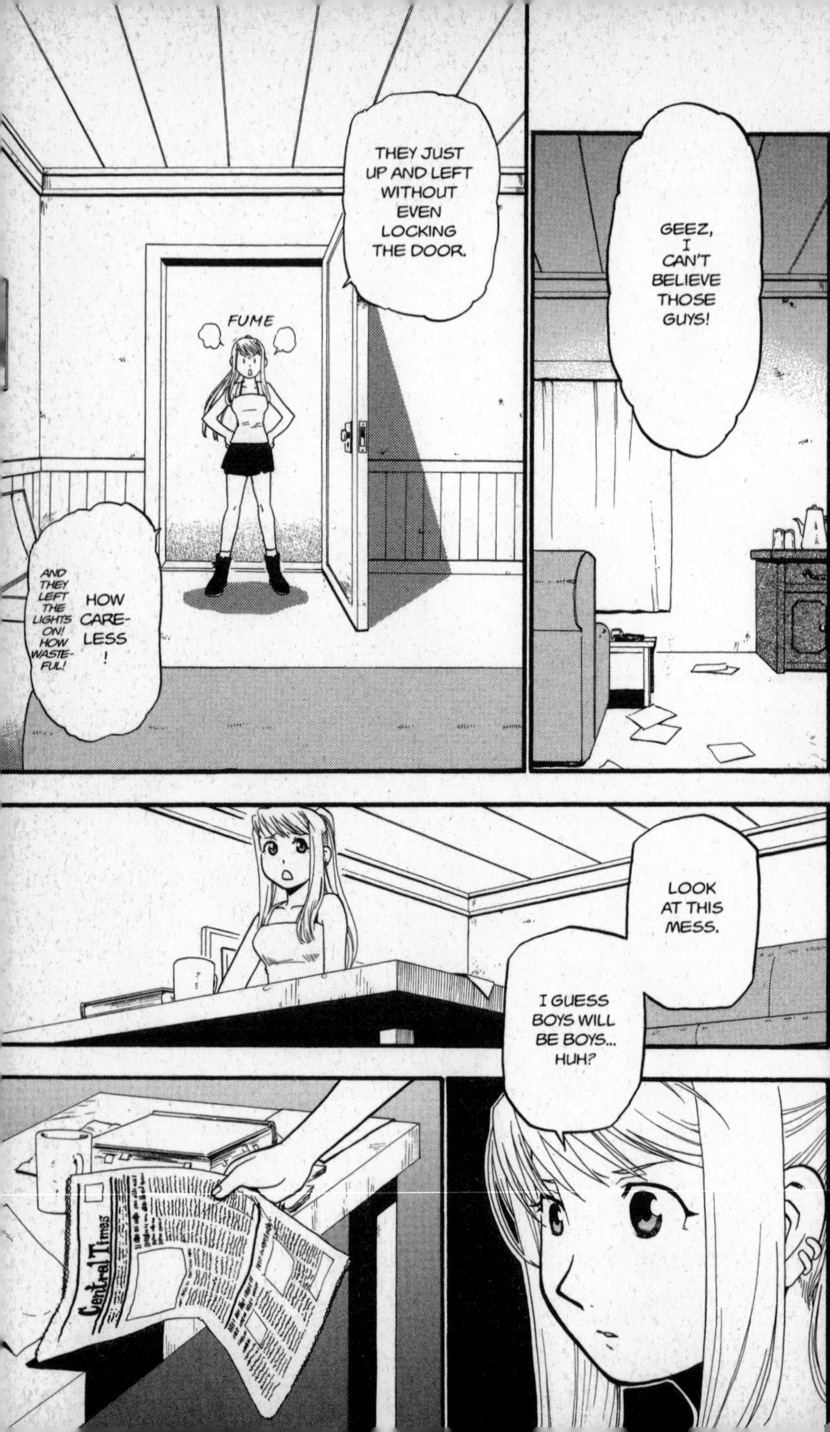
GEEZ, I CAN'T BELIEVE THOSE GUYS!
THEY JUST UP AND LEFT WITHOUT EVEN LOCKING THE DOOR.
FUME
HOW CARE-LESS!
AND THEY LEFT THE LIGHTS ON! HOW WASTE-FUL!
LOOK AT THIS MESS.
I GUESS BOYS WILL BE BOYS... HUH?
Central Times

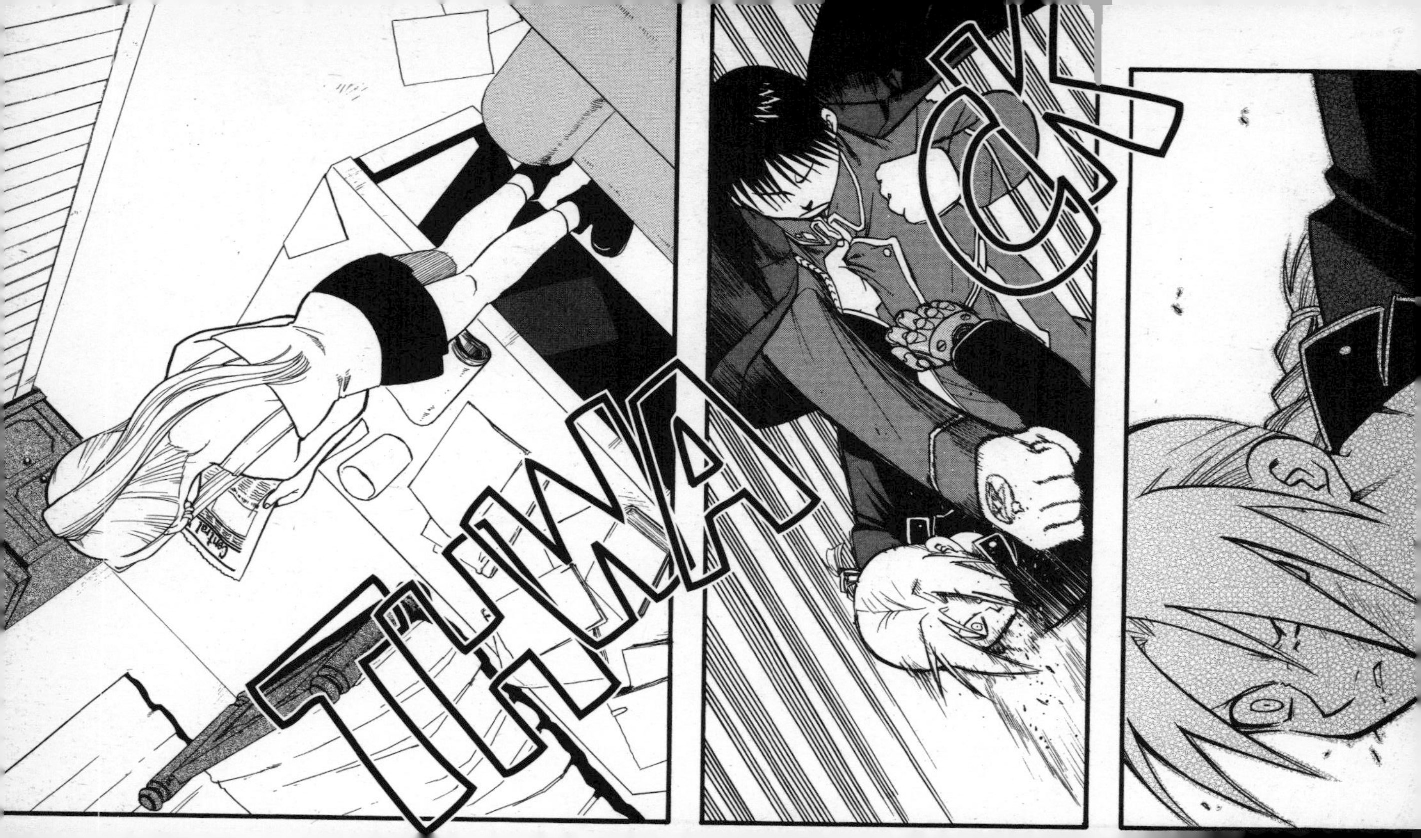
Central
THWACK

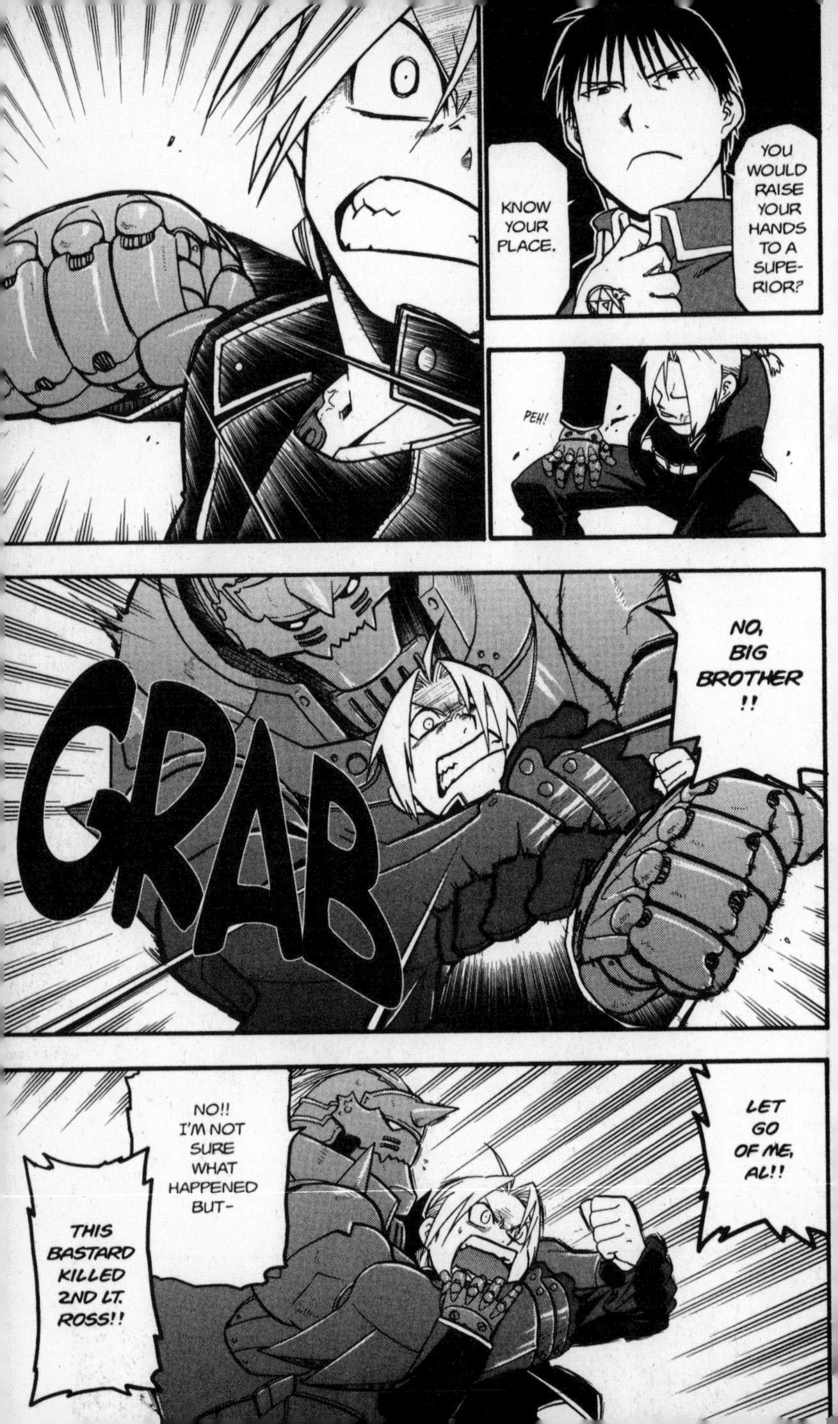
YOU WOULD RAISE YOUR HANDS TO A SUPERIOR?
KNOW YOUR PLACE.
PEH!
NO, BIG BROTHER!!
GRAB
LET GO OF ME, AL!!
NO!! I'M NOT SURE WHAT HAPPENED BUT-
THIS BASTARD KILLED 2ND LT. ROSS!!

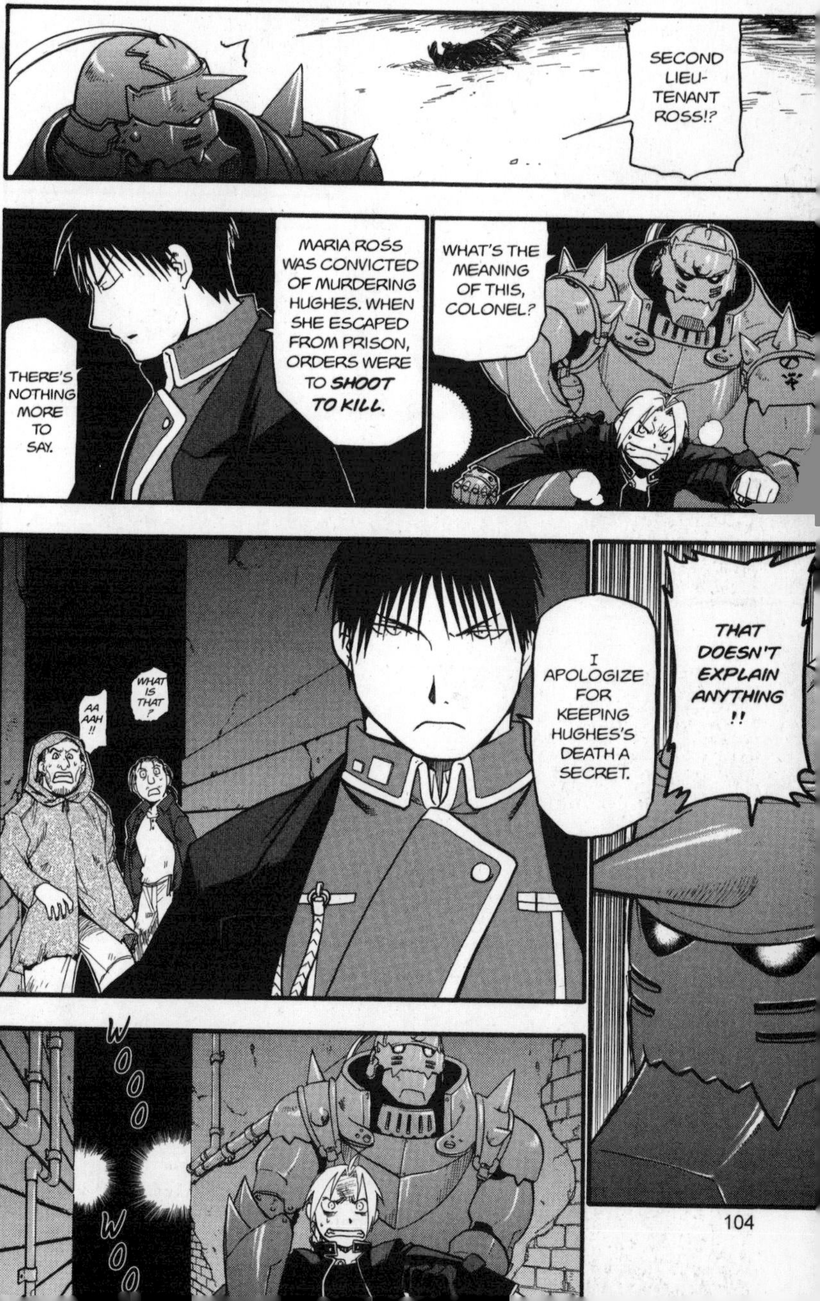
SECOND LIEU-TENANT ROSS!?
WHAT'S THE MEANING OF THIS, COLONEL?
MARIA ROSS WAS CONVICTED OF MURDERING HUGHES. WHEN SHE ESCAPED FROM PRISON, ORDERS WERE TO **SHOOT TO KILL.**
THERE'S NOTHING MORE TO SAY.
THAT DOESN'T EXPLAIN ANYTHING!!
I APOLOGIZE FOR KEEPING HUGHES'S DEATH A SECRET.
WHAT IS THAT?
AA AAH!!
WOOOO
WOO

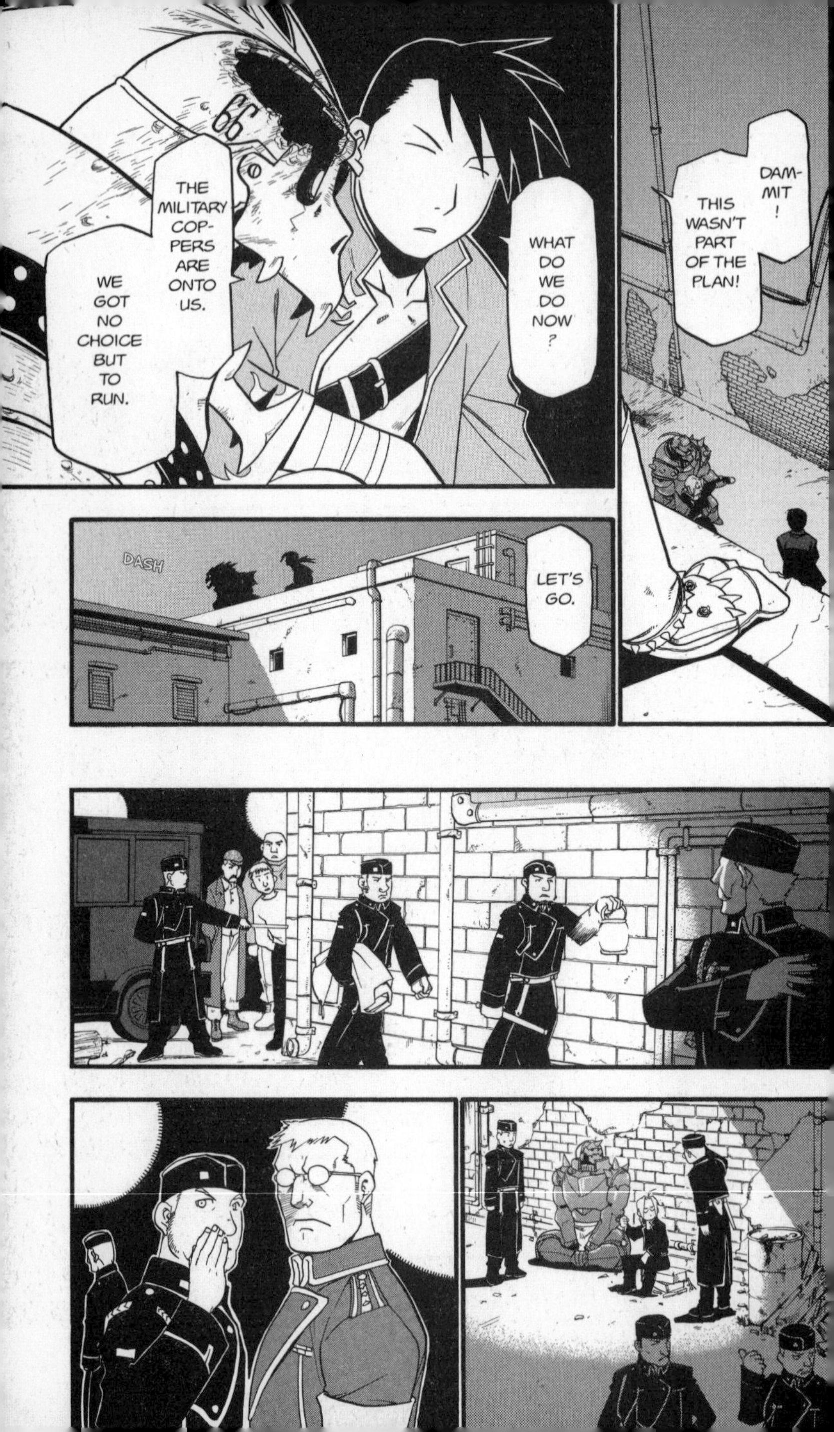
DAM-MIT!
THIS WASN'T PART OF THE PLAN!
WHAT DO WE DO NOW?
THE MILITARY COP-PERS ARE ONTO US.
WE GOT NO CHOICE BUT TO RUN.
LET'S GO.
DASH

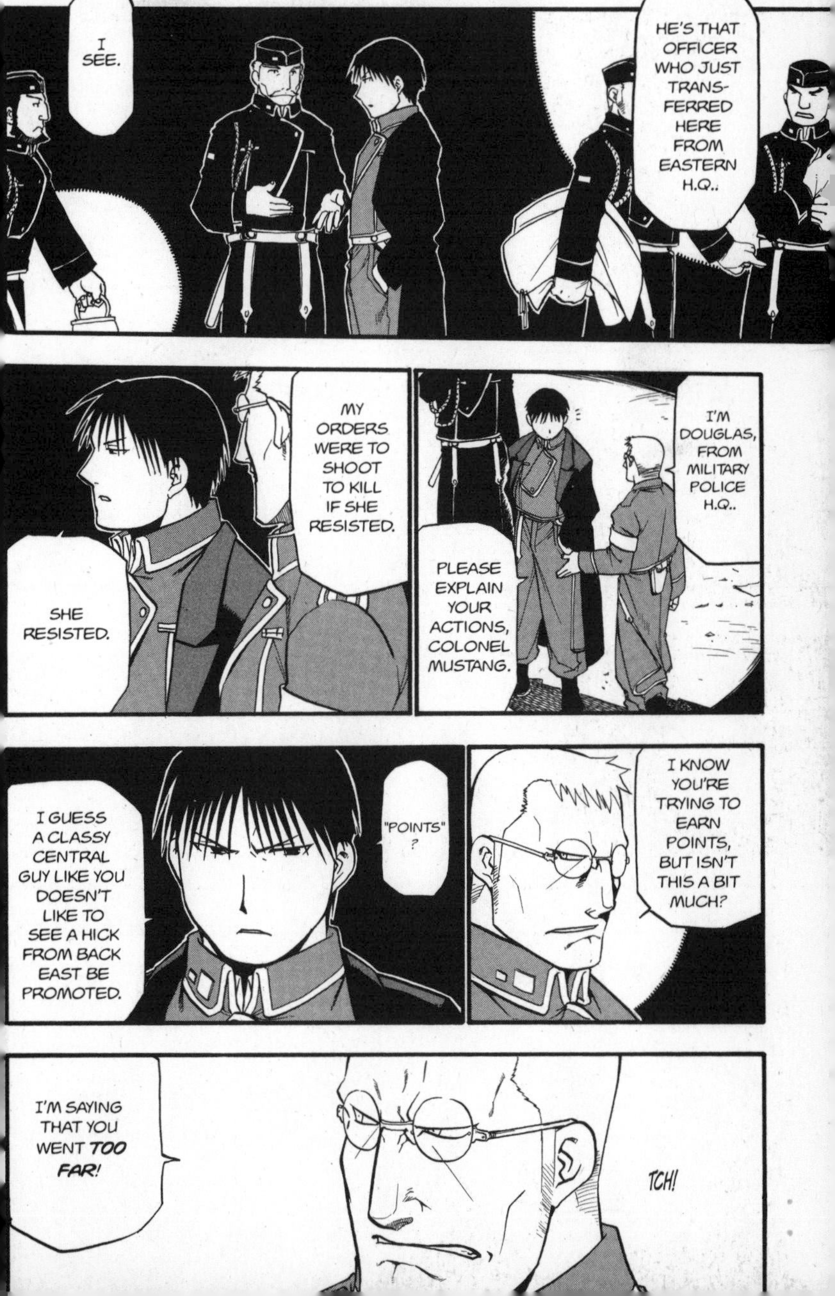
HE'S THAT OFFICER WHO JUST TRANS-FERRED HERE FROM EASTERN H.Q..
I SEE.
I'M DOUGLAS, FROM MILITARY POLICE H.Q..
PLEASE EXPLAIN YOUR ACTIONS, COLONEL MUSTANG.
MY ORDERS WERE TO SHOOT TO KILL IF SHE RESISTED.
SHE RESISTED.
I KNOW YOU'RE TRYING TO EARN POINTS, BUT ISN'T THIS A BIT MUCH?
"POINTS"?
I GUESS A CLASSY CENTRAL GUY LIKE YOU DOESN'T LIKE TO SEE A HICK FROM BACK EAST BE PROMOTED.
I'M SAYING THAT YOU WENT ***TOO FAR***!
TCH!

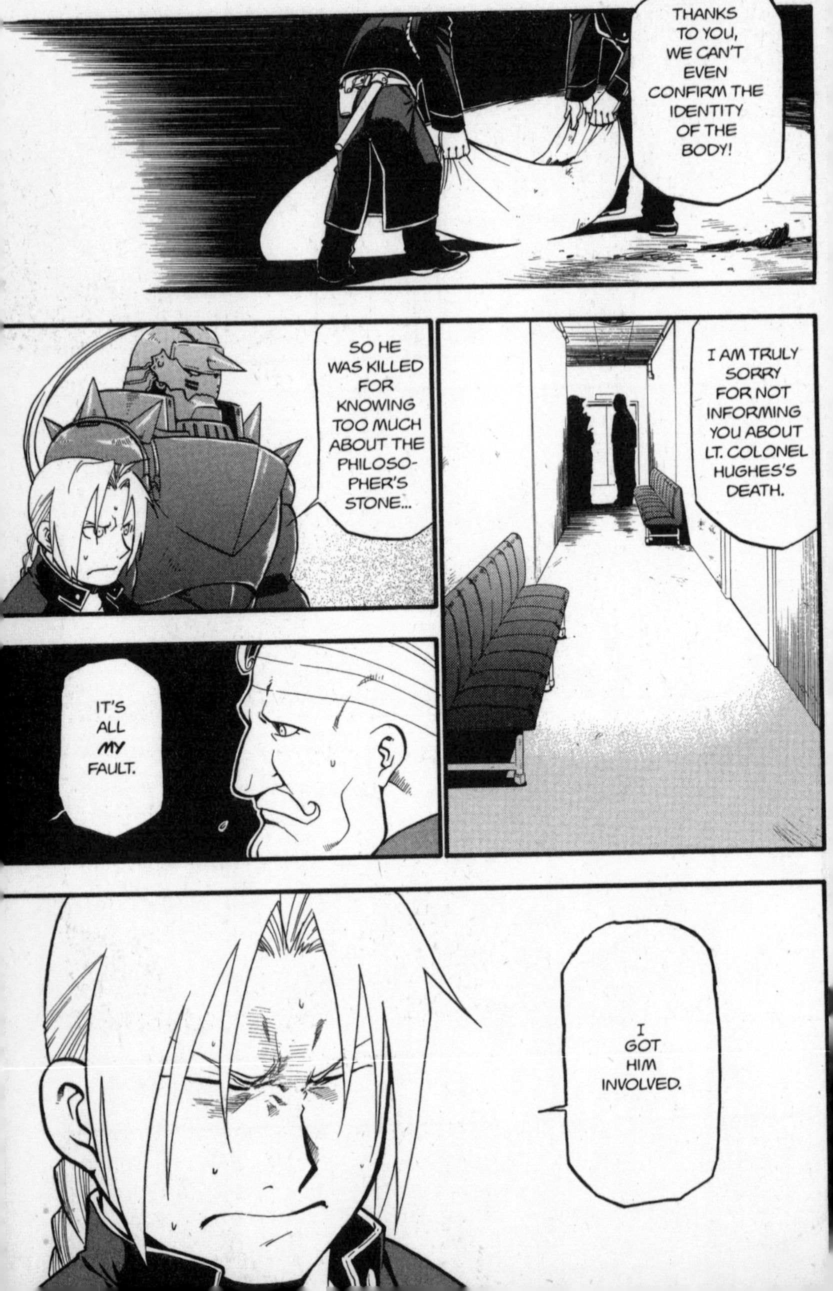
THANKS TO YOU, WE CAN'T EVEN CONFIRM THE IDENTITY OF THE BODY!
I AM TRULY SORRY FOR NOT INFORMING YOU ABOUT LT. COLONEL HUGHES'S DEATH.
SO HE WAS KILLED FOR KNOWING TOO MUCH ABOUT THE PHILOSO-PHER'S STONE...
IT'S ALL *MY* FAULT.
I GOT HIM INVOLVED.

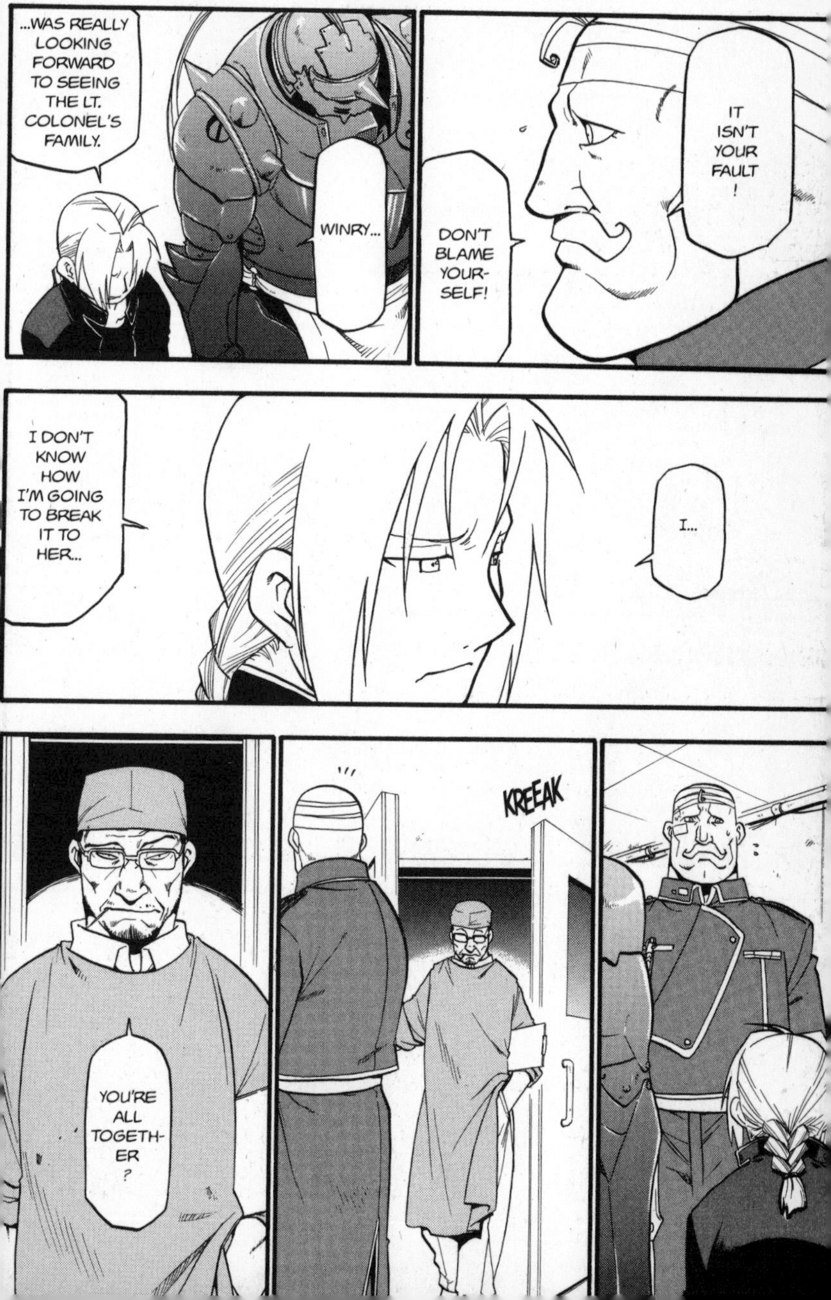
IT ISN'T YOUR FAULT!
DON'T BLAME YOURSELF!
WINRY...
...WAS REALLY LOOKING FORWARD TO SEEING THE LT. COLONEL'S FAMILY.
I...
I DON'T KNOW HOW I'M GOING TO BREAK IT TO HER...
KREEAK
YOU'RE ALL TOGETHER?

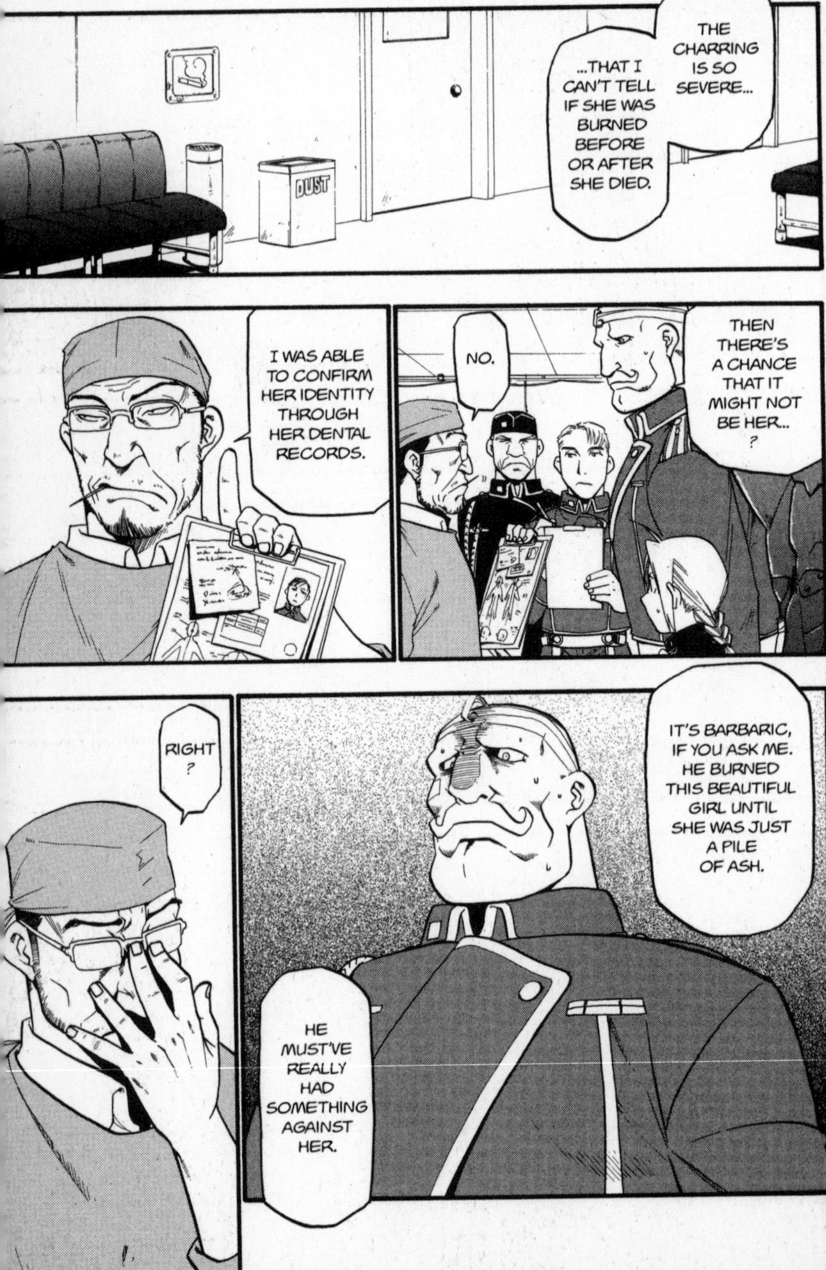
THE CHARRING IS SO SEVERE...
...THAT I CAN'T TELL IF SHE WAS BURNED BEFORE OR AFTER SHE DIED.
DUST
THEN THERE'S A CHANCE THAT IT MIGHT NOT BE HER...?
NO.
I WAS ABLE TO CONFIRM HER IDENTITY THROUGH HER DENTAL RECORDS.
IT'S BARBARIC, IF YOU ASK ME. HE BURNED THIS BEAUTIFUL GIRL UNTIL SHE WAS JUST A PILE OF ASH.
HE MUST'VE REALLY HAD SOMETHING AGAINST HER.
RIGHT?

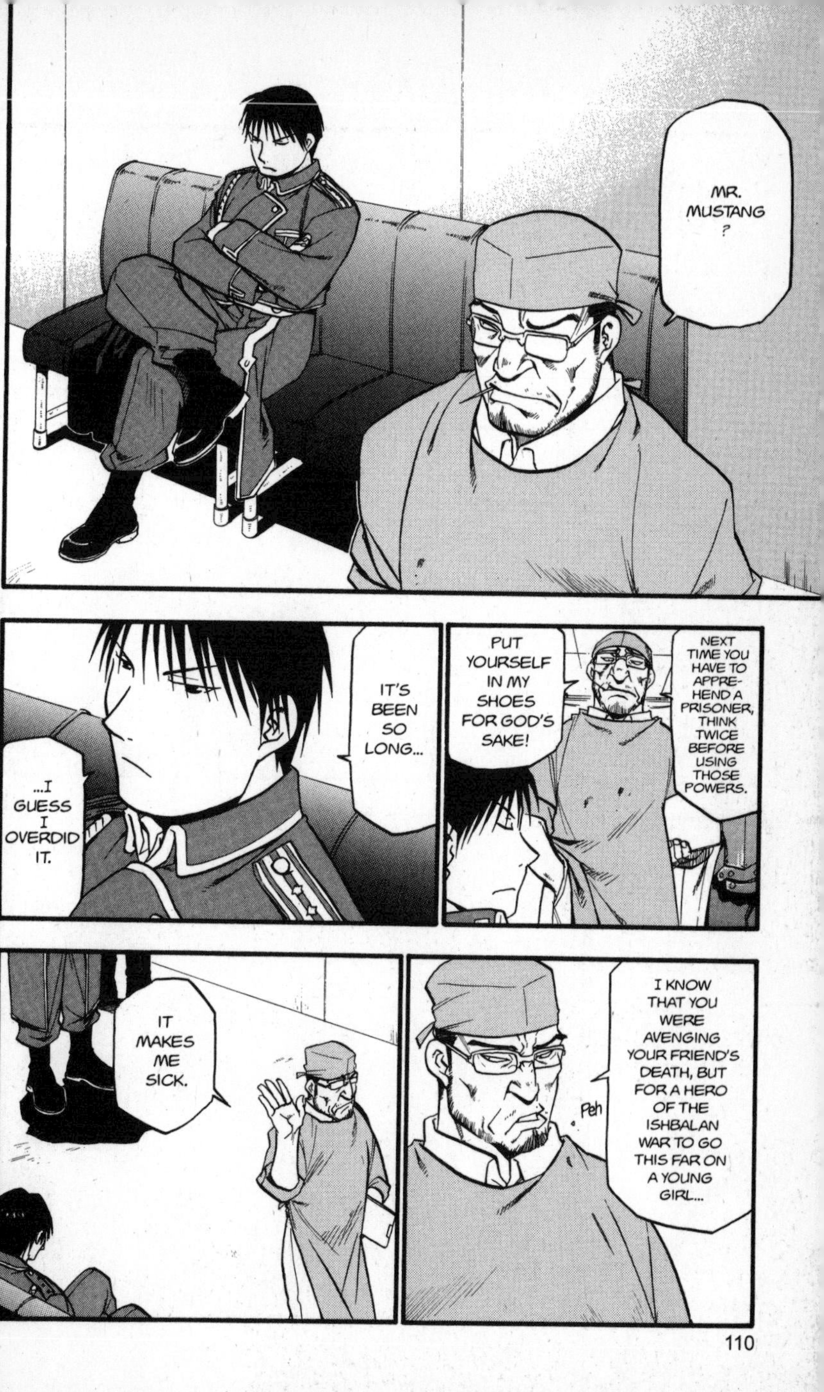
MR. MUSTANG?
NEXT TIME YOU HAVE TO APPREHEND A PRISONER, THINK TWICE BEFORE USING THOSE POWERS.
PUT YOURSELF IN MY SHOES FOR GOD'S SAKE!
IT'S BEEN SO LONG...
...I GUESS I OVERDID IT.
I KNOW THAT YOU WERE AVENGING YOUR FRIEND'S DEATH, BUT FOR A HERO OF THE ISHBALAN WAR TO GO THIS FAR ON A YOUNG GIRL...
Peh
IT MAKES ME SICK.

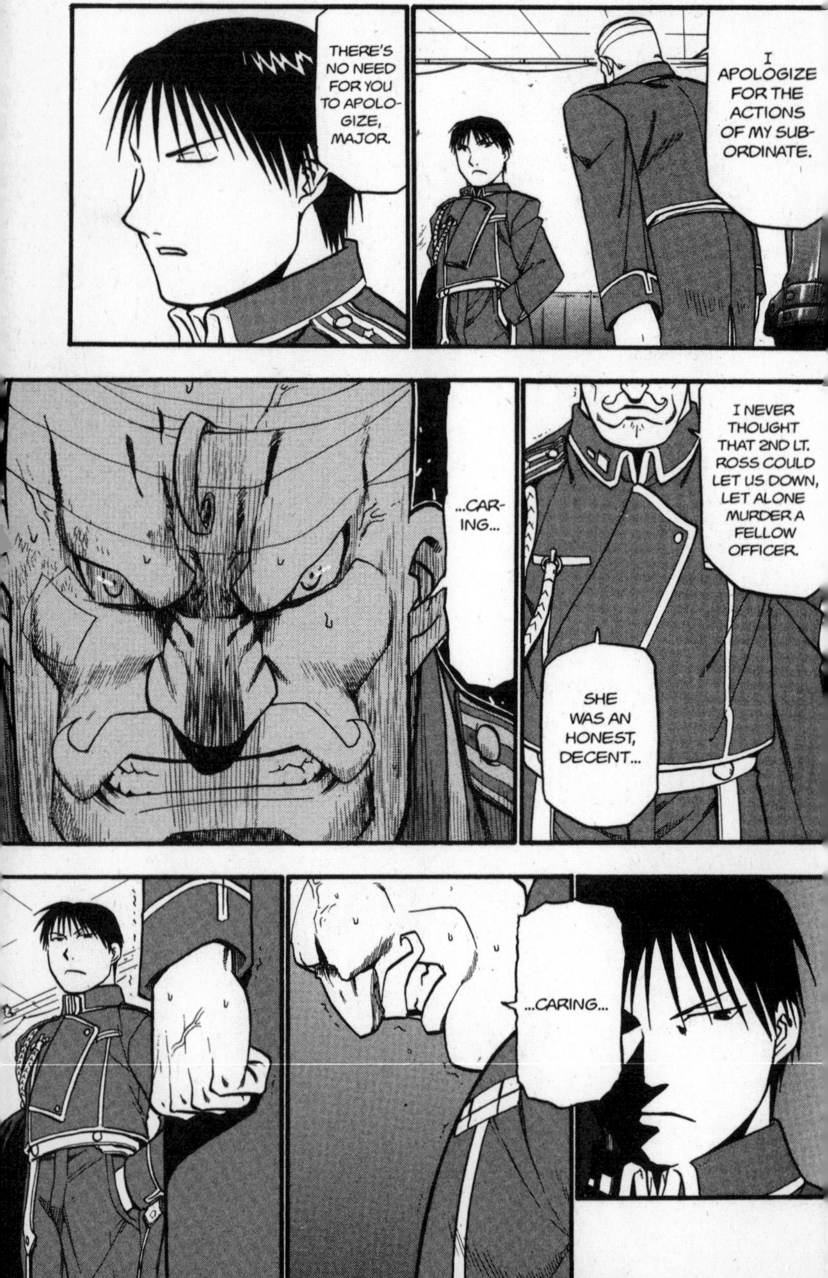
I APOLOGIZE FOR THE ACTIONS OF MY SUB-ORDINATE.
THERE'S NO NEED FOR YOU TO APOLO-GIZE, MAJOR.
I NEVER THOUGHT THAT 2ND LT. ROSS COULD LET US DOWN, LET ALONE MURDER A FELLOW OFFICER.
SHE WAS AN HONEST, DECENT...
...CAR-ING...
...CARING...

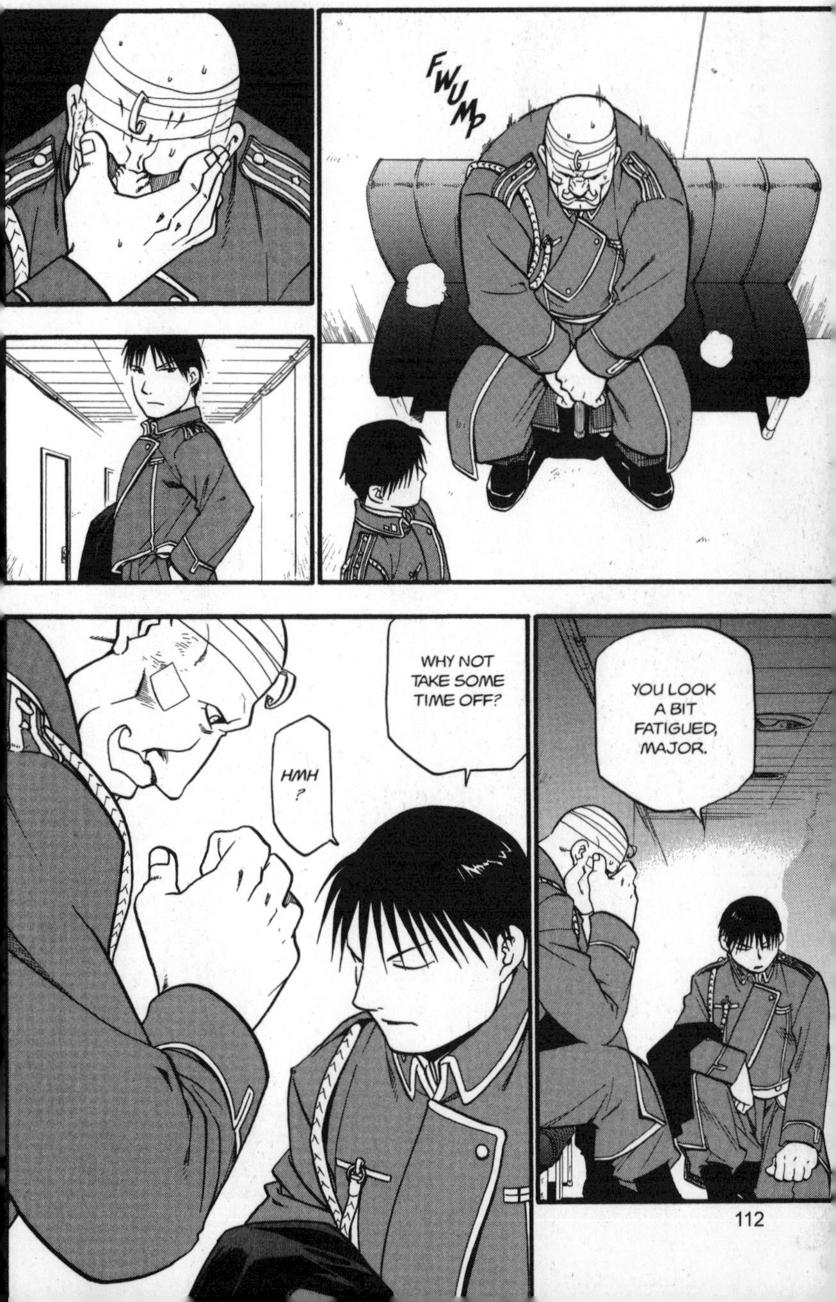
FWUMP
YOU LOOK A BIT FATIGUED, MAJOR.
WHY NOT TAKE SOME TIME OFF?
HMH?

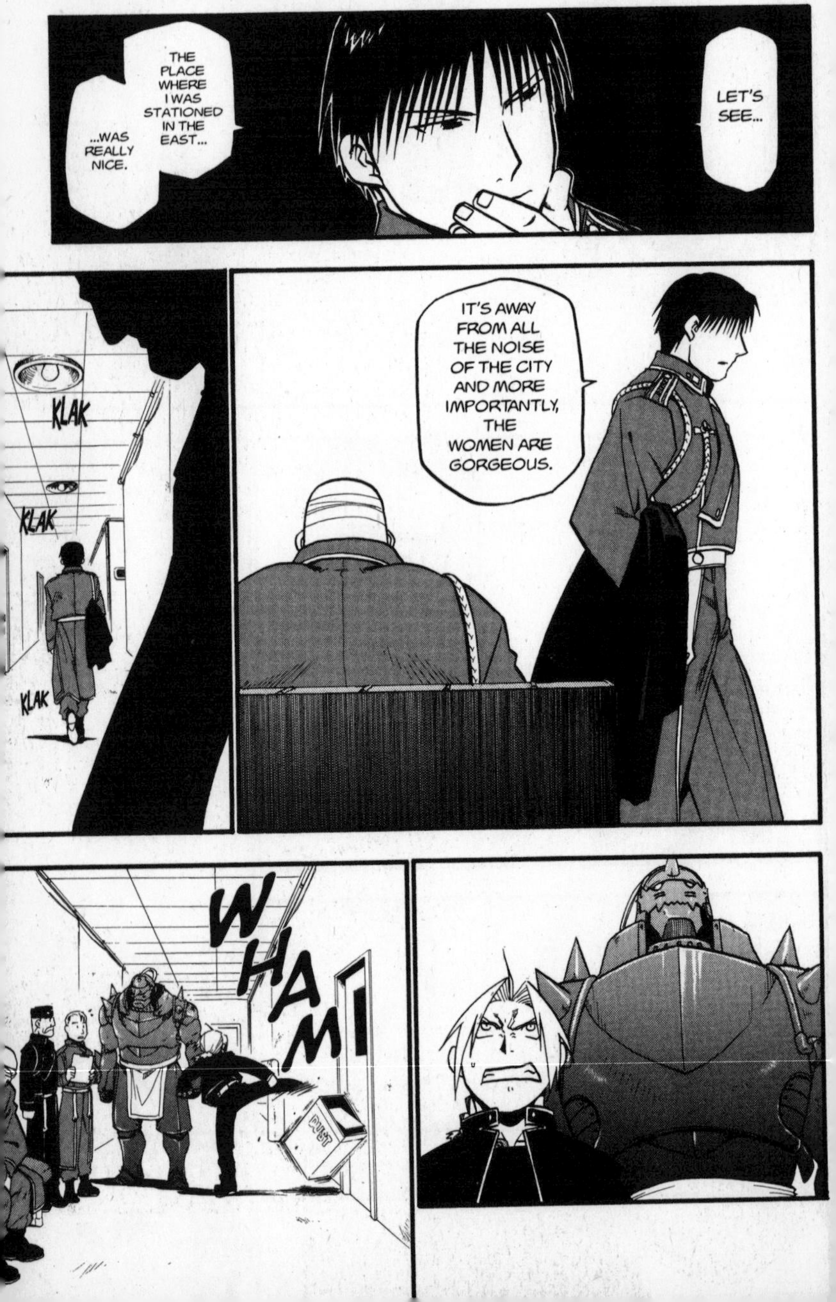
LET'S SEE...
THE PLACE WHERE I WAS STATIONED IN THE EAST...
...WAS REALLY NICE.
IT'S AWAY FROM ALL THE NOISE OF THE CITY AND MORE IMPORTANTLY, THE WOMEN ARE GORGEOUS.
KLAK
KLAK
KLAK
WHAM
DUST

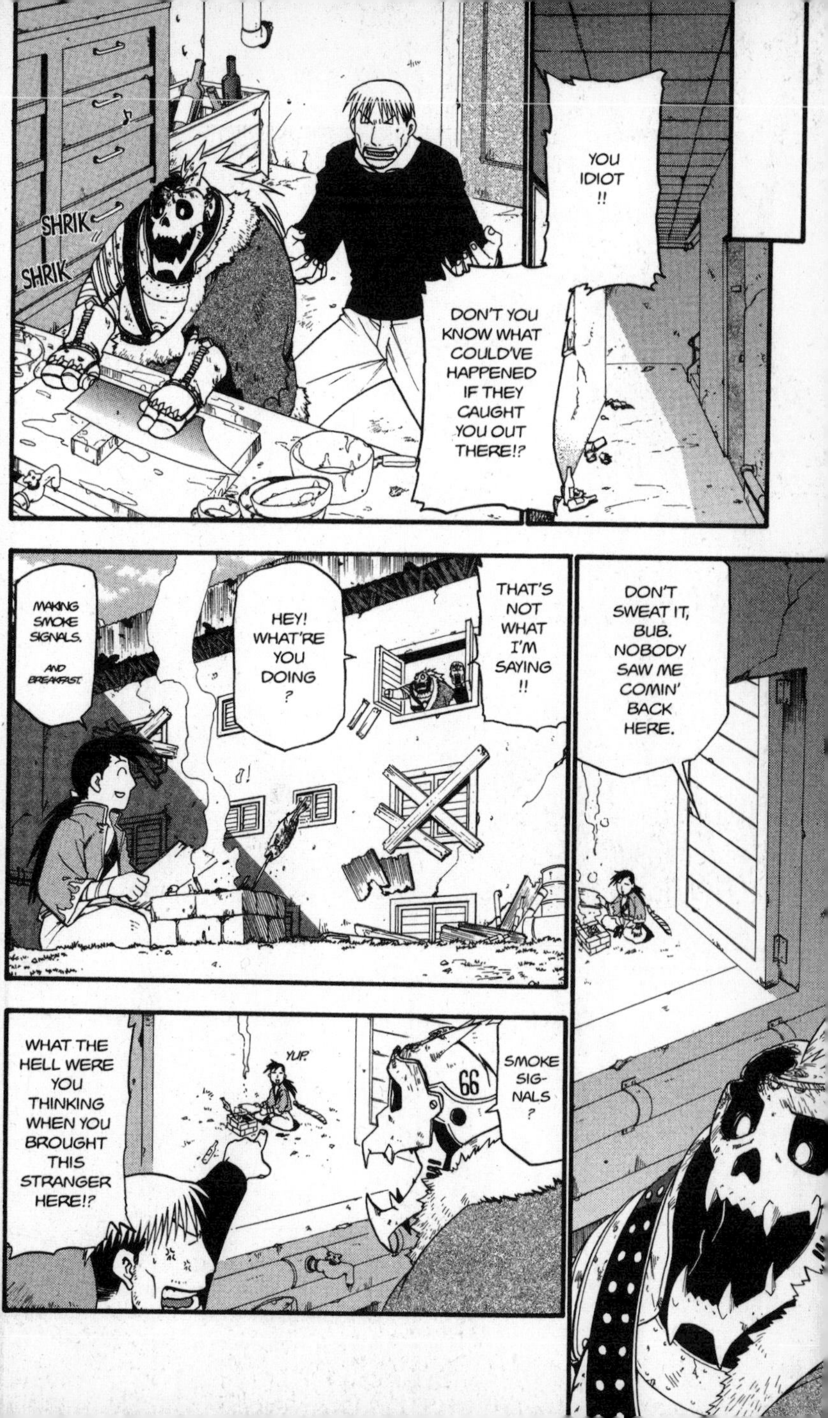
YOU IDIOT !!
DON'T YOU KNOW WHAT COULD'VE HAPPENED IF THEY CAUGHT YOU OUT THERE!?
SHRIK
SHRIK
DON'T SWEAT IT, BUB. NOBODY SAW ME COMIN' BACK HERE.
THAT'S NOT WHAT I'M SAYING !!
HEY! WHAT'RE YOU DOING ?
MAKING SMOKE SIGNALS.
AND BREAKFAST.
SMOKE SIG-NALS ?
66
YUP.
WHAT THE HELL WERE YOU THINKING WHEN YOU BROUGHT THIS STRANGER HERE!?

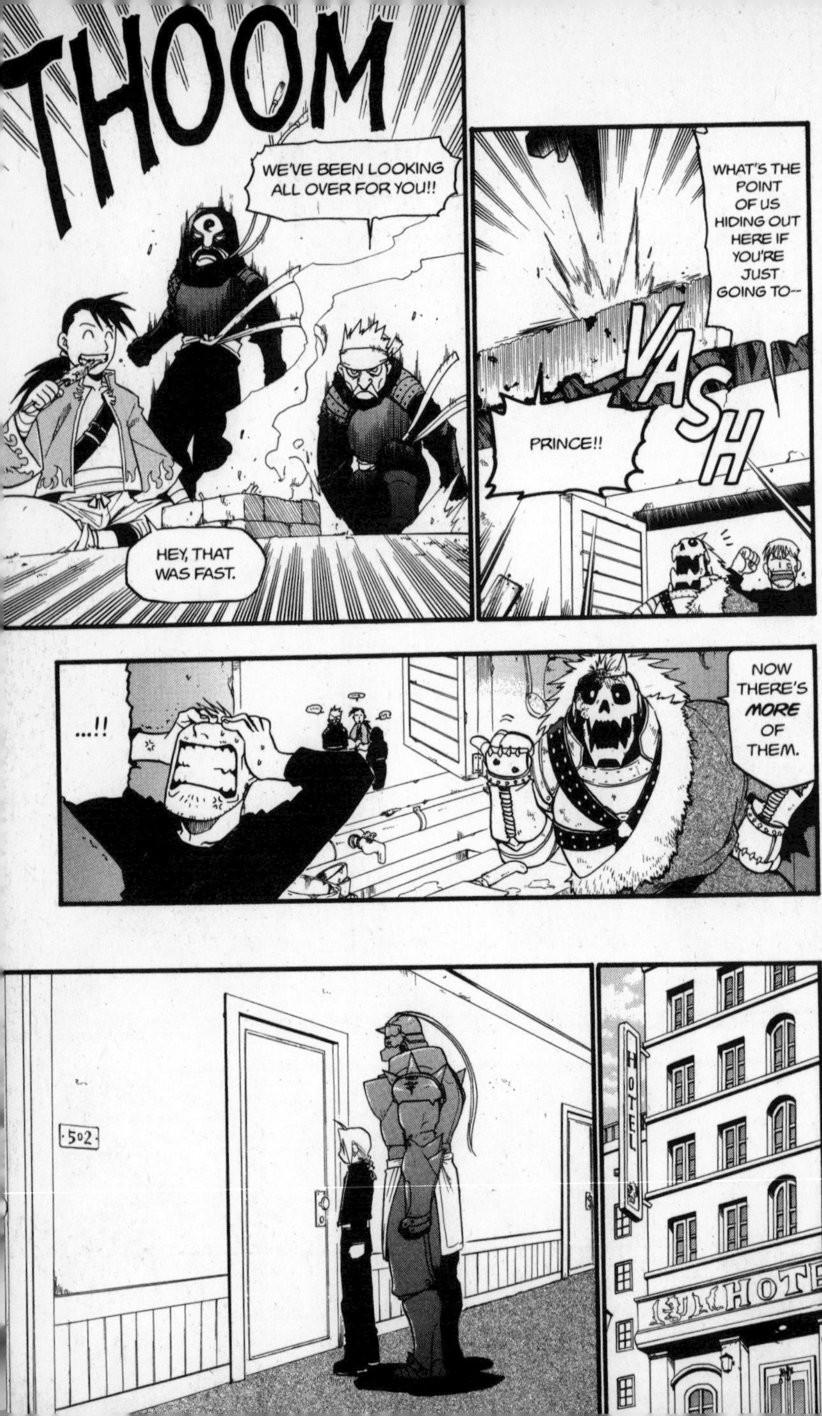

WHAT'S THE POINT OF US HIDING OUT HERE IF YOU'RE JUST GOING TO--
VASH
PRINCE!!
THOOM
WE'VE BEEN LOOKING ALL OVER FOR YOU!!
HEY, THAT WAS FAST.
NOW THERE'S *MORE* OF THEM.
...!!
HOTEL
HOTE
502

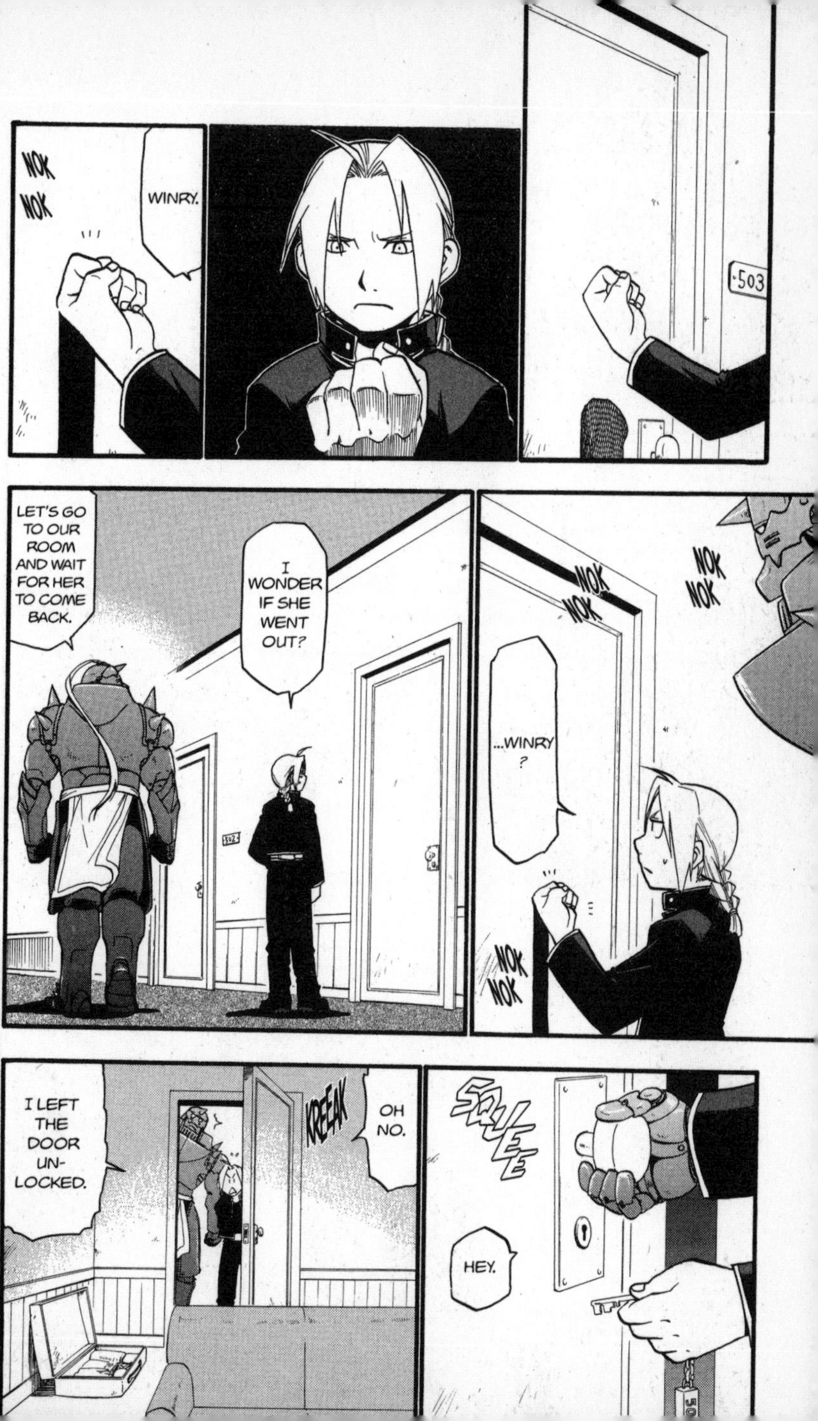
503
NOK NOK
WINRY.
NOK NOK
NOK NOK
...WINRY?
NOK NOK
I WONDER IF SHE WENT OUT?
LET'S GO TO OUR ROOM AND WAIT FOR HER TO COME BACK.
SQUEE
HEY.
OH NO.
KREEAK
I LEFT THE DOOR UNLOCKED.

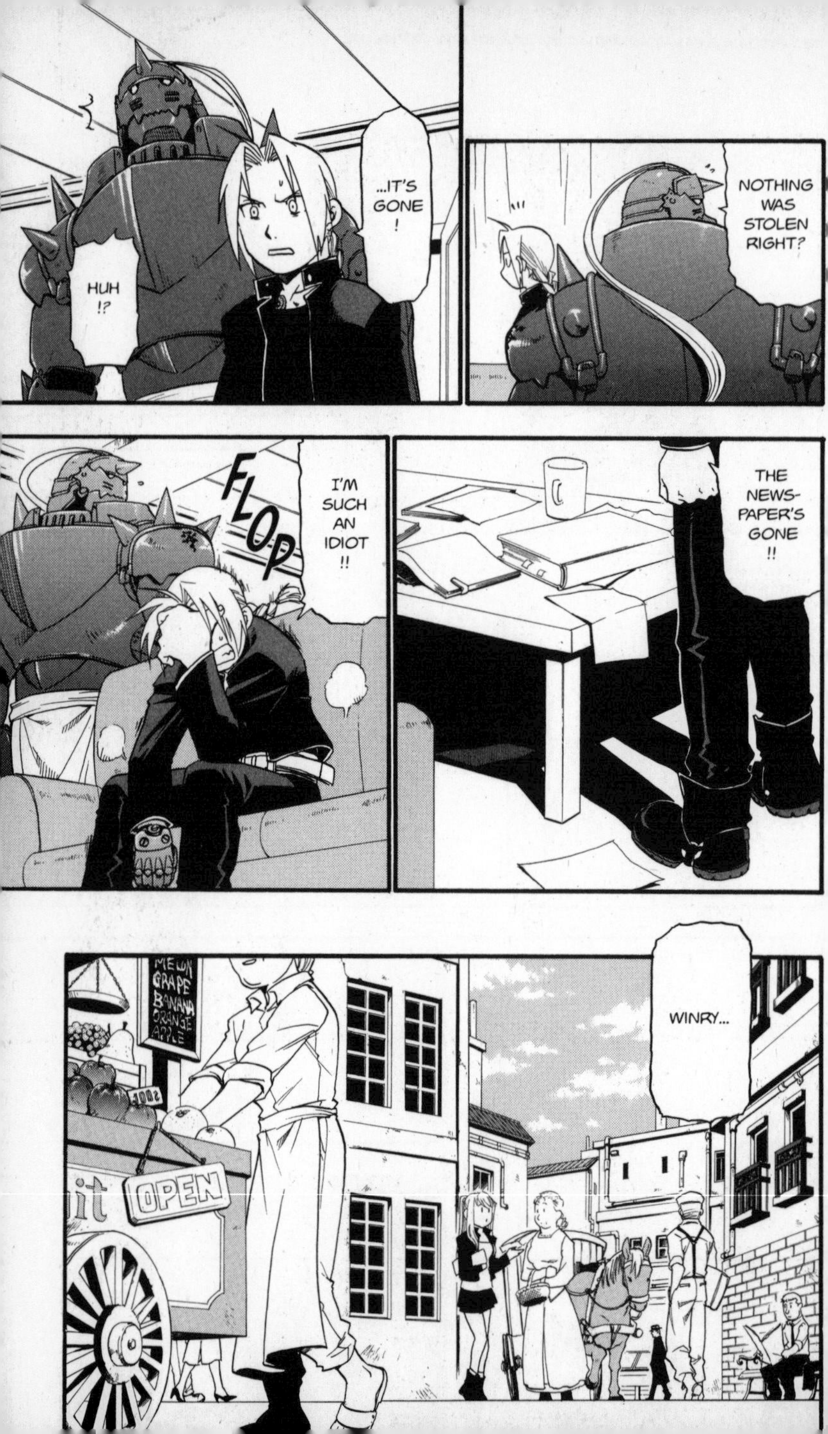
NOTHING WAS STOLEN RIGHT?
...IT'S GONE!
HUH!?
THE NEWS-PAPER'S GONE!!
FLOP
I'M SUCH AN IDIOT!!
WINRY...
MELON GRAPE BANANA ORANGE APPLE
OPEN

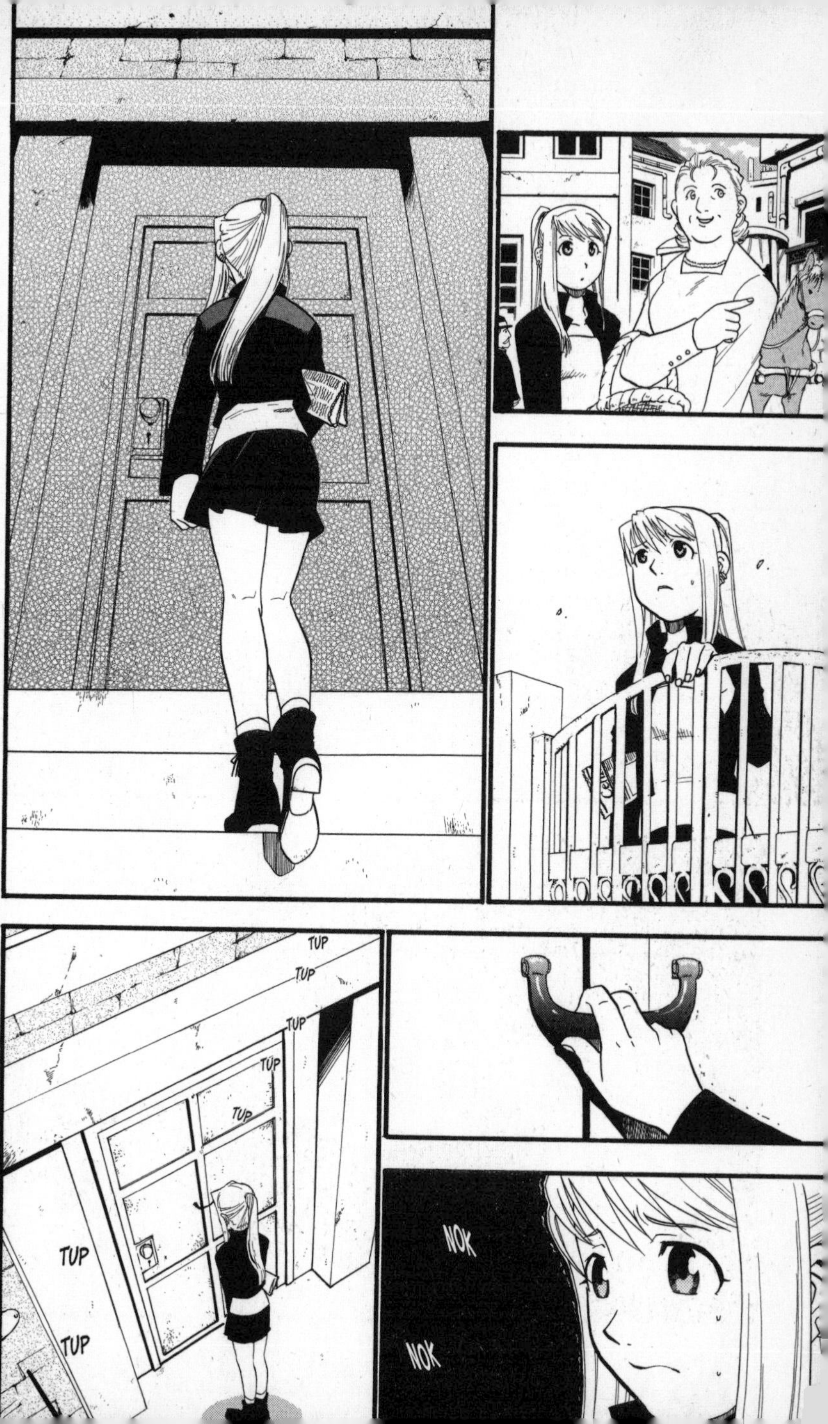
NOK
NOK
TUP
TUP
TUP
TUP
TUP
TUP
TUP

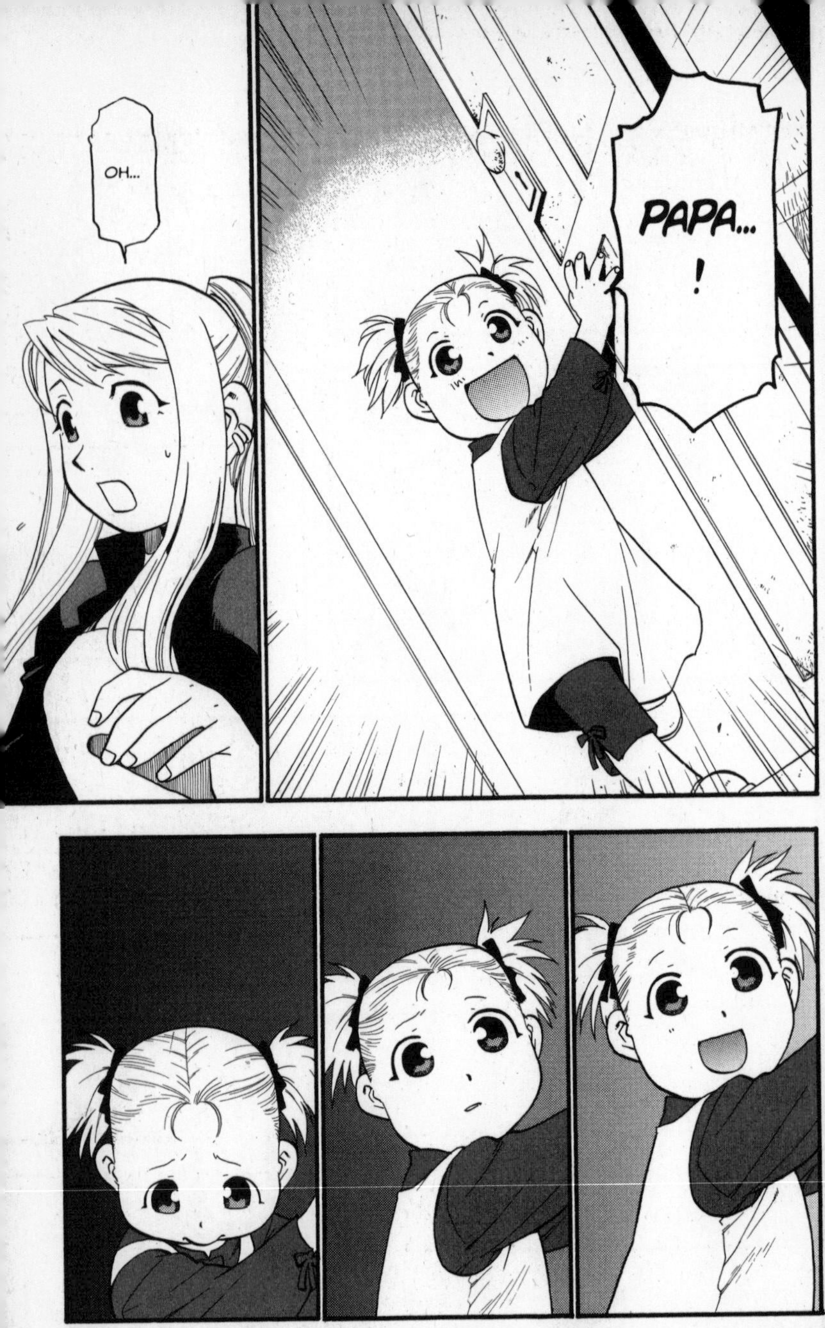
PAPA...
!
OH...

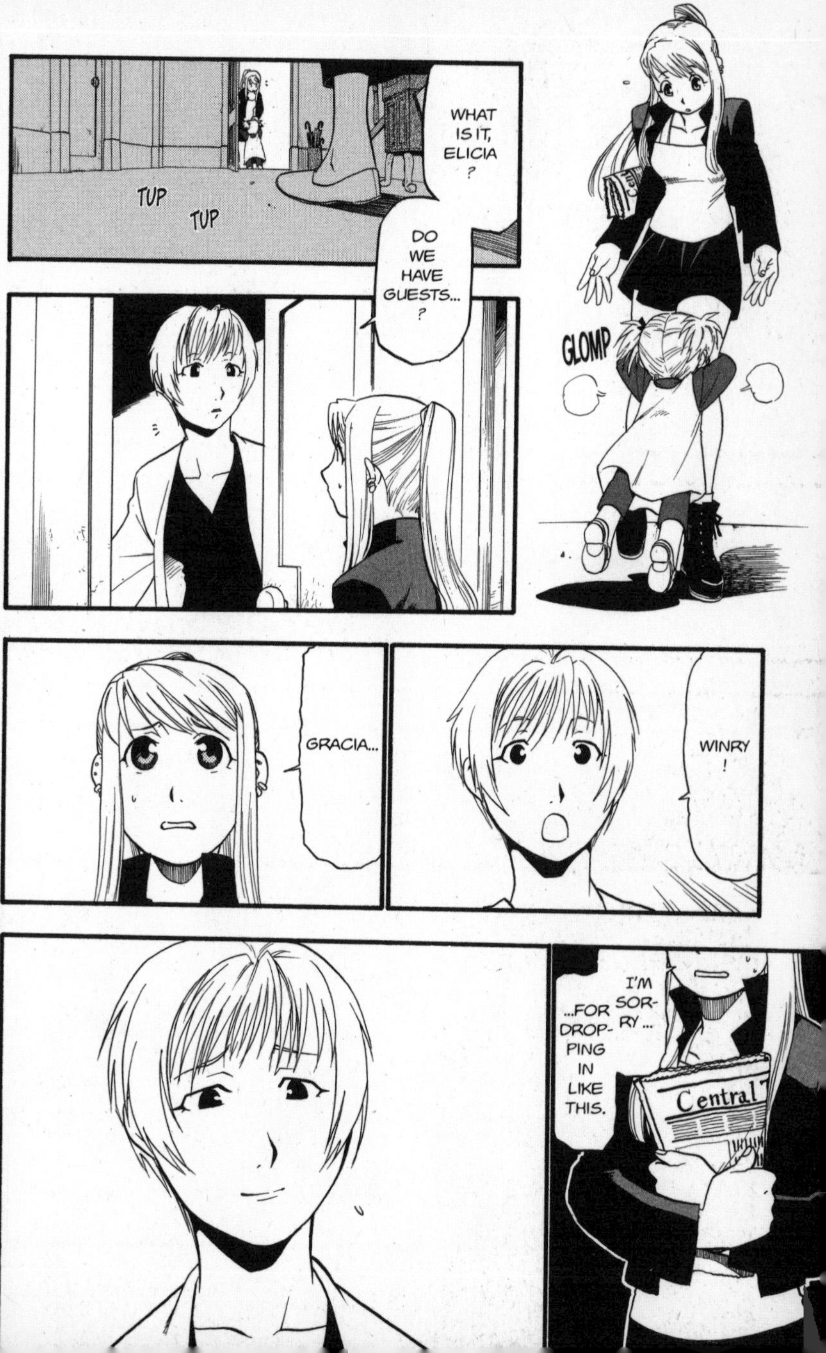
GLOMP
WHAT IS IT, ELICIA?
TUP
TUP
DO WE HAVE GUESTS...?
WINRY!
GRACIA...
I'M SORRY...
...FOR DROPPING IN LIKE THIS.
Central

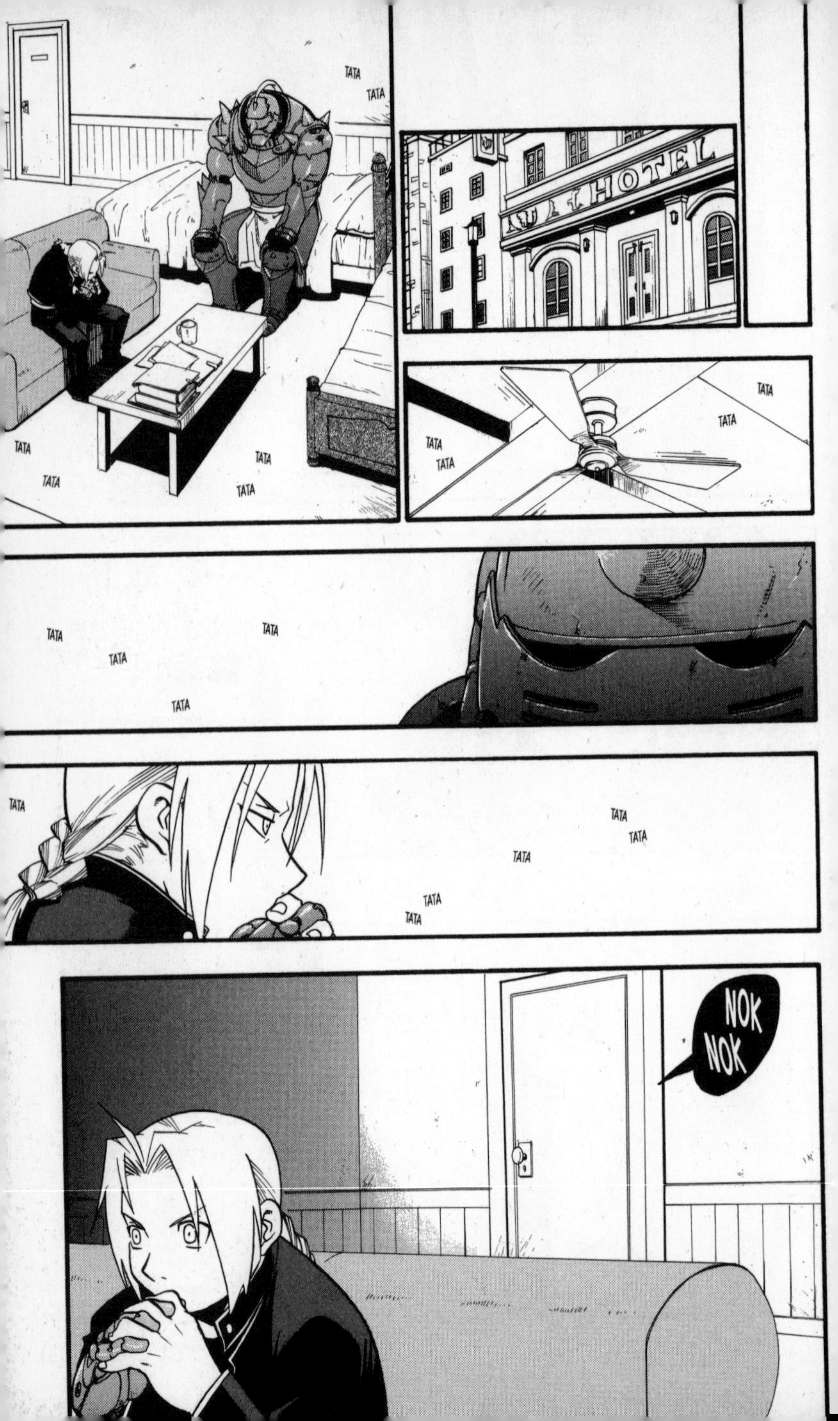

HOTEL
TATA
TATA
TATA
TATA
TATA
TATA
TATA
TATA
TATA
TATA
TATA
TATA
TATA
TATA
TATA
TATA
TATA
TATA
TATA
TATA
TATA
TATA
NOK NOK

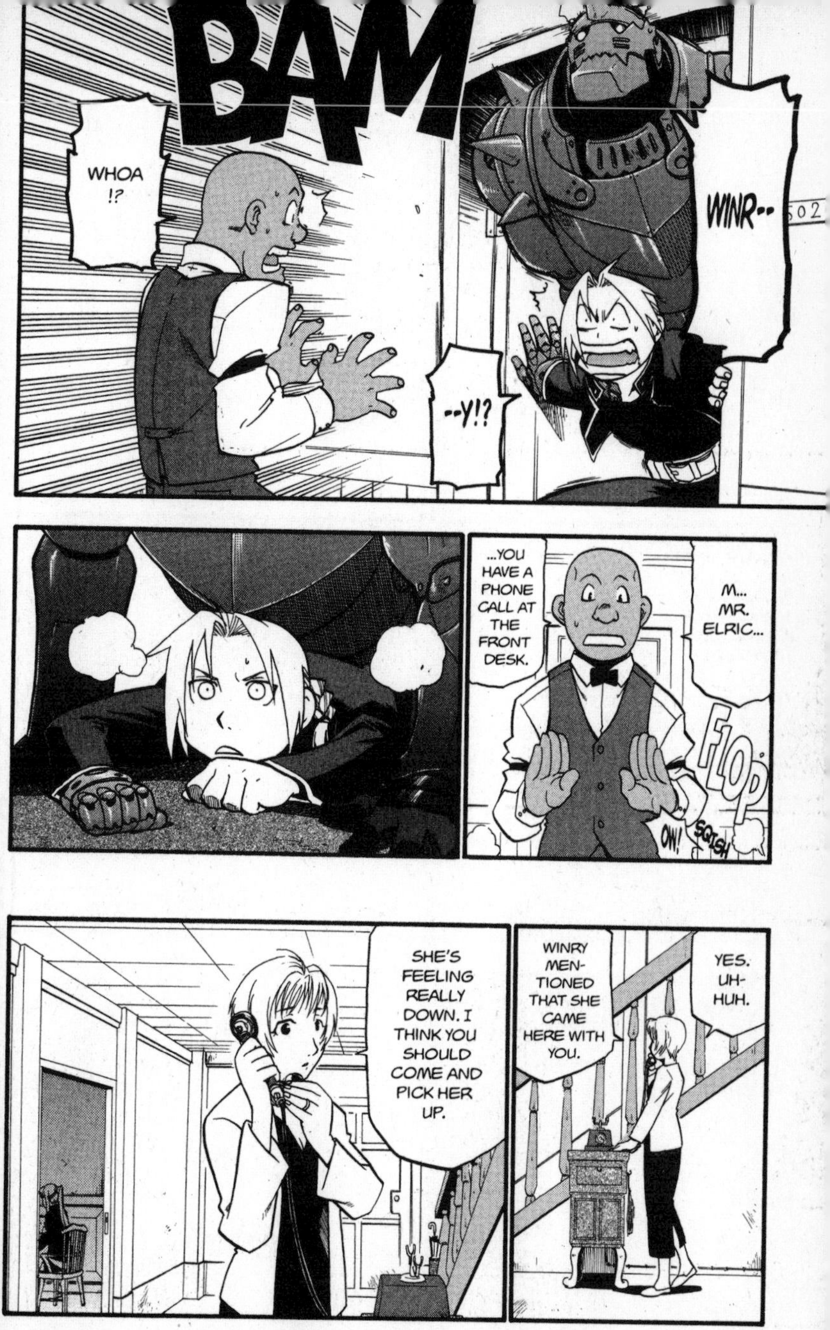
BAM
WINR--
502
--Y!?
WHOA !?
M... MR. ELRIC...
...YOU HAVE A PHONE CALL AT THE FRONT DESK.
FLOP
SQISH
OW!
YES. UH-HUH.
WINRY MEN-TIONED THAT SHE CAME HERE WITH YOU.
SHE'S FEELING REALLY DOWN. I THINK YOU SHOULD COME AND PICK HER UP.

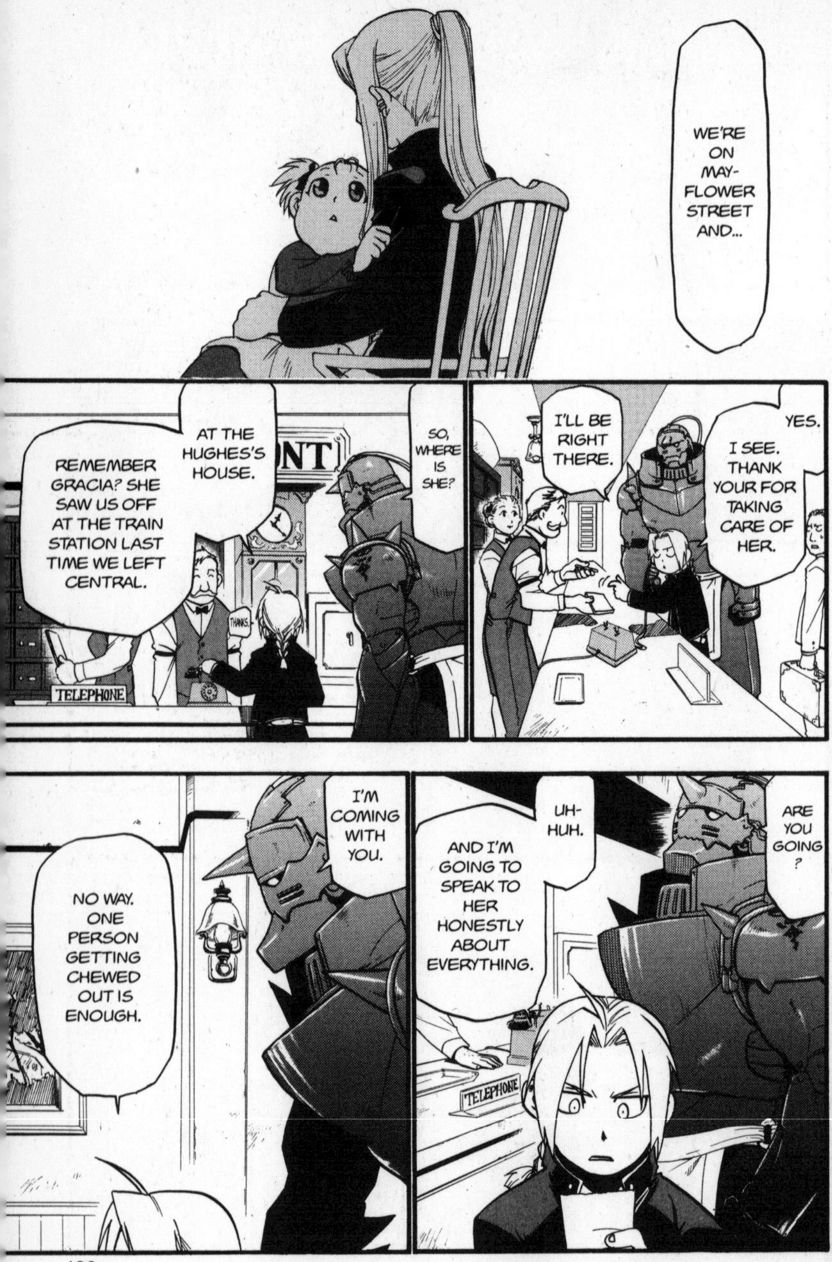
WE'RE ON MAY-FLOWER STREET AND...
YES.
I SEE. THANK YOUR FOR TAKING CARE OF HER.
I'LL BE RIGHT THERE.
SO, WHERE IS SHE?
AT THE HUGHES'S HOUSE.
REMEMBER GRACIA? SHE SAW US OFF AT THE TRAIN STATION LAST TIME WE LEFT CENTRAL.
THANKS.
TELEPHONE
ARE YOU GOING?
UH-HUH.
AND I'M GOING TO SPEAK TO HER HONESTLY ABOUT EVERYTHING.
TELEPHONE
I'M COMING WITH YOU.
NO WAY. ONE PERSON GETTING CHEWED OUT IS ENOUGH.

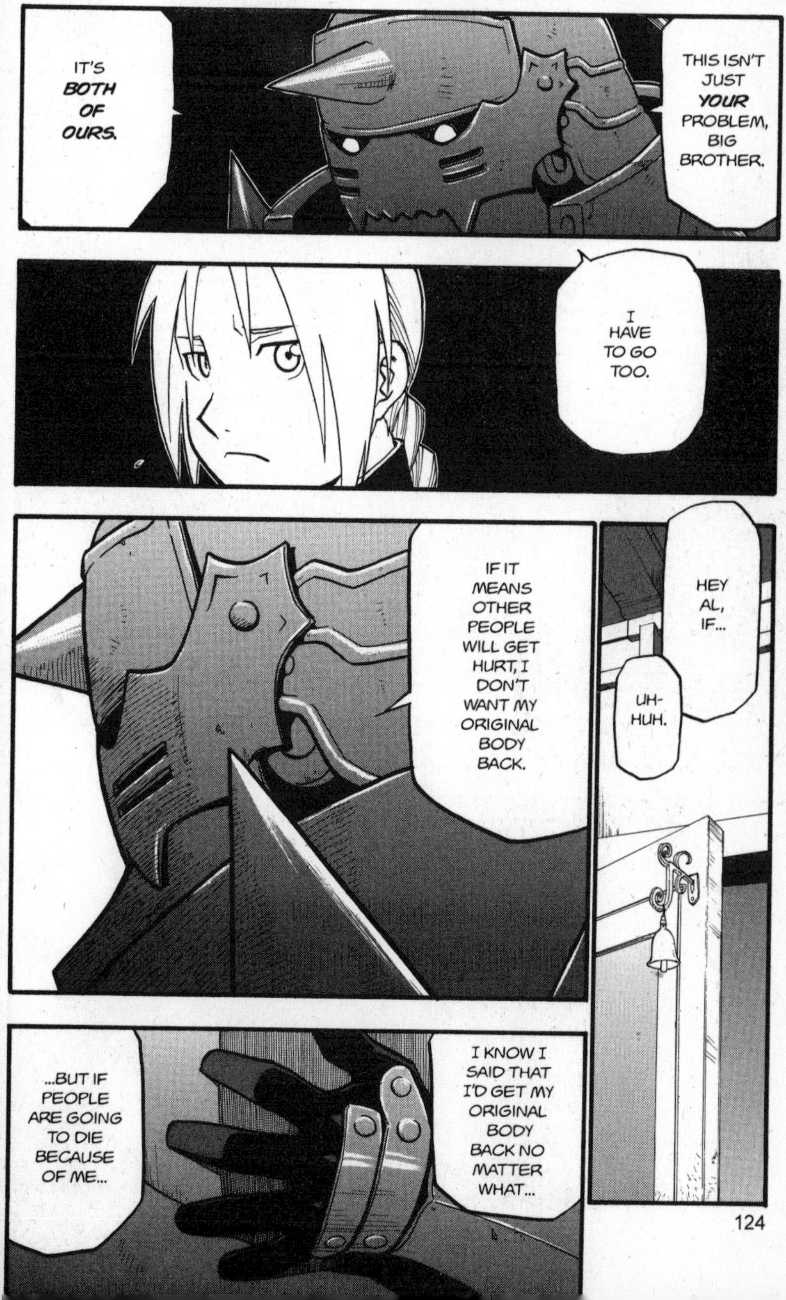
THIS ISN'T JUST *YOUR* PROBLEM, BIG BROTHER.
IT'S ***BOTH OF OURS.***
I HAVE TO GO TOO.
HEY AL, IF...
UH-HUH.
IF IT MEANS OTHER PEOPLE WILL GET HURT, I DON'T WANT MY ORIGINAL BODY BACK.
I KNOW I SAID THAT I'D GET MY ORIGINAL BODY BACK NO MATTER WHAT...
...BUT IF PEOPLE ARE GOING TO DIE BECAUSE OF ME...

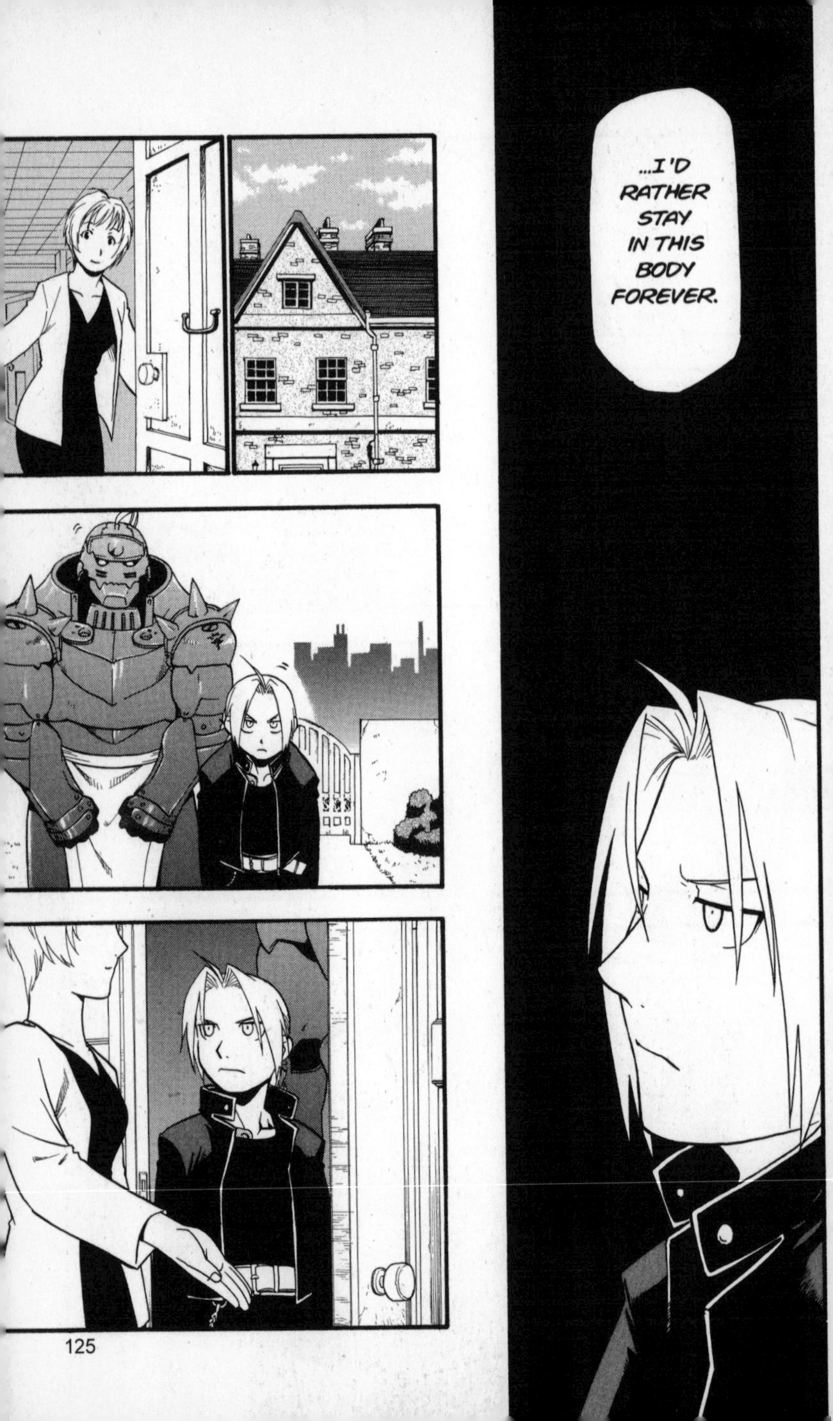
...I'D RATHER STAY IN THIS BODY FOREVER.

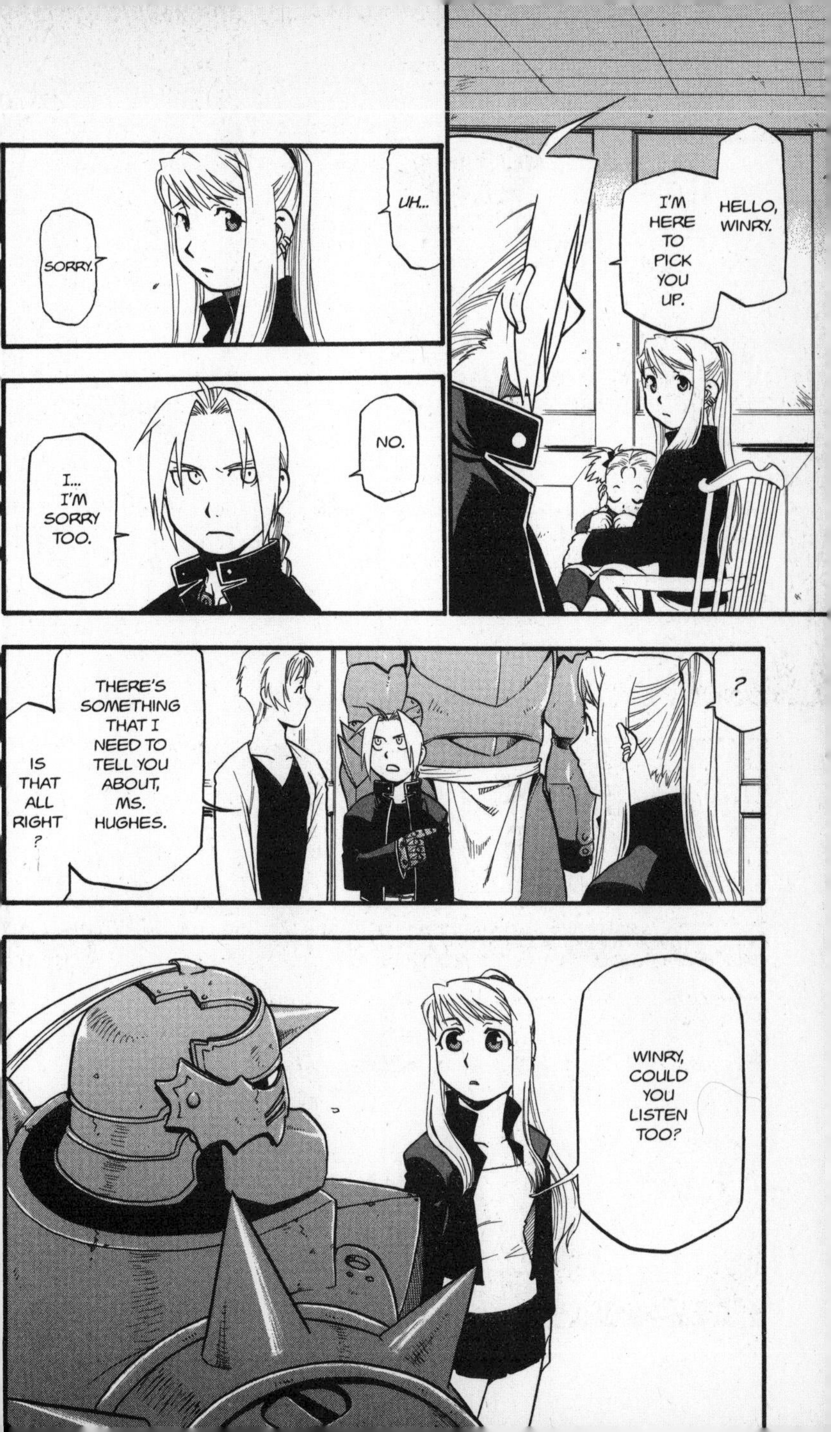
HELLO, WINRY.
I'M HERE TO PICK YOU UP.
UH...
SORRY.
NO.
I... I'M SORRY TOO.
?
THERE'S SOMETHING THAT I NEED TO TELL YOU ABOUT, MS. HUGHES.
IS THAT ALL RIGHT?
WINRY, COULD YOU LISTEN TOO?

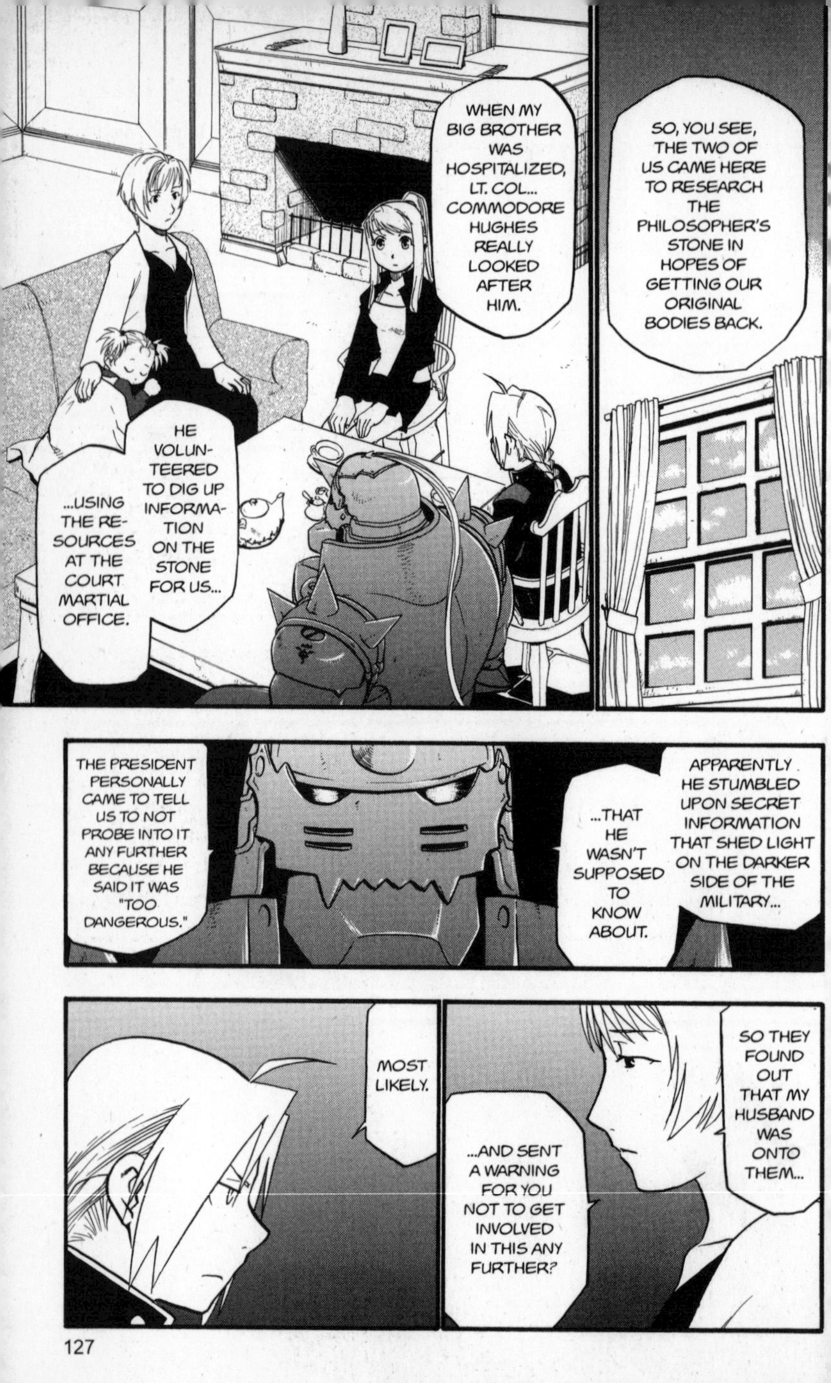
SO, YOU SEE, THE TWO OF US CAME HERE TO RESEARCH THE PHILOSOPHER'S STONE IN HOPES OF GETTING OUR ORIGINAL BODIES BACK.
WHEN MY BIG BROTHER WAS HOSPITALIZED, LT. COL... COMMODORE HUGHES REALLY LOOKED AFTER HIM.
HE VOLUN-TEERED TO DIG UP INFORMA-TION ON THE STONE FOR US...
...USING THE RE-SOURCES AT THE COURT MARTIAL OFFICE.
APPARENTLY HE STUMBLED UPON SECRET INFORMATION THAT SHED LIGHT ON THE DARKER SIDE OF THE MILITARY...
...THAT HE WASN'T SUPPOSED TO KNOW ABOUT.
THE PRESIDENT PERSONALLY CAME TO TELL US TO NOT PROBE INTO IT ANY FURTHER BECAUSE HE SAID IT WAS "TOO DANGEROUS."
SO THEY FOUND OUT THAT MY HUSBAND WAS ONTO THEM...
...AND SENT A WARNING FOR YOU NOT TO GET INVOLVED IN THIS ANY FURTHER?
MOST LIKELY.

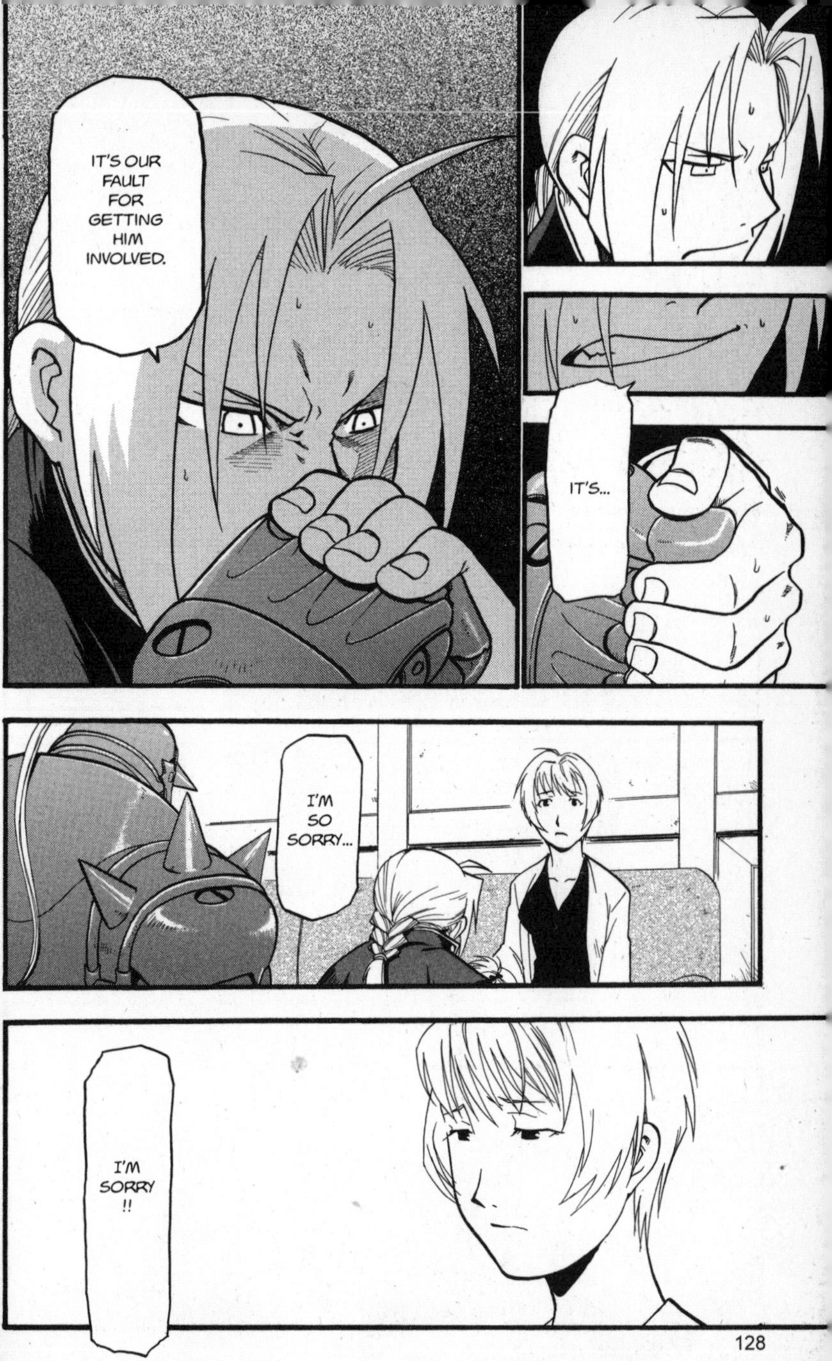
IT'S...
IT'S OUR FAULT FOR GETTING HIM INVOLVED.
I'M SO SORRY...
I'M SORRY !!

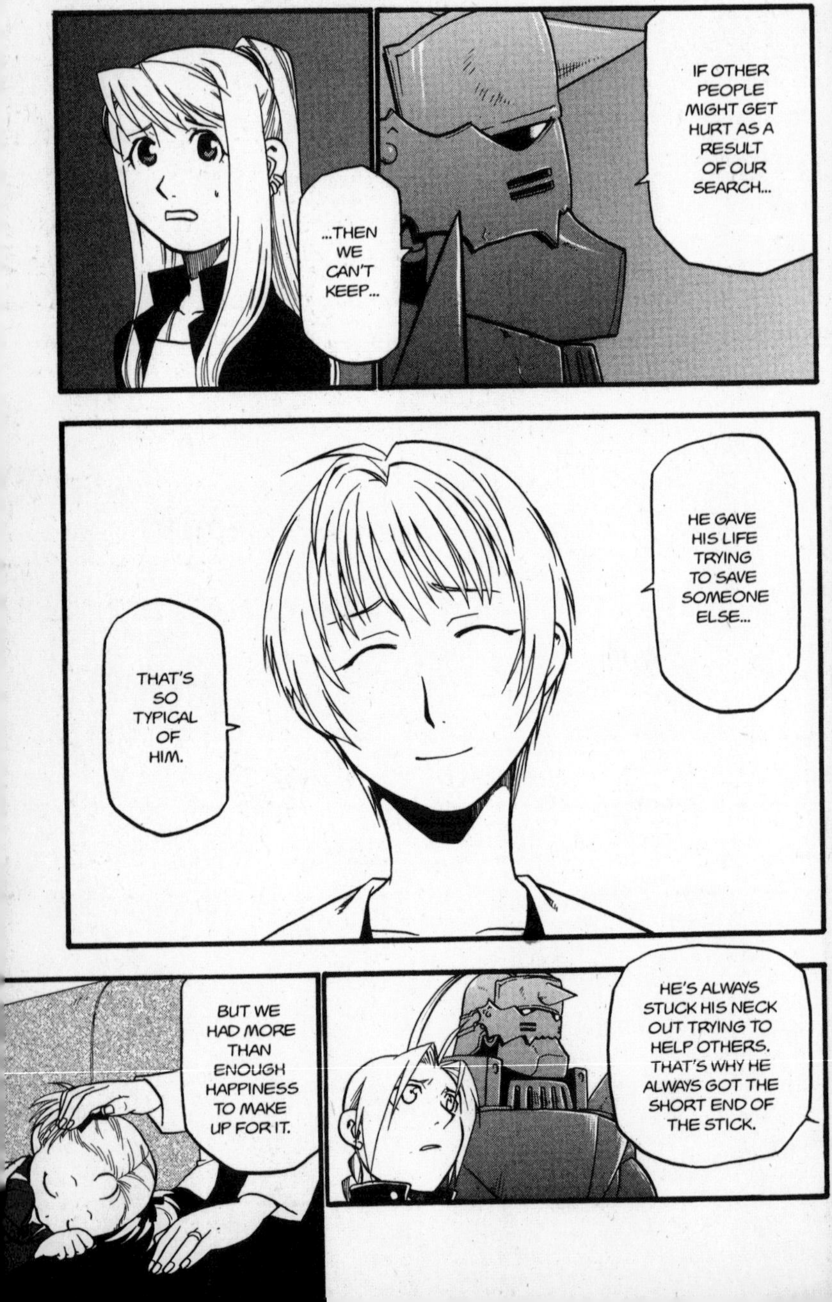
IF OTHER PEOPLE MIGHT GET HURT AS A RESULT OF OUR SEARCH...
...THEN WE CAN'T KEEP...
HE GAVE HIS LIFE TRYING TO SAVE SOMEONE ELSE...
THAT'S SO TYPICAL OF HIM.
HE'S ALWAYS STUCK HIS NECK OUT TRYING TO HELP OTHERS. THAT'S WHY HE ALWAYS GOT THE SHORT END OF THE STICK.
BUT WE HAD MORE THAN ENOUGH HAPPINESS TO MAKE UP FOR IT.

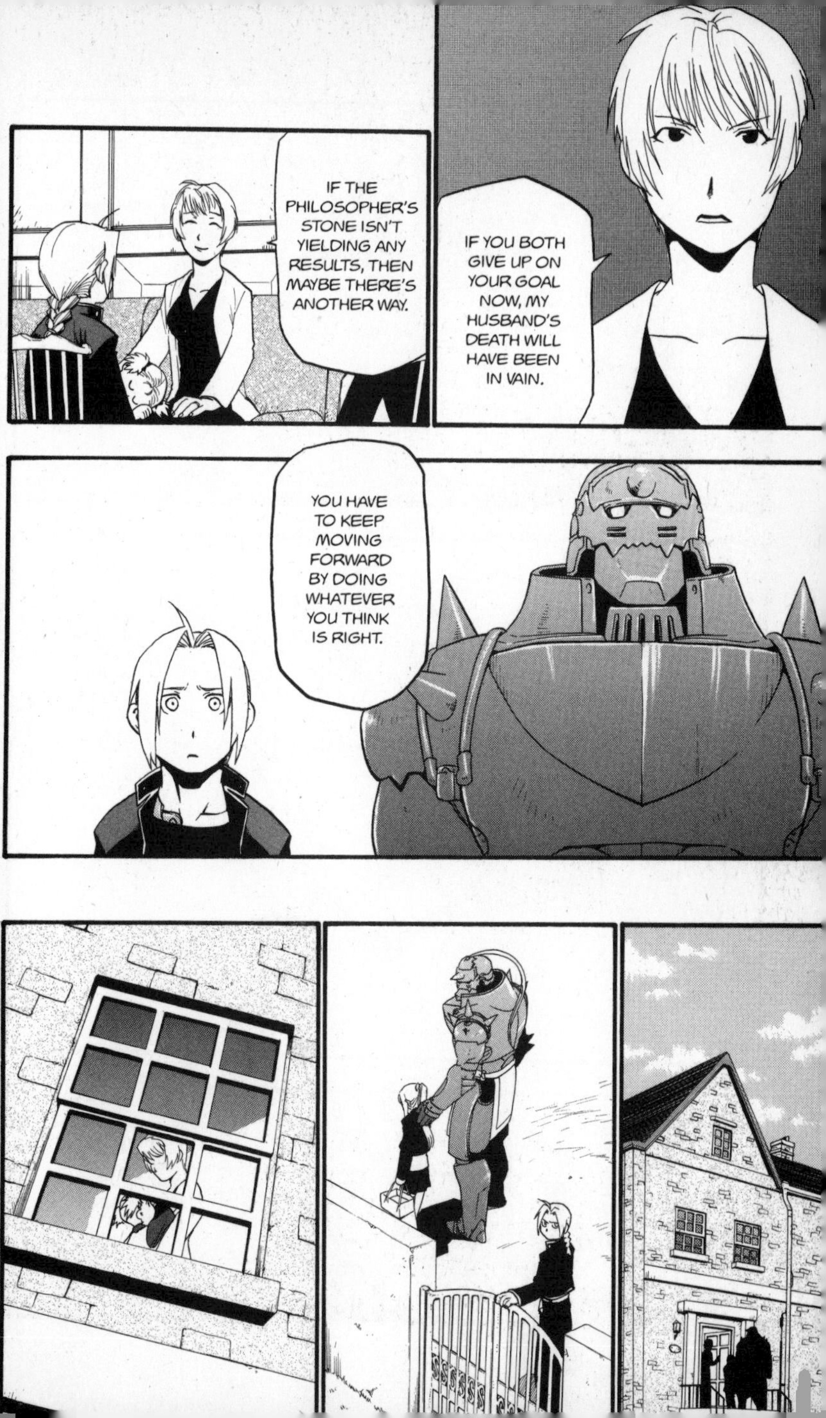
IF YOU BOTH GIVE UP ON YOUR GOAL NOW, MY HUSBAND'S DEATH WILL HAVE BEEN IN VAIN.
IF THE PHILOSOPHER'S STONE ISN'T YIELDING ANY RESULTS, THEN MAYBE THERE'S ANOTHER WAY.
YOU HAVE TO KEEP MOVING FORWARD BY DOING WHATEVER YOU THINK IS RIGHT.

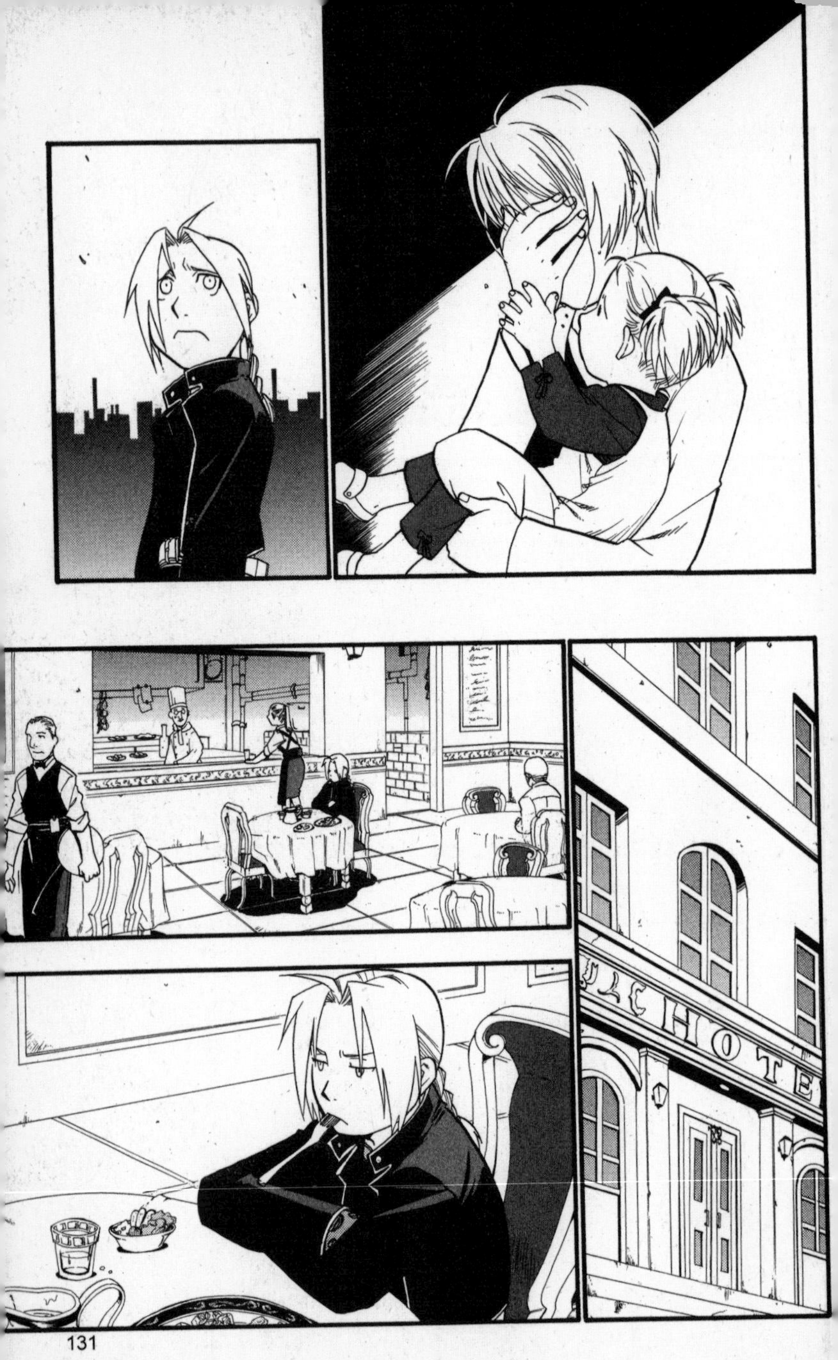

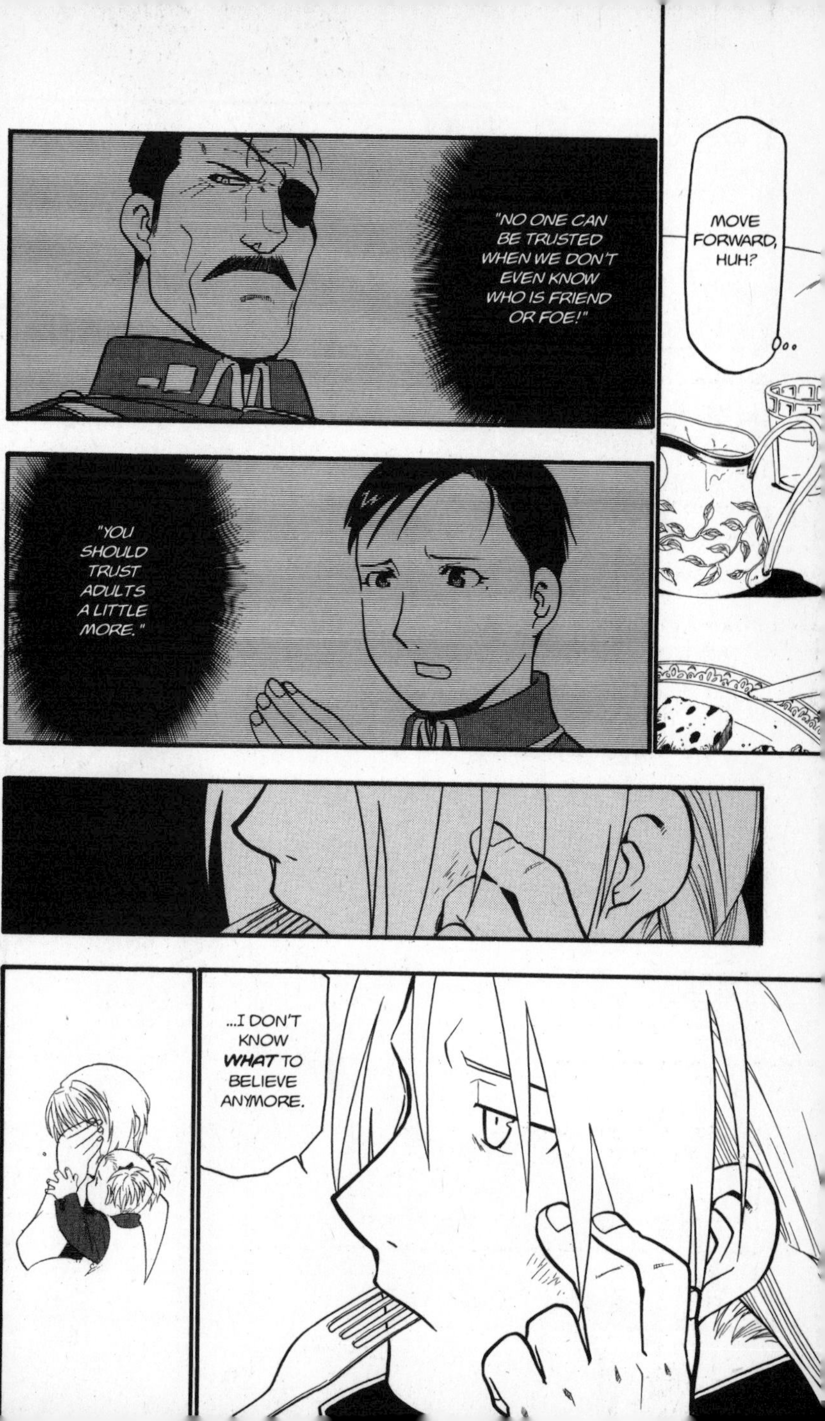
MOVE FORWARD, HUH?
"NO ONE CAN BE TRUSTED WHEN WE DON'T EVEN KNOW WHO IS FRIEND OR FOE!"
"YOU SHOULD TRUST ADULTS A LITTLE MORE."
...I DON'T KNOW **WHAT** TO BELIEVE ANYMORE.

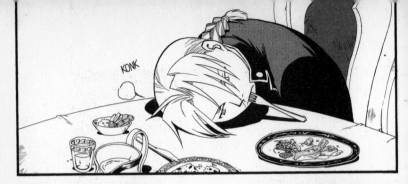

KONK
AW, GEEZ...
CLACK
SIR? ARE YOU FEEL-ING SICK, SIR?
SIR?
IT WOULD'VE BEEN EASIER...
...IF SHE HAD JUST CHEWED ME OUT.
NOK NOK
NOK NOK
503
NOK

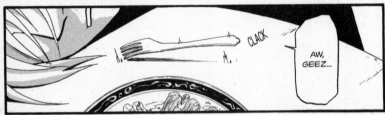

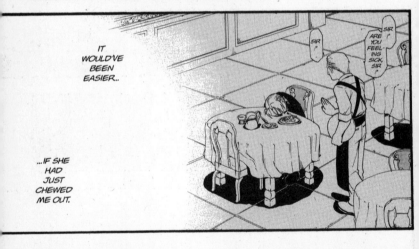

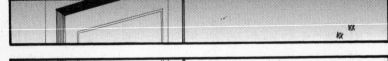

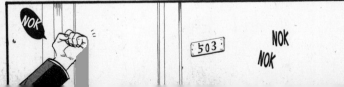

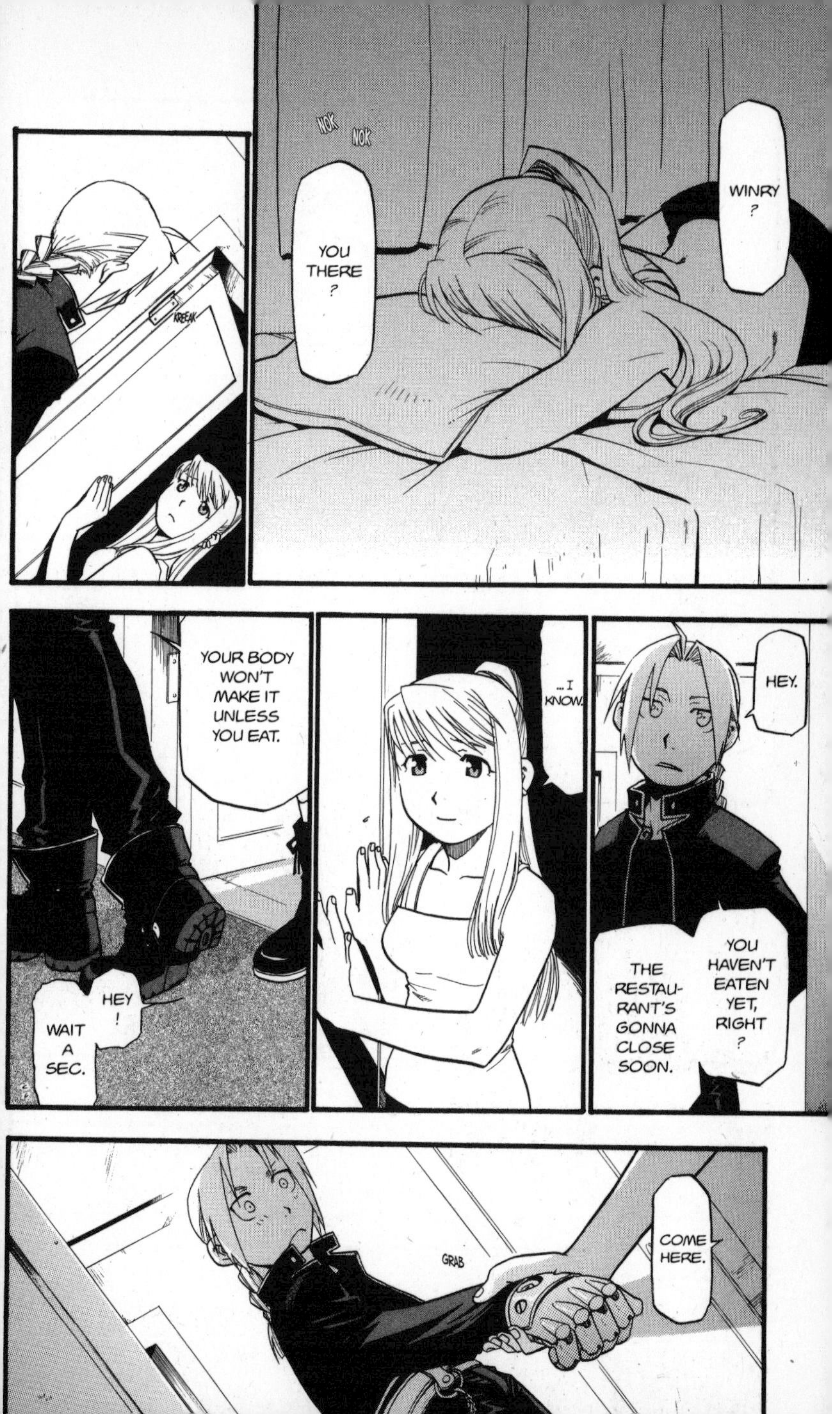
NOK NOK
WINRY ?
YOU THERE ?
KREEAK
HEY.
YOU HAVEN'T EATEN YET, RIGHT ?
THE RESTAU-RANT'S GONNA CLOSE SOON.
...I KNOW.
YOUR BODY WON'T MAKE IT UNLESS YOU EAT.
HEY !
WAIT A SEC.
COME HERE.
GRAB

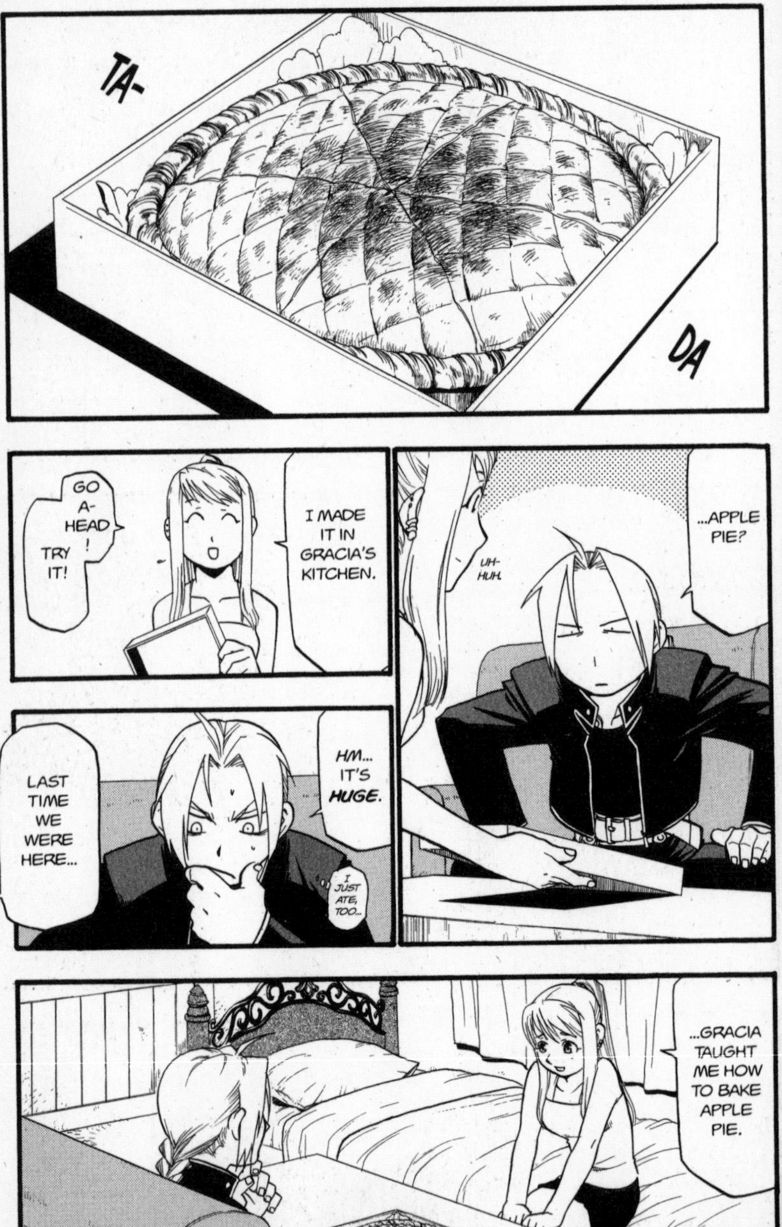
TA-
DA
...APPLE PIE?
UH-HUH.
I MADE IT IN GRACIA'S KITCHEN.
GO A-HEAD! TRY IT!
HM... IT'S **HUGE**.
I JUST ATE, TOO...
LAST TIME WE WERE HERE...
...GRACIA TAUGHT ME HOW TO BAKE APPLE PIE.

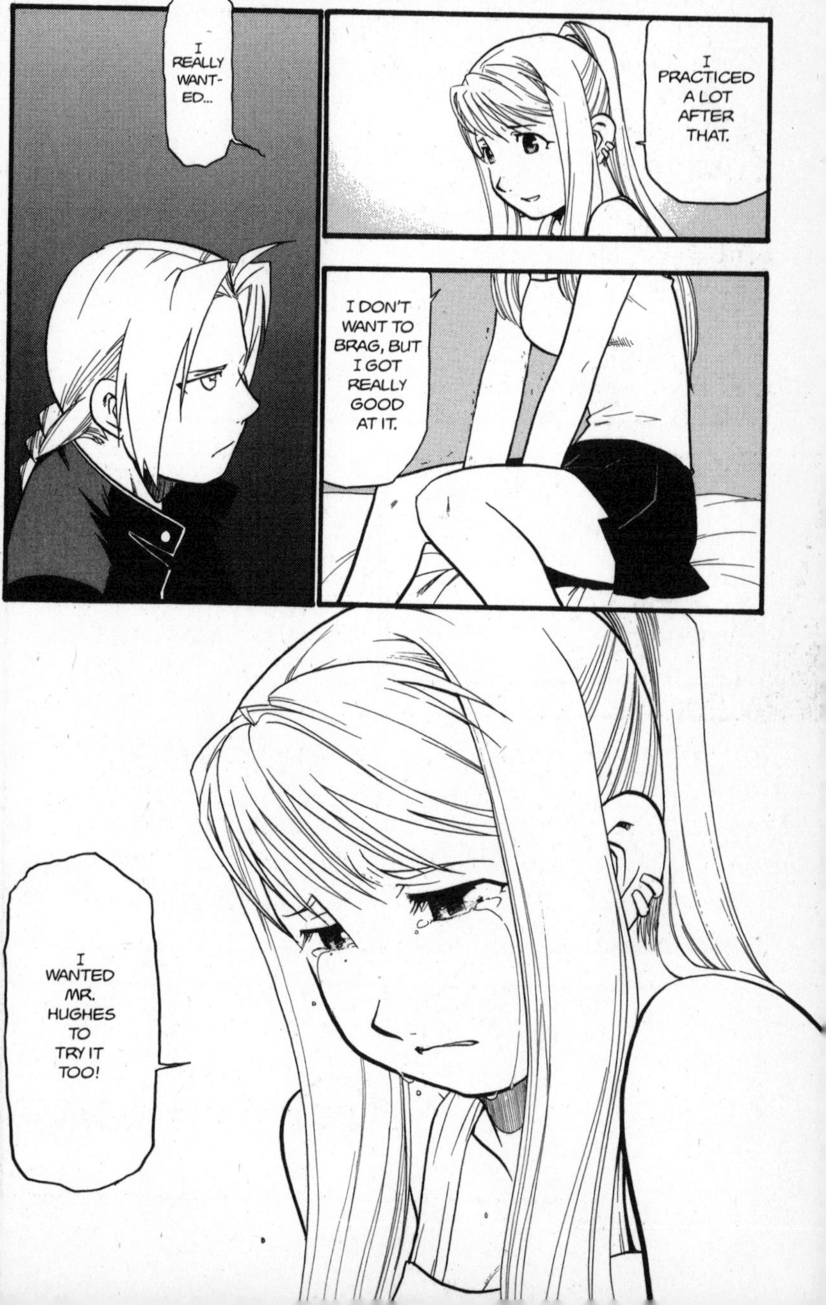
I PRACTICED A LOT AFTER THAT.
I DON'T WANT TO BRAG, BUT I GOT REALLY GOOD AT IT.
I REALLY WANT-ED...
I WANTED MR. HUGHES TO TRY IT TOO!

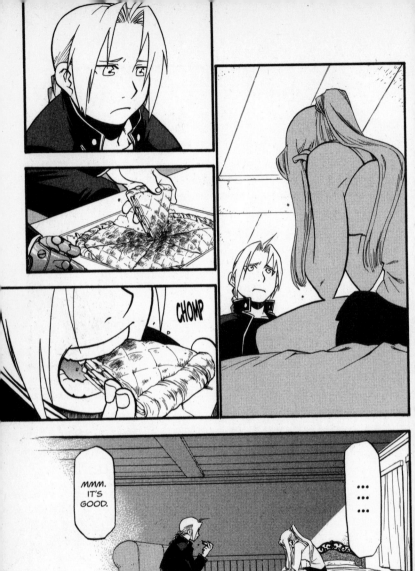

CHOMP

MMM.
IT'S
GOOD.

· · ·
· · ·
· · ·

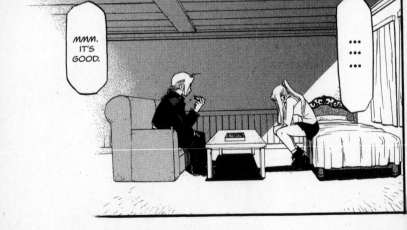

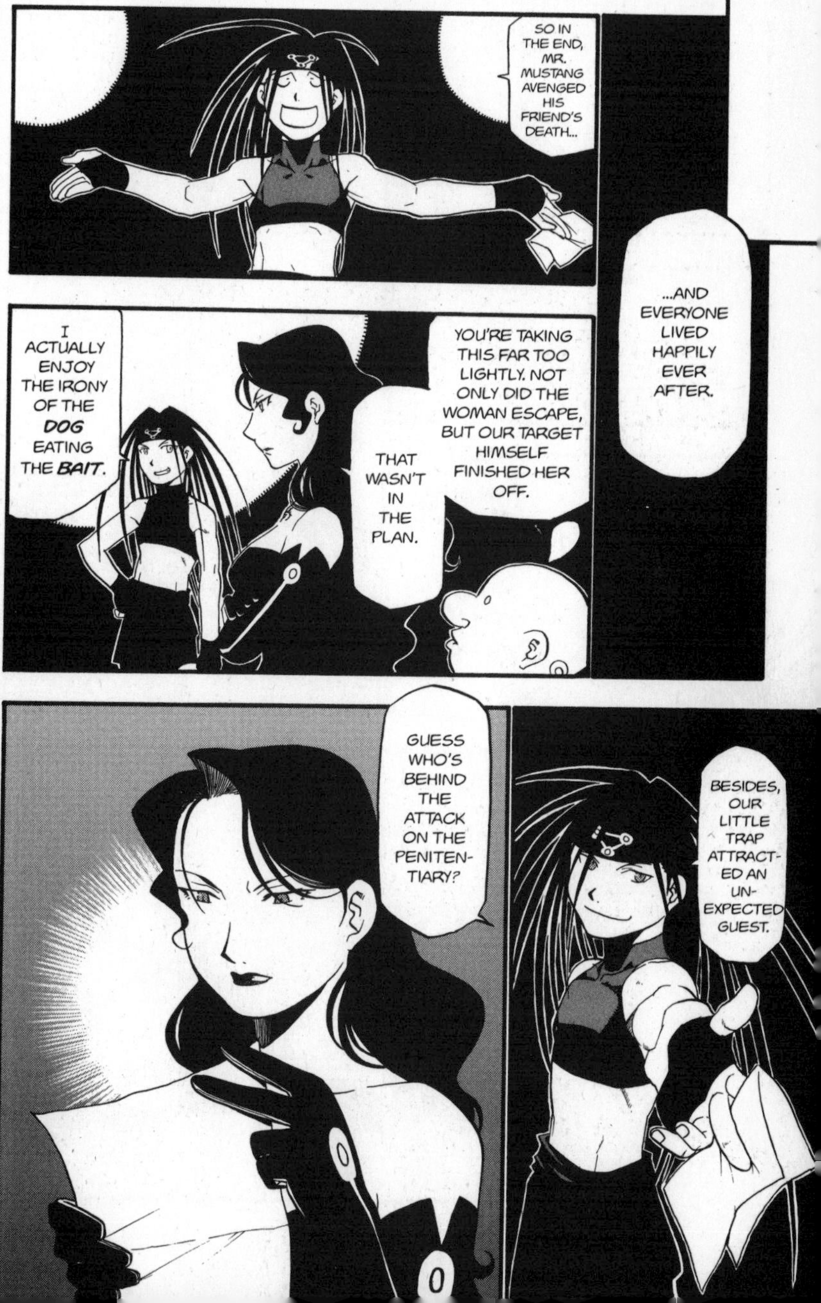
SO IN THE END, MR. MUSTANG AVENGED HIS FRIEND'S DEATH...
...AND EVERYONE LIVED HAPPILY EVER AFTER.
YOU'RE TAKING THIS FAR TOO LIGHTLY. NOT ONLY DID THE WOMAN ESCAPE, BUT OUR TARGET HIMSELF FINISHED HER OFF.
THAT WASN'T IN THE PLAN.
I ACTUALLY ENJOY THE IRONY OF THE *DOG* EATING THE *BAIT*.
BESIDES, OUR LITTLE TRAP ATTRACT-ED AN UN-EXPECTED GUEST.
GUESS WHO'S BEHIND THE ATTACK ON THE PENITEN-TIARY?

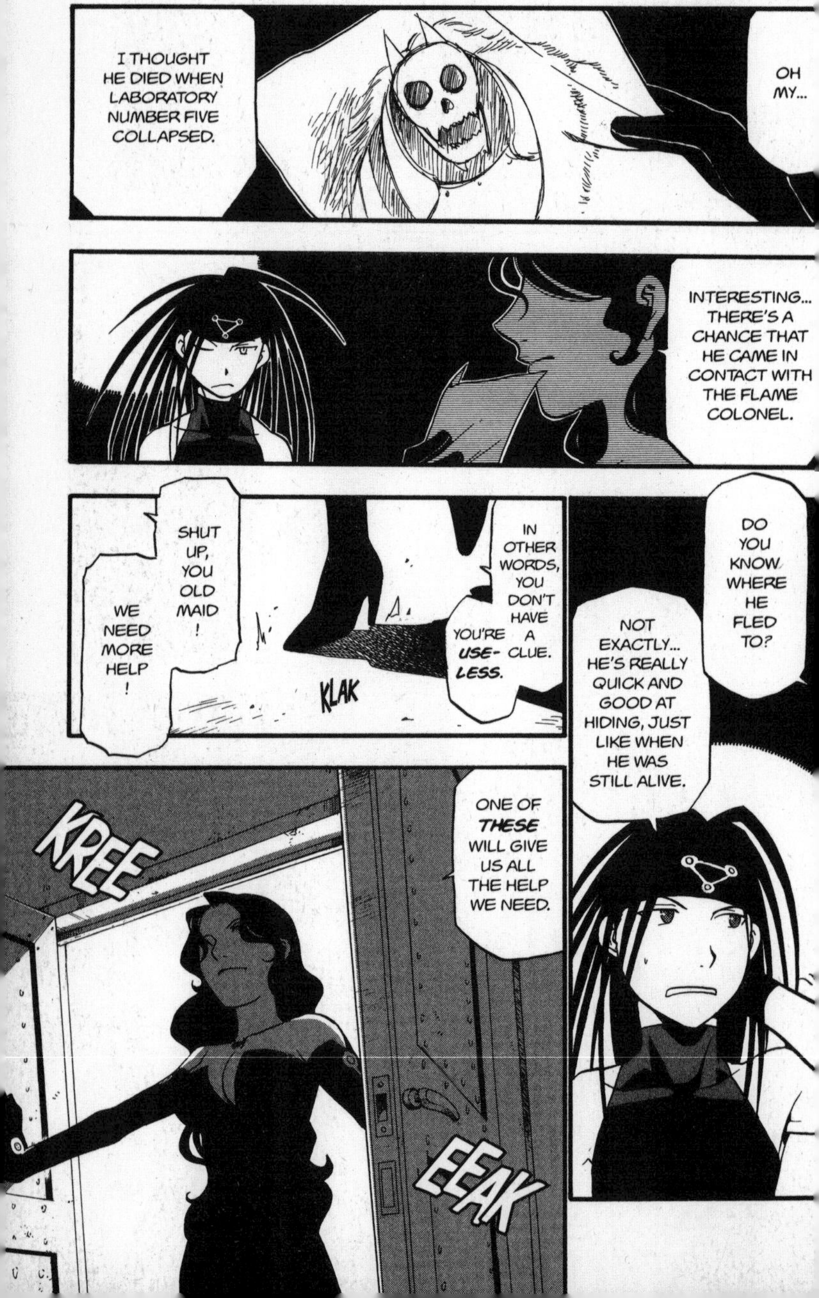
OH MY...
I THOUGHT HE DIED WHEN LABORATORY NUMBER FIVE COLLAPSED.
INTERESTING... THERE'S A CHANCE THAT HE CAME IN CONTACT WITH THE FLAME COLONEL.
DO YOU KNOW WHERE HE FLED TO?
NOT EXACTLY... HE'S REALLY QUICK AND GOOD AT HIDING, JUST LIKE WHEN HE WAS STILL ALIVE.
IN OTHER WORDS, YOU DON'T HAVE A CLUE.
YOU'RE *USELESS.*
KLAK
SHUT UP, YOU OLD MAID!
WE NEED MORE HELP!
ONE OF *THESE* WILL GIVE US ALL THE HELP WE NEED.
KREE
EEAK

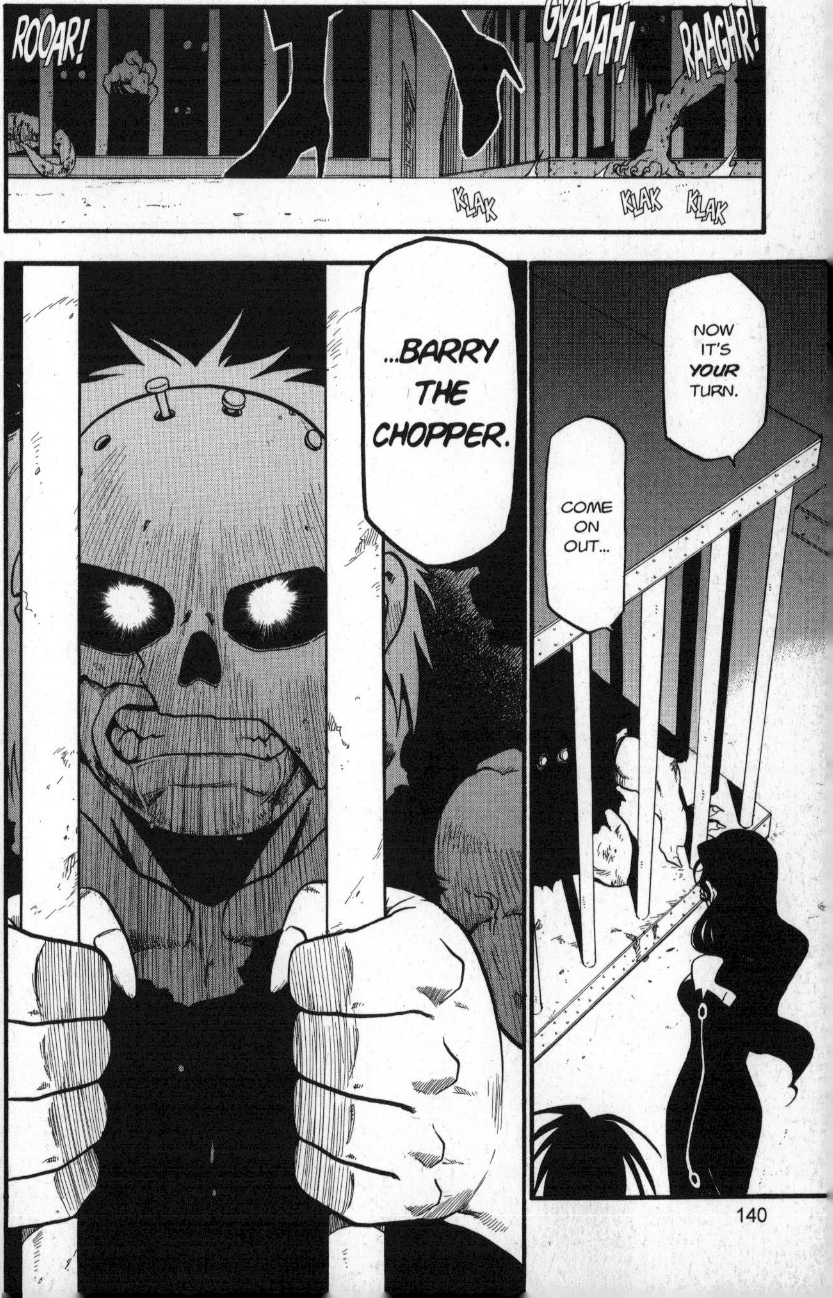
RAAGHR!
GYAAAH!
ROOAR!
KLAK
KLAK
KLAK
NOW IT'S YOUR TURN.
COME ON OUT...
...BARRY THE CHOPPER.

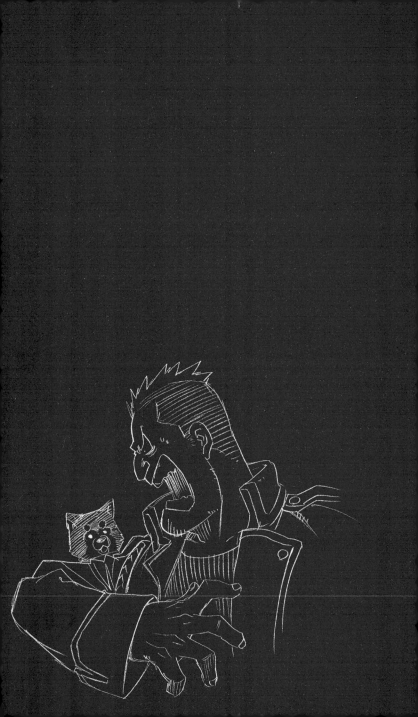

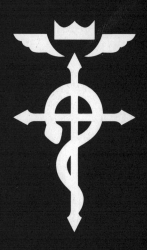

FULLMETAL
ALCHEMIST

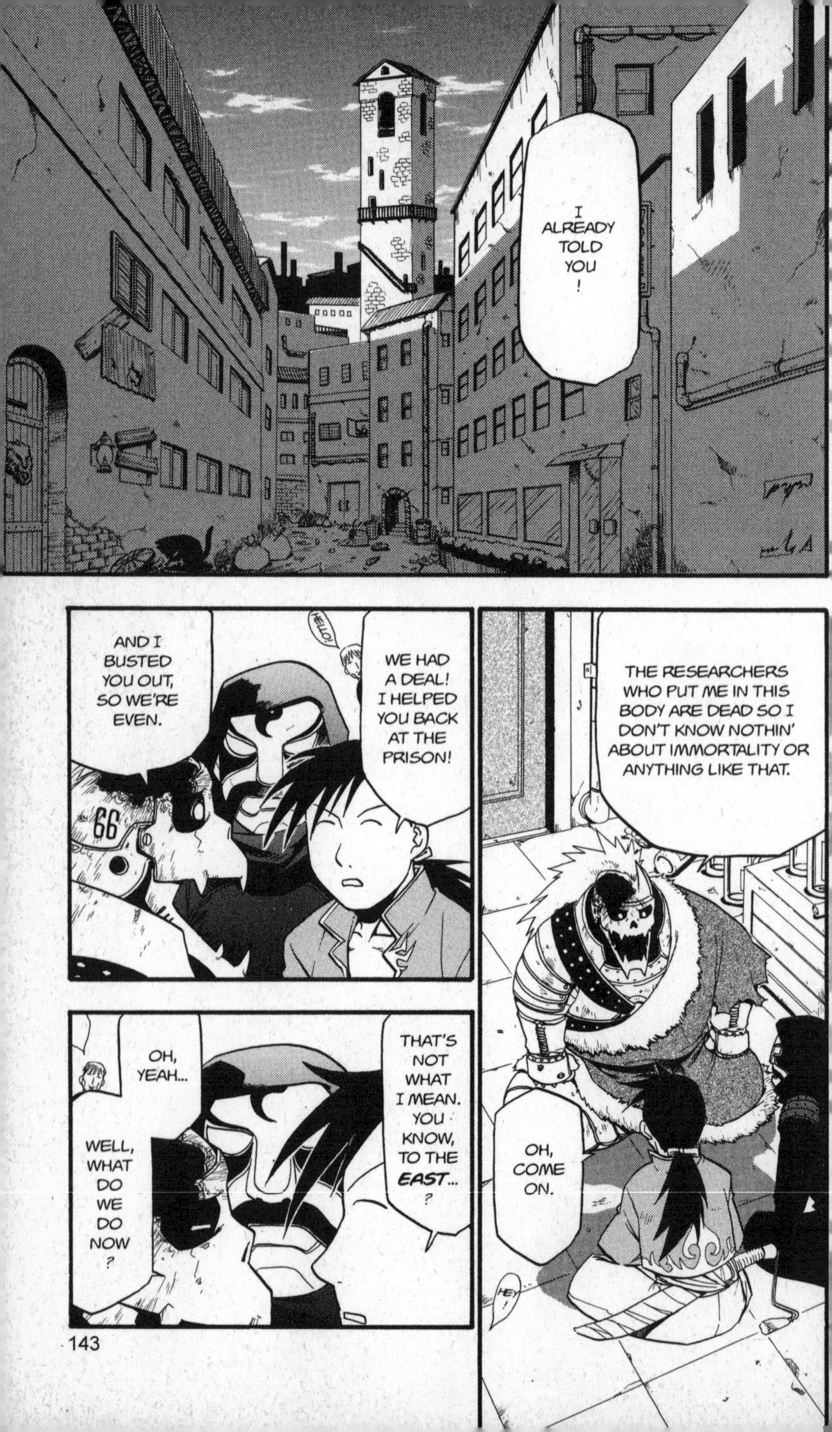
I ALREADY TOLD YOU!
THE RESEARCHERS WHO PUT ME IN THIS BODY ARE DEAD SO I DON'T KNOW NOTHIN' ABOUT IMMORTALITY OR ANYTHING LIKE THAT.
OH, COME ON.
HEY!
WE HAD A DEAL! I HELPED YOU BACK AT THE PRISON!
HELLO!
AND I BUSTED YOU OUT, SO WE'RE EVEN.
THAT'S NOT WHAT I MEAN. YOU KNOW, TO THE *EAST*...?
OH, YEAH...
WELL, WHAT DO WE DO NOW?

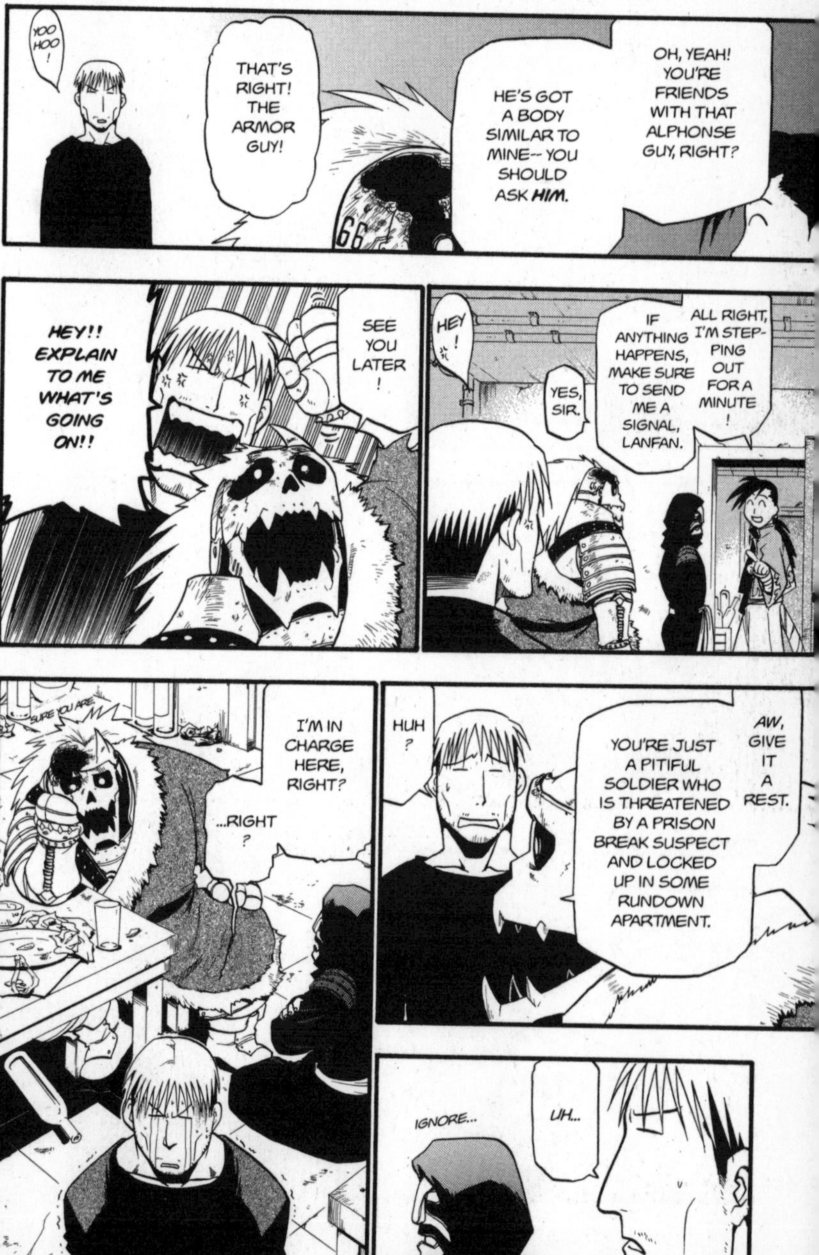
OH, YEAH! YOU'RE FRIENDS WITH THAT ALPHONSE GUY, RIGHT?
HE'S GOT A BODY SIMILAR TO MINE-- YOU SHOULD ASK **HIM**.
THAT'S RIGHT! THE ARMOR GUY!
YOO HOO!
ALL RIGHT, I'M STEPPING OUT FOR A MINUTE!
IF ANYTHING HAPPENS, MAKE SURE TO SEND ME A SIGNAL, LANFAN.
YES, SIR.
HEY!
SEE YOU LATER!
HEY!! EXPLAIN TO ME WHAT'S GOING ON!!
AW, GIVE IT A REST.
YOU'RE JUST A PITIFUL SOLDIER WHO IS THREATENED BY A PRISON BREAK SUSPECT AND LOCKED UP IN SOME RUNDOWN APARTMENT.
HUH?
UH...
IGNORE...
I'M IN CHARGE HERE, RIGHT?
...RIGHT?
SURE YOU ARE.

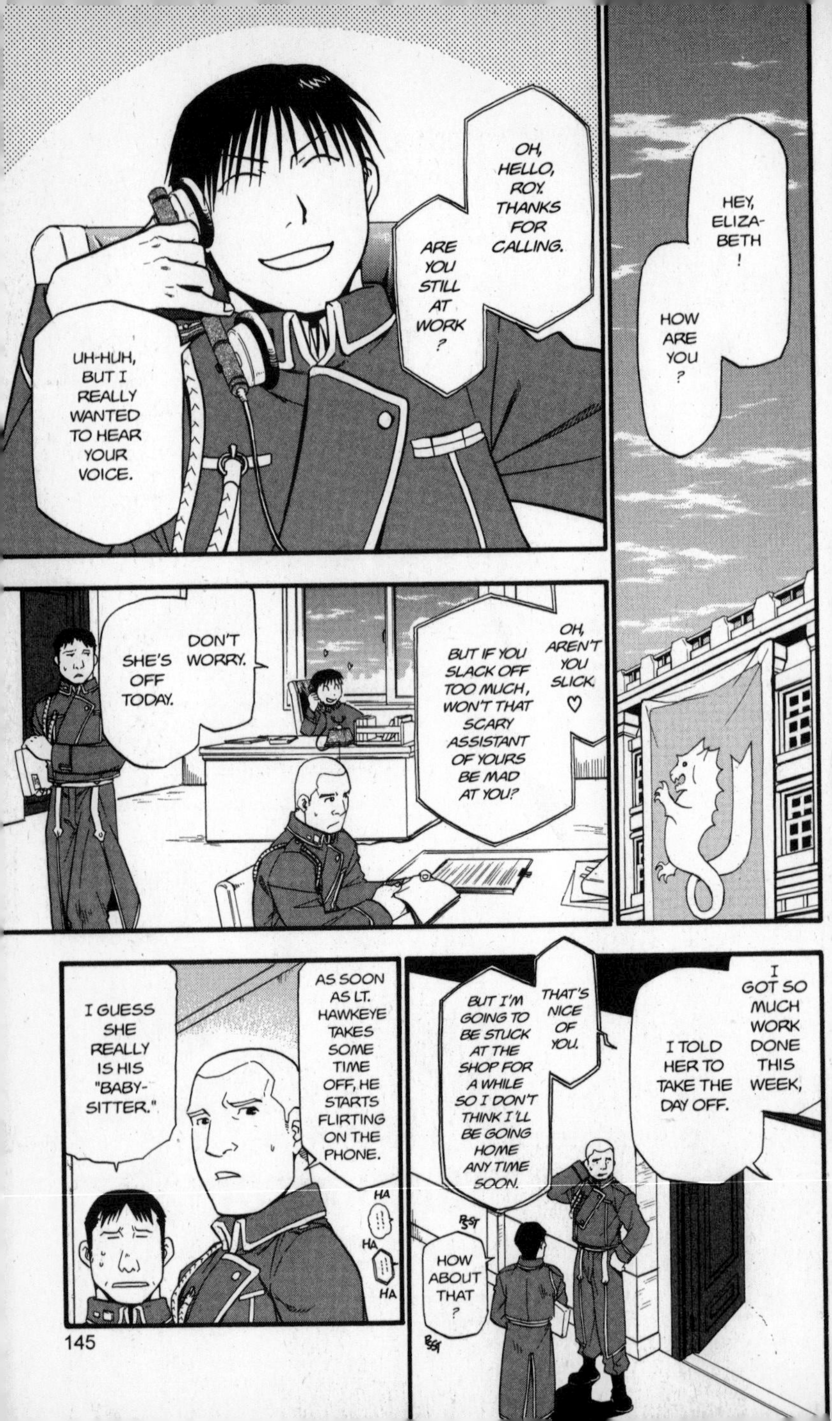
HEY, ELIZABETH!
HOW ARE YOU?
OH, HELLO, ROY. THANKS FOR CALLING.
ARE YOU STILL AT WORK?
UH-HUH, BUT I REALLY WANTED TO HEAR YOUR VOICE.
OH, AREN'T YOU SLICK. ♡
BUT IF YOU SLACK OFF TOO MUCH, WON'T THAT SCARY ASSISTANT OF YOURS BE MAD AT YOU?
DON'T WORRY.
SHE'S OFF TODAY.
I GOT SO MUCH WORK DONE THIS WEEK,
I TOLD HER TO TAKE THE DAY OFF.
THAT'S NICE OF YOU.
BUT I'M GOING TO BE STUCK AT THE SHOP FOR A WHILE SO I DON'T THINK I'LL BE GOING HOME ANY TIME SOON.
PSST
HOW ABOUT THAT?
PSST
AS SOON AS LT. HAWKEYE TAKES SOME TIME OFF, HE STARTS FLIRTING ON THE PHONE.
HA
HA
HA
I GUESS SHE REALLY IS HIS "BABY-SITTER."

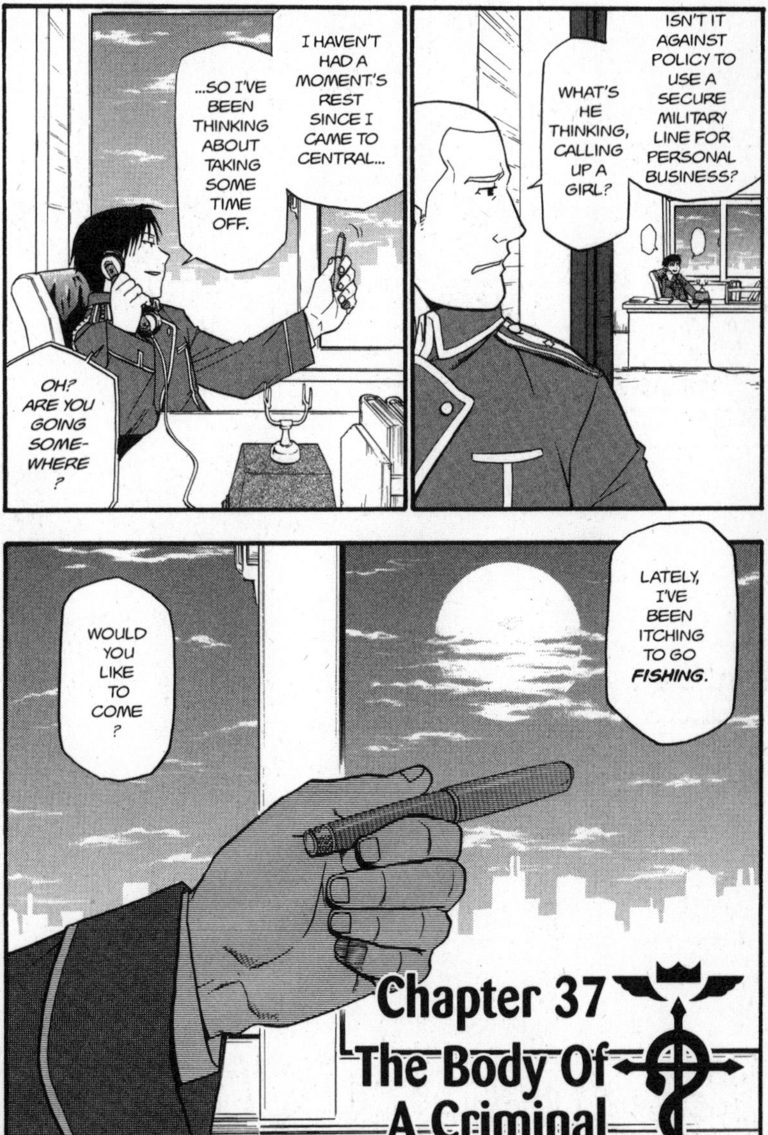
ISN'T IT AGAINST POLICY TO USE A SECURE MILITARY LINE FOR PERSONAL BUSINESS?
WHAT'S HE THINKING, CALLING UP A GIRL?
I HAVEN'T HAD A MOMENT'S REST SINCE I CAME TO CENTRAL...
...SO I'VE BEEN THINKING ABOUT TAKING SOME TIME OFF.
OH? ARE YOU GOING SOMEWHERE?
LATELY, I'VE BEEN ITCHING TO GO *FISHING*.
WOULD YOU LIKE TO COME?

Chapter 37
The Body Of A Criminal

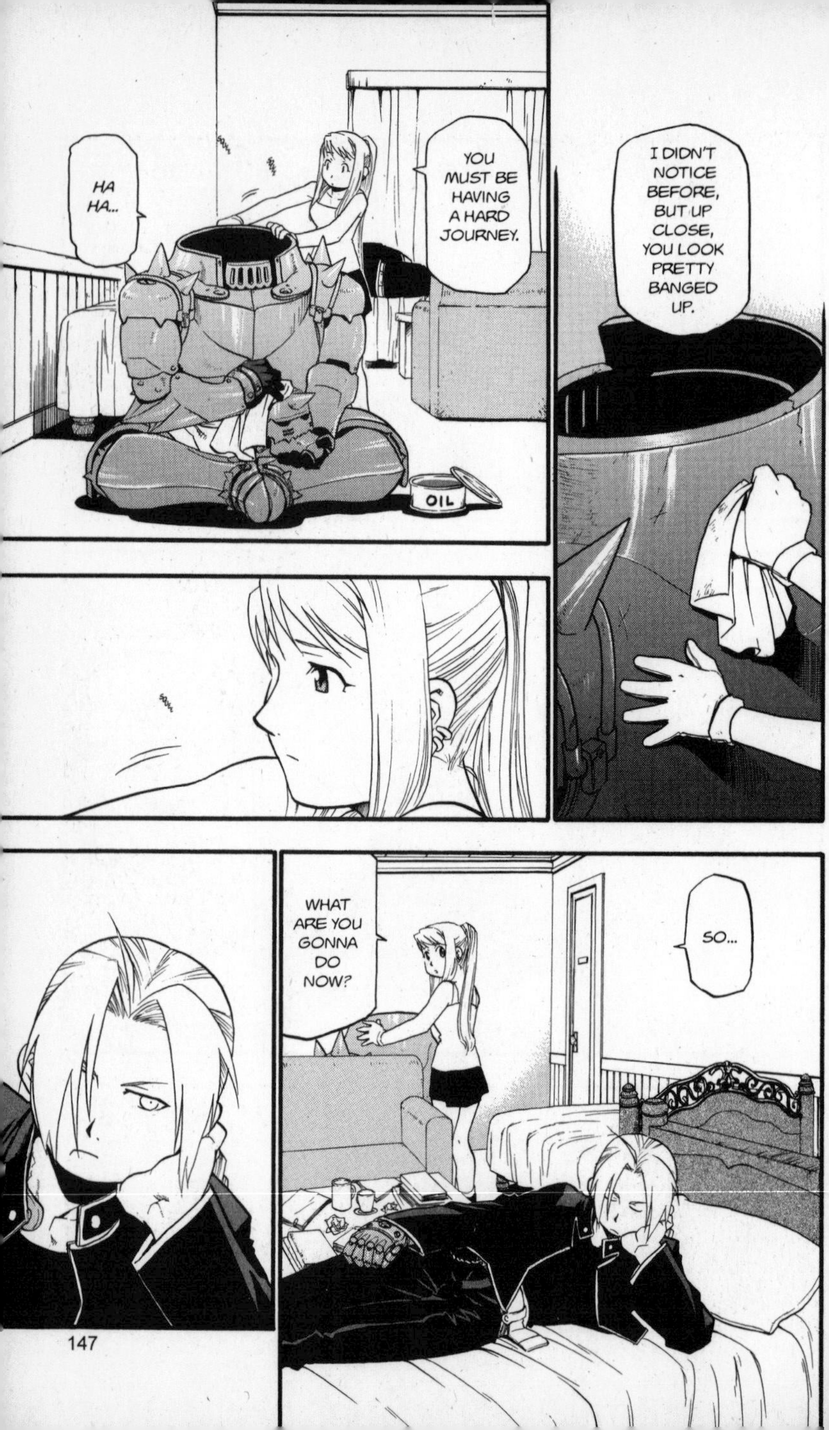
I DIDN'T NOTICE BEFORE, BUT UP CLOSE, YOU LOOK PRETTY BANGED UP.
YOU MUST BE HAVING A HARD JOURNEY.
HA HA...
OIL
SO...
WHAT ARE YOU GONNA DO NOW?

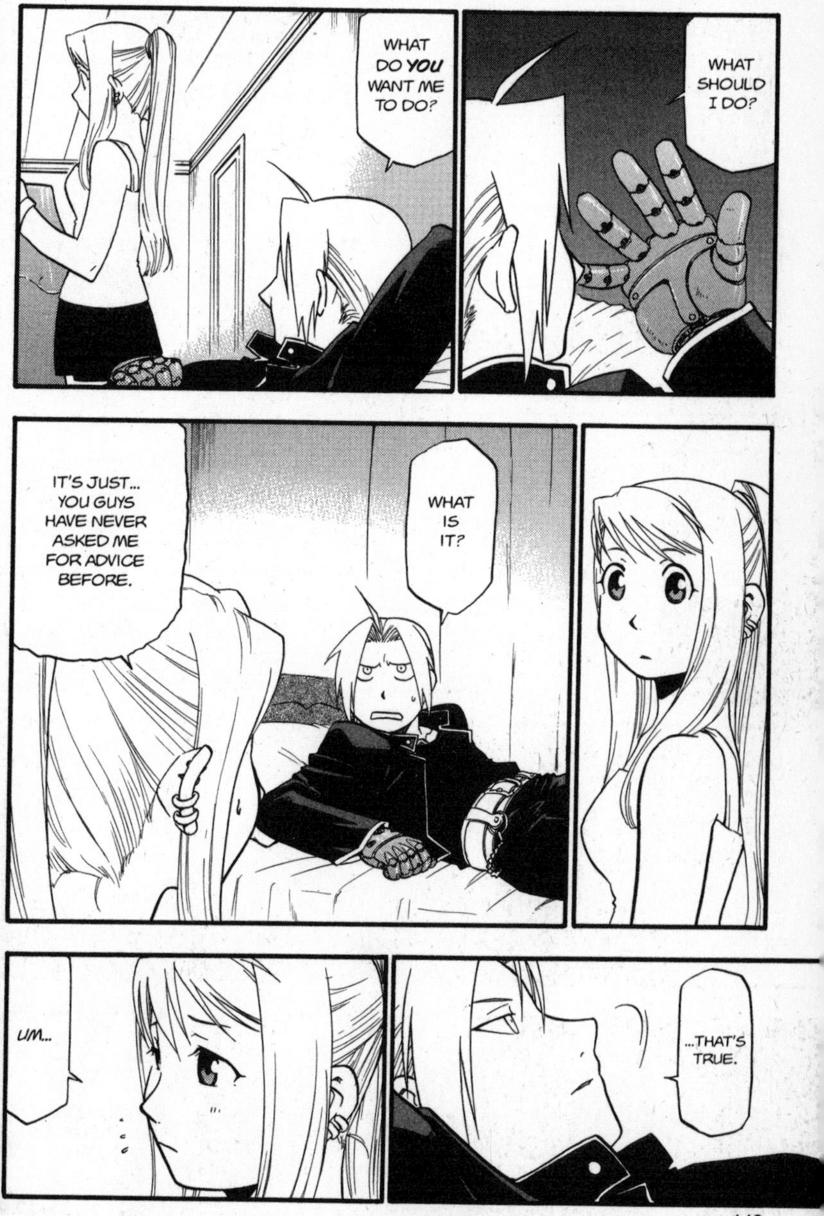
WHAT SHOULD I DO?
WHAT DO YOU WANT ME TO DO?
WHAT IS IT?
IT'S JUST... YOU GUYS HAVE NEVER ASKED ME FOR ADVICE BEFORE.
...THAT'S TRUE.
UM...

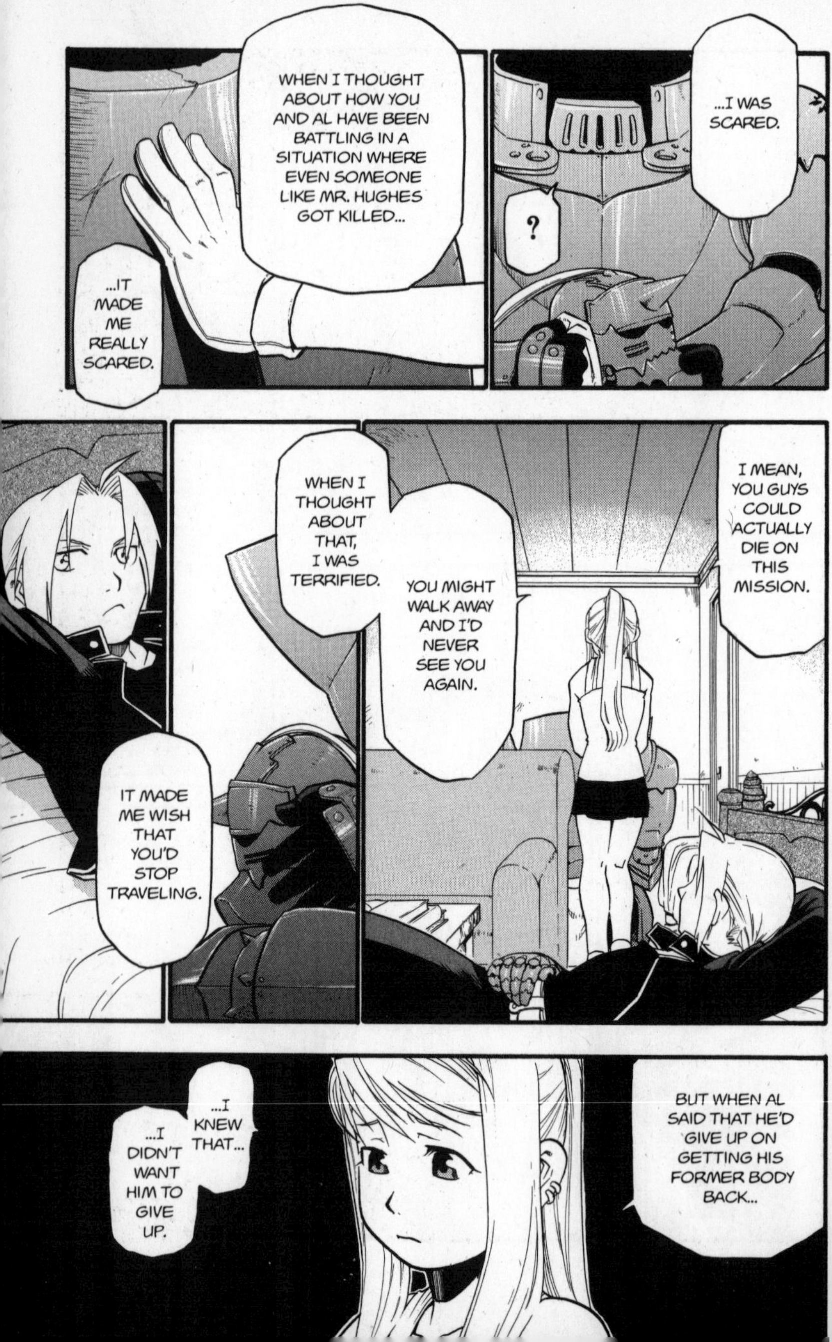
...I WAS SCARED.
?
WHEN I THOUGHT ABOUT HOW YOU AND AL HAVE BEEN BATTLING IN A SITUATION WHERE EVEN SOMEONE LIKE MR. HUGHES GOT KILLED...
...IT MADE ME REALLY SCARED.
I MEAN, YOU GUYS COULD ACTUALLY DIE ON THIS MISSION.
YOU MIGHT WALK AWAY AND I'D NEVER SEE YOU AGAIN.
WHEN I THOUGHT ABOUT THAT, I WAS TERRIFIED.
IT MADE ME WISH THAT YOU'D STOP TRAVELING.
BUT WHEN AL SAID THAT HE'D GIVE UP ON GETTING HIS FORMER BODY BACK...
...I KNEW THAT...
...I DIDN'T WANT HIM TO GIVE UP.

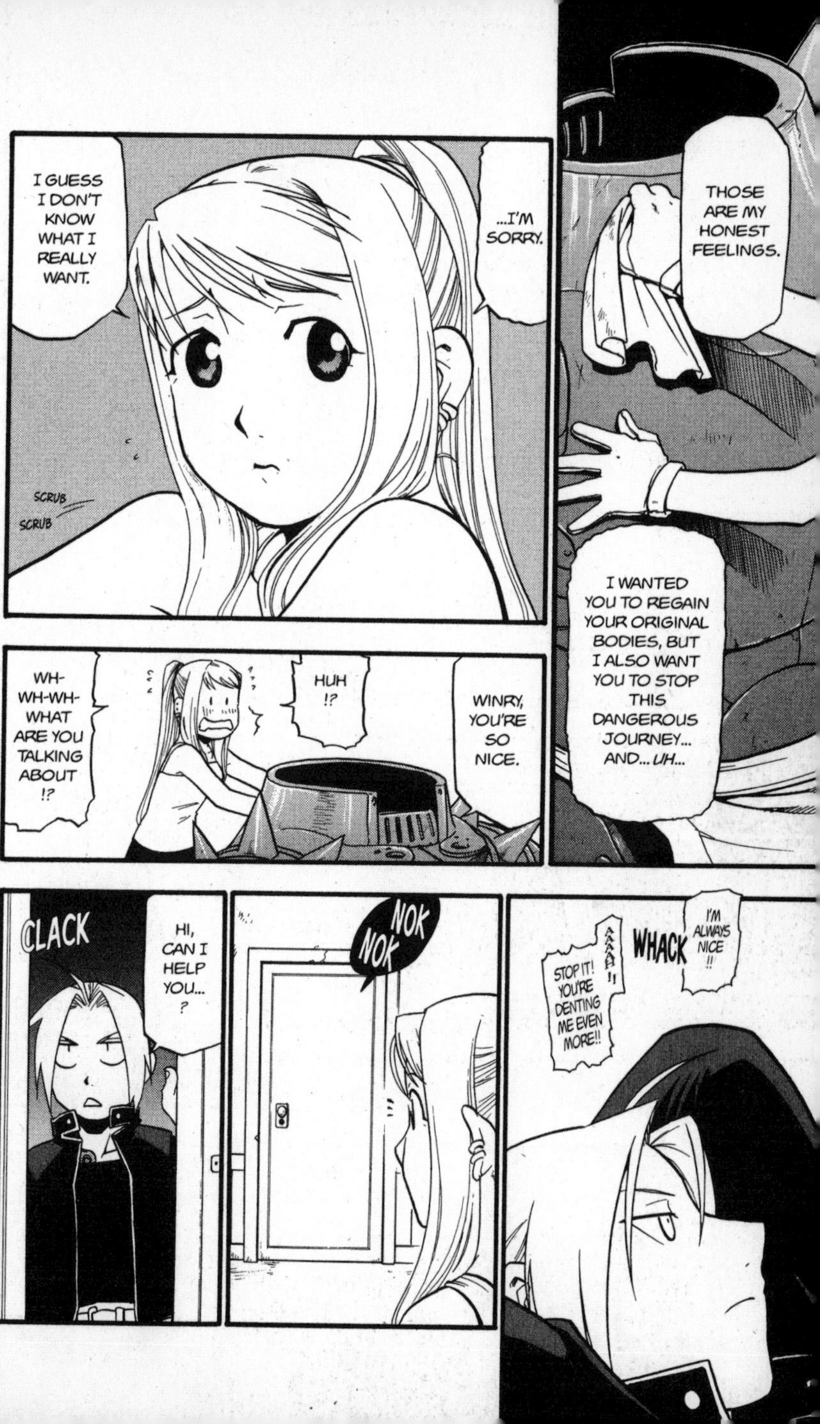
THOSE ARE MY HONEST FEELINGS.
I WANTED YOU TO REGAIN YOUR ORIGINAL BODIES, BUT I ALSO WANT YOU TO STOP THIS DANGEROUS JOURNEY... AND... UH...
...I'M SORRY.
I GUESS I DON'T KNOW WHAT I REALLY WANT.
SCRUB
SCRUB
WINRY, YOU'RE SO NICE.
HUH !?
WH-WH-WH-WHAT ARE YOU TALKING ABOUT !?
I'M ALWAYS NICE !!
WHACK
AAAAH !!
STOP IT! YOU'RE DENTING ME EVEN MORE!!
NOK NOK
HI, CAN I HELP YOU... ?
CLACK

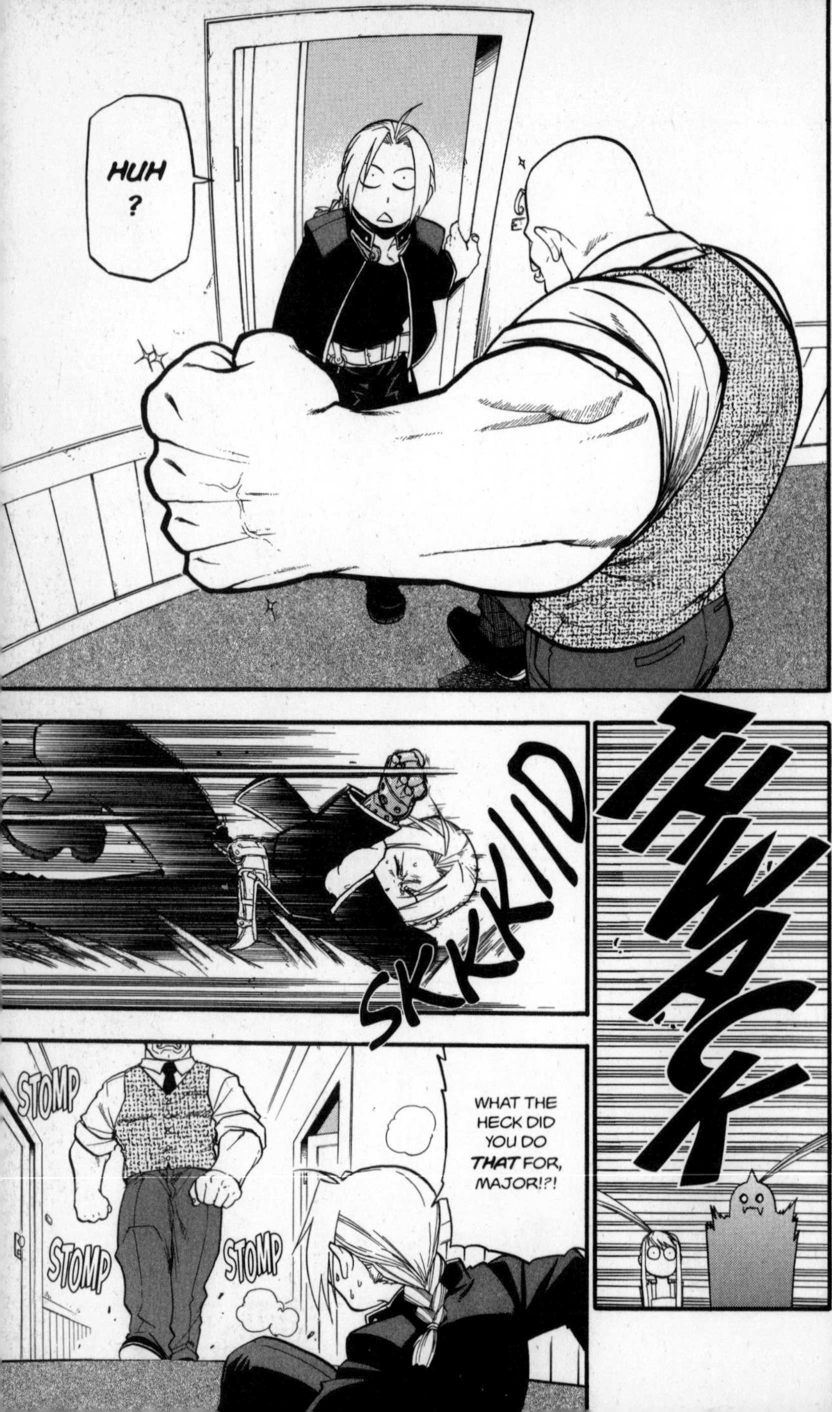
HUH
?
THWACK
SKKKIID
WHAT THE HECK DID YOU DO ***THAT*** FOR, MAJOR!?!
STOMP
STOMP
STOMP

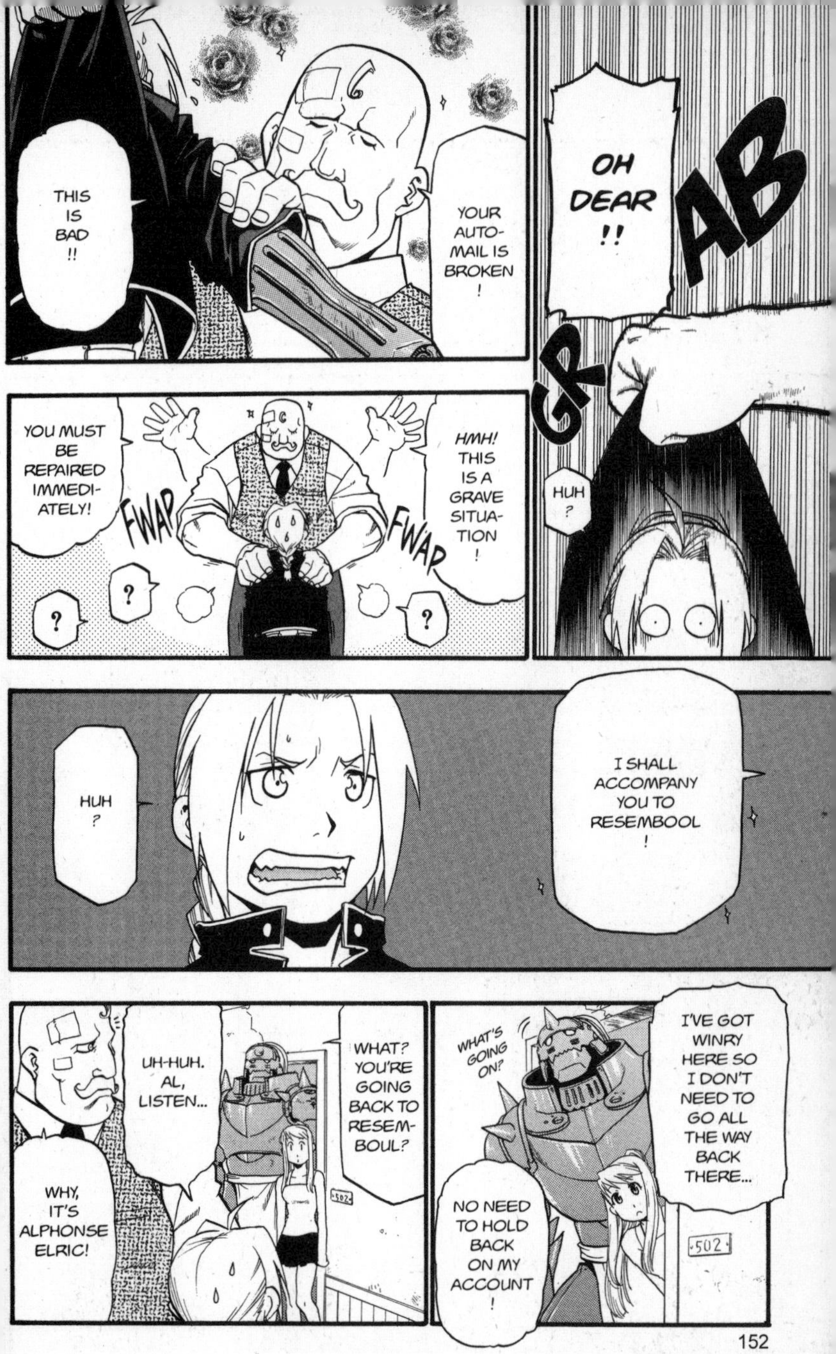
OH DEAR !!
GRAB
HUH ?
YOUR AUTO-MAIL IS BROKEN !
THIS IS BAD !!
HMH! THIS IS A GRAVE SITUATION !
YOU MUST BE REPAIRED IMMEDIATELY!
FWAP
FWAP
?
?
?
I SHALL ACCOMPANY YOU TO RESEMBOOL !
HUH ?
I'VE GOT WINRY HERE SO I DON'T NEED TO GO ALL THE WAY BACK THERE...
WHAT'S GOING ON?
NO NEED TO HOLD BACK ON MY ACCOUNT !
502
WHAT? YOU'RE GOING BACK TO RESEMBOUL?
UH-HUH. AL, LISTEN...
WHY, IT'S ALPHONSE ELRIC!
502

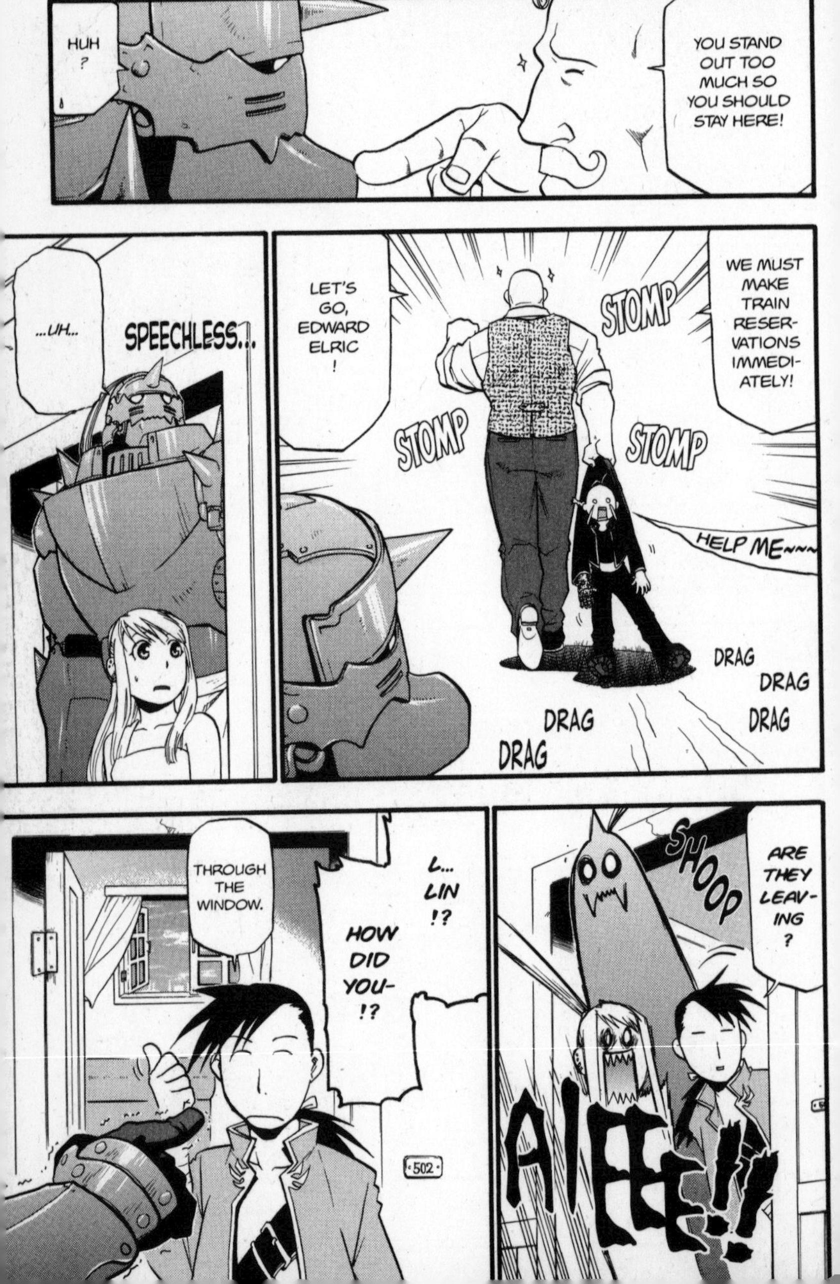
YOU STAND OUT TOO MUCH SO YOU SHOULD STAY HERE!
HUH ?
WE MUST MAKE TRAIN RESER-VATIONS IMMEDI-ATELY!
STOMP
LET'S GO, EDWARD ELRIC !
STOMP
STOMP
HELP ME~~~
DRAG
DRAG
DRAG
DRAG
DRAG
...UH...
SPEECHLESS...
ARE THEY LEAV-ING ?
SHOOP
AIEEE!!
L... LIN !?
HOW DID YOU-!?
THROUGH THE WINDOW.

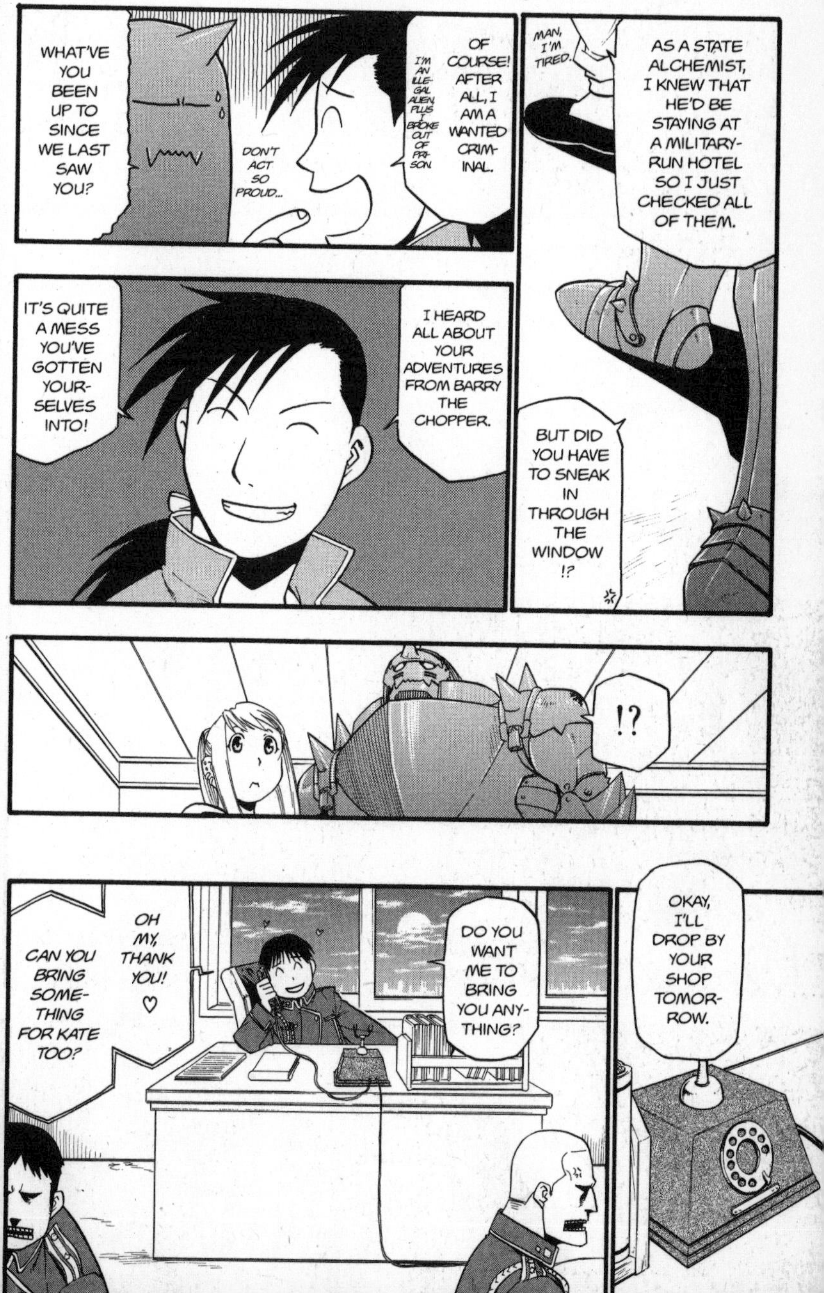
AS A STATE ALCHEMIST, I KNEW THAT HE'D BE STAYING AT A MILITARY-RUN HOTEL SO I JUST CHECKED ALL OF THEM.
MAN, I'M TIRED.
BUT DID YOU HAVE TO SNEAK IN THROUGH THE WINDOW !?
OF COURSE! AFTER ALL, I AM A WANTED CRIMINAL.
I'M AN ILLEGAL ALIEN, PLUS I BROKE OUT OF PRISON.
DON'T ACT SO PROUD...
WHAT'VE YOU BEEN UP TO SINCE WE LAST SAW YOU?
I HEARD ALL ABOUT YOUR ADVENTURES FROM BARRY THE CHOPPER.
IT'S QUITE A MESS YOU'VE GOTTEN YOURSELVES INTO!
!?
OKAY, I'LL DROP BY YOUR SHOP TOMORROW.
DO YOU WANT ME TO BRING YOU ANYTHING?
OH MY, THANK YOU! ♡
CAN YOU BRING SOMETHING FOR KATE TOO?

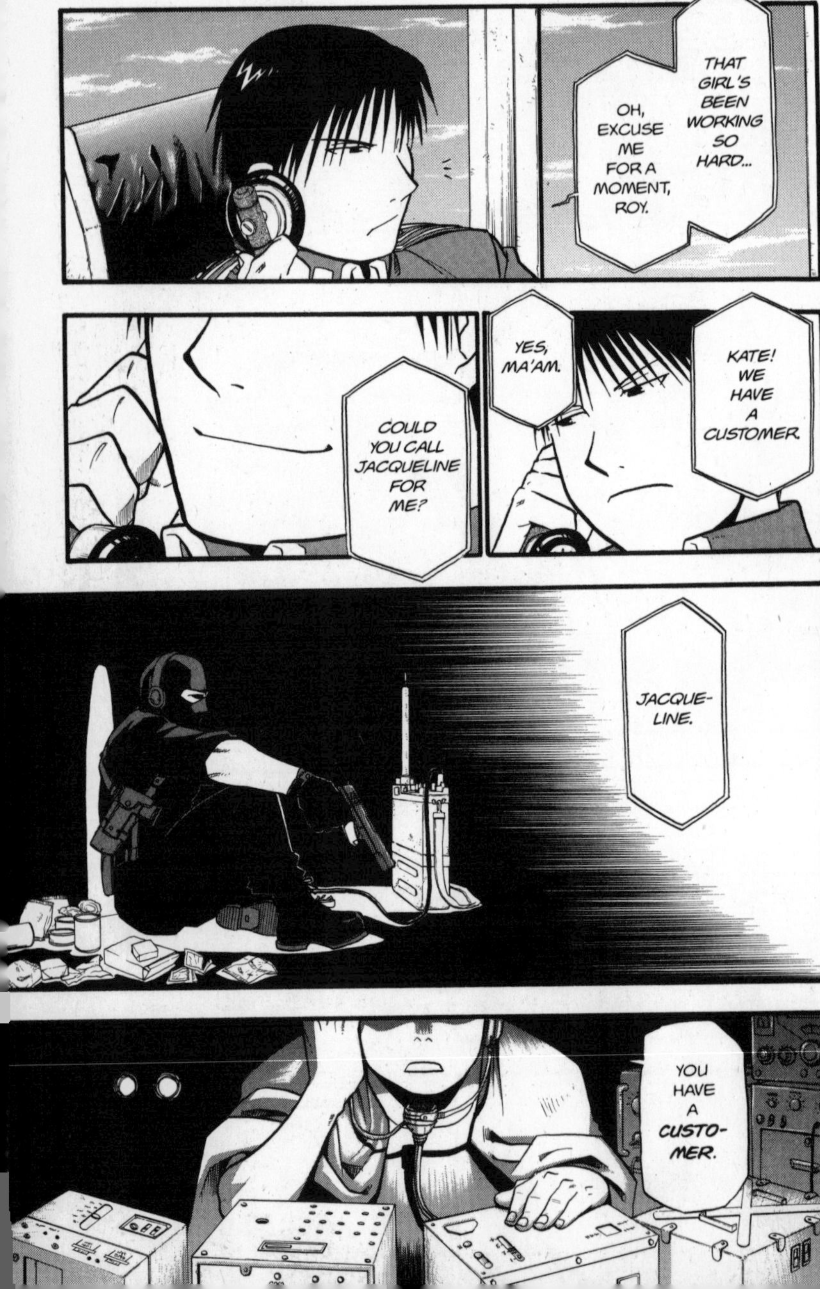
THAT GIRL'S BEEN WORKING SO HARD...
OH, EXCUSE ME FOR A MOMENT, ROY.
KATE! WE HAVE A CUSTOMER.
YES, MA'AM.
COULD YOU CALL JACQUELINE FOR ME?
JACQUE-LINE.
YOU HAVE A CUSTO-MER.

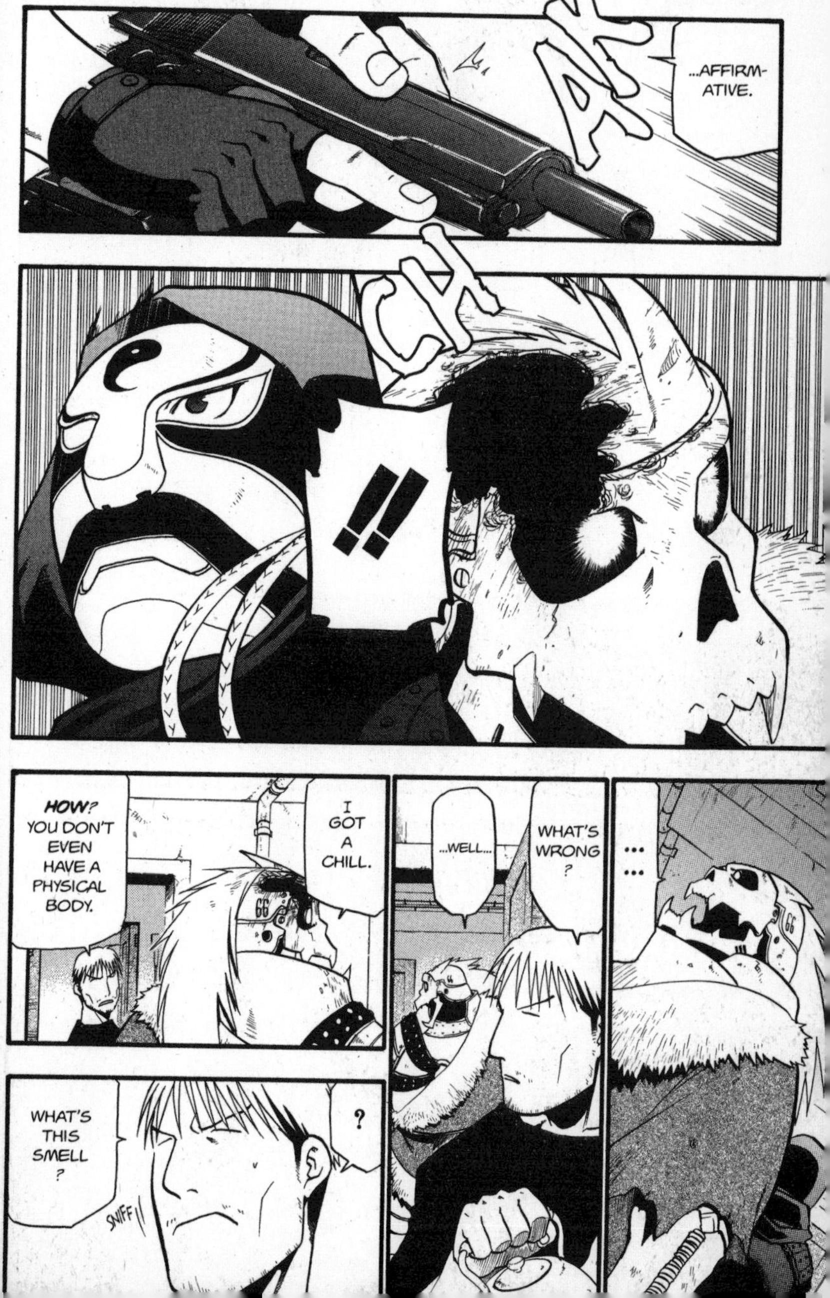
...AFFIRM-ATIVE.
CHAK
!!
...
...
WHAT'S WRONG?
...WELL...
I GOT A CHILL.
HOW? YOU DON'T EVEN HAVE A PHYSICAL BODY.
?
WHAT'S THIS SMELL?
SNIFF

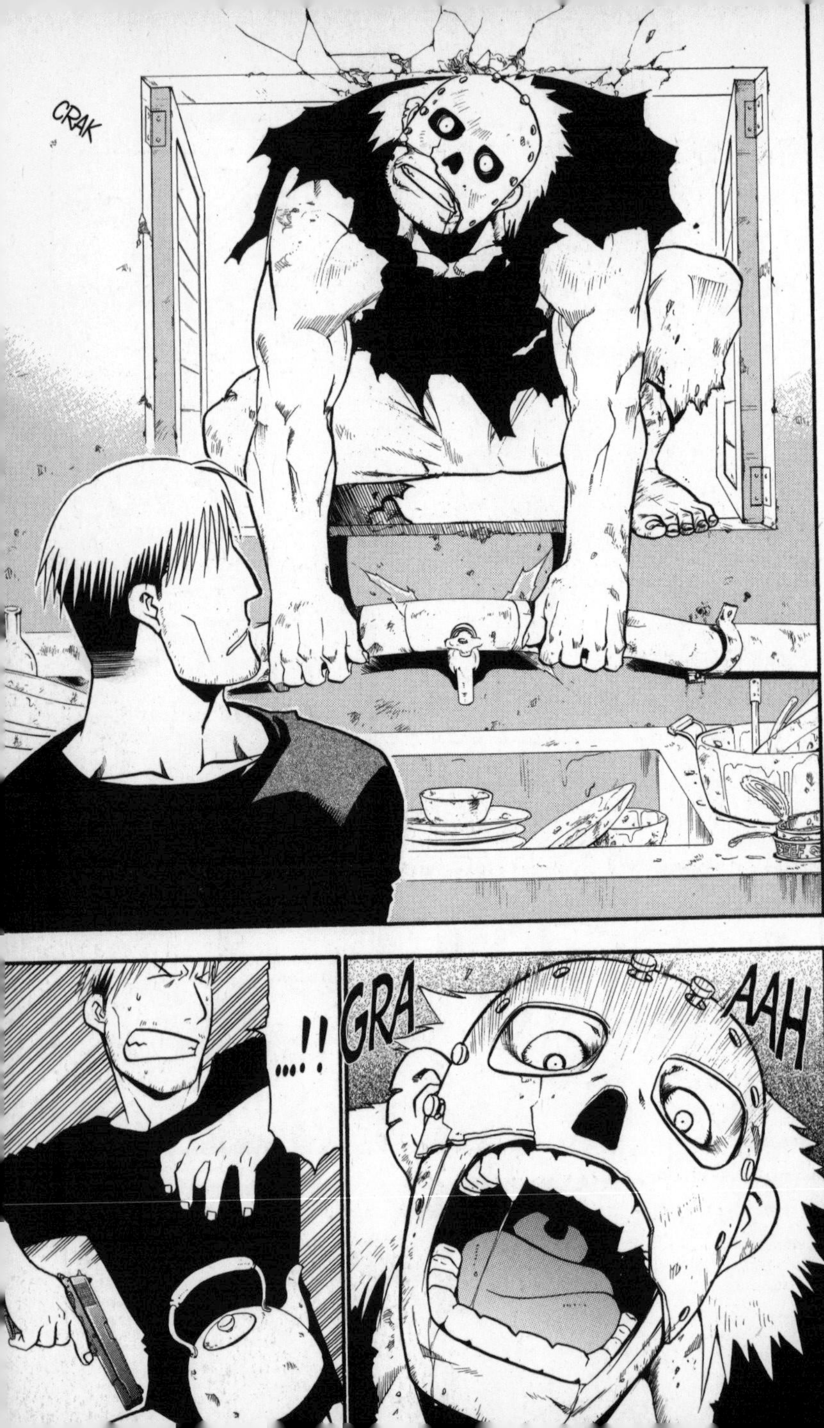
CRAK
GRA
AAH
...!!

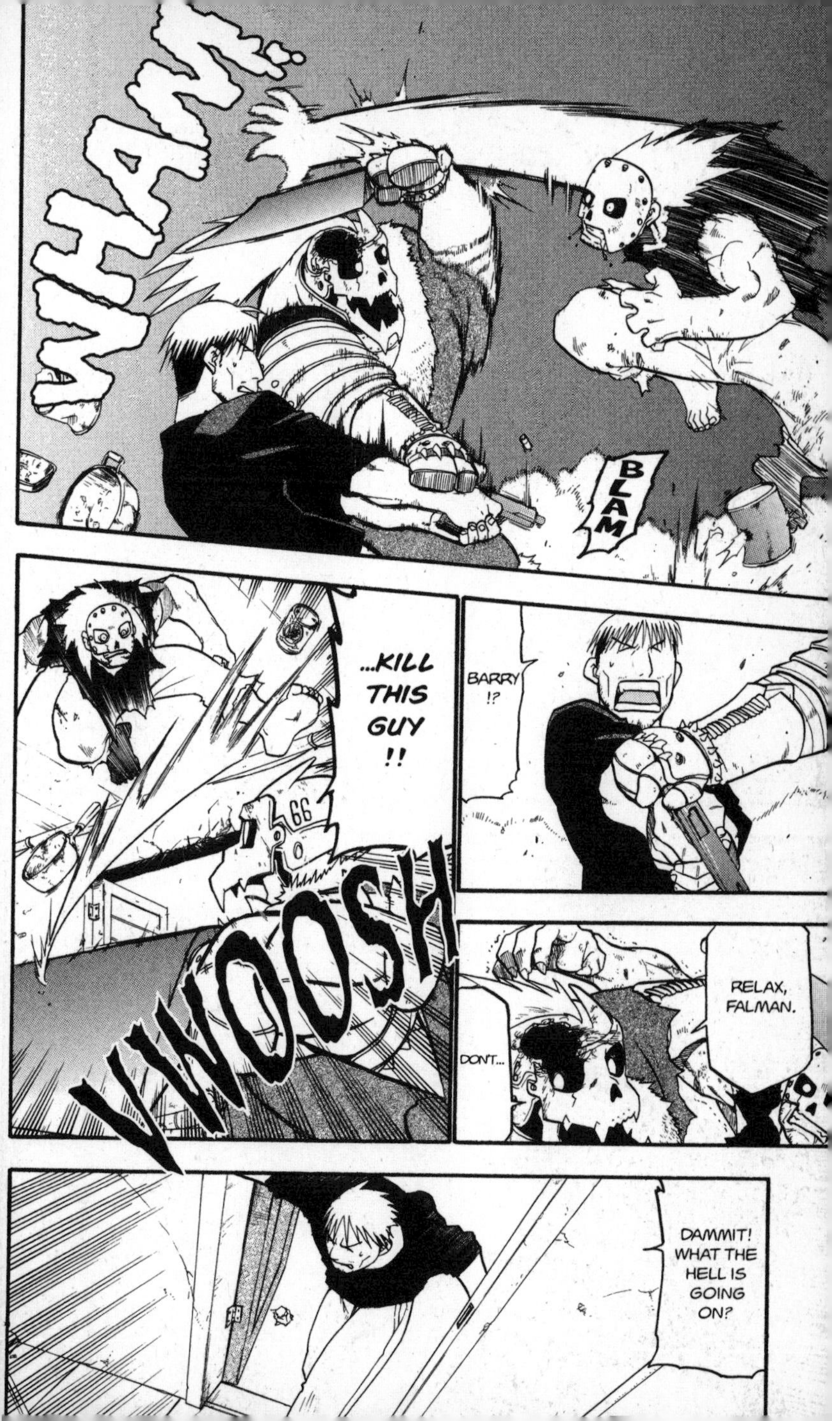
WHAM!
BLAM
BARRY !?
RELAX, FALMAN.
DON'T...
...KILL THIS GUY !!
VWOOSH
DAMMIT! WHAT THE HELL IS GOING ON?

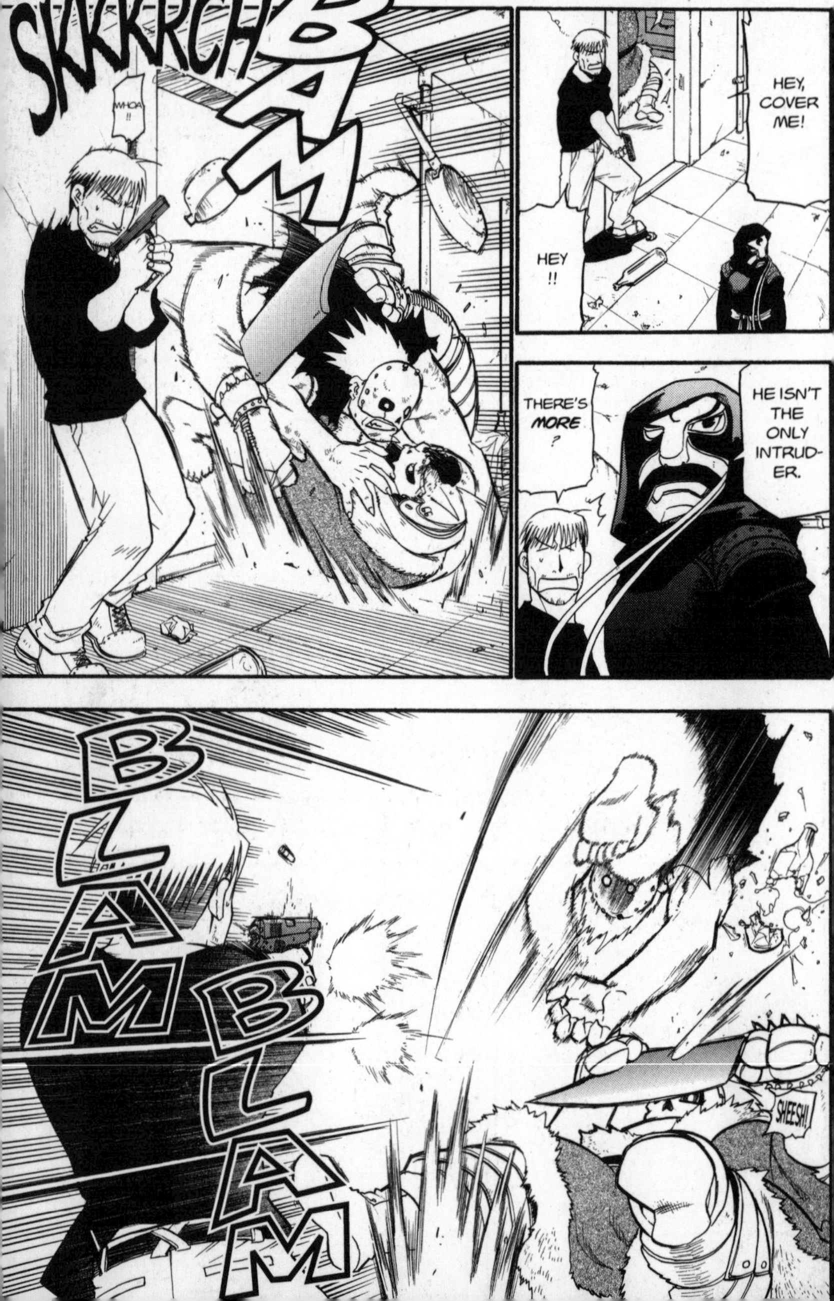
HEY, COVER ME!
HEY !!
HE ISN'T THE ONLY INTRUD-ER.
THERE'S MORE?
SKKKRCH
BAM
WHOA !!
BLAM
BLAM
SHEESH!

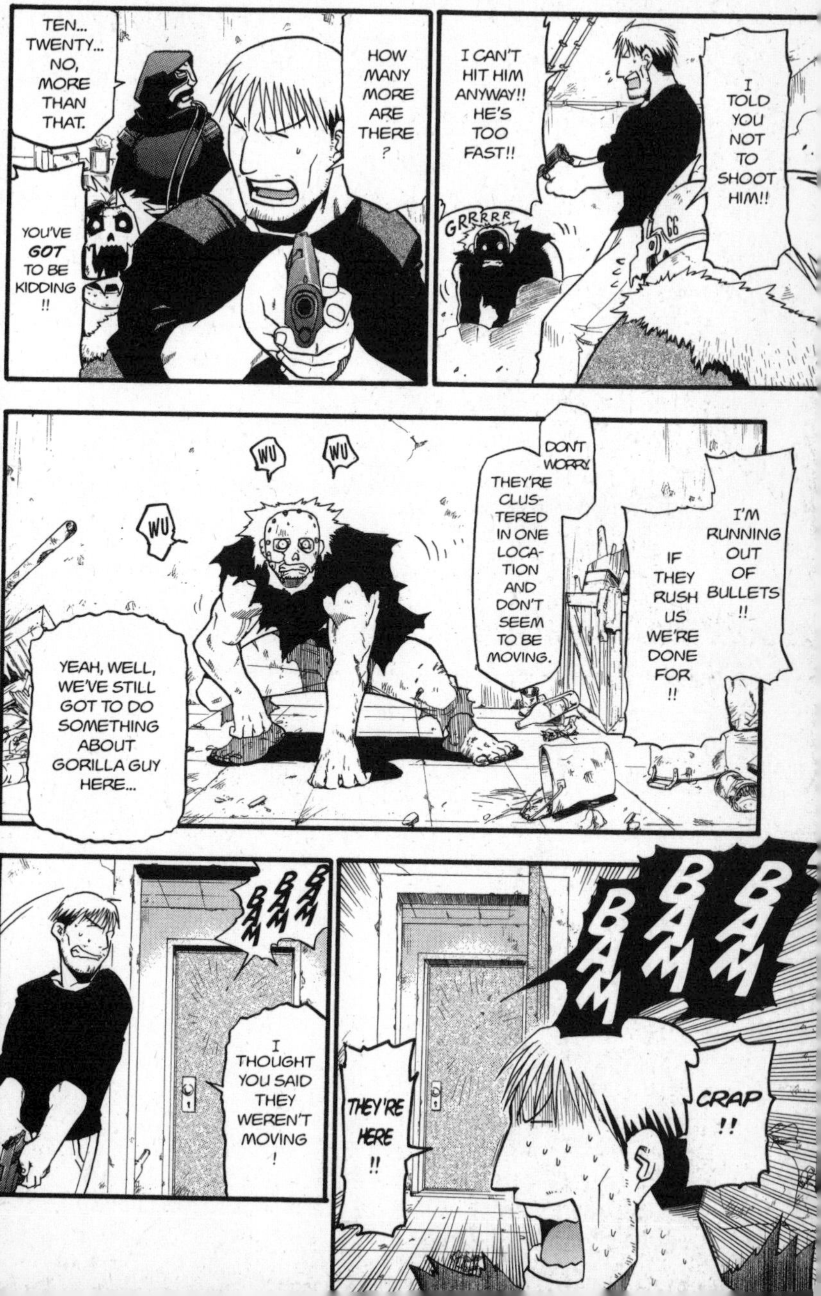
I TOLD YOU NOT TO SHOOT HIM!!
GRRRRR
I CAN'T HIT HIM ANYWAY!! HE'S TOO FAST!!
HOW MANY MORE ARE THERE?
TEN... TWENTY... NO, MORE THAN THAT.
YOU'VE *GOT* TO BE KIDDING!!
I'M RUNNING OUT OF BULLETS!!
IF THEY RUSH US WE'RE DONE FOR!!
DON'T WORRY. THEY'RE CLUSTERED IN ONE LOCATION AND DON'T SEEM TO BE MOVING.
WU
WU
WU
YEAH, WELL, WE'VE STILL GOT TO DO SOMETHING ABOUT GORILLA GUY HERE...
BAM BAM BAM
CRAP!!
THEY'RE HERE!!
BAM BAM BAM
I THOUGHT YOU SAID THEY WEREN'T MOVING!

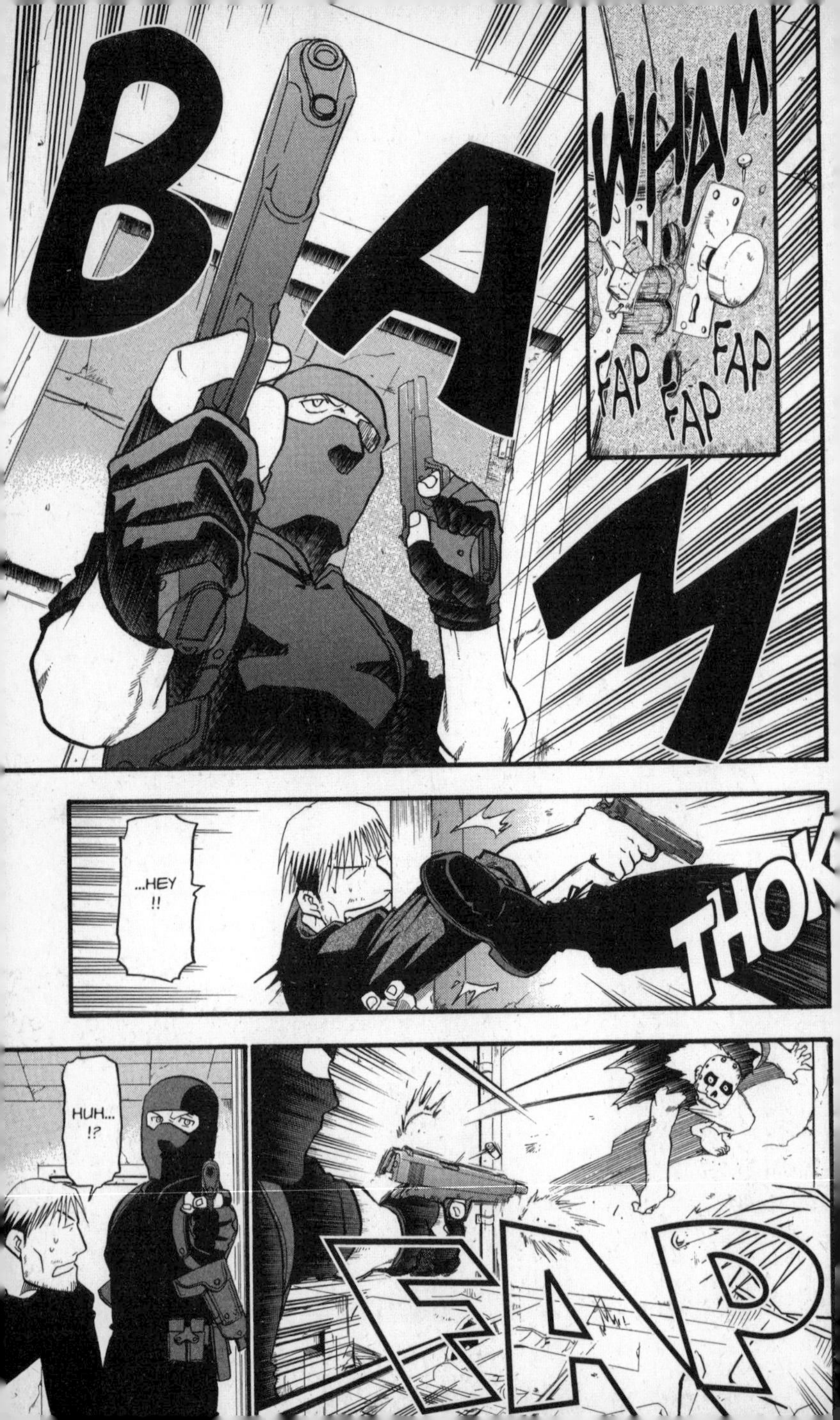
WHAM
FAP
FAP
FAP
BLAM
THOK
...HEY !!
FAP
HUH... !?

ARE YOU ON OUR SIDE ?
NOD
LEAP
VERY WELL.
HUH !?
I'LL LEAVE THIS TO YOU.
BLAM
BLAM
SNIFF
!
SMELLS LIKE A SMOKER...
HEY !
BLAM
BLAM
2ND LT. HAVOC ?
FREEZE

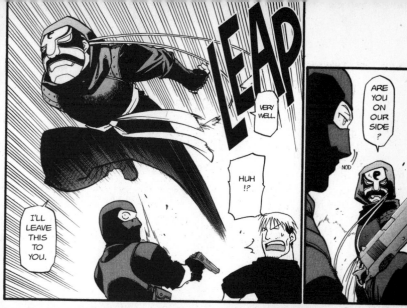

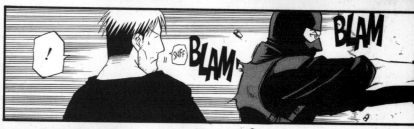

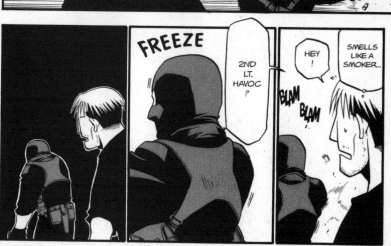

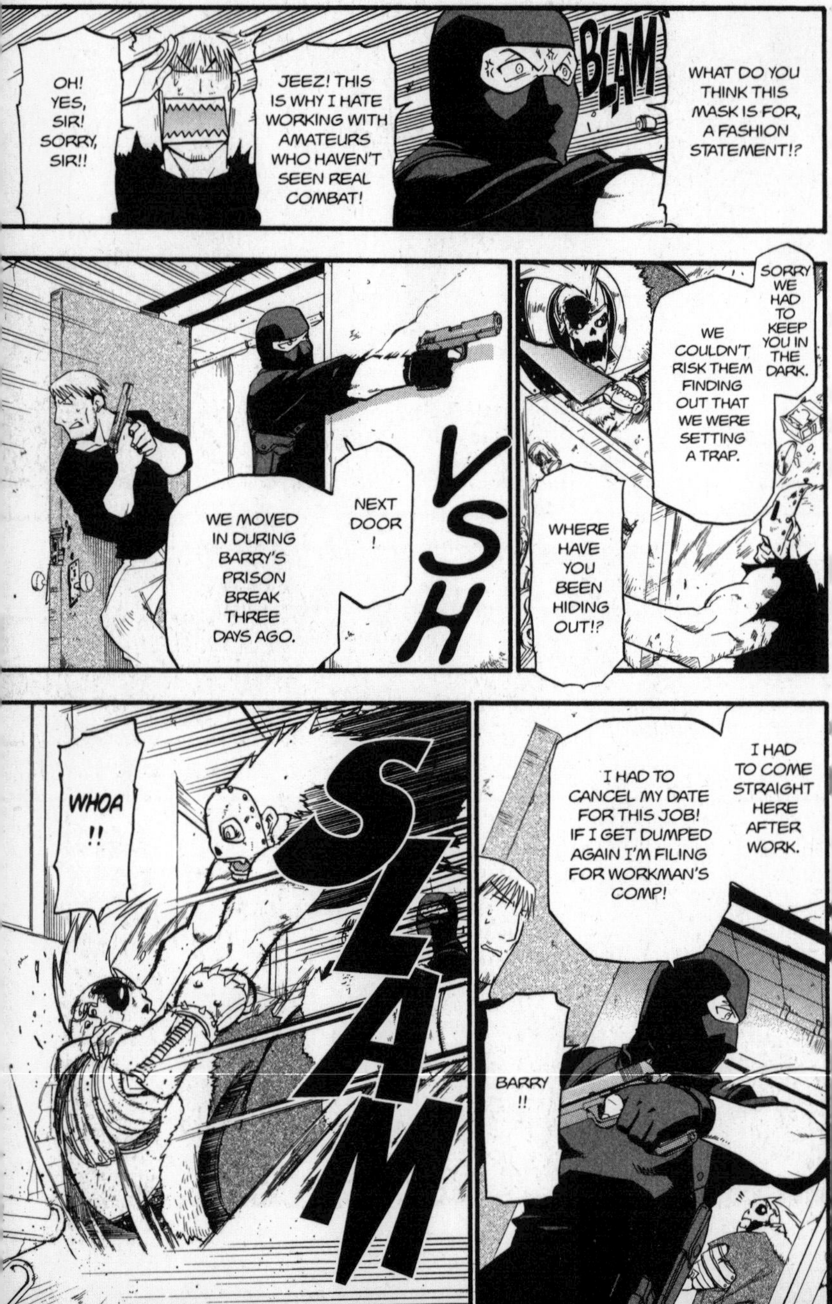

WHAT DO YOU THINK THIS MASK IS FOR, A FASHION STATEMENT!?
BLAM
JEEZ! THIS IS WHY I HATE WORKING WITH AMATEURS WHO HAVEN'T SEEN REAL COMBAT!
OH! YES, SIR! SORRY, SIR!!
SORRY WE HAD TO KEEP YOU IN THE DARK.
WE COULDN'T RISK THEM FINDING OUT THAT WE WERE SETTING A TRAP.
WHERE HAVE YOU BEEN HIDING OUT!?
VSH
NEXT DOOR!
WE MOVED IN DURING BARRY'S PRISON BREAK THREE DAYS AGO.
I HAD TO COME STRAIGHT HERE AFTER WORK.
I HAD TO CANCEL MY DATE FOR THIS JOB! IF I GET DUMPED AGAIN I'M FILING FOR WORKMAN'S COMP!
BARRY!!
SLAM
WHOA!!

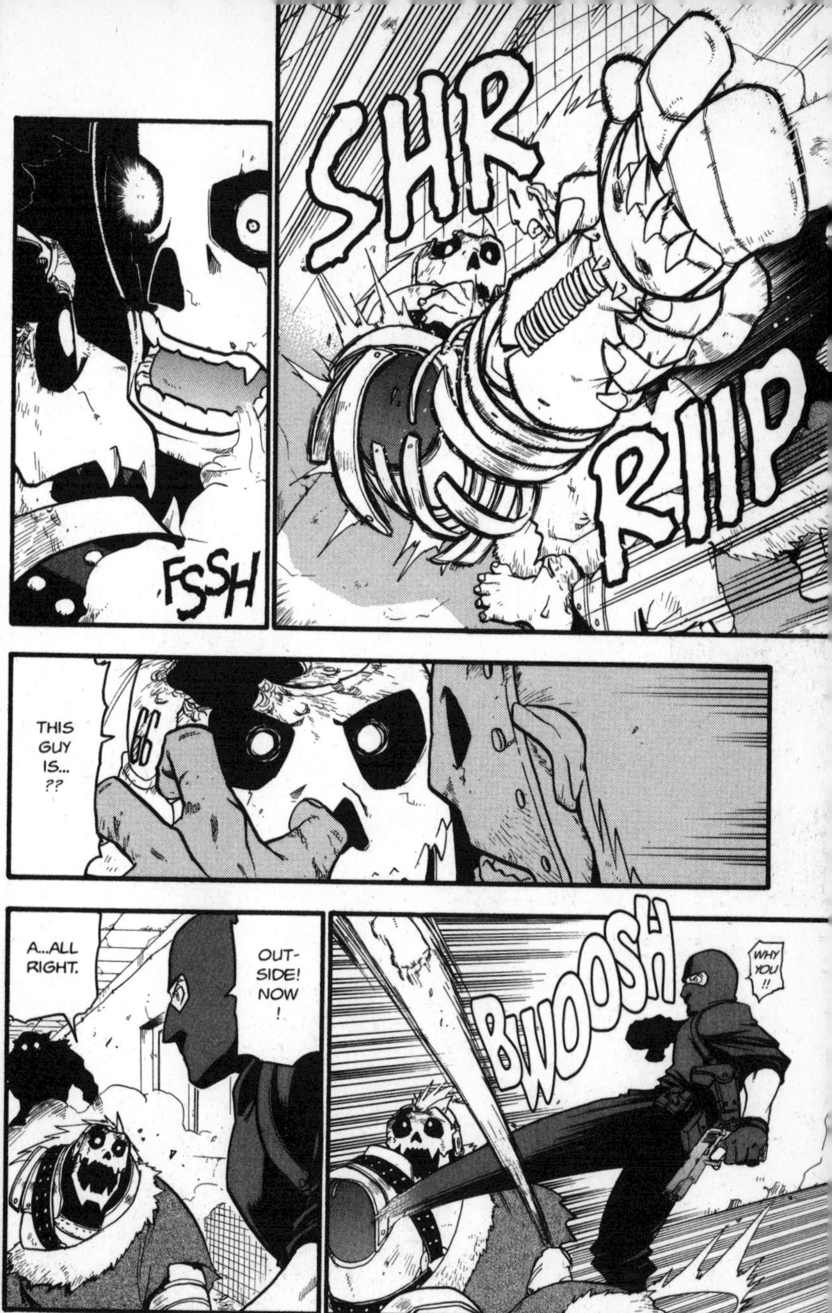
SHR-RIIP
FSSH
THIS GUY IS...??
WHY YOU!!
BWOOSH
OUT-SIDE! NOW!
A...ALL RIGHT.

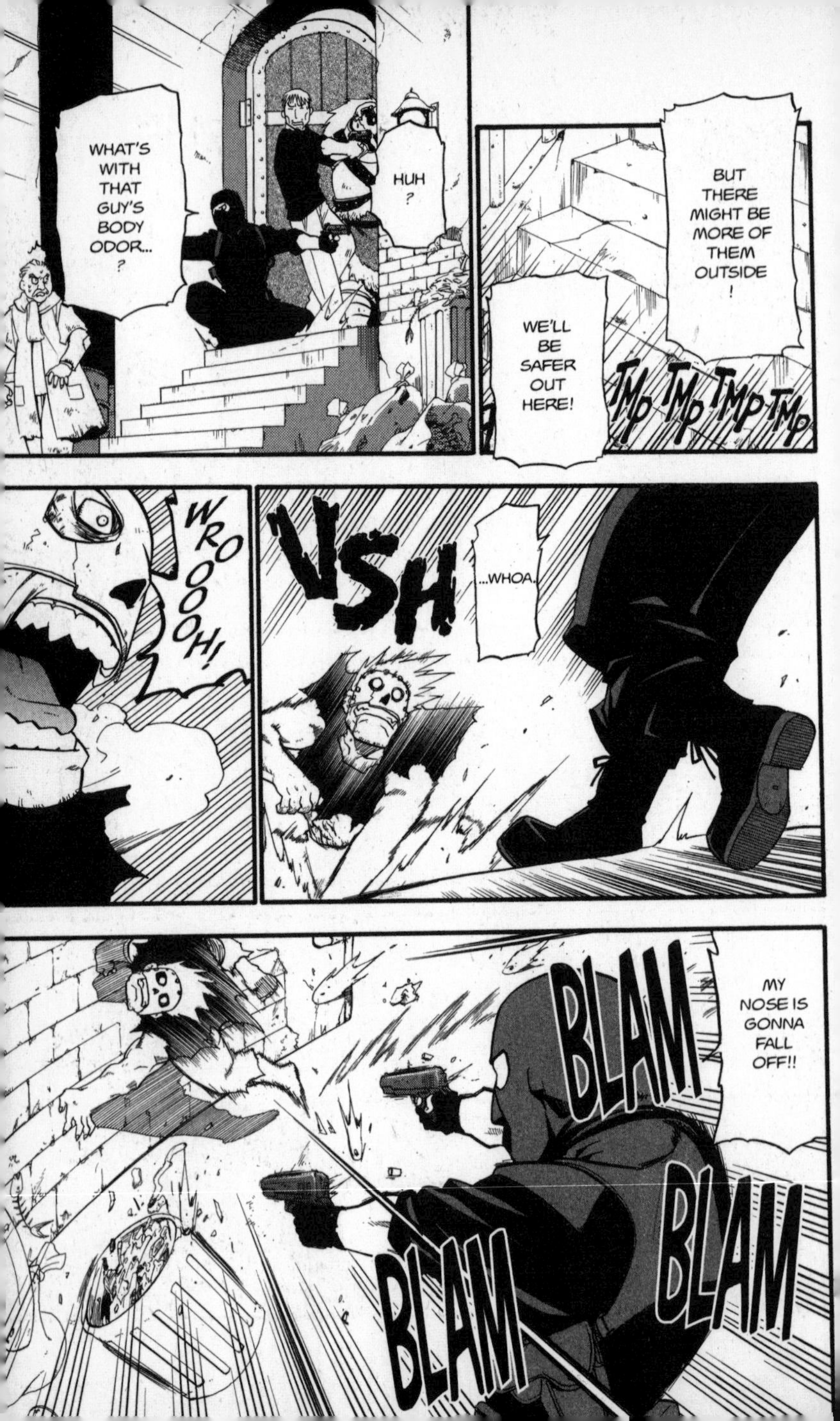
BUT THERE MIGHT BE MORE OF THEM OUTSIDE!
WE'LL BE SAFER OUT HERE!
TMP TMP TMP TMP
HUH?
WHAT'S WITH THAT GUY'S BODY ODOR...?
VSH
...WHOA.
WROOOOOH!
MY NOSE IS GONNA FALL OFF!!
BLAM
BLAM
BLAM

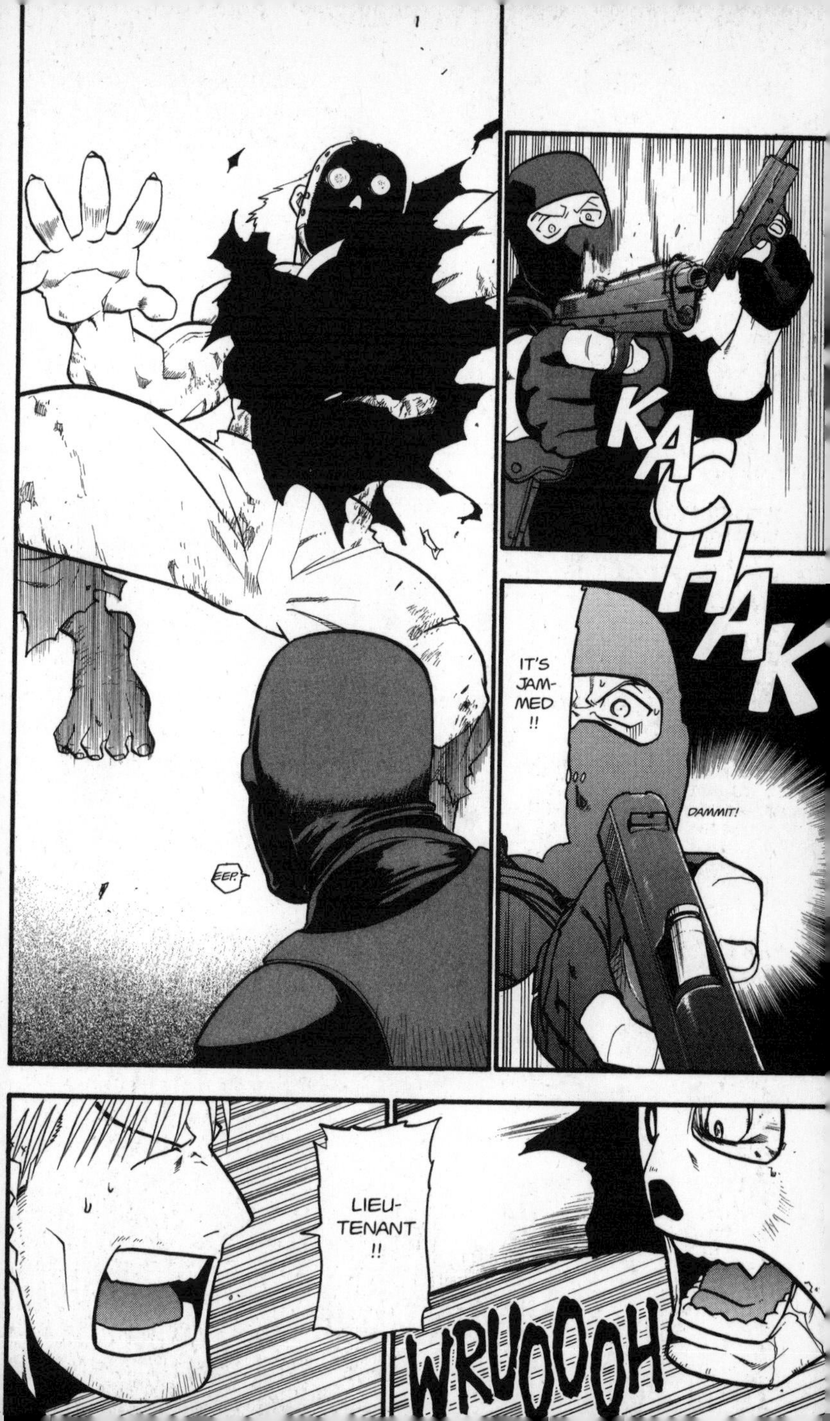
KACHAK
IT'S JAM-MED !!
DAMMIT!
EEP.
WRUOOOH
LIEU-TENANT !!

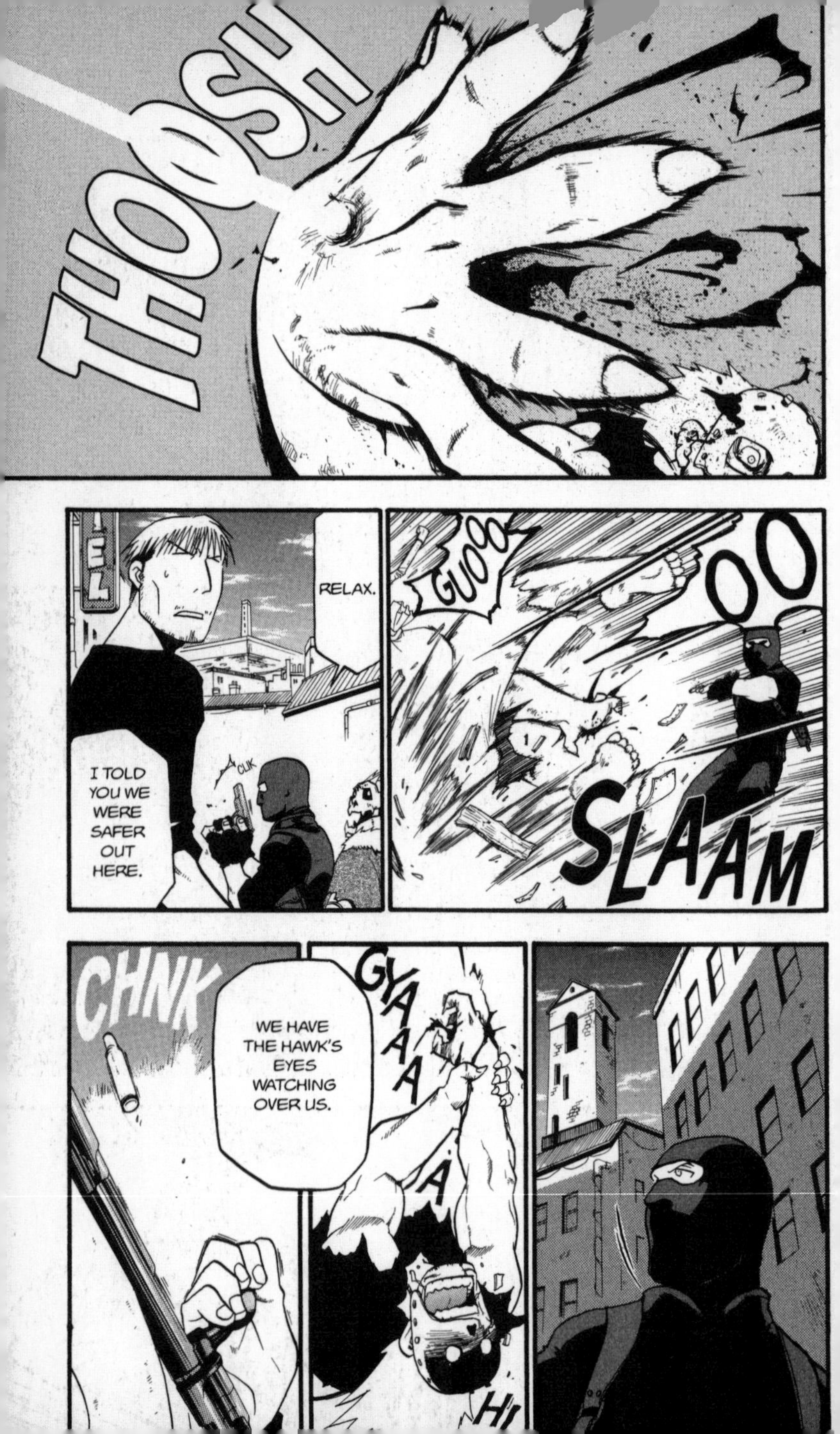
THOOSH
GUOOOO
SLAAM
RELAX.
I TOLD YOU WE WERE SAFER OUT HERE.
CLIK
GYAAAA
AA
HI
CHNK
WE HAVE THE HAWK'S EYES WATCHING OVER US.

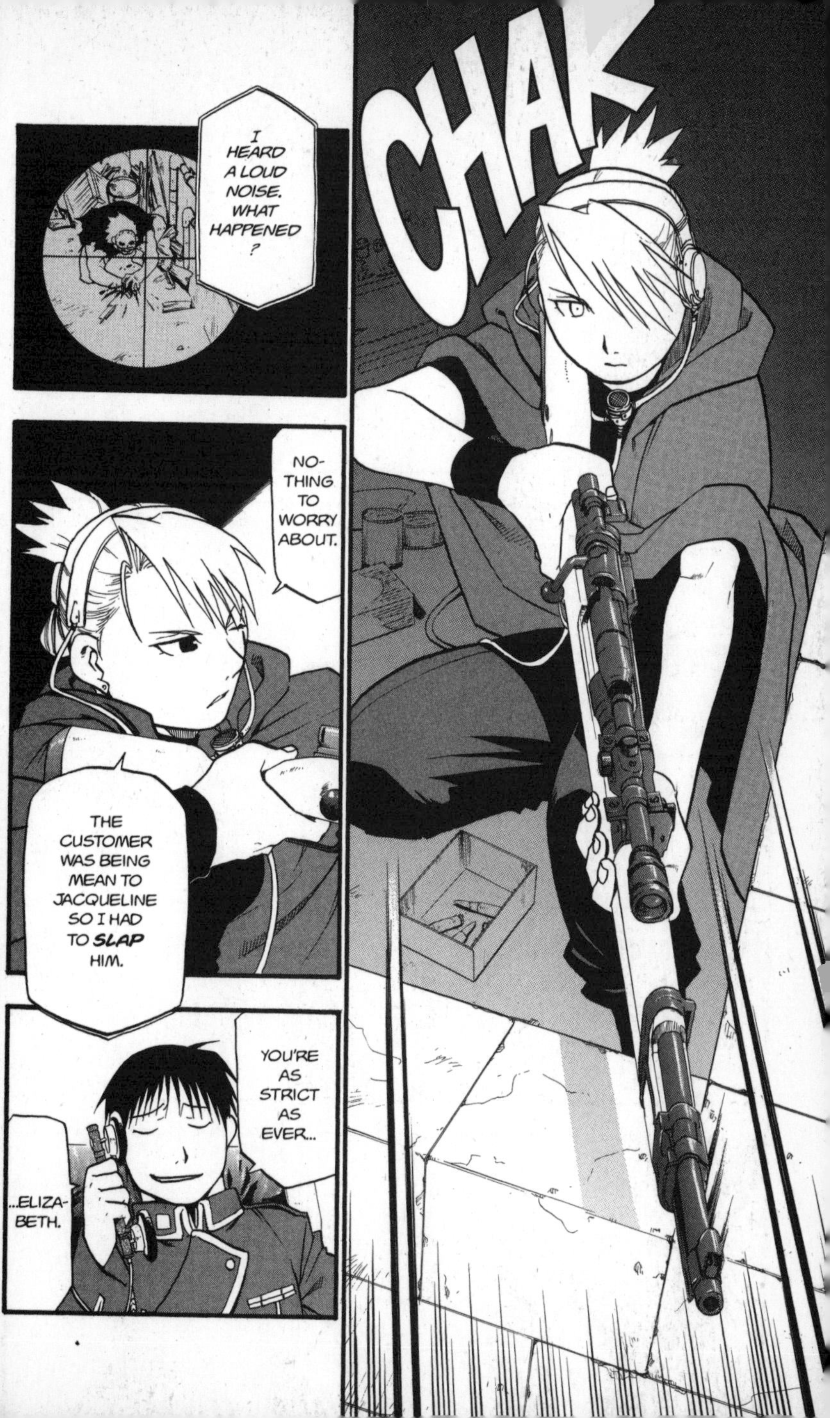
CHAK
I HEARD A LOUD NOISE. WHAT HAPPENED?
NO-THING TO WORRY ABOUT.
THE CUSTOMER WAS BEING MEAN TO JACQUELINE SO I HAD TO **SLAP** HIM.
YOU'RE AS STRICT AS EVER...
...ELIZA-BETH.

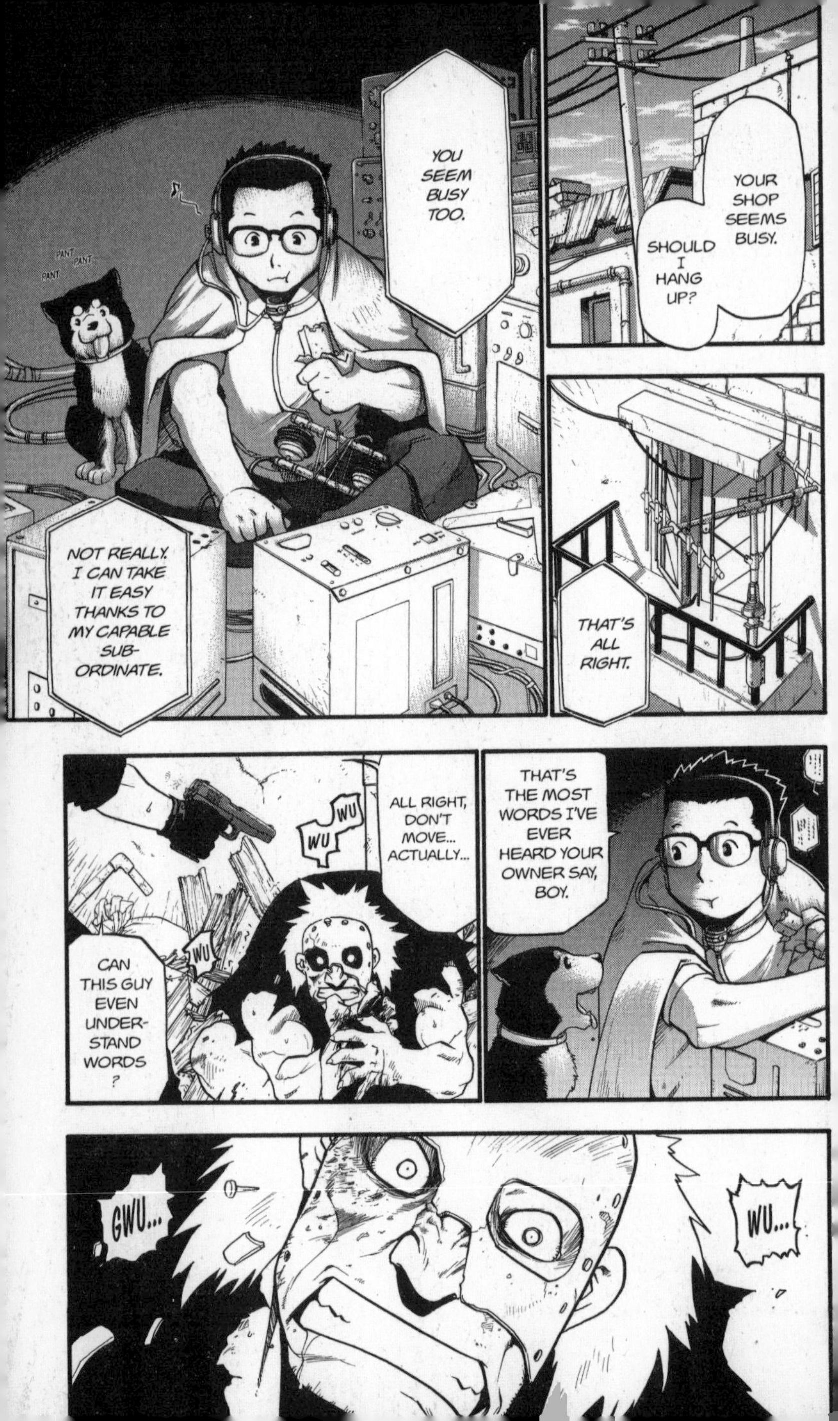
YOUR SHOP SEEMS BUSY.
SHOULD I HANG UP?
THAT'S ALL RIGHT.
YOU SEEM BUSY TOO.
PANT PANT PANT
NOT REALLY. I CAN TAKE IT EASY THANKS TO MY CAPABLE SUB-ORDINATE.
THAT'S THE MOST WORDS I'VE EVER HEARD YOUR OWNER SAY, BOY.
WU
WU
ALL RIGHT, DON'T MOVE... ACTUALLY...
WU
CAN THIS GUY EVEN UNDER-STAND WORDS ?
WU...
GWU...

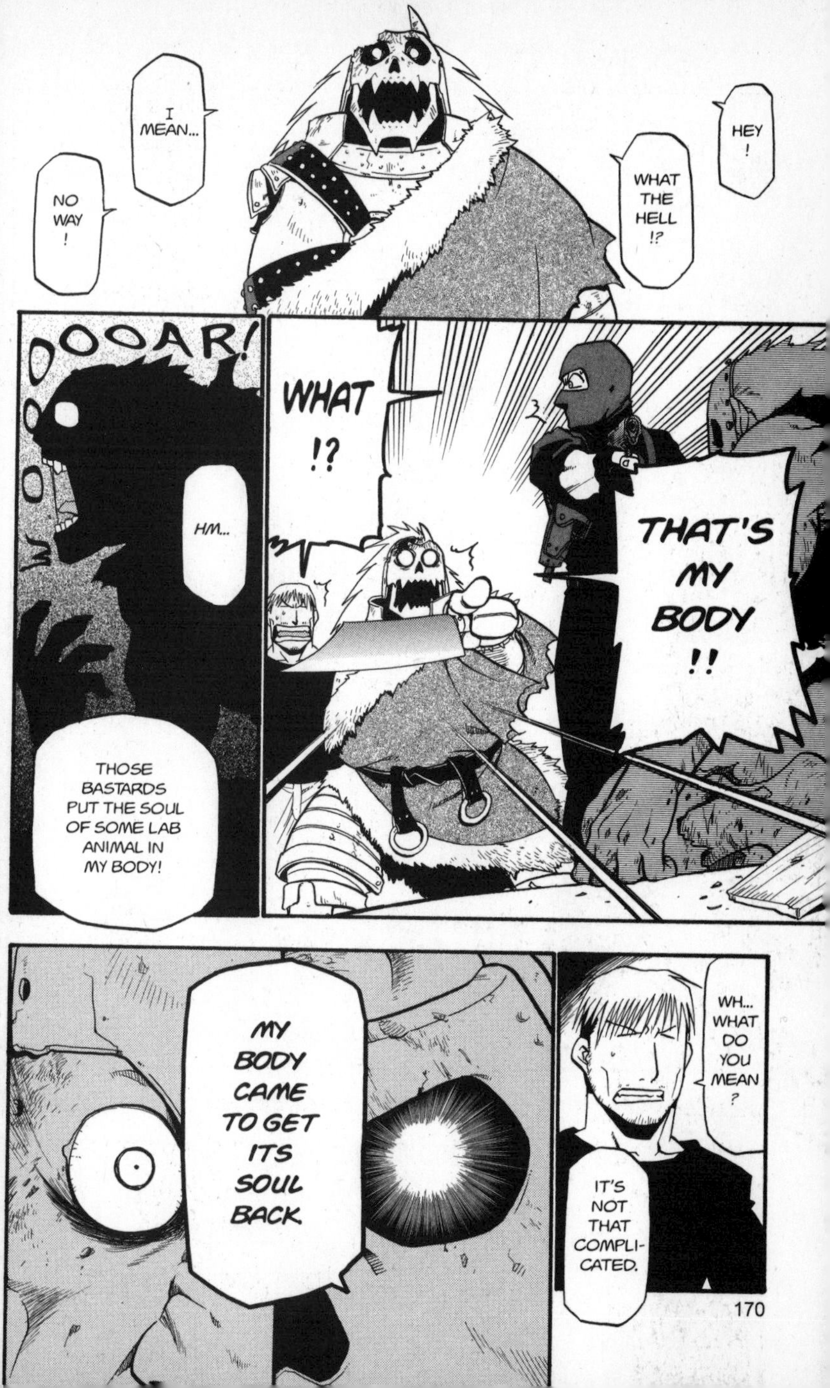
HEY!
WHAT THE HELL!?
I MEAN...
NO WAY!
THAT'S MY BODY!!
WHAT!?
WOOOOAR!
HM...
THOSE BASTARDS PUT THE SOUL OF SOME LAB ANIMAL IN MY BODY!
WH... WHAT DO YOU MEAN?
IT'S NOT THAT COMPLICATED.
MY BODY CAME TO GET ITS SOUL BACK.

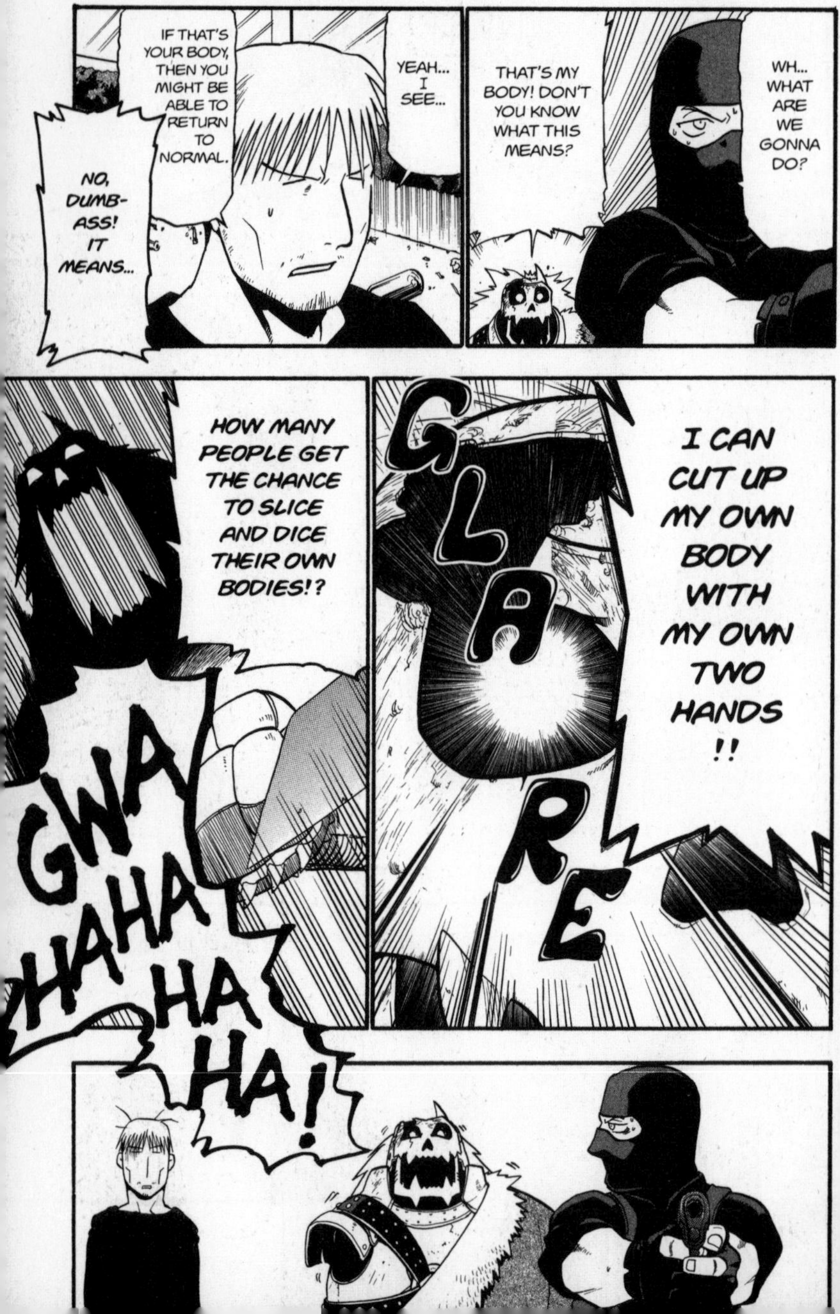
WH... WHAT ARE WE GONNA DO?
THAT'S MY BODY! DON'T YOU KNOW WHAT THIS MEANS?
YEAH... I SEE...
IF THAT'S YOUR BODY, THEN YOU MIGHT BE ABLE TO RETURN TO NORMAL.
NO, DUMB-ASS! IT MEANS...
I CAN CUT UP MY OWN BODY WITH MY OWN TWO HANDS !!
GLARE
HOW MANY PEOPLE GET THE CHANCE TO SLICE AND DICE THEIR OWN BODIES!?
GWAHAHAHAHA!

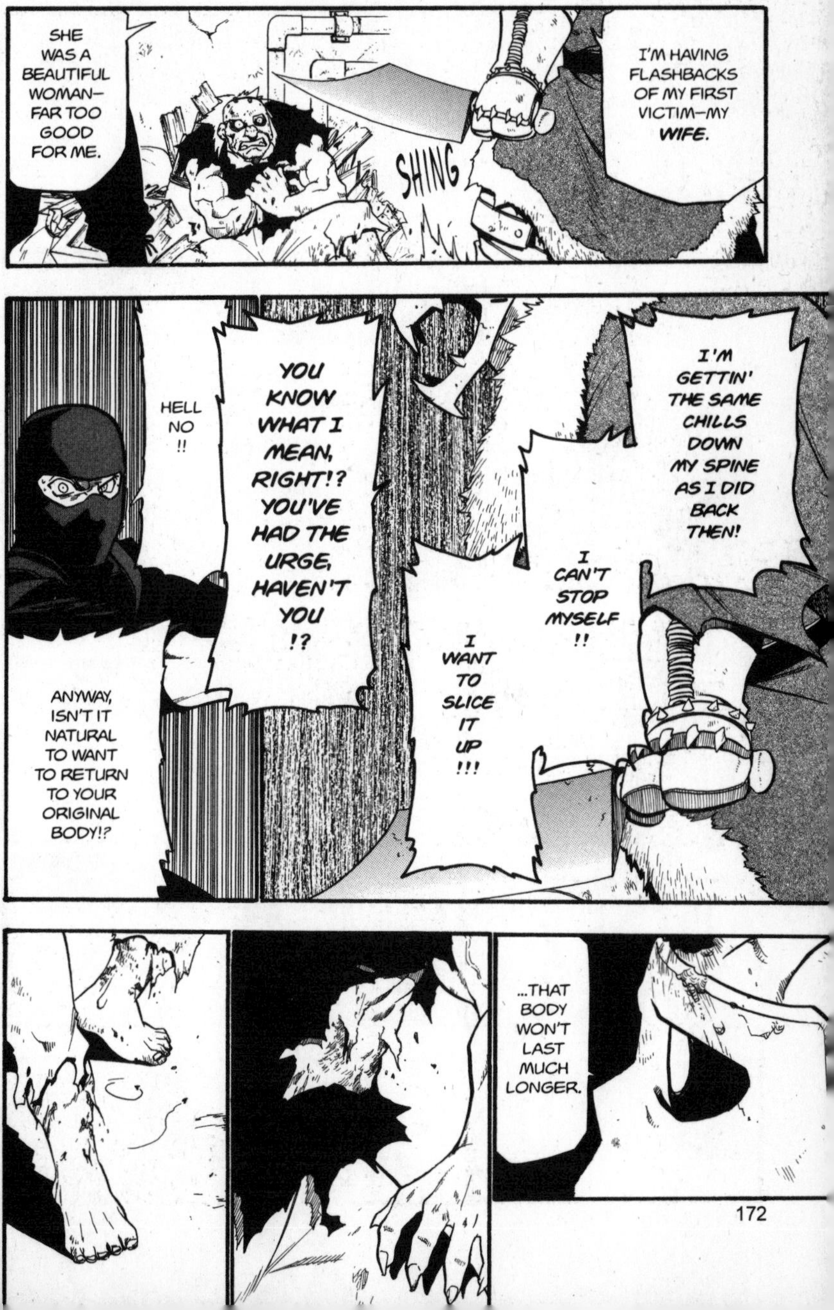

I'M HAVING FLASHBACKS OF MY FIRST VICTIM—MY WIFE.
SHING
SHE WAS A BEAUTIFUL WOMAN—FAR TOO GOOD FOR ME.
I'M GETTIN' THE SAME CHILLS DOWN MY SPINE AS I DID BACK THEN!
I CAN'T STOP MYSELF!!
I WANT TO SLICE IT UP!!!
YOU KNOW WHAT I MEAN, RIGHT!? YOU'VE HAD THE URGE, HAVEN'T YOU!?
HELL NO!!
ANYWAY, ISN'T IT NATURAL TO WANT TO RETURN TO YOUR ORIGINAL BODY!?
...THAT BODY WON'T LAST MUCH LONGER.

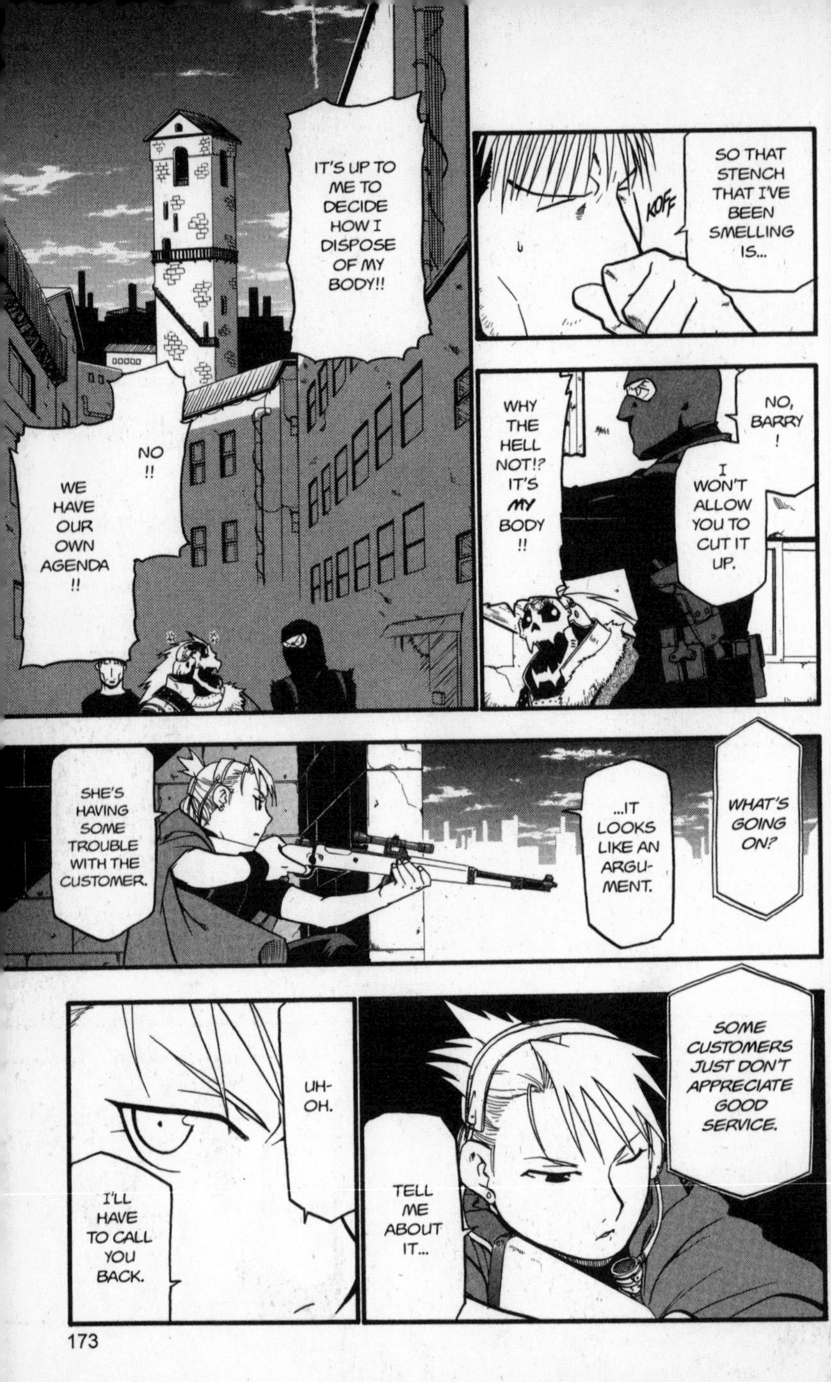
SO THAT STENCH THAT I'VE BEEN SMELLING IS...
KOFF
NO, BARRY!
I WON'T ALLOW YOU TO CUT IT UP.
WHY THE HELL NOT!? IT'S *MY* BODY!!
IT'S UP TO ME TO DECIDE HOW I DISPOSE OF MY BODY!!
NO!!
WE HAVE OUR OWN AGENDA!!
WHAT'S GOING ON?
...IT LOOKS LIKE AN ARGUMENT.
SHE'S HAVING SOME TROUBLE WITH THE CUSTOMER.
SOME CUSTOMERS JUST DON'T APPRECIATE GOOD SERVICE.
TELL ME ABOUT IT...
UH-OH.
I'LL HAVE TO CALL YOU BACK.

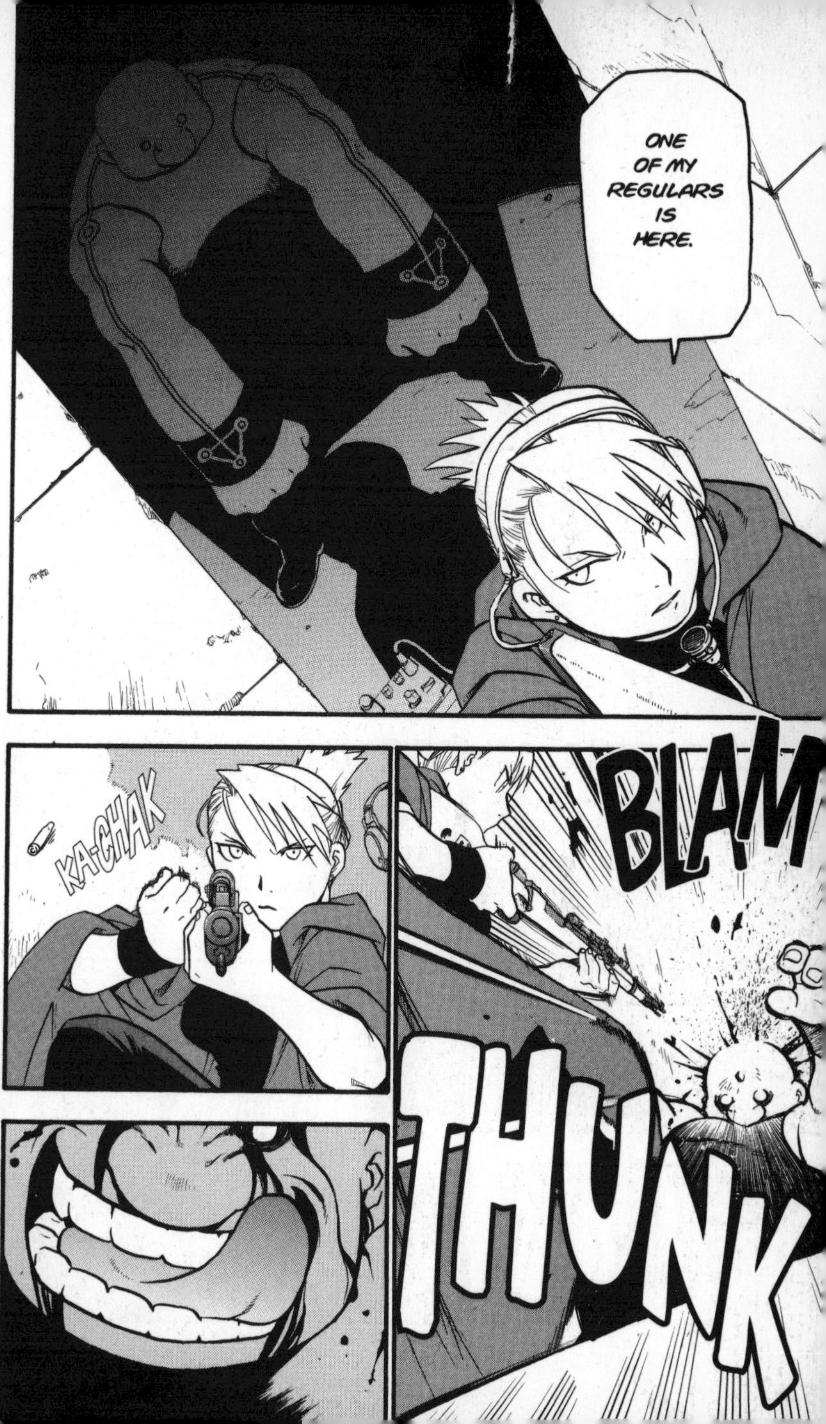
ONE OF MY REGULARS IS HERE.
BLAM
KA-CHAK
THUNK

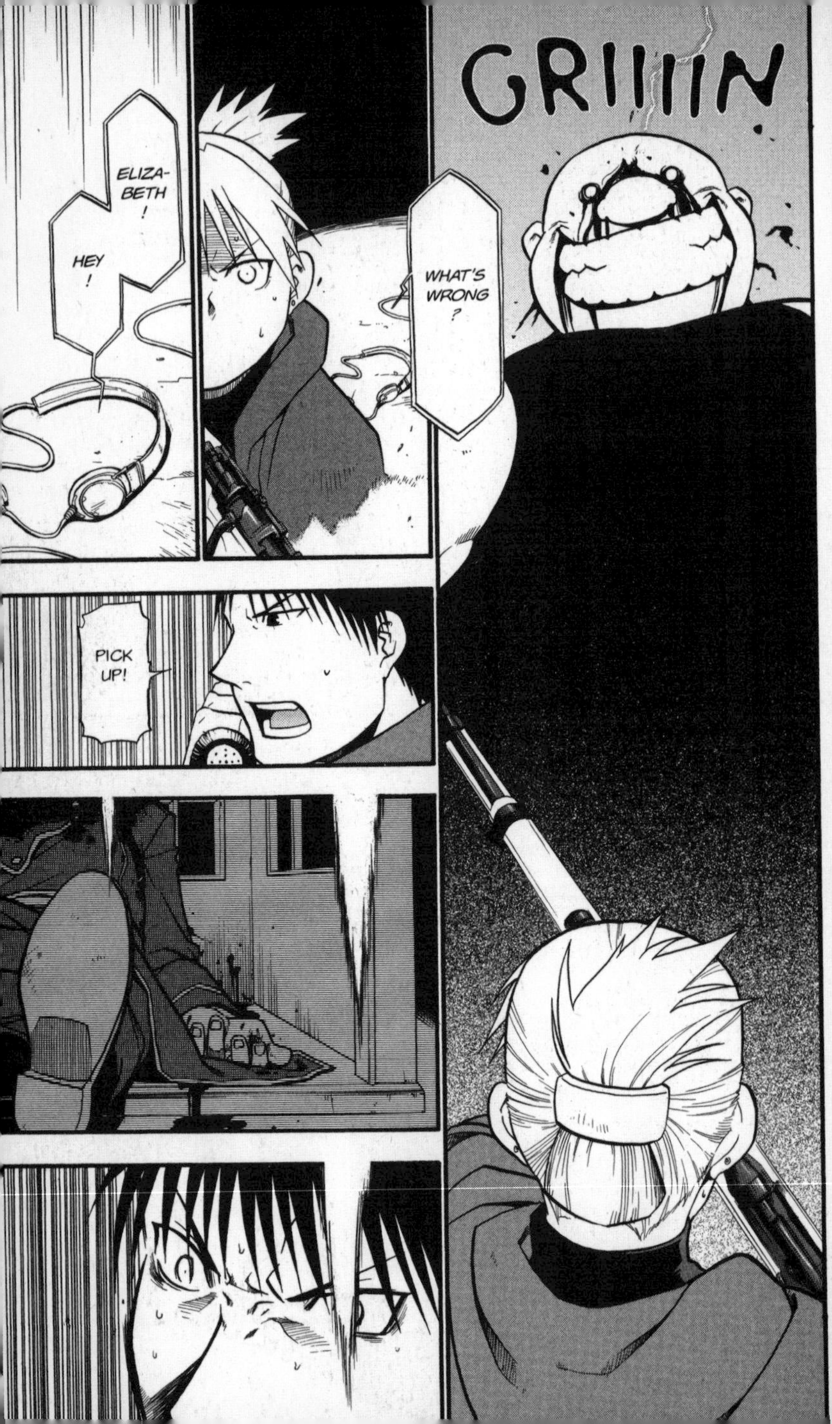
GRIIIN
WHAT'S WRONG?
ELIZA-BETH!
HEY!
PICK UP!

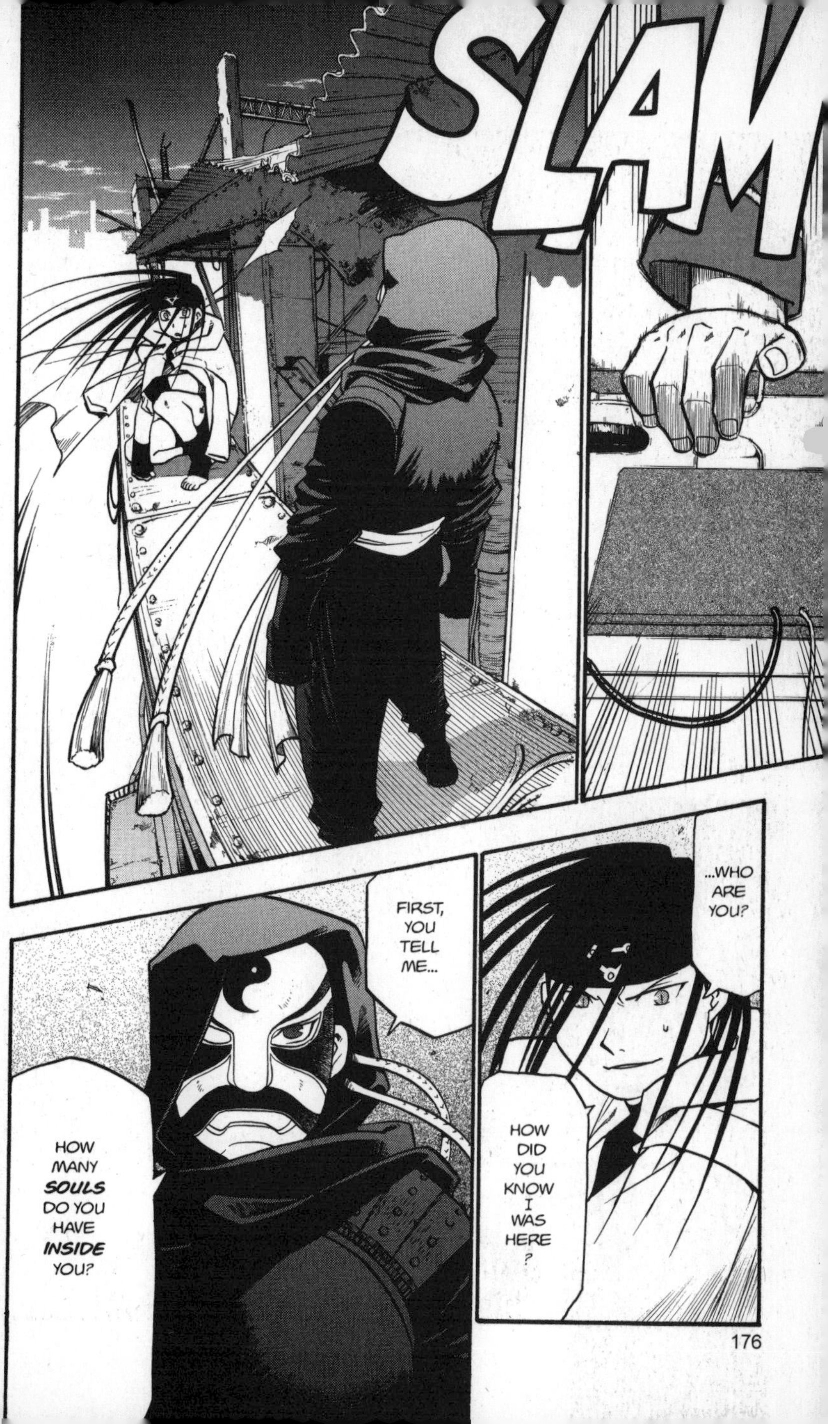
SLAM
...WHO ARE YOU?
HOW DID YOU KNOW I WAS HERE?
FIRST, YOU TELL ME...
HOW MANY **SOULS** DO YOU HAVE **INSIDE** YOU?

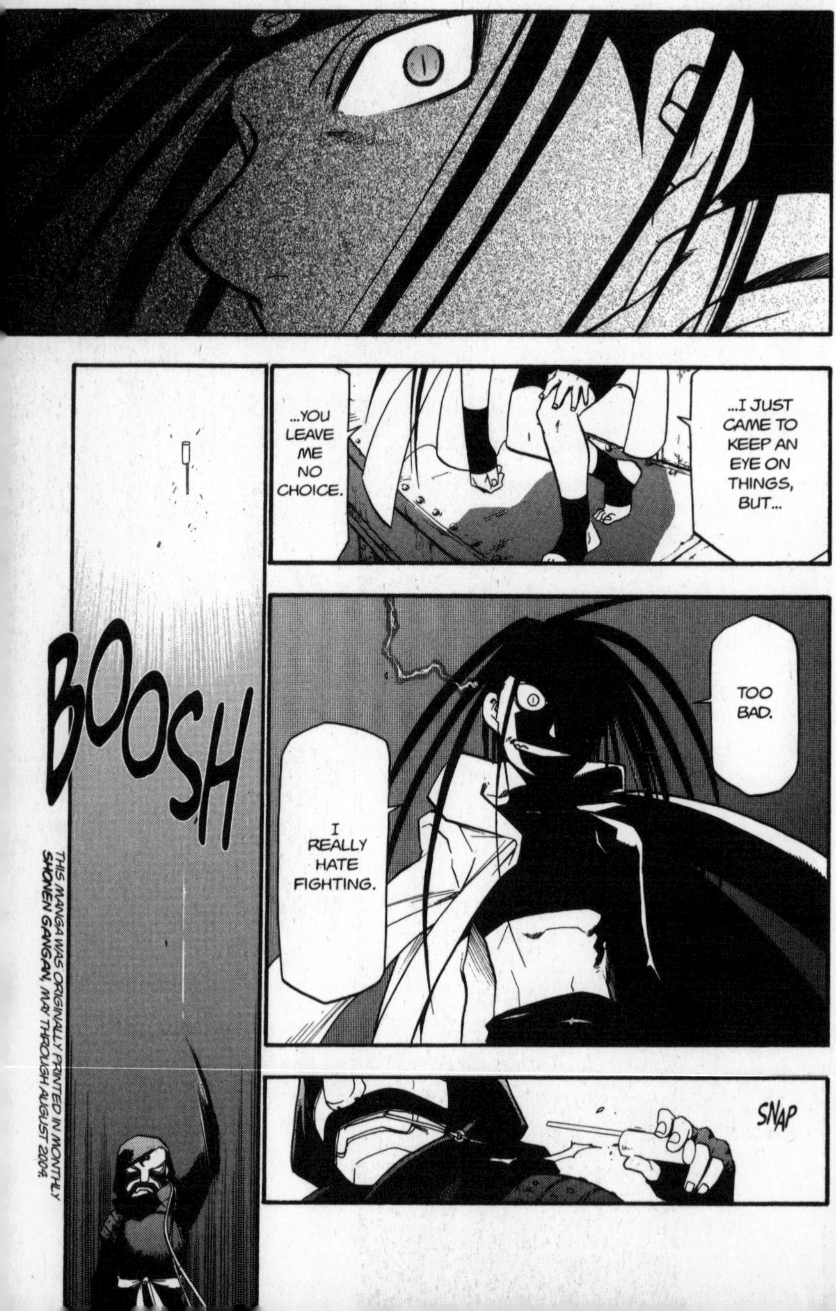
...I JUST CAME TO KEEP AN EYE ON THINGS, BUT...
...YOU LEAVE ME NO CHOICE.
TOO BAD.
I REALLY HATE FIGHTING.
SNAP
BOOSH

THIS MANGA WAS ORIGINALLY PRINTED IN MONTHLY SHONEN GANGAN, MAY THROUGH AUGUST 2004.

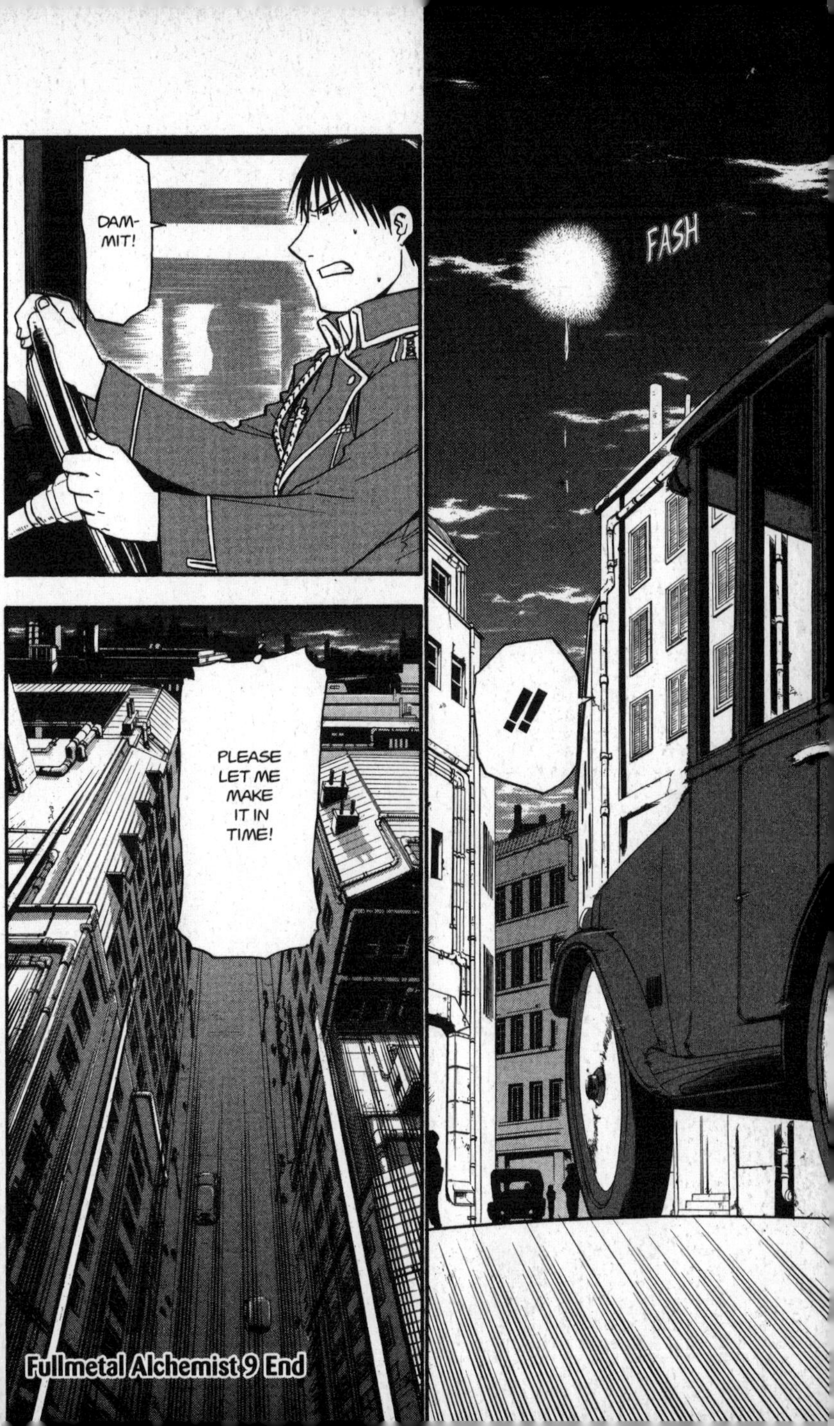
FASH
!!
DAM-MIT!
PLEASE LET ME MAKE IT IN TIME!
Fullmetal Alchemist 9 End

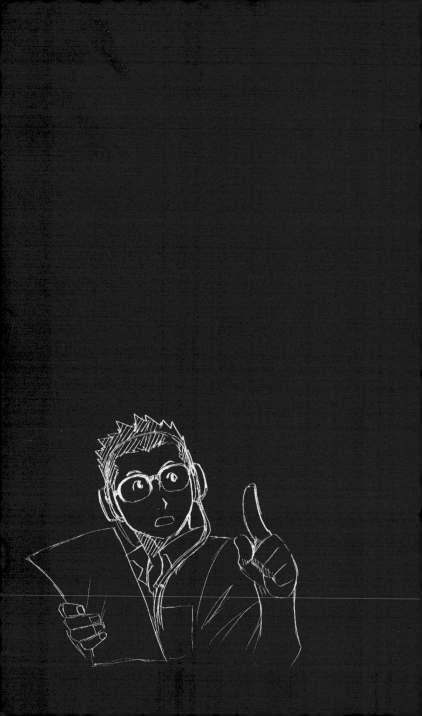

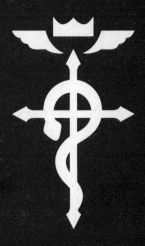

FULLMETAL
ALCHEMIST

EXTRAS

In the Next Volumn (Not)

WHAM
WHAK
THOCK
LIEUTENANT!!

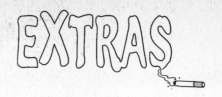

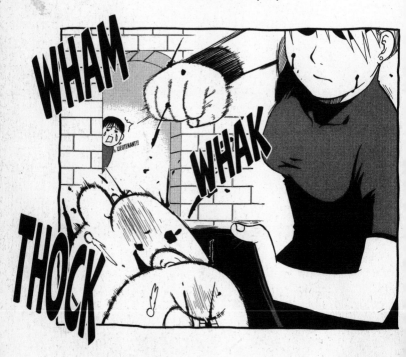

CRAMPED

MEEOW
YOU'RE HIDING A CAT IN THERE AGAIN-
GRAB
MEOW?
BIG CAT!!!
MEOW!
CRACK

A BAD SOLUTION

LOOK HERE!!
IT SAYS HERE THAT WEARING VERTICAL STRIPES MAKES YOU LOOK TALLER!!!
Book of Wisdom
VERTICAL STRIPES!? LEAVE IT TO ME, BIG BROTHER!!
ALL RIGHT! I KNEW I COULD DEPEND ON YOU, AL!!
SLASH
VERTICAL STRIPES!

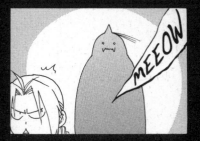

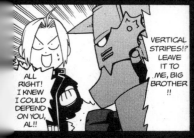

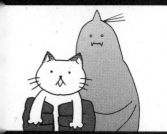

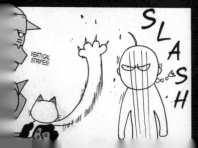

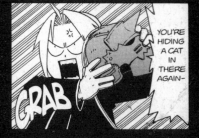

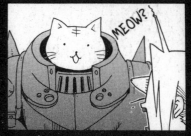

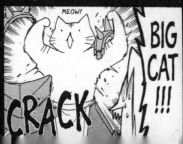

LIFELINE

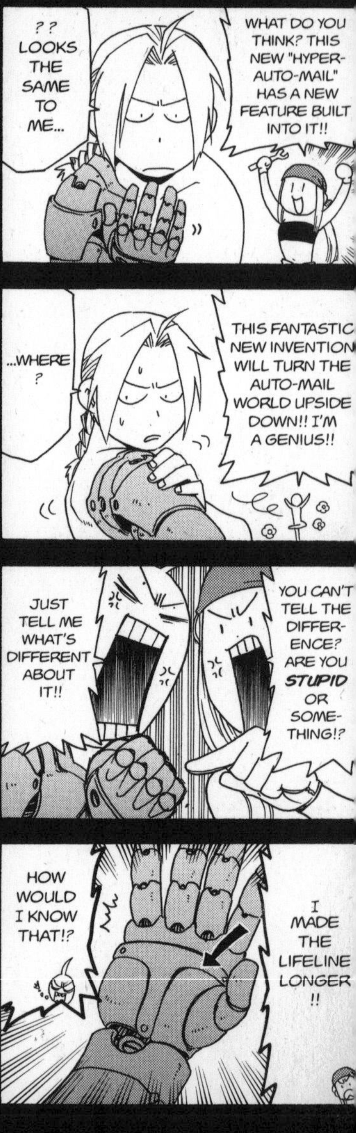
WHAT DO YOU THINK? THIS NEW "HYPER-AUTO-MAIL" HAS A NEW FEATURE BUILT INTO IT!!
? ? LOOKS THE SAME TO ME...
THIS FANTASTIC NEW INVENTION WILL TURN THE AUTO-MAIL WORLD UPSIDE DOWN!! I'M A GENIUS!!
...WHERE ?
YOU CAN'T TELL THE DIFFERENCE? ARE YOU **STUPID** OR SOMETHING!?
JUST TELL ME WHAT'S DIFFERENT ABOUT IT!!
I MADE THE LIFELINE LONGER !!
HOW WOULD I KNOW THAT!?

FULLMETAL ALCHEMIST 9

SPECIAL THANKS

MR. KEISUI TAKAEDA
MR. SANKICHI HINODEYA
MR. MASANARI YUZUKA
MR. JUNSHI BABA
MR. AIYAABALL
MR. JUN TOKO
MS. RIKA SUGIYAMA
MORITAISHI SENSEI

MANAGER—MR. YOICHI SHIMOMURA

AND YOU !!

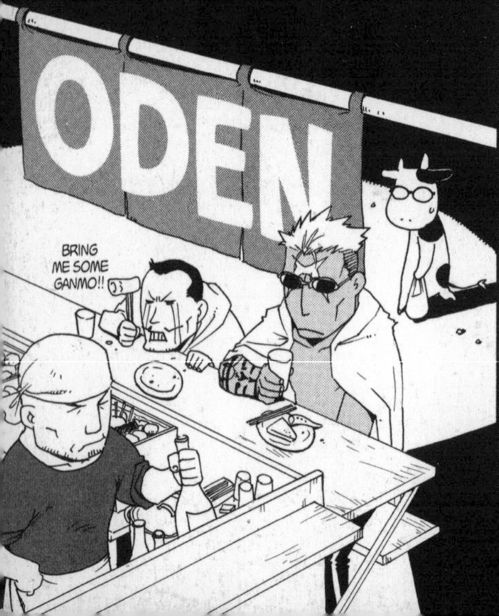
ODEN
BRING ME SOME GANMO!!

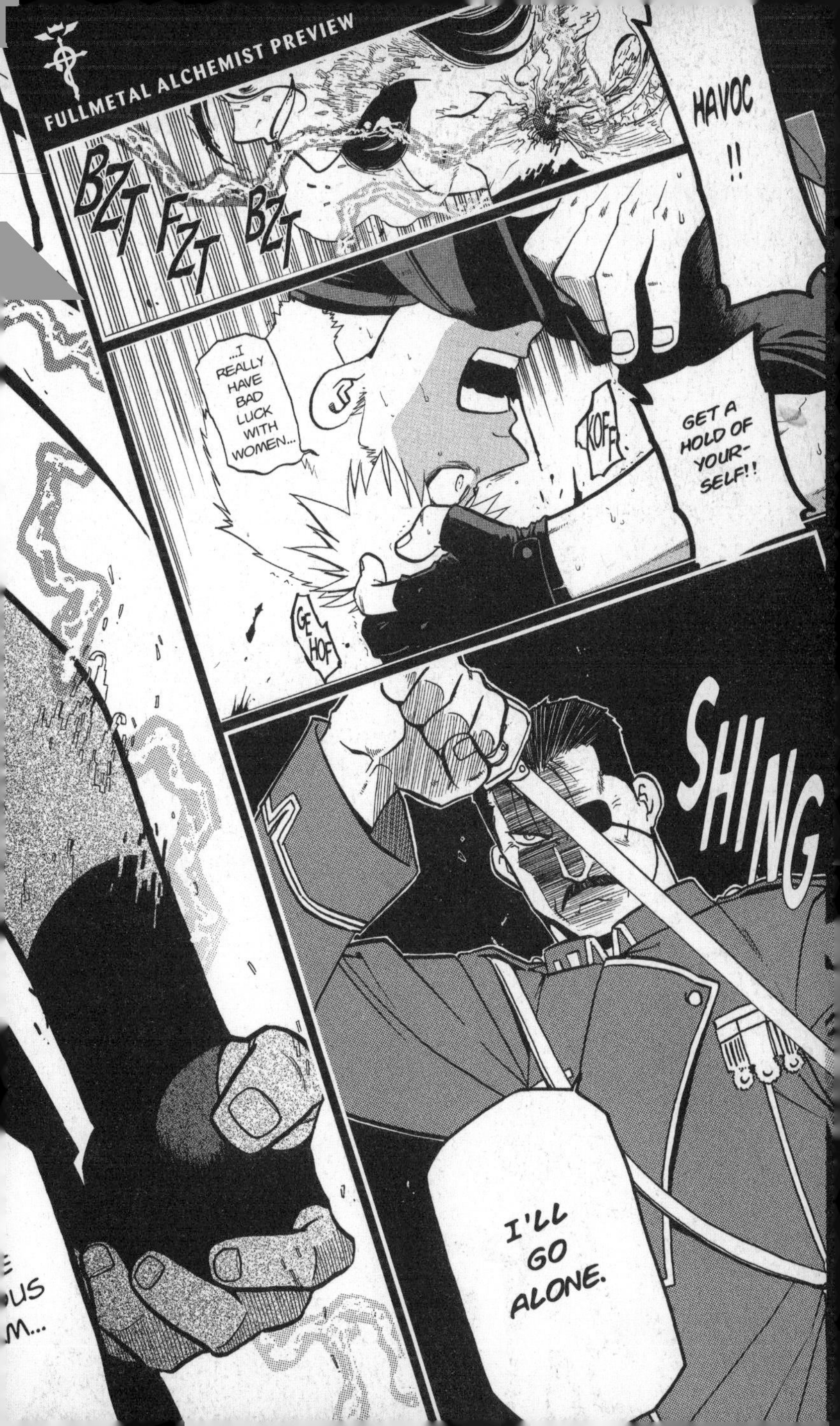
HAVOC !!
BZT FZT BZT
GET A HOLD OF YOUR-SELF!!
KOFF
...I REALLY HAVE BAD LUCK WITH WOMEN...
GEHOF
SHING
I'LL GO ALONE.

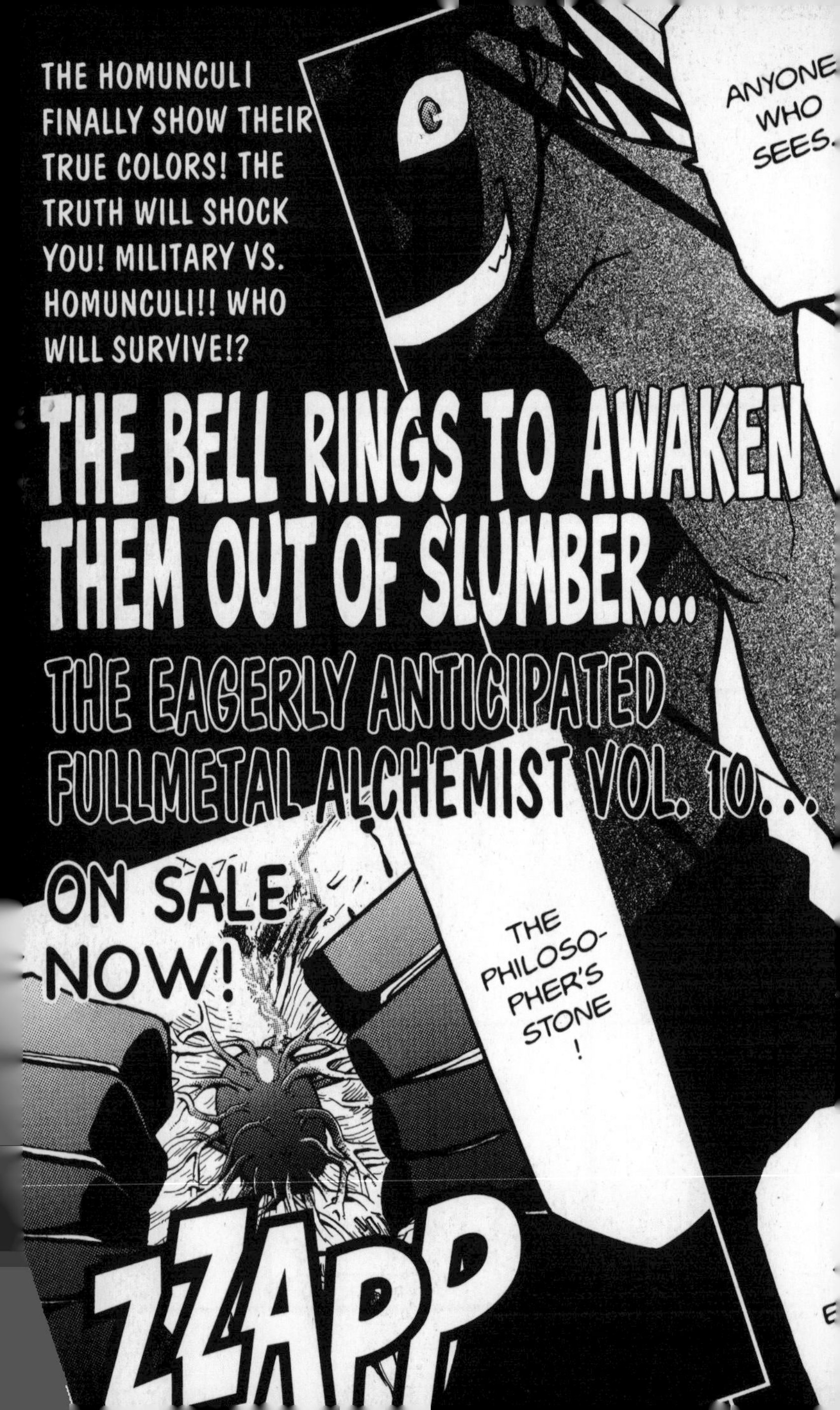
ANYONE WHO SEES.
THE HOMUNCULI FINALLY SHOW THEIR TRUE COLORS! THE TRUTH WILL SHOCK YOU! MILITARY VS. HOMUNCULI!! WHO WILL SURVIVE!?
THE BELL RINGS TO AWAKEN THEM OUT OF SLUMBER...
THE EAGERLY ANTICIPATED FULLMETAL ALCHEMIST VOL. 10...
ON SALE NOW!
THE PHILOSOPHER'S STONE!
ZZAPP

Fullmetal Alchemist 9 Special Guest Comic: On Location

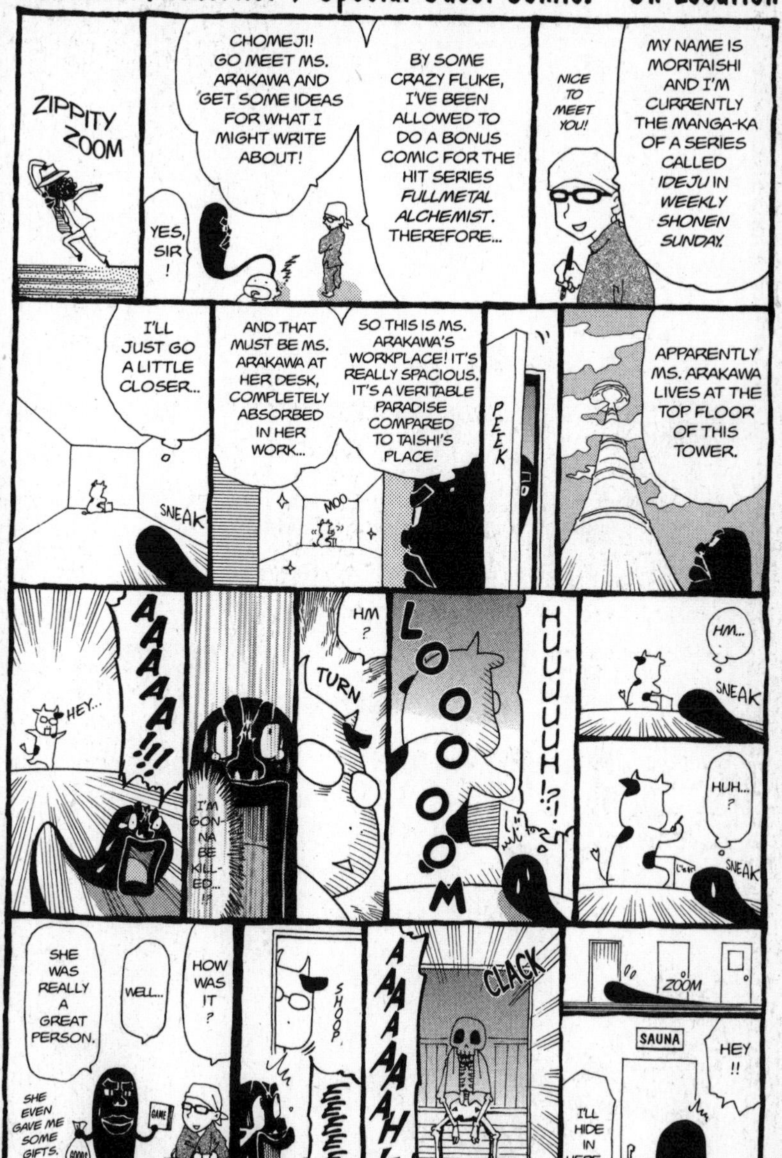

MY NAME IS MORITAISHI AND I'M CURRENTLY THE MANGA-KA OF A SERIES CALLED *IDEJU* IN *WEEKLY SHONEN SUNDAY.*
NICE TO MEET YOU!
BY SOME CRAZY FLUKE, I'VE BEEN ALLOWED TO DO A BONUS COMIC FOR THE HIT SERIES *FULLMETAL ALCHEMIST*. THEREFORE...
CHOMEJI! GO MEET MS. ARAKAWA AND GET SOME IDEAS FOR WHAT I MIGHT WRITE ABOUT!
YES, SIR!
ZIPPITY ZOOM
APPARENTLY MS. ARAKAWA LIVES AT THE TOP FLOOR OF THIS TOWER.
PEEK
SO THIS IS MS. ARAKAWA'S WORKPLACE! IT'S REALLY SPACIOUS. IT'S A VERITABLE PARADISE COMPARED TO TAISHI'S PLACE.
AND THAT MUST BE MS. ARAKAWA AT HER DESK, COMPLETELY ABSORBED IN HER WORK...
MOO
I'LL JUST GO A LITTLE CLOSER...
SNEAK
HM...
SNEAK
HUH...?
SNEAK
HUUUUUH!?!
LOOOOOOM
HM?
TURN
I'M GON-NA BE KILL-ED...!?
AAAAA!!!
HEY...
ZOOM
SAUNA
HEY!!
I'LL HIDE IN HERE...
CLACK
AAAAAAAH!!!
SHOOP
EEEEEEK!
HOW WAS IT?
WELL...
SHE WAS REALLY A GREAT PERSON.
SHE EVEN GAVE ME SOME GIFTS.
GAME
GOODS

CONGRATULATIONS ON THE PUBLICATION OF VOLUME 9, MS. ARAKAWA!

↑TRUE STORY.

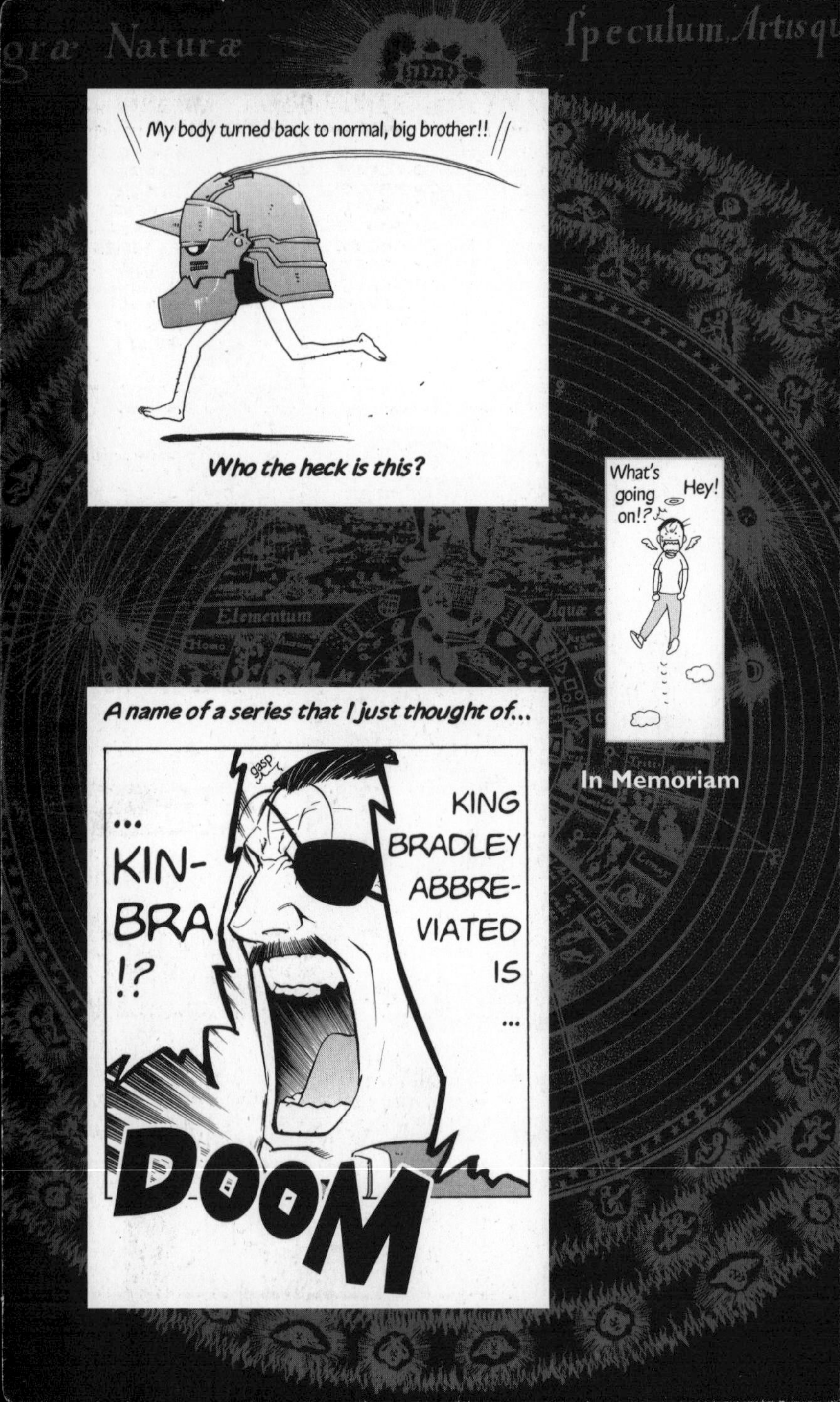
What's going on!?
Hey!
In Memoriam
My body turned back to normal, big brother!!
Who the heck is this?
A name of a series that I just thought of...
KING BRADLEY ABBREVIATED IS ...
gasp
... KIN-BRA !?
DOOM
grae Naturae
Speculum Artisque
Elementum

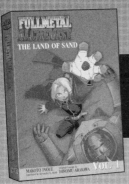
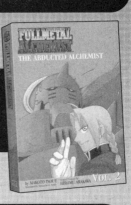
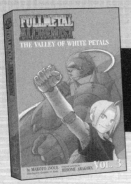
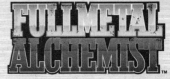

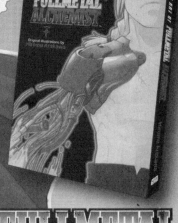

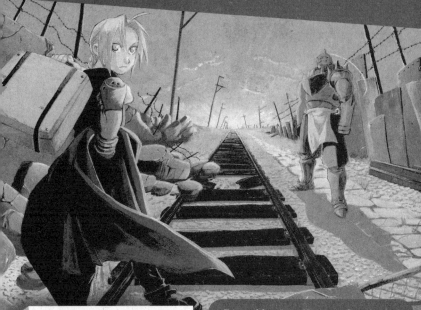

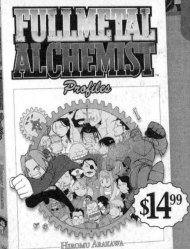

$14.99

HIROMU ARAKAWA

Everything You Need to Get Up to *FULLMETAL Speed*

Fullmetal Alchemist Profiles is an encyclopedia for old fans and new ones. Whether you love the manga, anime, video games, or all of the above, everything you need to know is now available in one handy volume!

- Story background & world history
- Character bios
- New & original artwork
- Interviews with creator Hiromu Arakawa
- Bonus manga pages

It's the who's who and what's what in Edward and Alphonse's world—buy *Fullmetal Alchemist Profiles* today at store.viz.com!

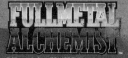

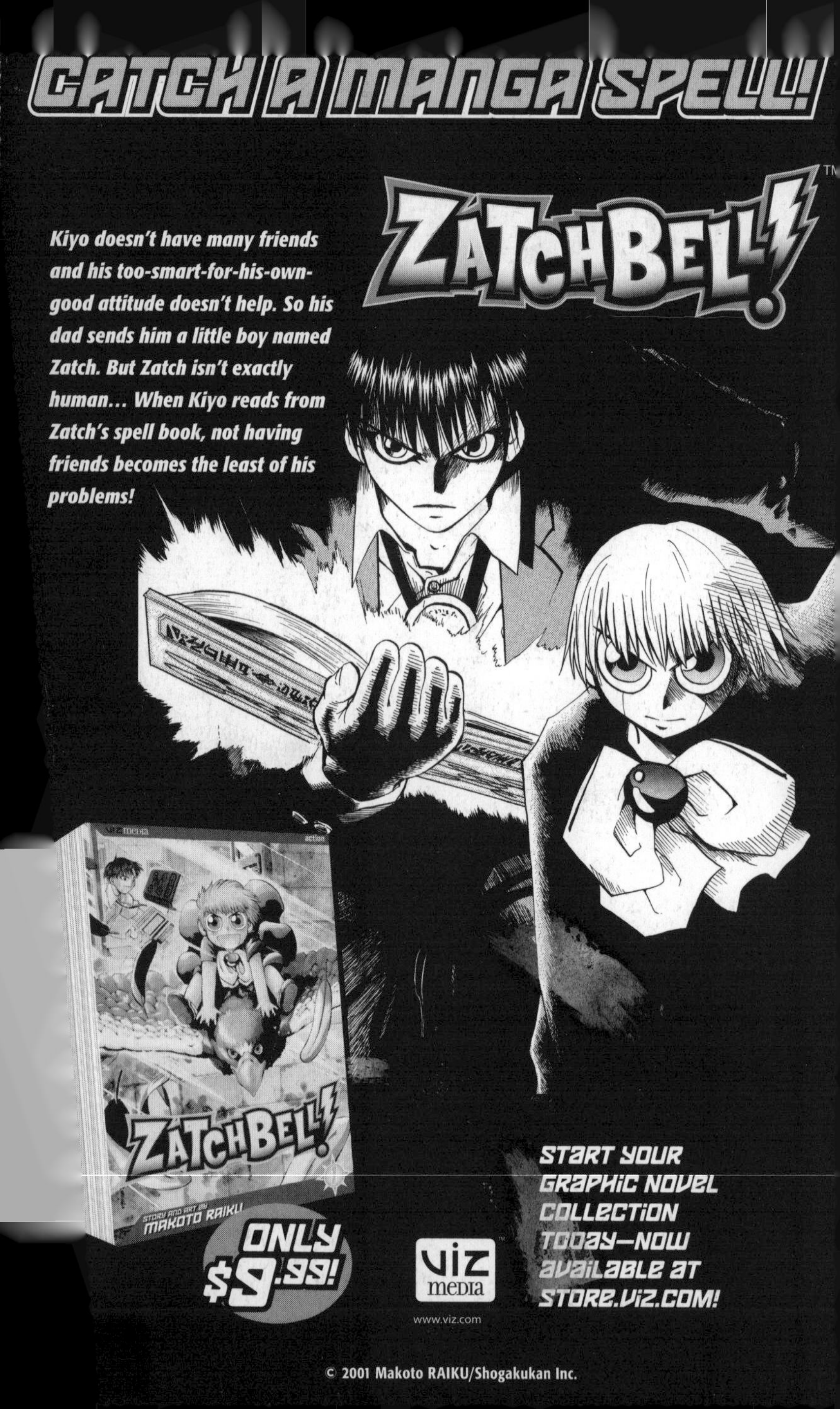

CATCH A MANGA SPELL!
ZATCHBELL!™
Kiyo doesn't have many friends and his too-smart-for-his-own-good attitude doesn't help. So his dad sends him a little boy named Zatch. But Zatch isn't exactly human… When Kiyo reads from Zatch's spell book, not having friends becomes the least of his problems!
viz media
action
ZATCHBELL!
STORY AND ART BY
MAKOTO RAIKU
ONLY $9.99!
viz media
www.viz.com
START YOUR GRAPHIC NOVEL COLLECTION TODAY—NOW AVAILABLE AT STORE.VIZ.COM!
© 2001 Makoto RAIKU/Shogakukan Inc.

LOVE MAN[GA]

LET US KNOW WHAT YOU THINK!

OUR MANGA SURVEY IS NOW
AVAILABLE ONLINE. PLEASE VISIT:
VIZ.COM/MANGASURVEY

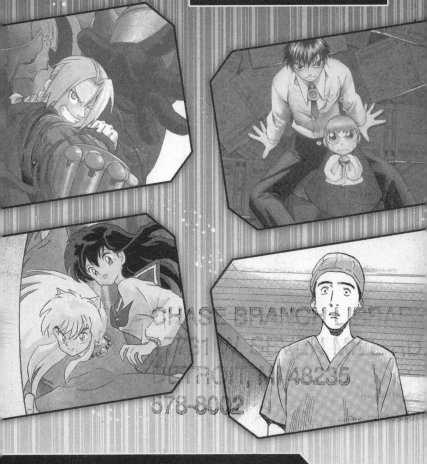

HELP US MAKE THE MANGA
YOU LOVE BETTER!